The Illustrated Guide to Yachting Volume 2

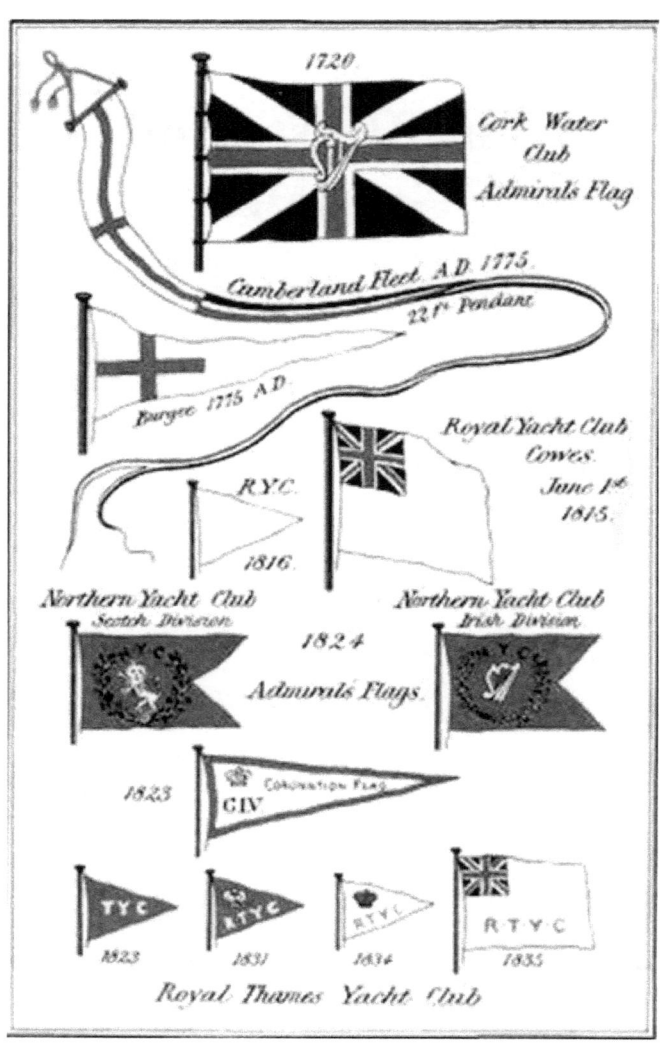

OLD FLAGS

The Illustrated Guide to Yachting Volume 2
A Classic Guide to Yachts & Sailing from the Turn of the 19th & 20th Centuries

R. T. Pritchett, The Marquis of Dufferin and Ava, James Mcferran, Rev. G. L. Blake, T. B. Middleton, Edward Walter Castle, Robert Castle, Christopher Davies, Lewis Herreshoff, The Earl of Onslow, H. Horn and Sir George Leach

LEONAUR

The Illustrated Guide to Yachting
Volume 2
A Classic Guide to Yachts & Sailing from the Turn of the 19th & 20th Centuries
by R. T. Pritchett, The Marquis of Dufferin and Ava, James Mcferran,
Rev. G. L. Blake, T. B. Middleton, Edward Walter Castle, Robert Castle
G. Christopher Davies, Lewis Herreshoff, The Earl of Onslow, H. Horn and
Sir George Leach

First published under the title
*The Badminton Library of Sports and Pastimes
Yachting Volume 2*

Leonaur is an imprint of Oakpast Ltd
Copyright in this form © 2013 Oakpast Ltd

ISBN: 978-1-78282-118-2 (hardcover)
ISBN: 978-1-78282-119-9 (softcover)

http://www.leonaur.com

Publisher's Notes

The views expressed in this book are not necessarily those of the publisher.

Contents

Royal Yachts and English Yacht Clubs	7
Scottish Clubs	80
Irish Clubs	111
The Thames Clubs and Windermere	161
Yachting on the Norfolk Broads	193
Yachting in America	224
Yachting in New Zealand	279
Foreign and Colonial Yachting France	293
Some Famous Races	312
Racing in a 40-Rater in 1892	320
Yacht Racing in 1893	337
The American Yachting Season of 1893	382
The America Cup Races, 1893	395
Appendix	402

Chapter 1
Royal Yachts and English Yacht Clubs

Royal Yachts
By R. T. Pritchett

The innate love of the English for everything connected with seafaring, roving and adventure, burst prominently forth in the time of Queen Elizabeth, when Drake and Raleigh showed what could be done in small craft in 'ocean cruising,' and, with early Corinthian crews from Devon and the brave West, sallied forth and straightway laid the foundation of our navy, and our present numerous fleet of yachts. In 1604 an early designer, one Phineas Pett, built a yacht for Henry of Wales; and to him the navy was much indebted for general improvement in line and build throughout the early part of the Stuart dynasty.

At the Restoration we begin in earnest the History of Yachting, and find King Charles II. taking most enthusiastically to yacht building and even racing. That mine of wealth for the details of every-day life, that minute recorder of modes and fashions, Samuel Pepys, Esq., F.R.S., Secretary to the Admiralty, first brings to our notice the aquatic taste of His Majesty. In his delightful *Diary* we find:—

July 15, 1660.—Found the king gone this morning by 5 of the clock to see a Dutch pleasure boat below bridge, where he dines and my Lord with him.

In a further notice we find His Majesty winning the first yacht race in the Thames, over the course of the R.T.Y. Club, Greenwich to Gravesend and back—a wager of one hundred guineas.

January 13, 1660-1661.—Lord's Day. To the Globe to dinner, then to Commissioner Pett, to his lodgings there, which he hath for the present while he is building the king's yacht, which will be a very pretty thing and much beyond the Dutchman's.

January 15.—The king hath been this afternoon to Deptford to see the yacht that Commissioner Pett is building, which will be very pretty, as also that his brother Christopher Pett (son of Phineas Pett) at Woolwich is making.

November 8.—On board the yacht, which indeed is one of the finest things that ever I saw, for neatness and room in so small a vessel.

May 21, 1661.—To Deptford and took barge and were overtaken by the king in his barge, he having been down the river in his yacht this day for pleasure to try it; and I hear Commissioner Pett's do prove better than the Dutchman, and that his brother did build at Woolwich.

October 1, 1661.—Between Charles II. and his brother the Duke of York for 100 guineas. Sailing match from Greenwich to Gravesend and back. The king won.

July 22, 1662.—Lord Sandwich in yacht to Boulogne in foul weather.

September, 1662.—By water to Woolwich, on my way saw the yacht lately built by our *virtuosos*. My Lord Brunkard and others, with the help of Commissioner Pett also, set out from Greenwich with the little Dutch *Bezan* to try for mastery; and before they got to Woolwich the Dutch beat them half a mile. And I hear this afternoon that in coming home it got above three miles, which all our people were glad of.

July 31, 1663.—Sir William Petty's vessel, which he hath built on two keeles, a model whereof built for the king he showed me, hath this month won a wager of 50*l.* in sailing between Dublin & Holyhead with the pacquett boat. The best ship or vessel the king hath there, and he offers to lay with any vessel in the world.

It is about thirty tons in burden, and carries 30 men with good commodation, as much more as any ship of her burden also as any vessel of this figure shall carry more men. She carries 10 guns of about 5 tons weight. In coming back from Holyhead they started together, and this vessel came to Dublin by 5 at night and the Pacquett boat not before eight the next morning.[1]

---

1. Sloane MSS., Brit. Mus., and model sent to, and deposited by, Petty in Wadham College

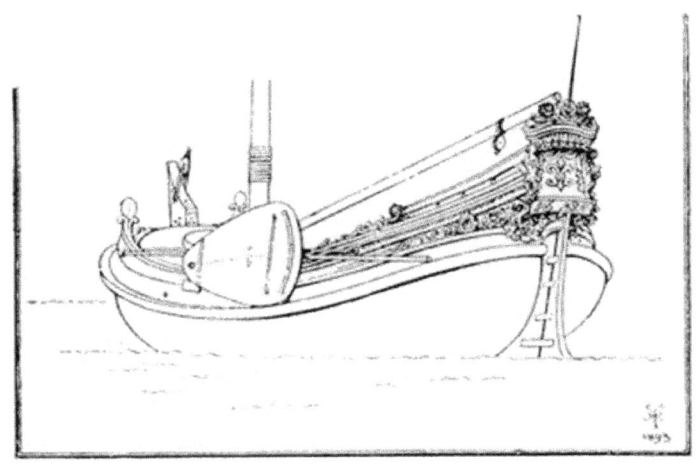

Dutch yacht. From drawing by Vandervelde dated 1640.

Een Bezan Jagt, 1670.

September 17, 1665.—Lord's Day. To church to Gravesend in the *Bezan* yacht, and then to anchor for all night—and with much pleasure at last to sleep—having very good lodging upon cushions in the cabbin.

October 1, 1665.—Lord's Day. Embarked on board the *Bezan*. . . . After supper on board the *Bezan*, then to cards for a while and so to sleep; but Lord! the mirth it caused me to be waked in the night by the snoring around me.

1690.—Macaulay in his *History* mentions a yacht. Caermarthen's eldest son—bold and volatile, fond of the sea, and living much among sailors—had a small yacht of marvellous speed.

1697.—Peter the Great is known to have added to the advancement of sailing and building yachts during his visit to this country.

1720-1737.—The Water Club of the harbour of Cork was established, to be held once every spring tide in April to the last in September, inclusive. The details of this doyen club will be found in its proper place, further on.

Amidst all the voluminous MSS. of the Admiralty secured and appropriated by Samuel Pepys, it is unfortunate that no sketch or drawing of the Royal yacht of Charles II. is to be found. Search is vain among the papers at Cambridge, where most of the Diarist's gleanings are preserved. We must, therefore, start with existing Royal yachts, beginning with that built for King George III. in 1814, and now lying in Portsmouth Harbour.

The Royal yacht *Royal George* was laid down at Deptford, May 1814, designed by Sir Henry Peake, Surveyor of the Navy, and she was launched at Deptford in July, 1817. Her dimensions were as follow:

	Ft.	In.
Length between perpendiculars	103	00
" keel for tonnage	84	4½
Breadth, extreme	26	80
" for tonnage	26	60
Depth of hold	11	60
Burden in tons 330 tons		

The *Royal George* was used on Her Majesty's accession, 1837; she was rigged as a ship, and was remarkable for excellent sailing qualities. The captain appointed was Lord Adolphus FitzClarence, G.C.B., &c.

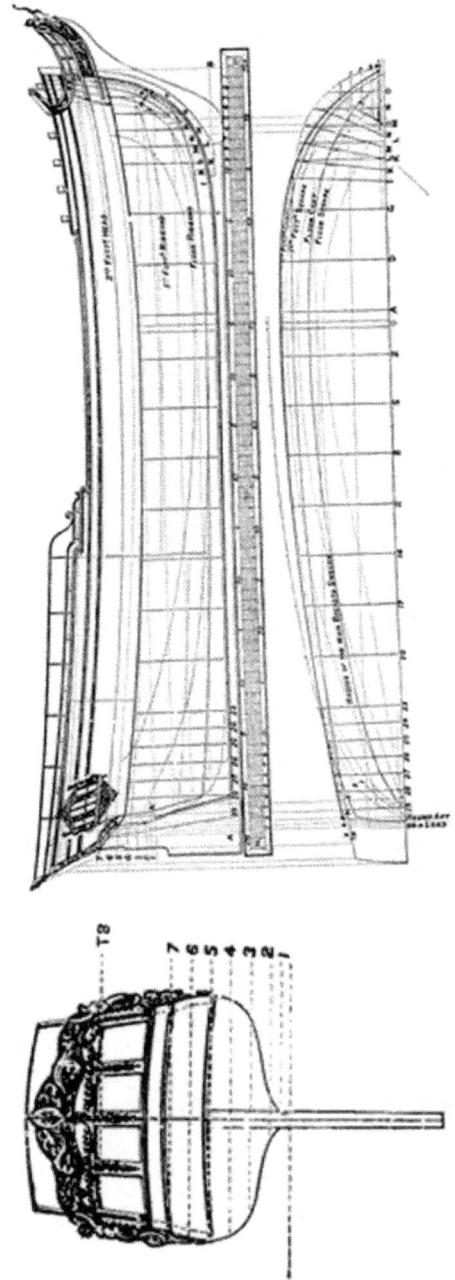

Cutter, 141 tons, from Stalkart's 'Naval Architecture,' 1781.

Yacht stern, 1781.

The *Royal George* was laid up in Portsmouth Harbour, in charge of the Master and only fitted out when specially required for Royal service. The lieutenants, mates, assistant-surgeon, and crew were stationed on board a 10-gun brig, H.M.S. *Pantaloon*, attached to the Royal yacht as tender. This vessel was employed in looking after fishermen, carrying mails, and on other services that might be required.

Esmeralda, cutter, under command of the second master, was also attached to the Royal yacht as tender.

On November 7, 1842, a new steam yacht, *Victoria and Albert*, was laid down at Pembroke Dockyard, and on April 26 next year she was launched. She was designed by Sir William Symonds, Surveyor of the Navy. Construction: diagonal principle, Dantzic oak without, horizontal planking of Italian larch. This yacht, it may here be stated, was subsequently, when a new *Victoria and Albert* was built, known as the *Osborne*.

Dimensions

	Ft.	In.
Length	200	00
Extreme length	225	00
Beam	39	00
Over paddle boxes	59	00

In 1844, it is to be noted, it was ordered that the Royal yacht should carry the Royal standard at the main, the Admiralty flag at the fore, and the Union Jack at the mizzen, which order remains in force at the present time. In this year, it should perhaps be added, the queen stayed at Osborne House, and in the following year the estate was purchased from Lady Isabella Blatchford by Her Majesty. The steam yacht *Fairy* (screw) was built at this period.

	Ft.	In.
Length	160	00
Beam	39	00

Burden, 317 tons.
Speed, 13.25 knots, and carrying 18 tons of coal

The paddle steam yacht *Elfin* appeared in 1849. It was built at Chatham, from the design of Mr. Oliver Lang, of mahogany and on the diagonal principle.

	Ft.	In.
Length over all	112	3

TRINITY YACHT   H.M.S.   1842   H.M.S.   H.M.S.   G.S.N.O.'s
            MONARCH   THE ROYAL YACHT ROYAL GEORGE SHEARWATER BLACK EAGLE TRIDENT
VESTAL   Her Majesty the Queen going to Scotland.

Length	103	6
Beam	13	2
Over boxes	25	6
Burden in tons, 96 tons.		
Speed, 12 knots.		
Draught,	4	10
H.P. nominal 40.		
Indicated 192 H.P.		

Amongst interesting details which should here be recorded, it may be remarked that in August of this year Her Majesty in the Royal yacht visited Cork, and the Cove was henceforth called Queenstown. As regards the speed and capacity of the *Victoria and Albert*, her capabilities for long cruises were tested in 1850. Leaving Plymouth Sound June 26, 8.45, she arrived in the Tagus off Belem, June 29, 3.10. Distance 772 miles in 66 hrs. 25 mins. Average speed $11^6/_{10}$ knots. Tried at a measured mile with anthracite and Merthyr coal mixed, three years afterwards, her average speed was 11 knots.

A new yacht, under the temporary name of the *Windsor Castle*, was started at Pembroke in February 1854, but a few weeks later its progress was suspended to facilitate work for the Baltic and Black Sea fleets.

On January 16, 1855, the 'new' *Victoria and Albert* was launched and christened, and the name of the old yacht (built 1843) changed to *Osborne*. The new *Victoria and Albert* was designed by Oliver Lang, Master Shipwright at Pembroke Yard.

	Ft.	In.
Length figure-head to stern	336	4
" between perpendiculars	300	0
Beam outside paddle boxes	66	6
Burden in tons 2,342 tonnage		
Breadth of wales	40	0
Diameter of paddle-wheel	31	0

	h. p.	
Engines' power nominal	600	
Indicated	2,700	

	miles	knots
Speed	16.813	14.592
July 23	17.762	15.416

Her Majesty's first cruise in the new yacht took place on July 12, and next day she steamed round the Isle of Wight in 3 hrs. 25 mins. The *Victoria and Albert* proved an excellent sea-boat. In a heavy gale soon afterwards four line-of-battle ships drove; but Captain Denman reported of the new Royal yacht, 'Splendid sea-boat, and rode out the gale with extraordinary ease, not pitching at all, or bringing the smallest jerk on the cable.'

As for speed, she was tried from Cork to Madeira, and returned from the island, 1,266 miles, at an average rate of 10.8 knots. Cork to Portsmouth, 341 miles, 22 hrs. 7 mins., average 15.4 knots, is also noted.

The new yacht *Alberta* (paddle steamer) was built in 1863.

	Ft.	In.
Extreme length	179	0
Extreme breadth	22	8
Over paddle-boxes	41	0

Burden in tons, 390.
Coal stowage, 33 tons.
Speed, 14 knots.

All the fittings of the Royal yachts are as simple as possible, but the perfect quality of material is not to be surpassed.

The appointments on these vessels are as follows: The commander, three years; lieutenants, two years. One promoted at end of each year. Names of all officers to be submitted to the queen.

The *Victoria and Albert* always lies off Cowes during the queen's residence at Osborne in the summer. During the winter, when the queen is at Osborne, she is in Portsmouth Harbour. The *Alberta* always brings the queen from Gosport to Cowes, and *vice versâ*, and, as a rule, members of any Royal family. The *Elfin* runs regularly with messengers, bringing despatches as may be from time to time required; the whole fleet is under the command of Admiral Fullerton, A.D.C., who is always on board any of the yachts in which the Queen may embark. The *Osborne* brings the Prince of Wales across to Cowes in the summer, when the prince and princess and family live on board, remaining generally for about three weeks.

The *Osborne* is an independent command, being the Prince's Royal yacht. The grandest view of the Royal yachts is obtained when Her Majesty inspects a fleet at Spithead. On these occasions the *Victoria and Albert*, with the Queen and Royal family, the Lords of the Admi-

The Royal Yacht 'Victoria and Albert,' 1843.
(*First cruise, 1843.*)

ralty in attendance on board, is preceded by the Trinity yacht *Irene*, the *Alberta* being on the starboard, and the *Elfin* on the port quarter. Next come the Admiralty yacht *Enchantress*, and the Lords and Commons,—generally in troopships such as the *Himalaya*,—others according to precedence.

The stately five-knot approach of these vessels is always very impressive, and forms a nautical pageant well worthy of the Queen of England and Empress of India, who has bestowed such munificent patronage on the various yacht clubs of her realms, having presented since the Accession no fewer than seventy-two valuable challenge cups to be sailed for by all classes, besides the annual cups to the R.Y.S. since 1843. The details of these will be recorded later on.

THE ROYAL YACHT SQUADRON

The present club-house of the Royal Yacht Squadron is of no modern date, but a continuance of Cowes Castle, a fort built in the time of Henry VIII. for the protection of the Medina River, which runs south and forms a fine harbour for laying-up yachts of all sizes and classes, with building yards on either side; and a very busy scene it presents during the fitting-out season.

The castle was continued as a fort, and on the death of the last governor, the Marquis of Anglesey, who was a very great patron of yachting small and great, the Marquis Conyngham took a lease of the property from the Crown and passed it on in 1856 to the Royal Yacht Squadron, which was established in 1812, as the seal shows. In 1815 a meeting of the then club was held at the Thatched House Tavern, St. James's Street, Lord Grantham in the chair, supported by Lords Ashbrook, Belmore, Buckingham, Cawdor, Craven, Deerhurst, Fitzharris, Kirkwall, Nugent, Ponsonby, Thomond, Uxbridge, Sirs W. Curtis, J. Hippesley, G. Thomas, Godfrey Webster, Colonels Sheddon and Wheatley, &c. when new life was infused into the Association, and from that time the squadron has held the proud position of being the first yacht club in the world, with the much-envied privilege and distinction of flying the White Ensign.

After 1815, the R.Y.S. met for some years at the Medina Hotel, East Cowes, and later on the Gloucester Hotel, at West Cowes, was taken for the club-house, close to the Fort and Castle, whither, as just remarked, they moved in 1856. It was at once rebuilt and enlarged. The situation is beautiful, backed by large elm-trees. The platform commands a grand view—towards the Motherbank, Ryde, and the forts to

Cowes Castle, from drawing by Louterburg.

Seal of Royal Yacht Club, Cowes.

the eastward, with Calshot Castle, Portdown Hill, and Southampton Water to the northward, and, away to the westward, Lymington.

Two of the old guns, formerly in the fort, have been happily preserved, and are now placed in the grounds which have recently been added to the castle property on the west side, towards Egypt.

THE HISTORY OF THE ROYAL CUPS

The first Royal Cup was presented by His Majesty King William IV., 1830, to be competed for by yachts belonging to members of the Squadron; and the gift was continued during His Majesty's reign. The table appended furnishes details.

Year	Yacht	Rig	Tons	Owner
1830	*Alarm*	Cutter	193	Jos. Weld
1831	*Alarm*	"	193	Jos. Weld
1832	*Alarm*	"	193	Jos. Weld
1833	—	—	—	—
1834	*Harriet*	"	65	G. W. Heneage
1835	*Columbine*	"	90	J. Smith-Barry
1836	*Breeze*	"	55	James Lyons
1837	*Amulet*	"	51	J. Mecklam
1838	*Alarm*	"	193	Joseph Weld

At a meeting of the Royal Yacht Squadron in 1837, it was moved and seconded:

> That the commodore be requested to seek an interview or audience with Her Majesty, with a view to the continuance of the Royal Cup to be presented to the Yacht Club at Cowes.

The request was graciously accorded. The list of Cups presented by Her Majesty is given further on.

On the occasion of the emperor and empress of the French visiting Osborne, and landing in Osborne Bay in 1857, the Royal Yacht Squadron boats formed an escort round the Royal barge.

The squadron has always been characterised by the large and powerful class of vessels composing it; and the oil picture now hanging in the dining-room at the castle, painted by W. Huggins, 1835, shows the leading craft of that date, with the commodore's yacht in the centre. This is the *Falcon*, 351 tons, full ship rigged, carrying eleven guns on the broadside. The *Pearl*, 130 tons, belonging to the Marquis of Anglesey, is coming up on the left side, dipping her gaff-topsail to the

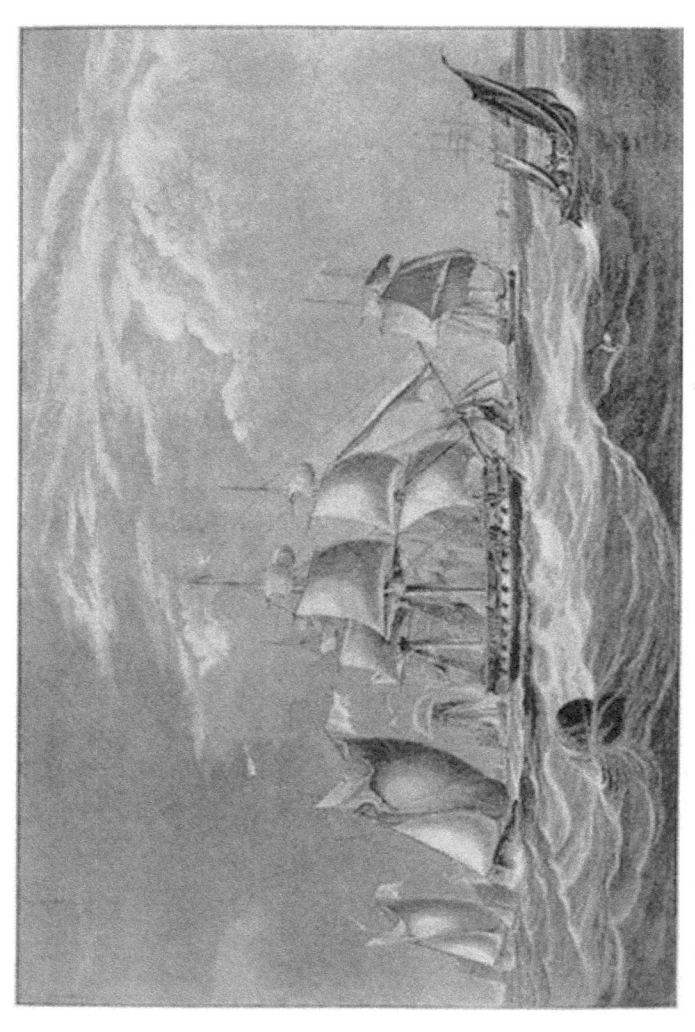

'Pearl,' The 'Falcon' 'Waterwitch.'
351 tons (Earl of Yarborough),
Off Spithead with the Royal Yacht Squadron on their voyage to Cherbourg, 1832.

commodore, who is under topsails with top-gallant sails loose; in the distance is a yacht, *Pantaloon*, belonging to the Duke of Portland, brig rigged, with her topsail aback; a large schooner and several cutters are included. An engraving of this picture is lettered thus:

> The Right Honourable Lord Yarborough's yacht *Falcon*, of 351 tons, off Spithead with the Royal Squadron, on their voyage to Cherbourg. Painted by W. Huggins, Marine Painter to His Majesty, and published by him at 105 Leadenhall Street. January 10, 1835.

This was a grand period in the club's history for large yachts. These included the *Pearl* and *Alarm* cutters, and the schooners *Dolphin* (217 tons), *Xarifa*, *Kestrel*, and *Esmeralda*. A picture of this schooner, by Condy, is still, (at first publication), in the possession of Lord Llangattock of The Hendre. Then came the *Arrow* cutter of *Chamberlayne* fame, with the well-known parti-coloured streak. She won and won until she was requested not to enter, which was hardly reasonable, as the enthusiastic owner improved her year by year, and kept well ahead of his day.

In 1843 the Royal Yacht Squadron gave a cup to be sailed for by the Royal Thames Yacht Club at Cowes. A very good picture of the race was painted by Condy of Plymouth. At that time the 25-tonners were the representative craft in the Thames, and *Mystery*, *Blue Bell*, *Phantom*, *Cygnet*, and *Gnome* were generally to the fore. When the Thames matches were sailed there were invariably some representatives from the Royal Yacht Squadron to attend the racing, and everyone looked out for the white ensign. The *Pearl*, belonging to the Marquis of Anglesey, always ran up alongside the club steamer, and dipped her ensign as her owner waved his glazed hat, standing by the gunwale of his grand craft.

In those days there certainly was intense enthusiasm about the 25-tonners, and great was the enjoyment they afforded the visitors.

In 1851 the Royal Yacht Squadron gave a cup to be sailed for, and it was won by the *America* schooner, belonging to Commodore J. C. Stevens, of the New York Club. In America it is always called the Queen's Cup, and in England the 'America' Cup, but it is really the Royal Yacht Squadron Cup. The Americans have held it ever since.

Luggers as yachts were common. In 1827 Lord Harborough had a large lugger, the *Emmetje*, of 103 tons, of which he was so proud that he entered Ramsgate Harbour flying the coach whip of the Royal Navy, until the officer of the Coastguard came on board and hauled it down.

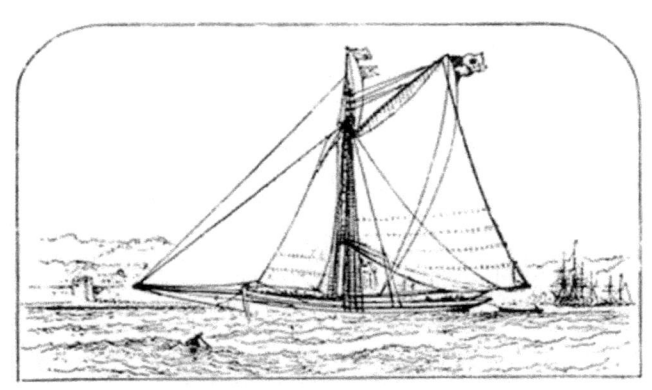

'Pearl,' R.Y.S., 130 tons (Marquis of Anglesey). Launched 1821.

'Dolphin,' R.Y.S., 217 tons, 1839. (G. H. Ackers, Esq.)

'Esmeralda,' R.Y.S., 1846.

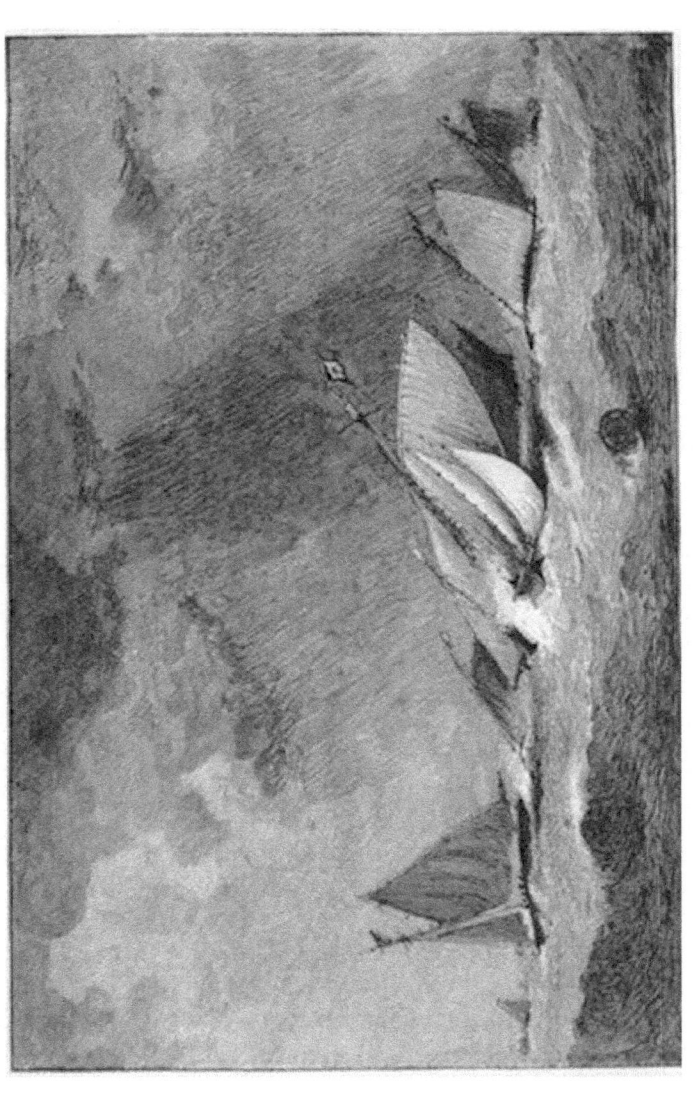

The 'Mystery' winning the cup presented by R.Y.S. to be sailed for by yachts of R.T.Y. Club.(*August 1843.*)

Some thirty years afterwards came a revival when Lord Willoughby De Eresby brought out in 1859 his celebrated lugger the *New Moon*. She was larger than Lord Harborough's—209 tons, 134 ft. long, 18 ft. 5 in. beam, constructed at Hastings. Her highest speed was attained on long reach, and was shown on the occasion of her racing back to Harwich. In a fine breeze she went away from the other yachts, going 14 or 15 knots; but ill fate awaited her; she had to make two boards to fetch the Cork Lightship and the Bell Buoy. That was her destruction; the time taken to dip the enormous lugs in going about allowed the others, who had been nearly hull down, to overhaul her, so necessary is it to have a craft that comes round like a top with canvas easily handled.

The Jubilee of the Yacht Club was celebrated at Cowes in 1865, and another notable event took place on the occasion of the Queen's Jubilee, June 21, 1887. A procession of the Royal Yacht Squadron manoeuvred in two columns, canvas and steam, finishing up with a signal from the commodore: 'Steam ahead full speed.' A drawing of this spectacle, by Sir Oswald Brierley, is at the Castle, Cowes.

The fastest yachts in the Royal Yacht Squadron are shown, of course, in the list of Queen's Cup winners, which forms a befitting annual history. Yachting in early days, however, was real yachting in its truest sense, cruising about, that is to say, for the sake of peace and rest; the vessels were generally schooners of considerable tonnage for sea cruising. We have no longer *Alarm*, 248 tons, *Aurora Borealis*, 252 tons; but the faithful *Egeria*, 152 tons, belonging to Mr. Mulholland, now Lord Dunleath, is still with us. In 1852-53 there were only two steam yachts in the Squadron, which was averse to the new comers; but by degrees a fine schooner class with auxiliary steam was introduced, including, of well-known boats, *Sunbeam*,[2] 1874; *Czarina*, 1877; *Wanderer* and *Lancashire Witch*, 1878. New members from 1890 to 1892 added 7,000 tons to the fleet, principally steamers up to 1,000 tons and more.

The squadron at the time of writing is composed of 227 members, and the fleet consists of 107 vessels, as follows: 44 steam yachts, 10 steam schooners, 28 schooners, 13 cutters, 12 yawls, 107 vessels, making 20,367 total tonnage. The minimum tonnage is 30 tons register for sailing vessels, and 30 tons net for steamers (rule, May 1870).

The Queen's Cups are sailed for by yachts belonging to members of the Royal Yacht Squadron only, but other prizes are given during

---

2. Described by Lord Brassey, in his chapter on Ocean Cruising, Vol. 1.

'DE EMMETJE,' LUGGER, 103 TONS, 1827 (LORD HARBOROUGH).

'NEW MOON,' R.Y.S., 209 TONS, 1859 (LORD WILLOUGHBY DE ERESBY).

'CORSAIR,' R.Y.S., WINNING THE QUEEN'S CUP AT COWES, 1892.
40-RATER (ADMIRAL THE HON. VICTOR MONTAGU).

the Squadron Week, generally the first week in August.

Names and dates of yachts owned by H.R.H. the Prince of Wales:

Date	Name	Rig	Tonnage
1865	*Dagmar*	Cutter	36
1871	*Alexandra*	"	40
1872	*Princess*	"	40
1873	*Zenobia*	S.-steam	38
1877	*Hildegarde*	Schooner	205
1880	*Formosa*	Cutter	104
1882	*Aline*	Schooner	210
1893	*Britannia*	Cutter	220

Beside several steam launches and sailing boats.

The German emperor, who became a member in 1891, in that year brought over the *Meteor*, née *Thistle*, to compete for the Queen's Cup, and evinced the greatest enthusiasm, sailing in her for the prize, August 3. The 'Meteor' finished first, but the *Corsair*, 40 tons, Rear-Admiral Victor Montague, R.N., came up with a smart breeze, saved her time, and won.

Much interest was also taken in the presence of a 40-tonner, designed by Mr. G. L. Watson for Prince Henry of Prussia, and steered by the Prince, who seemed thoroughly to enjoy it, and remained all day at the tiller—a sort of thing the British public fully appreciate. Unfortunately the wind was not true.

The queen has always graciously encouraged yachting in every way. The list of challenge cups presented by Her Majesty will amply confirm the assertion.

List of Yacht Clubs to which the queen has occasionally given Regatta Cups:

Royal Yacht Squadron (Cowes) Every year since 1843, annually
Dublin Yacht Club 1849
Royal St. George's Club 1851, 1866, 1870, 1874, 1878, 1884, 1892
Royal Thames Club 1851, 1868, 1874, 1880, 1885
Royal Victoria (Ryde) Club 1851, 1852, 1856, 1888
Royal Southern Club 1851, 1857, 1870, 1891
Royal Irish Club 1852, 1865, 1871, 1877, 1881, 1885
Royal Cork Club 1850, 1852, 1858, 1865, 1869, 1889
Royal Yorkshire Club 1853

Royal Mersey Club 1853, 1857, 1861, 1866, 1881
Royal Western (Plymouth) Club 1858, 1861, 1867, 1878, 1882
Royal Northern Club 1859, 1869, 1882, 1890
Royal West of Ireland Club 1863, 1867, 1873
Royal Cornwall 1871, 1884
Royal Alfred Yacht Club 1872, 1879, 1886
Royal Albert Club 1873, 1890
Royal Cinque Ports Club 1875, 1891
Royal Clyde Club 1876, 1883, 1888
Royal Ulster Club 1880, 1887
Royal Harwich Club 1883
Royal London Club 1886
Royal Dorset Club 1887
Royal Portsmouth Corinthian Club 1889
Royal Forth Club 1892

Cups given by the queen to Clubs not Royal
Canada Yacht Club 1891
Upper Thames Sailing Clubs (Challenge Cup) 1893

The majority of members of the squadron own, and chiefly use, large yachts, but not a few of them are practical seamen. One prominent member, Lord Dufferin, is specially notable as a keen devotee of single-handed sailing, and is the owner of a famous boat, *The Lady Hermione*. The editor has thought this an appropriate place to insert a description of the pastime kindly contributed by his lordship, followed by an account of his well-known boat.

SINGLE-HANDED SAILING
By the Marquis of Dufferin and Ava

The wind blows fair, the vessel feels
The pressure of the rising breeze,
And, swiftest of a thousand keels,
She leaps to the careering seas.

The following description of *The Lady Hermione* has been written by my friend Mr. McFerran, who is a much better sailor than myself; but, as the editor has asked me to prefix a few observations of my own on single-handed boat sailing, I have great pleasure in recommending to the attention of the readers of the *Badminton Library* that exceptionally pleasant form of sea adventure.

Probably the proudest moment of the life of anyone who loves the

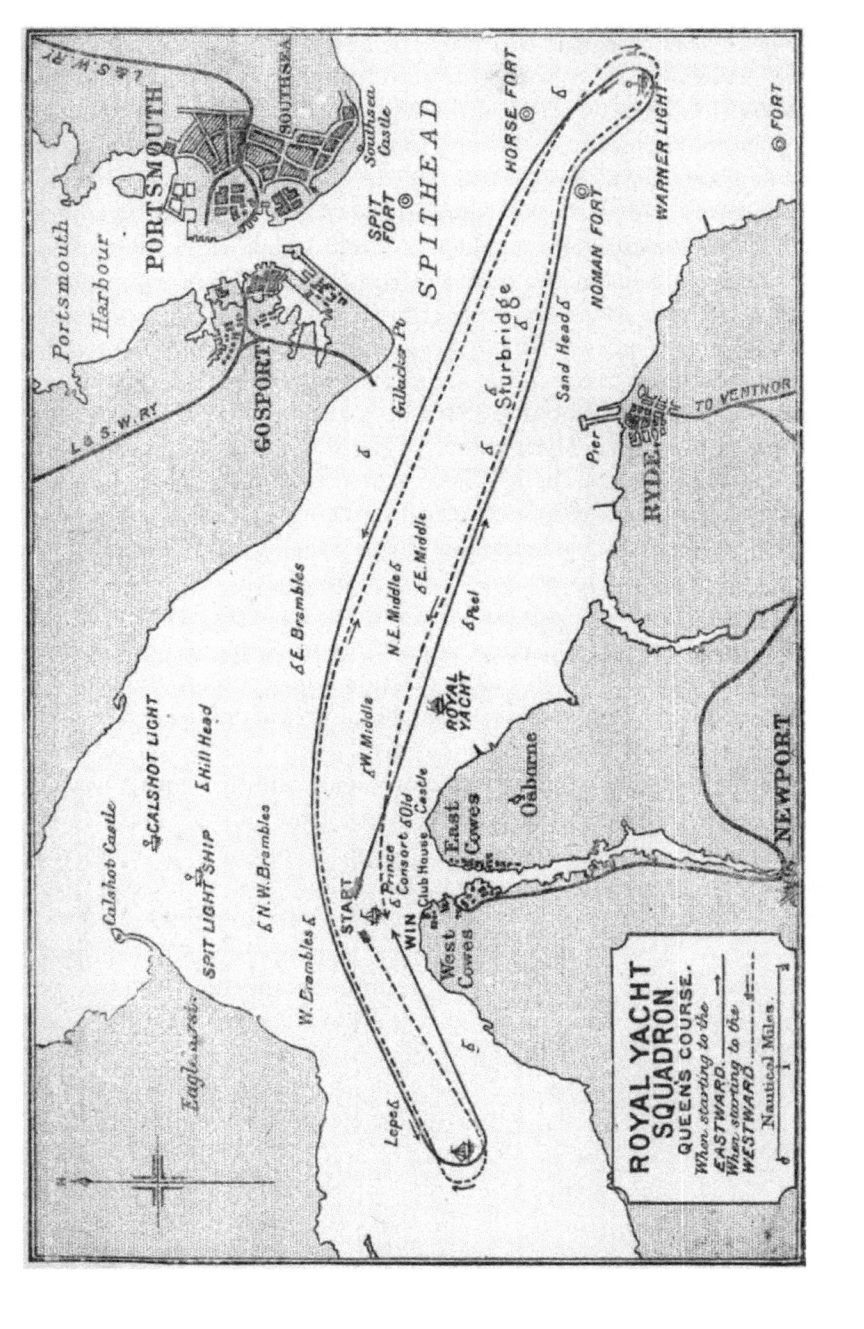

sea, not even excepting the analogous epoch of his marriage morning, is the one in which he weighs anchor for the first time on board his own vessel. It is true that from the first hour he could call her his own his existence has been a dream of delight, unless perhaps for the passing cloud cast by the shadow of the cheque he has been required to draw for her payment. As soon as she has come into his possession, her ungainly naked bulk, as she lies upon the mud, assumes divine proportions; and as by slow degrees her '*toilette*' proceeds, her decks whiten, her masts assume a golden hue and clothe themselves with sail and rigging, his happiness becomes unspeakable. If he is animated by the proper spirit, he has at once set himself to learn navigation; he has plunged deep into the *Sailor's Manual*; and, to the amazement of his female relations, he is to be seen busily employed in tying and untying knots on short pieces of rope. But his principal preoccupation is the fitting of his cabins. The mystery of the ship's practical garniture he leaves to his master, as being beyond the utmost effort of his intellect, though he has a certain satisfaction in knowing that he possesses a pretty accurate knowledge of the way in which the framework of the vessel has been put together.

At last everything is reported ready. He gives the order to weigh anchor, and, as if by a magical impulse, he finds that the being upon whom he has lavished so much affection has become a thing of life, has spread her wings, and is carrying him into the unknown. He paces the deck with telescope under his arm, in the proud consciousness that he is absolute master of her movements, and that with a wave of his hand he can direct her to the golden islands of the west or to the fabled homes of Calypso and the Cyclops, according as his fancy may suggest. No emperor or autocrat has ever been so conscious of his own majesty. But soon a most unwelcome and humiliating conviction damps his exaltation. He discovers that for all practical purposes of command and government he is more incompetent than his own cabin-boy or the cook's mate: that the real ruler of the ship's movements and destiny is his 'master,' whom his crew call the 'captain'; and that the only orders he can issue with a certainty that they are not open to criticism are those he gives for his breakfast and his dinner, if indeed he is in a position to partake of either.

Officially he is gratified with the ambiguous title of 'owner,' while he is painfully conscious that his real social status is that of a mere passenger, and that this unwelcome servitude has every likelihood of enduring during his whole career as a yachtsman. He may indeed, as a man of education, or perhaps of scientific attainments, become in course of time a better navigator than many of the splendid rough and ready sailormen who command the ships of our squadron; but, unless he has been able to spend more time on board than their multifarious occupations allow most owners of yachts to devote to seafaring, he must know that it is idle for him to pretend to compete either in seamanship or experience with the man whom he employs to sail his vessel for him. In short, he remains an amateur to the end of the chapter, and, if he is sensible and honest, is always ready to acknowledge himself the disciple of the professional sailor.

But in single-handed boat sailing this humiliating sense of dependence and inferiority disappears. For the first time in his life, no matter how frequent may have been his cruises on bigger vessels, he finds himself the *bona fide* master of his own ship, with that delightful sense of unlimited responsibility and co-extensive omnipotence which is the acme of human enjoyment. The smallness of his craft does not in the slightest degree diminish the sense of his importance and dignity; indeed, there is no reason why it should. All the problems which task the intelligence and knowledge of the captain of a thousand-tonner during the various contingencies of its nautical manoeuvres have to be dealt with by him with equal promptness and precision.

Anchored in a hot tideway and amongst a crowd of other shipping, he has perhaps a more difficult job to execute in avoiding disaster when getting under way or picking up his moorings than often confronts under similar circumstances the leviathans of the deep; and his honour is equally engaged in avoiding the slightest graze or sixpence worth of injury either to himself or his neighbours as would be the case were a court-martial or a lawsuit and 5,000*l*. damages involved in the misadventure. The same pleasurable sentiments stimulate his faculties when encountering the heavy weather which waits him outside; for, though the seas he encounters may not be quite so large as Atlantic rollers, nor break so dangerously as in the Pentland Firth, they are sufficiently formidable in proportion to the size of his craft to require extremely careful steering, and probably an immediate reduction of canvas under conditions of some difficulty.

Nor are even misfortunes when they occur, as occur they must, utterly devoid of some countervailing joys. He has neglected to keep his lead going when approaching land; he has misread the perverse mysteries of the tides, and his vessel and his heart stop simultaneously as her keel ploughs into a sandbank. The situation is undoubtedly depressing, but at least there is no one on board on this and on similar occasions to eye him with contemptuous superiority or utter the aggravating, 'I told you so.' Nay, if he is in luck, the silent sea and sky are the only witnesses of his shame, and even the sense of this soon becomes lost and buried in the ecstacy of applying the various devices necessary to free his vessel from her imprisonment. He launches his Berthon boat, and lays out an anchor in a frenzy of delightful excitement; he puts into motion his tackles, his gipsy winches, and all the mechanical appliances with which his ingenuity has furnished his beloved; and when at last, with staysail sheet a-weather, she sidles into deep water, though, as in the case of Lancelot, '*his honour rooted in dishonour stood,*' the tragic origin of his present trial quickly fades into oblivion, and during after years he only recalls to his mind, or relates with pride to his friends, the later incidents of the drama.

Another happiness attending his pursuit is that he is always learning something new. Every day, and every hour of the day, the elements of each successive problem with which he has to deal are perpetually changing. As Titian said of painting, seamanship is an art whose horizon is always extending; and what can be more agreeable than to be constantly learning something new in a pursuit one loves?

I have heard it sometimes objected that single-handed boat-sailing is dangerous. Well, all sport is dangerous. People have been killed at golf, at football, and at cricket; nor is sitting in an easy-chair exempt from risk; but during an experience of five and twenty years, though laying no claim to much skill as a mariner, I have never had a serious accident, though occasionally a strong tide may have swept me whither I had not the least intention of going; nor have I ever done more than 10*l.* worth of damage either to my own vessel or my neighbour's. The principal thing one must be careful about is not to fall overboard, and in moving about the ship one should never leave go one holdfast till one's hand is on another. It is also advisable not to expose one's head to a crack from the boom as one is belaying the jib and staysail sheets in tacking, for it might very well knock one senseless.

In conclusion, I would submit that to anyone wearied with the business, the pleasures, the politics, or the ordinary worries of life, there is no such harbour of refuge and repose as single-handed sailing. When your whole thoughts are intent on the management of your vessel, and the pulling of the right instead of the wrong string, it is impossible to think either of your breakdown in your maiden speech in the House of Commons, of your tailor's bills, or of the young lady who has jilted you. On the other hand, Nature, in all her beauty and majesty, reasserts her supremacy, and claims you for her own, soothing your irritated nerves, and pouring balm over your lacerated feelings. The complicated mysteries of existence reassume their primeval simplicity, while the freshness and triumphant joyousness of early youth return upon you as you sweep in a dream past the magic headlands and islands of the Ionian Sea or glide along the Southern coast of your native land, with its sweet English homes, its little red brick villages and homesteads nestling in repose amid the soft outlines of the dear and familiar landscape. The loveliness of earth, sea, and sky takes possession of your soul, and your heart returns thanks for the gift of so much exquisite enjoyment in the pursuit of an amusement as manly as it is innocent.

N.B.—Single-handed sailing need not preclude the presence of a lady passenger. On the contrary, she will be found very useful on occasion, whether in starting the sheets, in taking a spell at the wheel (for they are all familiar with the art of despotic guidance), in keeping a sharp look-out, in making tea, or in taking her part in a desultory conversation.

'THE LADY HERMIONE,' SINGLE-HANDED SAILING YAWL
By James Mcferran

In the course of two summers passed on the shores of the Gulf of Naples the writer had frequent opportunities of becoming acquainted with the details of the construction, fittings, and equipment of a very remarkable little yacht, whose white canvas for a couple of seasons was constantly to be seen on that unrivalled sheet of water between the months of June and October. He has thought that a description of the vessel in question may prove interesting, not only to such of the readers of these volumes as are devoted to the art of single-handed sailing—that most delightful, manly, and invigorating of all sports—but also to the general body of yachtsmen who, during the summer and autumn months, fill, in ever-increasing numbers, our various yachting ports with the most perfect specimens of the shipwright's craft that the world can produce.

The Lady Hermione, as the vessel whose qualities and characteristics it is proposed to describe is called, is the property of Her Majesty's Ambassador at Paris, his Excellency the Marquis of Dufferin and Ava. His Lordship, as is well known, has from very early days been a keen yachtsman, and though for some time past he has had no opportunities of indulging in his favourite pastime in large yachts, he has long been devoted to sailing in vessels in which he comprises in his own person the hierarchy of owner, master, and crew. During the last fifteen years, in whatever part of the world he may have been, provided sailing were possible, he has never been without a little ship specially constructed for this form of amusement. In each succeeding vessel some new invention or arrangement for her safer, easier, and more efficient handling has suggested itself, and been worked out under the owner's direct supervision. In the present boat the development of the single-handed sailing yacht seems at last to have reached perfection, and it would hardly be possible for the most inventive mind to suggest an improvement in her.

The Lady Hermione is a yawl-rigged yacht (fig. 1), built by Forrest & Son, of Wivenhoe, to the order of her owner. She is 22 ft. 9 in. long between perpendiculars, 4 ft. 2 in. in depth, has a beam of 7 ft. 3 in., and a registered tonnage of four tons. She is built with mild-steel frames, galvanised so as to resist the corrosive action of sea-water—a mode of construction which has recently been adopted for torpedo-boats—and is sheathed with East Indian teak and coppered. A novel feature in the hull of so small a boat is its division into water-tight compartments by transverse and longitudinal bulkheads, composed of galvanised steel plates riveted to the steel frames. These bulkheads form a large forward compartment, two compartments on each side of the cabin, and a compartment at the stern, thus rendering the vessel water-tight as long as they remain intact.

On the deck, forward and aft, are hatchways which give entrance to the bow and stern compartments respectively. The hatches to these openings, which are kept constantly closed at sea, are fastened down with strong gun-metal screws fitted with butterfly nuts, the screws being fastened to the deck and made to fold down on it with joint when not in use. The coamings of the hatchways, as well as the inner edges of the hatches themselves, are lined with india-rubber, so as to render the covers perfectly water-tight. Access to the side compartments is obtained by means of manholes opening from the cabin, and covered with steel plates screwed into the bulkhead. In the event of the yacht's shipping any water, it is removed by a pump leading through the deck near to the cockpit and within easy reach of the steersman's hand. The cover of the pump works on a hinge, and lies flush with the deck when closed. The pump-handle is made to ship and unship at will, and is in the form of a lever, which renders the operation of pumping

Fig. 1.—'The Lady Hermione.'

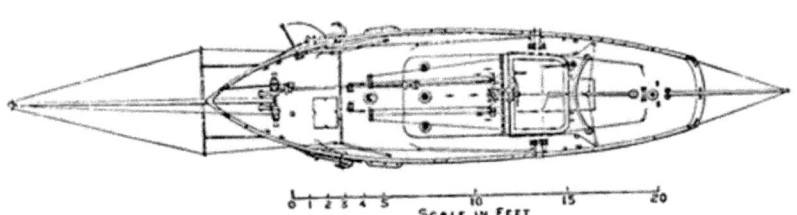

Fig. 3.—'The Lady Hermione.' Deck plan.

more easy than in the ordinary form of pump usually employed in small boats (c, figs. 2 and 11).

The Lady Hermione is ballasted with lead, the greater portion of which is carried outside in the form of a keel, which weighs about two tons. On trial, it was found that the little craft was too quick on her helm—a quality which, however useful in racing vessels, is undesirable in a single-handed boat, where the operation of getting aft the sheets when going about naturally requires somewhat more time than it does when the crew is composed of more than one hand. In order to remedy this defect a deep oak keel has been fixed outside the lead keel, and has to a considerable extent answered its purpose. It has also added immensely to the boat's stiffness; and it is blowing very hard indeed when a reef requires to be taken down. In fact, owing to her deep build and her heavy outside keels, *The Lady Hermione* is virtually uncapsizable, while her water-tight compartments render her unsinkable. It is impossible to overrate the value of these two elements of safety in a boat which is always worked by one person and is taken out in all weathers.

Stepping on board *The Lady Hermione*, the visitor, however much he is accustomed to yachts, is struck by the number and apparent complication of the contrivances which meet his eye (fig. 3), the interior of the vessel looking, as a witty naval officer once observed on being shown over her, 'something like the inside of a clock'; but, after a few explanations, the usefulness and practical efficiency of the various devices become evident. The principle which has been adhered to throughout in the rigging and fittings is, that all operations connected with the handling and management of the boat shall be performed by one person without the application of any considerable physical force. It has also been laid down as a *sine quâ non* that everything shall work perfectly in all weathers and under all conditions of wind and sea. The result of the owner's ingenuity is, that the sails can be hoisted and lowered, the sheets attended to, the anchor let go and weighed, and the tiller fixed and kept fixed in any desired position, without the necessity of the one person, who composes the crew leaving the cockpit. The arrangements for carrying out these objects will now be described in detail.

The first contrivance which claims attention is that for keeping the rudder fixed at any desired angle (figs. 4 and 5A). In his account of his cruise in the yawl *Rob Roy* the late Mr. Macgregor says that he had never seen any really satisfactory method of accomplishing this object;

but the difficulty has been solved by Lord Dufferin, who, indeed, has had fitted in many of his previous boats an apparatus similar to that in the present one. On the deck aft, about a couple of feet in advance of the rudder-head, are fitted two brass stanchions. These support a brass bar which on its lower side is indented with notches similar to the teeth of a saw, and of a depth of about half an inch (A, fig. 4).

On the tiller there is fitted a brass tube or cylinder made so as to slide backwards and forwards within a limit of some eight or ten inches, and bearing on its upper surface a triangular fin of brass (A, fig. 5). When it is desired to fix the tiller in any particular position, the cylinder is instantaneously slipped back until the fin catches one of the notches of the bar, and the tiller is thus securely fixed. The tiller is unlocked by simply flicking forward the cylinder with the hand, the locking and unlocking being done in a second. The toothed brass bar, it may be mentioned, is curved so that the fin may fit into any desired notch, no matter at what an angle it may be desired to fix the rudder (A, fig. 4). The cockpit of the yacht being somewhat small, it was found that when there was a lady passenger on board the movement of the tiller interfered with her comfort, and, in order to obviate this difficulty, a steering-wheel has recently been fixed on the top of the cabin immediately in front of where the helmsman stands (fig. 6).

When the wheel is used a short tiller is employed, with steel tackles leading from it through pulleys and fair-leads to the wheel itself. The axis of the wheel carries a brass cap fitted with a screw, by half a turn of which the steering apparatus can be locked or unlocked, and the helm fixed in any position. If it is desired at any time to substitute steering with the tiller for steering with the wheel, the process is very simple. A brass handle of the requisite length, and bearing a cylinder and fin as above described, is screwed on to the short tiller, and the tiller ropes are cast off, the whole operation being performed in a few seconds. The wheel, the stand for which slides into brass grooves on the cabin top, can also be unshipped and stowed out of the way in a very short time.

We now proceed to examine the gear for letting go the anchor, which, though difficult to describe, will readily be understood from the drawing (fig. 7). The anchor, a Martin's patent, when stowed, rests upon two crescent-shaped supports, which project from the bulwarks just forward of the main rigging (A, A', fig. 7). These supports are fixed to a bar or tumbler lying close to the inside of the bulwark, and arranged so as to turn on its axis (B, fig. 7; and C, fig. 12). Fixed to the

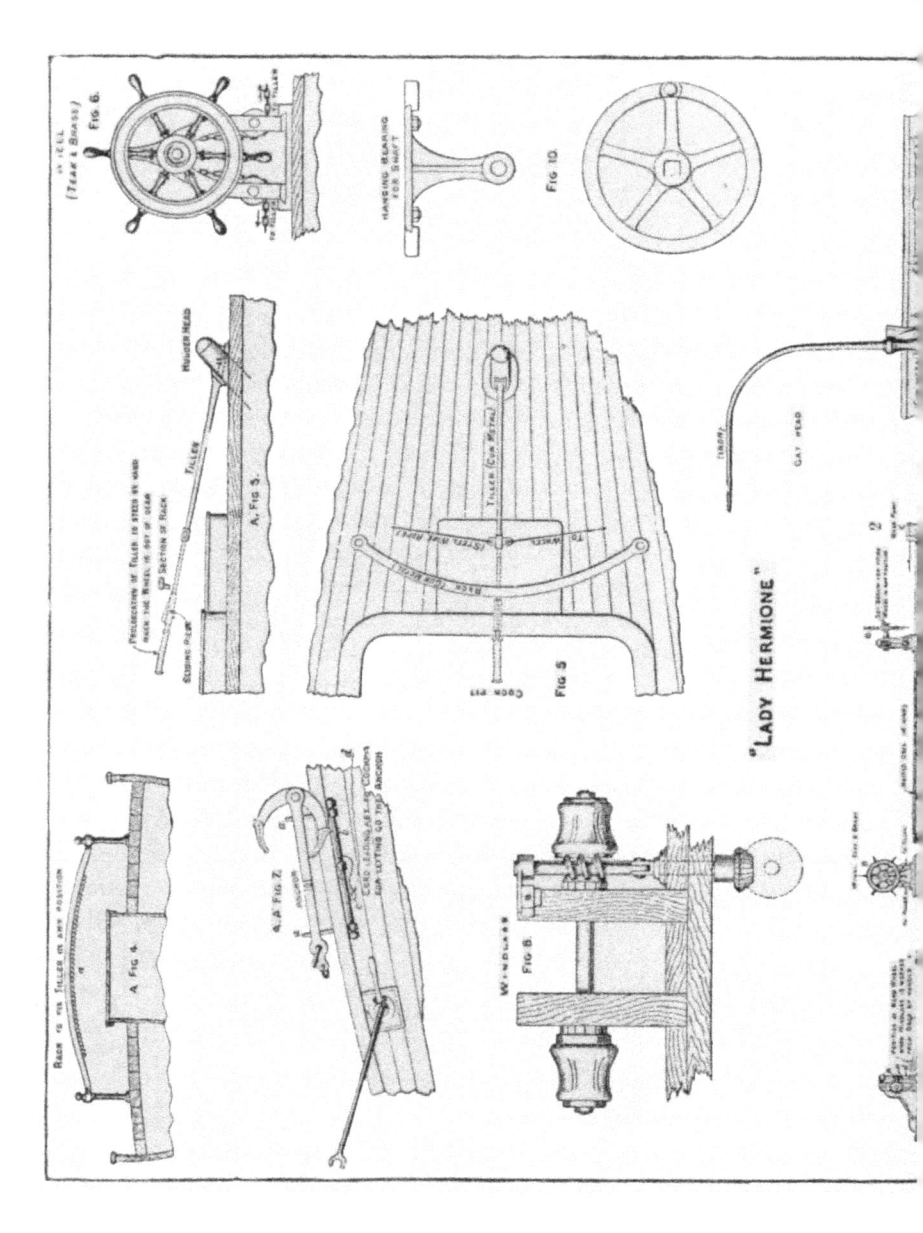

Fittings of 'The Lady Hermione.'

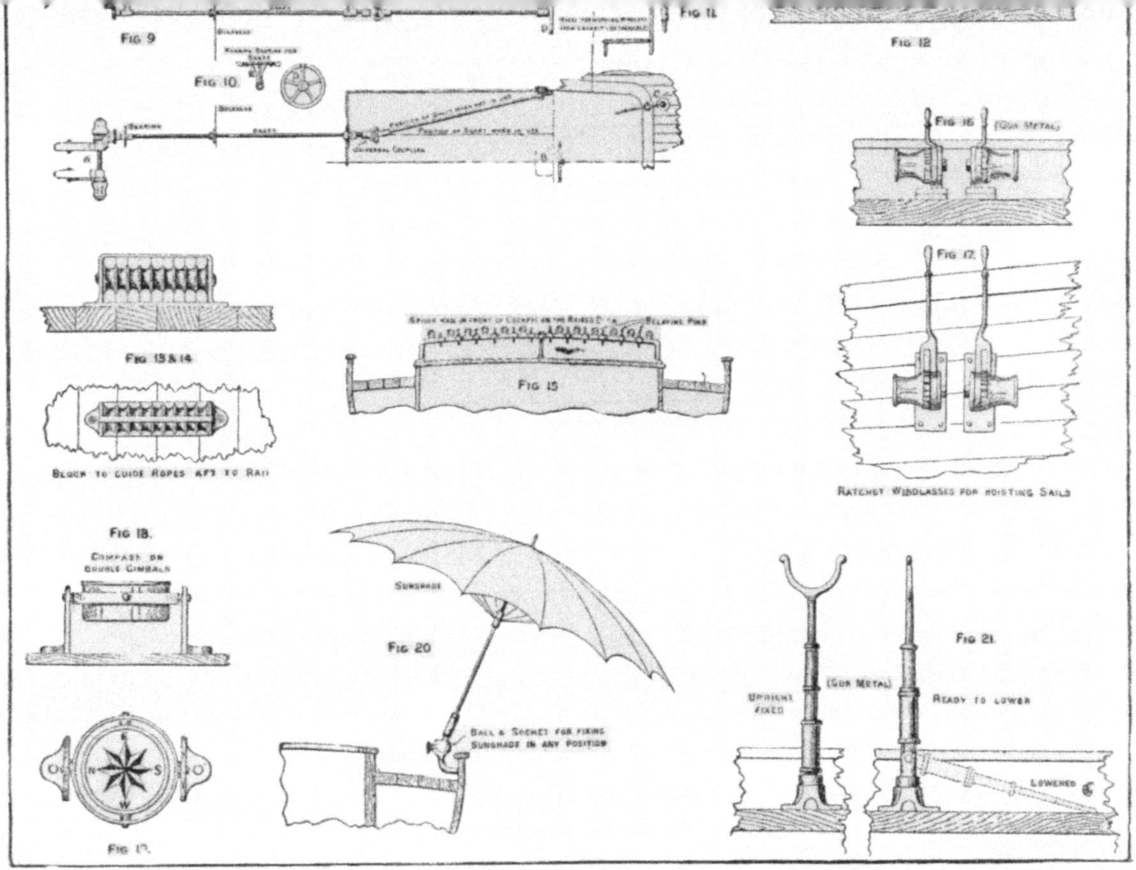
Fig 9
Fig 10.
Fig 11
Fig 12
Bulkhead
Bearing
Shaft
Universal Coupling
Fig 16
(Gun Metal)
Fig 17
Ratchet Windlasses for hoisting Sails
Fig 13 & 14
Block to guide Ropes aft to Rail
Fig 15
Belaying Pins
Fig 18.
Compass on double Gimbals
Fig 19.
Sunshade
Fig 20
Ball & Socket for fixing Sunshade in any position
Fig 21
Upright fixed
(Gun Metal)
Ready to lower
Lowered

tumbler inboard there is a small bar which fits into a socket attached to the covering board. On the socket is a trigger (C, fig. 7, and D, fig. 12) from which a line leads along the inside of the bulwarks to within easy reach of the cockpit (D, fig. 7). By pulling this line the socket is made to revolve, so as to release the arm; the weight of the anchor forces the tumbler to turn on its axis, bringing down with it the crescent-shaped supports, and the anchor falls into the sea.

This operation having been completed, it will probably be thought that now at last the crew must leave his point of vantage, and go forward to stopper and bit his cable. But no; we have not by any means yet reached the limits of ingenuity displayed in this extraordinary little ship. The chain cable runs out through a hawse-pipe in the bow, and across the hawse-hole a strong steel plate or compressor, with a notch cut in it to fit the links of the cable, runs in grooves. By pulling a line which leads to the cockpit this compressor is drawn over the hawse-hole, and the cable is thus effectually snubbed. When the anchor has to be got up, or it is required to let out more chain, the compressor can be drawn back by another line which also leads to the cockpit. These two contrivances for letting go and stopping the anchor, together with the apparatus for weighing it without leaving the cockpit, which will now be dealt with, get rid of that fruitful source of discomfort in boats manned by one hand—namely, the necessity of the solitary mariner's having to go forward to deal with his ground tackle at a time when perhaps he has other pressing calls on his attention in connection with the management of his vessel.

Equally as ingenious as the means of letting go the anchor is the machinery employed for weighing it. The windlass used is an ordinary yacht's windlass, except that on its outer end on its starboard side it carries a cogged wheel (fig. 8). Close alongside the windlass there rises from the deck a spindle cut with an endless screw (A, fig. 9), the threads of which take the teeth of the cogged wheel. This spindle runs through the deck, and has at its lower extremity a cogged wheel (B, fig. 9), fitting into another cogged wheel attached to a shaft, which runs aft on bearings in the ceiling of the cabin to the cockpit (C, fig. 9). At the cockpit end it is furnished with a large wheel (D, fig. 9, and fig. 10), on turning which the motion is communicated through the shaft and a system of cog-wheels (figs. 9 and 11), to the Archimedean screw rising up through the deck forward, and this screw in its turn revolves the windlass, and the anchor comes merrily home. The slack of the chain, as it comes in, drops perpendicularly through the hawse-pipe to the chain-locker below, and requires no attention or handling. The machinery for getting the anchor possesses great power, and, even when the anchor has a tight hold of the bottom, the wheel in the cockpit can be turned almost with one finger. The wheel is made to ship and unship, and when not in use is hung up to the side of the cabin.

As a general rule, especially when weighing in a crowded harbour, the anchor is simply hove up close to the hawse-hole until open water has been gained, the ropes carefully coiled down, and everything made snug and shipshape. The vessel is then laid to, or the helm fixed so as to keep her on her course, as circumstances may determine, and the crew goes forward to do the one thing he cannot perform from aft, the catting and fishing of his anchor. Suspended from the head of the mainmast is a tackle of the kind known to seamen as a 'Spanish burton,' with a long iron hook attached to its lower block. In fishing the anchor this burton is first overhauled, and, leaning over the bow, the operator fixes the hook in a ring let into the shank of the anchor at a point where the anchor exactly balances itself when suspended horizontally. He then passes the various parts of the fall of the tackle through an eye at the end of a fish-davit—similar in shape to the boat-davits used in large ships—which stands up from the deck close to the bulwarks, a little forward of the supports for the anchor already mentioned (A, fig. 12).

By pulling on the hauling part of the burton the anchor is raised close to the end of the davit, and the davit, by an ingeniously arranged spring, on a lever at its base (B, fig. 12), being pressed with the foot, can be swung round until the anchor is suspended immediately above its resting-place, into which it is then lowered, the crescent-shaped supports already referred to having been previously placed in position, and the trigger locked. Here it rests in perfect security, and is ready to be let go by pulling on the line attached to the trigger. On the port side a second anchor is carried, an Admiralty pattern, weighing about fifty pounds, and secured in precisely the same way as the starboard or working anchor, though in weighing it the windlass is used with an ordinary ratchet, as the windlass barrel on the port side is not connected with the shaft previously described. It may here be mentioned that the starboard barrel of the windlass can also be used in the ordinary way, as the spindle with the endless screw already mentioned is made with a joint, so that it can be disconnected from the cogged wheel and laid down flat on deck out of the way whenever necessary

(C, fig. 8; and D, fig. 9).

We now pass on to what is the most important thing in all single-handed sailing boats, the arrangement of the halliards and sheets in such a manner that all operations connected with making and shortening sail can be performed from the cockpit. In *The Lady Hermione* this essential principle has been carried out to its fullest extent. At the foot of the mainmast on each side is a brass fair-lead fitted with ten or twelve sheaves (figs. 13 and 14). Through these sheaves all the halliards (except, of course, those connected with the mizzen) are rove, and then led aft over the top of the cabin to within a few inches of the cockpit (fig. 3). Here they are belayed to a large belaying-pin rack which crosses the cabin top in front of the steersman and within easy reach of his hand (fig. 15). The frame of this rack is pierced with horizontal holes for the ropes to pass through, after which they are belayed to the pins, while the falls are allowed to drop down on to the cabin floor, where they are snugly coiled away in a box with a number of compartments which has been made to receive them.

The object of passing the halliards through holes in the belaying-pin rack is to afford a straight pull when getting up sail, and to prevent the ropes from flying away out of the steersman's reach when they are let go. *The Lady Hermione* is, or rather was originally, fitted with all the running rigging that would be employed in the largest-sized yacht, and this will give some idea of the number of ropes that have to be dealt with by one person:—main and peak halliards, two topping-lifts, tack tackle and tack tricing line, topsail tack, sheets, halliards, and clew line, jib and staysail halliards, and jib and staysail down-hauls. As originally rigged, main, peak, and jib purchases were employed for getting the mainsail and jib well up, but the introduction of the gipsy winches mentioned in the next paragraph rendered these ropes unnecessary, and they have consequently been dispensed with.

The system employed, however, has always worked without the slightest hitch, and enables whoever may be sailing the boat to attend to all the halliards without leaving the helm. On the belaying-pin rack each pin has the name of the rope for which it is intended engraved on a small brass plate, so that no confusion can arise as to what part of the gear it may at any time be desired to deal with; though, after a little practice, whoever is sailing the boat knows the lead of each rope by instinct. At the foot of the mizzen-mast fair-leads, similar to those near the mainmast, bring the gear of the mizzen to within reach of the cockpit. The jib and staysail sheets also lead aft, through bull's-eye fair-leads fixed inside the bulwarks, and are belayed to cleats screwed on to the coamings of the cockpit.

Even in a boat of the size now under description, it will be understood that the hoisting of the sails and the getting aft of the head-sheets in a strong breeze would tax the strength of an ordinary person; but, still carrying out the principle of doing everything with the least possible exertion, small gipsy winches of a peculiar pattern are largely employed, and form a very remarkable feature in the fittings of the vessel (figs. 16 and 17). These winches are all made so as to be easily shipped and unshipped at will, as they slide into brass grooves affixed to the deck, and are worked with ratchet handles, to which are attached strong steel springs in order to insure the ratchets always biting in the cogs. Altogether, there are ten gipsy winches on board, two on the deck on each side of the cockpit, two on the cabin top just forward of the belaying-pin rack, and two on the deck in front of the mainmast. The two on each side of the cockpit are used for the head-sheets. The sheets, led aft as previously described, are given a couple of turns round the barrel of the winch, and then belayed to their cleats. In getting them in after going about, they are first hauled hand-taut, then the ratchet handle is worked until they are as tight as may be desired, after which they are belayed. These operations are performed in a very few seconds, and the power of the winches is so great that the sheets are got in flatter than would be possible by any other means. The four winches on the cabin top are employed in the same manner for the main and peak halliards, or for the topsail tack, sheet and halliards, as may be required. The two forward of the mast are used for any purpose for which it may be required to use a purchase. The winches have all worked admirably from the time they were first fitted; they are not in the least in the way, and the simplicity of their operation and the extraordinary power which can be developed from them would scarcely be credited by anyone who has not seen them in actual use. The jib and staysail sheets were at first fitted with tackles; but the introduction of the winches has rendered tackles unnecessary. For the same reason, the main, peak and jib purchases, which were fitted when the little vessel was first prepared for sea, have been dispensed with, as the winches give all the power that can be desired.

Forward of, and attached to, the mainmast a long hawser is kept constantly stowed, to be used as a tow-rope in case towing by a steam-launch or tug should be necessary, as sometimes happens in a calm. This hawser is bulky and unwieldy to handle when wet, and it is understood that on the first opportunity there is to be substituted for it a light steel-wire hawser wound on a miniature but sufficiently strong drum, carried forward, in the same manner that steel hawsers are disposed of on the decks of large vessels.

Having now completed the description of the main features of the vessel, a word or two may be said about her minor fittings, which are also worthy of notice.

In most single-handed boats the helmsman is constantly bothered by his head-sheets, especially when there is a strong breeze, getting foul of something, thus necessitating his going forward to clear them. In 'The Lady Hermione' this inconvenience is entirely obviated by brass guards placed over all the projections upon which it is possible for a rope to catch. In this way the fair-leads in the bow, the windlass and the gipsy winches forward, are all protected, so that it is impossible for a rope to get foul anywhere.

In order to harmonise with the rest of the metal-work, the screws by which the rigging is set up are all of gun-metal, instead of the galvanised iron usually employed for the purpose.

Round the entire gunwale there runs a steel-wire ridge-rope, supported on brass stanchions, so that anyone moving about the deck in heavy weather may have something to hold on by.

In front of the mast there is a ladder made of steel-wire rope with wooden steps, leading from the deck to the crosstrees, which is very convenient in case anything has to be done aloft. This ladder is set up to the deck with brass screws, similar to those used for the rigging.

On the top of the cabin, in front of the steersman and between the gipsy winches, is a lifeboat liquid-compass fitted with a binnacle, the compass, like almost every fitting on board, being made to ship and unship, so as to be stowed out of the way when not in use (figs. 18 and 19).

As the little vessel when abroad was frequently sailed in the winter months, when, even in the Mediterranean, it is somewhat bitterly cold, a brass charcoal stove or chafing-dish of the kind used in Turkey, and there called a 'mangal,' is fitted at the bottom of the cockpit. It is covered with a brass grating, which forms a floor for the helmsman to stand on; and the heat from below keeps him comfortably warm, even in the coldest weather.

Another provision against the weather is a large umbrella for the use of any lady passenger when sailing under a strong sun. When in use the handle is fitted into a socket on the coaming of the hatchway, the socket being fitted with a universal joint, so that the umbrella may be adjusted in any desired position. There are two sockets, one on either side of the cockpit, in order that the umbrella may be carried on whichever side is most convenient (fig. 20).

On either side of the gunwale aft is fitted a brass crutch for supporting the main boom when the vessel is at anchor (fig. 21). At sea the clutches also serve the purpose of receiving the topsail-yard, one end of which is stowed in a crutch, while the other is made fast with a tying to the outside of the main rigging, thus getting rid of the inconvenience of having such a long spar on deck.

A very important fitting is a hatch by which the cockpit can be completely covered in in heavy weather. The hatch is made in sections hinged together, its two halves being also hinged to the back of the seats in the cockpit on either side. When unfolded and fixed in position it covers the entire cockpit, with the exception of a small circular opening left for the steersman, and the vessel is rendered almost as water-tight as a corked bottle. This small circular opening can also be closed, if necessary, by a wooden-hinged cover made for the purpose.

Most of the running rigging is of white cotton rope, which looks exceedingly smart and has answered its purpose fairly well; but it has not the durability of manilla, and when wet it has a great tendency to kink.

The cabin is very plainly fitted up, and is without berths or seats, its only furniture being some racks and cupboards used for stowing away a few necessary articles. When anyone sleeps on board, a mattress is spread on the floor and forms a very comfortable bed.

In the cabin there is carried, folded up, a 10-ft. Berthon dinghy, which can be expanded and launched in a few minutes. This does away with the necessity of towing a dinghy, while there is not room to carry one on deck.

In conclusion, it may be said that *The Lady Hermione* presents a very smart appearance and is an extraordinarily good sea-boat. The writer has frequently seen her out in the Gulf of Naples in weather which even the largest native craft would not venture to face. She is also admirably sailed by her owner, and it is a great pleasure to watch her being handled by him under sail, everything being done with great method and system and in a highly seamanlike style. Her cruising ground has now been transferred to the stormier regions of the English Channel; and two summers ago she was sailed to Trouville, where she remained for some time, running back to the Solent in

LORD DUFFERIN'S 'FOAM,' R.Y.S. 'IN HIGH LATITUDES,' 1856.

VIEW FROM THE ROYAL WESTERN YACHT CLUB, PLYMOUTH.

October in half a gale of wind, during which she behaved admirably, and made better weather than many large vessels could have done.

This paper has run to a greater length than the writer at first intended; but he trusts he will be forgiven in consideration of his having made known to his fellow-yachtsmen the existence of what is really a most unique and wonderful little craft. A model of her hull was included in Messrs. Forrest & Son's exhibit in the late Naval Exhibition at Chelsea, and it is to be regretted that the vessel herself, or, at all events, an accurate model showing her rigging and all her fittings, was not on view also, for she would not have been by any means the least attractive of the many nautical objects of interest contained in the collection in question, which has done so much to make the British public acquainted with the maritime history and greatness of their country.

Royal Western Yacht Club, Plymouth.

No wonder Plymouth was early in the field with yachting, in view of the tempting facilities for every variety of aquatic pastime which nature has there provided in the midst of lovely scenery, with shelter close at hand in case of sudden change of weather; in fact, the whole atmosphere is nautical with mighty precedents, for is not this the West-country long famed for mariners with stirring historical associations? Who can walk on the Hoe without thinking of Drake, of Armada fame, and the stout hearts that gathered round him in the hour of need for the defence of England against an overwhelming force? Plymouth is a delightfully picturesque spot. On the S.-W. is the seat of the Earl of Mount Edgcumbe, where the timber is specially fine on the hills which afford shelter from the prevalent S.-W. wind, and blow it truly can on occasions, not infrequently at the Regatta time, when it is least wanted, now that the small raters are in such force.

Still it is surprising what weather some of these little fellows make of it as they round the Breakwater. The present club-house of the Royal Western Yacht Club is situated at the west end of the Hoe. The view from the club-house is extremely fine. On the right the wooded heights of Mount Edgcumbe, with the Hamoaze beneath, a little to the right, also Drake's Island and the starting point for yacht and trawler racing; due south the great Breakwater, and in clear weather the new Eddystone Lighthouse. Bearing to the left beyond the Breakwater is the well-known *Mewstone* and familiar *Shag Rock*, whilst inside lie a variety of craft. Any foreign men-of-war visiting Plymouth generally

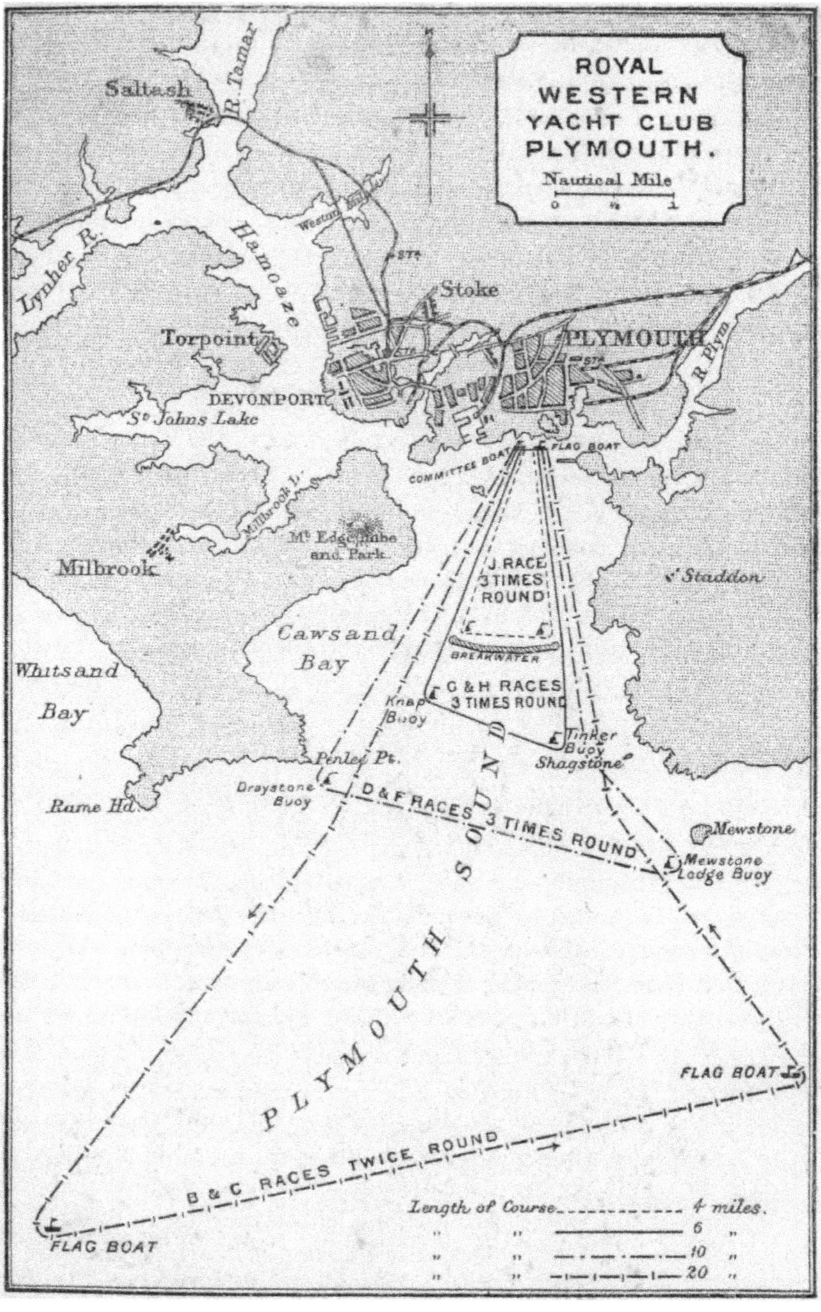
ROYAL WESTERN YACHT CLUB PLYMOUTH.
Nautical Mile
0 ½ 1
Saltash
R. Tamar
Lynher R.
Hamoaze
Stoke
Torpoint
PLYMOUTH
R. Plym
DEVONPORT
St Johns Lake
COMMITTEE BOAT
FLAG BOAT
Millbrook L.
Mt Edgcumbe and Park
Milbrook
Staddon
J. RACE 3 TIMES ROUND
BREAKWATER
Cawsand Bay
Whitsand Bay
G & H RACES 3 TIMES ROUND
Knap Buoy
Tinker Buoy
Shagstone
Penlee Pt.
Draystone Buoy
Rame Hd.
D & F RACES 3 TIMES ROUND
Mewstone
Mewstone Ledge Buoy
PLYMOUTH SOUND
FLAG BOAT
B & C RACES TWICE ROUND
FLAG BOAT
Length of Course 4 miles.
" " 6 "
" " 10 "
" " 20 "

bring up at this spot, and the training brigs *Seaflower, Pilot,* and *Martin* give quite an idea of old days in the British Navy, imparting much life to the whole sea view, for the lads are always getting under way, or loosing sails, going out or coming in. On still to the left is a range of high hills running out to the Start Point and Prawle Point, and just beyond the Hoe to the eastward is the Catwater, where yachts get a snug berth clear of the entrance to the inner harbour full of trawlers and every possible variety of hookers, fishing craft, &c.

The Royal Western Yacht Club was established in 1827, and was at that time known as the Port of Plymouth Royal Clarence Regatta Club; in 1833 it became the Royal Western Yacht Club. H.R.H. the Duke of Sussex consented to become patron and H.R.H. the Duchess of Kent patroness, eight presidents were appointed, one of whom, Sir T. D. Acland, is still living in Devonshire. The vice-presidents, twenty-one in number, were all men of high position and great influence. A most interesting list of the yachts in 1835, giving the names of the boats, is still in the possession of the club. Unfortunately there is not space to print this in full, valuable as it would be as a record; still certain points must be noted. There were 43 yachts in the list: of these 17 were clinker-built, like the *Harriet* cutter of Cowes, 96 tons, belonging to Sir B. R. Graham, Bart., a very handsome craft carrying a crew of eleven hands. Ten were carvel-built, 16 not classified. This was the period of general introduction of carvel surfaces. Sir T. D. Acland's yacht *Lady St. Kilda* was the largest schooner and largest yacht belonging to the Royal Western Yacht Club. Her complement of hands was eleven. Another point worthy of attention is the proportion of rigs adopted: out of 43 vessels, 29 were cutters, 5 schooners, 4 yawls, 5 no rig given.

The regattas were held at first on the anniversary of the coronation of His Majesty George IV., and the members were to be distinguished by a uniform worn on the day of the regatta, and at such other times as they might think proper.

Undress: Short blue jacket with round collar, single-breasted—six buttons in front, and three on each cuff. White or blue kerseymere waistcoat, with six buttons. White trousers. Blue and white shirt.

Full dress: Blue coat, with buttons on breast and cuffs. White kerseymere waistcoat. White shirt, black handkerchief, white trousers. The president, the vice-presidents, and the stewards were to have three buttons on a slash cuff, and to wear blue pantaloons.

The regatta takes place about September 1, when there is generally a great meeting. About four hundred members and one hundred yachts belong to the club. The Royal Navy contributes innumerable classes of craft to compete in the racing, whilst the trawlers and fishing vessels all come in for the sports, producing one of the most picturesque gatherings to be seen anywhere. The secretary is Capt. H. Holditch, who has kindly furnished the information here given.

The Royal Victoria Yacht Club, Ryde

The R.V.Y.C., established in 1844, made a strong start, as the foundation stone of the present house was laid by H.R.H. the Prince Consort in March 1846. It is well placed close to the end of Ryde Pier, having a commanding view of very wide range from its windows. The club has always been noted for its encouragement of yacht racing, and has endeavoured to bring about international contests. In 1890 a Gold Challenge Cup was instituted, value 600 guineas, subscribed for by the members, and the famous race for the trophy in 1893 between H.R.H. the Prince of Wales's *Britannia* and Mr. Carroll's *Navahoe* will be found described in the account of the sport which took place in that memorable year. The R.V.Y. Club at Ryde is often called the Red Squadron, in contradistinction to the R.Y.S. with the White Ensign.

In 1891 the club started regattas for the small classes which were then becoming so prominent. These have been warmly taken up and attended with great success.

International Gold Cup,
Royal Victoria Yacht Club, 1883.
Won by 'Britannia.'

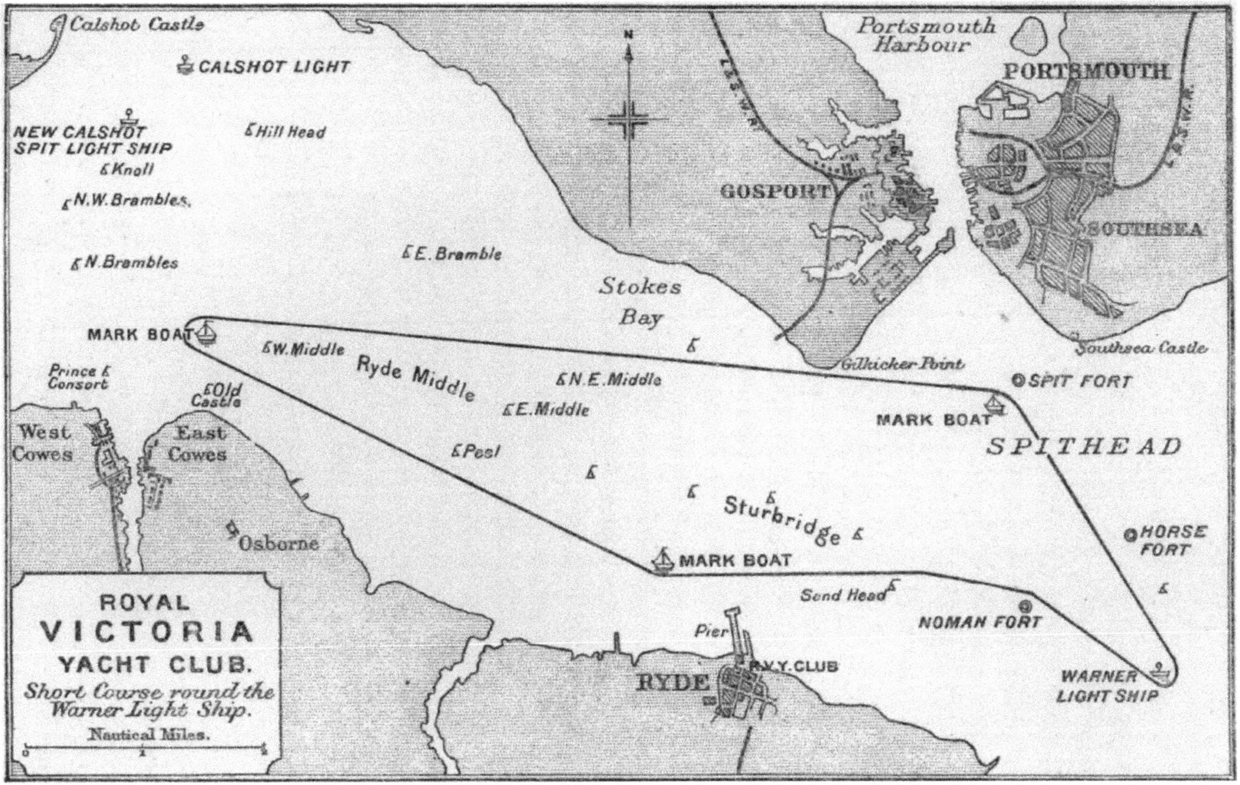
Calshot Castle
CALSHOT LIGHT
NEW CALSHOT SPIT LIGHT SHIP
Hill Head
Knoll
N.W. Brambles
N. Brambles
E. Bramble
Stokes Bay
Portsmouth Harbour
PORTSMOUTH
GOSPORT
SOUTHSEA
L & S.W.R.
N
Southsea Castle
Gilkicker Point
SPIT FORT
MARK BOAT
W. Middle
Ryde Middle
N.E. Middle
E. Middle
Prince Consort
Old Castle
West Cowes
East Cowes
Pesl
Osborne
Sturbridge
SPITHEAD
HORSE FORT
Sand Head
NOMAN FORT
Pier
R.V.Y. CLUB
RYDE
WARNER LIGHT SHIP
ROYAL VICTORIA YACHT CLUB.
Short Course round the Warner Light Ship.
Nautical Miles.
0
1
2

There is yet another Challenge Cup in the hands of the Committee, value 100 guineas. As yet it has not been sailed for, but it is decided that the course is to be in the open Channel, not less than 150 miles, such as Ryde, round Plymouth Breakwater, Cherbourg Breakwater, and back to Ryde for the finish. The cup was presented by Mr. T. B. C. West, of *Wendur* and *Queen Mab* fame. Probably the length of the course has deterred competition; at least, a well-known skipper, Captain John Nichols, who sailed *Alarm, Mosquito,* and *Cygnet,* always says that 'nine hours at the tiller is quite enough to do it properly'; and his experience spreads over many years and many a tough tussle for mastery. Mr. Fife of Fairlie declares that the *Cuckoo*, 90 tons, never showed her real capability until 'Captain John' sailed her. The Royal Victoria Yacht Club has recently added a very large room fronting the sea, and acquired a 'look-out' at the end of the Pier, which seems almost like sitting in an armchair at Spithead. The small raters have a good friend in the Secretary, Mr. Percy Thellusson, who dearly loves them, without neglecting in any way the interests of the larger craft.

An eccentric finish to a yacht race occurred in connection with this club, in the contest for Ryde Town Purse, August 11, 1892, and other prizes for smaller classes. There was a nice breeze from the eastward at 10 a.m., and like a flight of swans the yachts were away together. At 2 p.m., when off the Peel Bank, not a breath of wind was there to help them. The committee decided to run up signal to shorten course and conclude at the first round. No sooner was this done and carried out than a brave westerly breeze sprang up and brought in about fifteen of the craft, all classes together, both great and small, all with feathered bows. The whole of the starters returned together within about ten minutes. The uncertainty of the turf is proverbial, but the uncertainty of the sea is no less remarkable.

The Royal Mersey Yacht Club

This club, which was established in 1844, originally had its headquarters at Liverpool, the first commodore having been Dr. Grinwood, whose brother is now the only original member left. About 1878 the club quarters were moved to a large house in Birkenhead, close to the river, on the banks of which a pavilion has been constructed, as well as a large slip and two gridirons. During the whole time the club has only had two honorary secretaries, the past and the present. To the late secretary, Mr. Henry Melling, we are indebted for the two illustrations; he drew and published them himself, much to his

'Princess Royal,' steamer 'Leda,' 'Seagull,' 'Hebe,' 'Phœbe.'
First race of Mersey Yacht Club, June 16, 1845.

'Queen of the Ocean,' R.M.Y.C.,
Commodore Littledale, saving emigrants from 'Ocean Monarch,'
August 24, 1848.

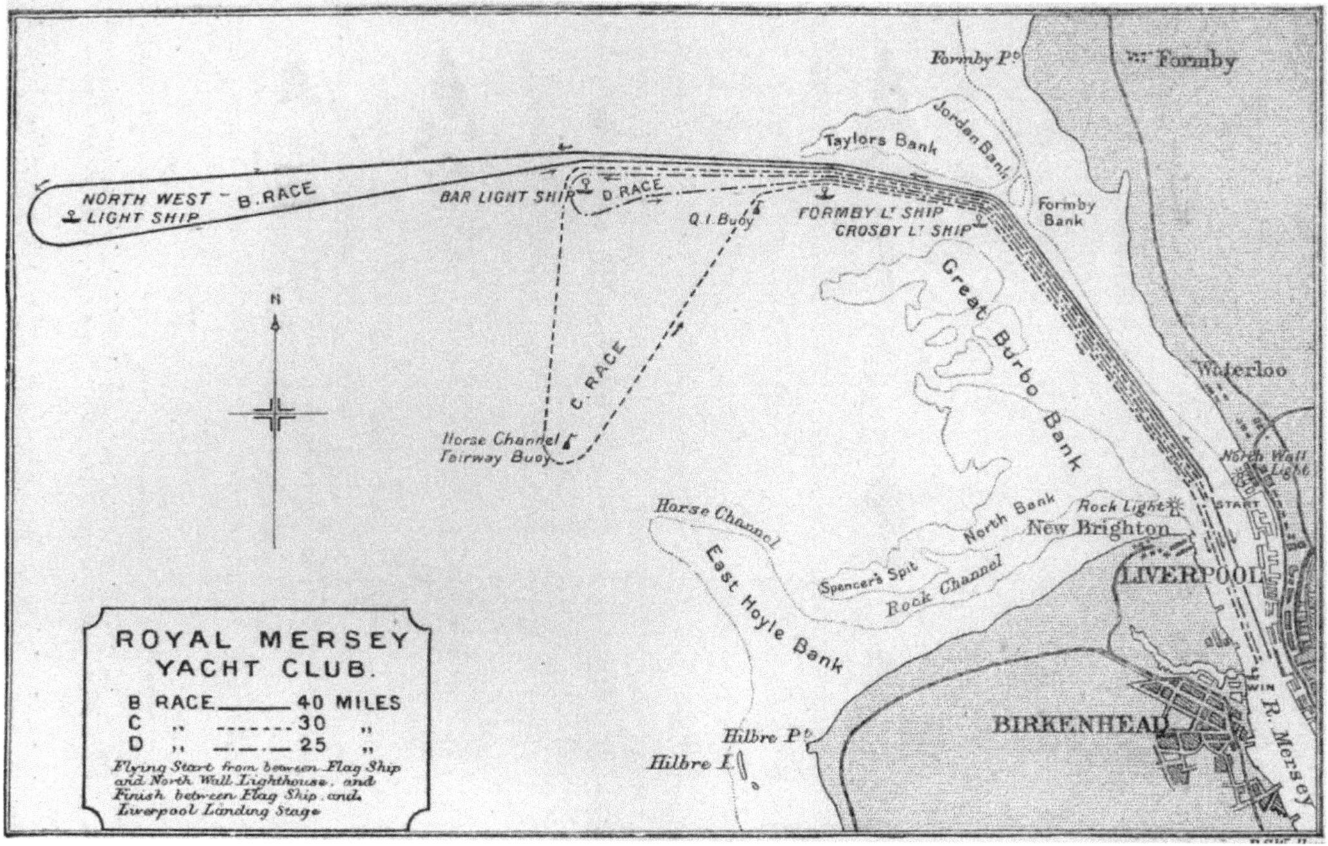
ROYAL MERSEY
YACHT CLUB.
B RACE 40 MILES
C ,, 30 ,,
D ,, 25 ,,
Flying Start from between Flag Ship and North Wall Lighthouse, and Finish between Flag Ship and Liverpool Landing Stage
NORTH WEST LIGHT SHIP
B. RACE
BAR LIGHT SHIP
D. RACE
C. RACE
Q.I. Buoy
Horse Channel Fairway Buoy
FORMBY Lt SHIP
CROSBY Lt SHIP
Formby Pt
Formby
Jordan Bank
Taylors Bank
Formby Bank
Great Burbo Bank
Waterloo
North Wall Light
START
Rock Light
North Bank
New Brighton
Horse Channel
East Hoyle Bank
Spencer's Spit
Rock Channel
LIVERPOOL
BIRKENHEAD
WIN
R. Mersey
Hilbre Pt
Hilbre I.
N

YACHT CLUB BURGEES.

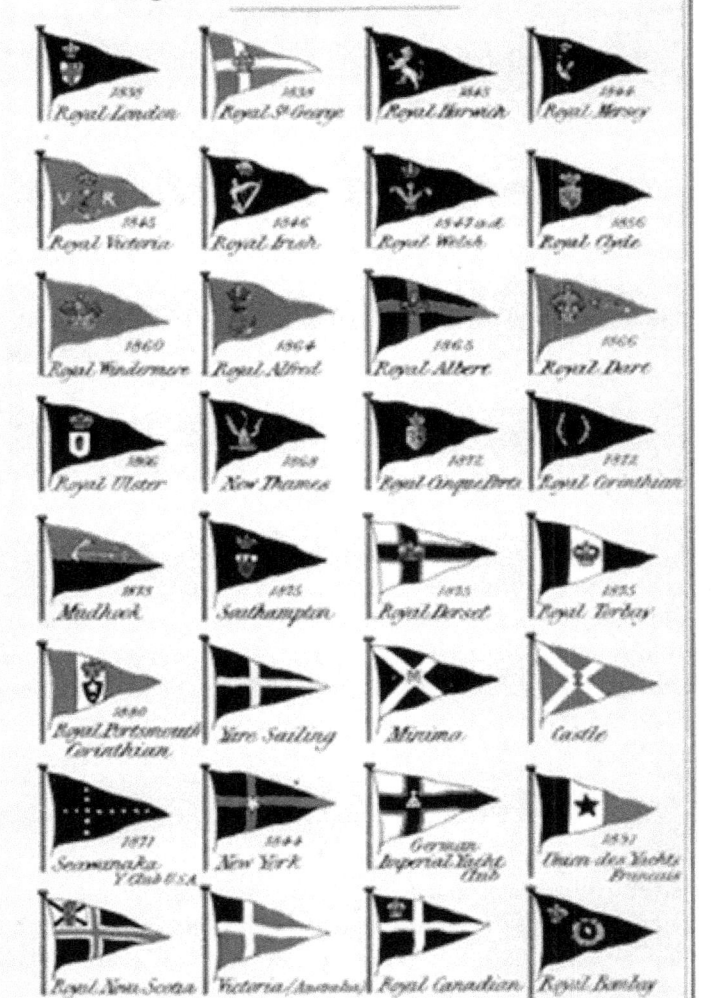

credit, as valuable data showing the rig of the time. The annual regatta is generally held at the latter end of June, the great drawback to Liverpool yachting being the tides and the bar, to diminish which great efforts are being made by dredging on an enormous scale. 1893 was the Jubilee Regatta. This was a great success. *Britannia, Satanita, Iverna,* took part in the races, which were accompanied by the club steamer, carrying the Commodore, Col. Gamble, C.B., and the Hon. Secretary, Captain James Gladstone.

The first illustration is most interesting as bearing the names of the yachts which sailed in the first match of the club, Monday, June 16, 1845. The bowlines on the luff of the gaff topsails should be particularly noticed as a feature of this period. The bowline is also shown in the drawing of the *Cygnet*, 35 tons, in a following chapter on Thames Clubs.

The second outline represents the *Queen of the Ocean* yacht, Commodore Littledale, R.M.Y.C., going to the rescue of the *Ocean Monarch*, emigrant ship, on fire in Abergele Bay, North Wales, Thursday, August 24, 1848.

The Royal Portsmouth Corinthian Yacht Club
By G. L. Blake

What the Clyde is to Scotland, and Kingstown and Queenstown are to Ireland, that the Solent and Southampton Water (which constitute the waters more or less shut off from the Channel by the Isle of Wight) are to the South of England. It is no matter of wonderment, then, that attempts should have been made from time to time, and dating back some generations, to form clubs which would have for their express purpose the encouragement of seamanship, and the racing and building of yachts.

To many old yachtsmen the 'ups and downs' of some of these societies which are still in existence form a history of no small interest; while the rise, doings, and fall of those now defunct ought to teach many valuable and important lessons to the officers and committees that are working hard for the prosperity and welfare of present day yacht clubs.

The club which above all others has tended to encourage the proficiency of amateur salts, so that they have become capable of manning, piloting, and steering their own or their friends' vessels to glory, is the Royal Portsmouth Corinthian Yacht Club. Instituted at a time when small-yacht sailing and amateur seamanship had little or no patronage from the big clubs, and when no ruling spirit appeared willing to come forward to help them on to any great degree, when the annual local regattas of the Itchen Ferry, Ryde, and Cowes Town, Southampton, and a few other seaside resorts, were the only opportunities afforded for sport and racing among the small fry, perhaps no club deserves more notice among those south of London than the one in question.

Its birth took place at a meeting held on Saturday, May 22, 1880, in the committee-room of the Prince of Wales Club, High Street, Portsmouth, under the patronage of the late Admiral Ryder, R.N., and General H.S.H. Prince Edward of Saxe-Weimar, at that time the Commander-in-Chief and Governor of Portsmouth, Rear-Admiral the Honourable F. A. C. Foley, R.N., and Major-General Sir F. Fitz-Wygram, with Captain Garrett, R.A., in the chair. A provisional committee was elected, among whom were Messrs. W. Gilman, C. Johnson, Thomas and Charles McCheane, F. Ruck, R.E., W. C. Storey, W. V. Dickenson, 69th Regiment, J. Bewicke, 69th Regiment, Colonel Savory, Admiral Hallowes, Commander Britten, R.N., H.M.S. *St. Vincent*, Captains Sutton, R. Kennedy, Rasch, the Reverends C. P. Grant, Vicar of Portsmouth, and J. F. Brown, R.C. Military Chaplain. General Prince Edward of Saxe-Weimar, Captain Garrett and Captain Sutton were the first officers appointed to serve as Commodore, Vice- and Rear-commodores, and Messrs. Gilman and C. McCheane with Captain Kennedy undertook other duties.

Among the yachts owned at that period by the young club, the best known were the *Vega*, 40 tons, belonging to Captain Garrett; Mr. Gilman's little *Zephyr*, 11 tons (for many seasons one of the fastest of the old 12-ton class); and the *Zoe*, one of the most successful 21-ft. boats on the Solent, which was fortunate in being owned and piloted by one of the best amateur helmsmen and sailormen in the south of England—the late Mr. C. Johnson, of Gosport.

At the third meeting the Yacht Racing Association rules were adopted, while the fourth settled that very much vext and troublesome question as to what constitutes 'a yachting amateur,' and accordingly drew out the rule that 'No person shall be considered an amateur who has been at any time engaged in the navigation or sailing of a yacht for pay,' the wording of which has since been altered to the following:

An amateur is a gentleman who has never received pay for

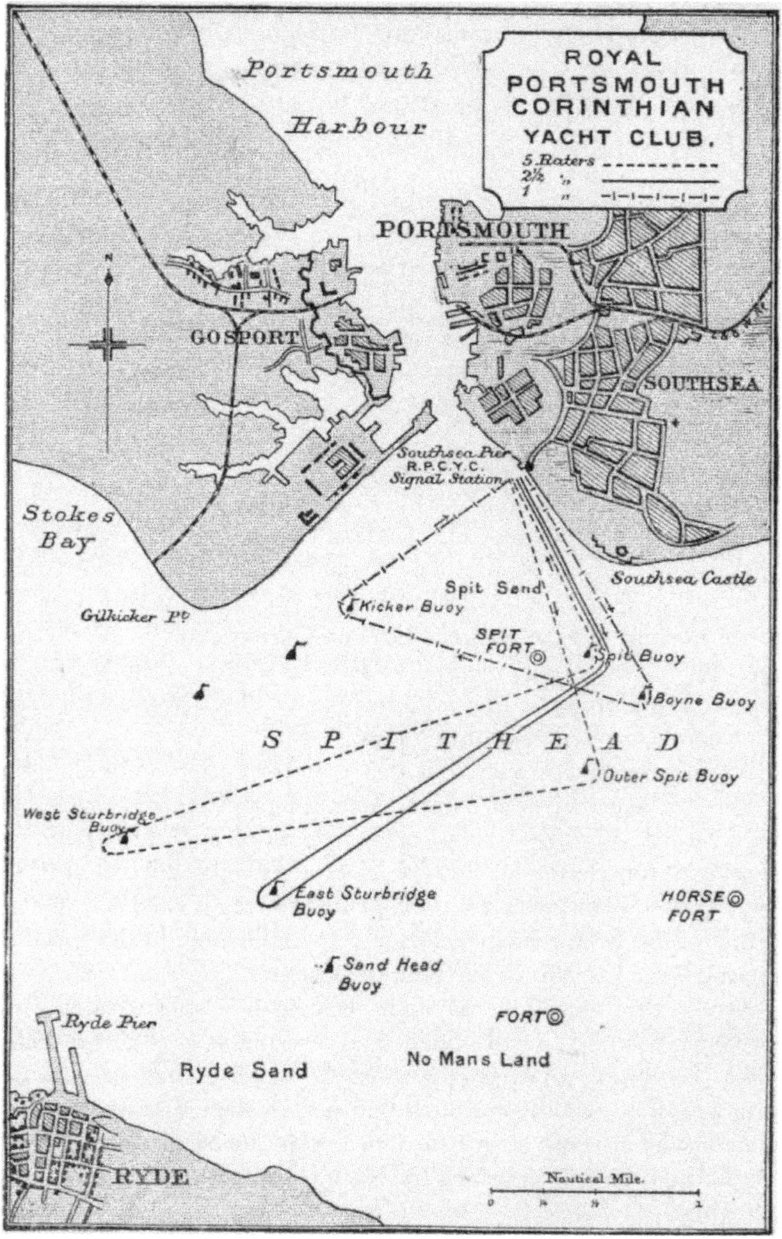
ROYAL PORTSMOUTH CORINTHIAN YACHT CLUB.
5 Raters
2½ „
1 „
Portsmouth
Harbour
PORTSMOUTH
GOSPORT
SOUTHSEA
Southsea Pier
R.P.C.Y.C.
Signal Station
Stokes Bay
Southsea Castle
Spit Sand
Kicker Buoy
Gilkicker Pt
SPIT FORT
Spit Buoy
Boyne Buoy
S P I T H E A D
Outer Spit Buoy
West Sturbridge Buoy
East Sturbridge Buoy
HORSE FORT
Sand Head Buoy
FORT
Ryde Pier
Ryde Sand
No Mans Land
RYDE
Nautical Mile
0
¼
½
1

sailing in a fore-and-aft vessel, officers of the Royal Navy and Mercantile Marine excepted.

At the same meeting Mr. C. McCheane undertook the sole duties of honorary secretary in place of Captain Kennedy.

On June 26, 1880, the first regatta of the newly formed club was held, when five events were pulled off under the most favourable auspices. So successful was this first attempt at bringing the local boats together, that the next regatta, which was similar in its classes, brought out no fewer than eight entries in the race for the service boats of Her Majesty's ships, all of which were steered by naval members of the club, with the one exception of the *Wren*, which, it is interesting to chronicle, was steered by Miss Foley, daughter of the Admiral commanding the Portsmouth Steam Reserve. She was the first lady member, and one of the first ladies—if indeed there was one before her—to pilot home the winning yacht in a race. Now that so many ladies enter into the sport of yacht racing and come out as famous helmswomen, the position held by Miss Foley is one to be proud of. In the fourth race Mr. Baden-Powell's old boat, the *Diamond*, 5 tons, at this time owned by Messrs. Sutton, put in an appearance as a 25-ft. boat; and in the fifth race Mr. J. H. Baillie's 20-ft. boat *Kate*, the earliest of Mr. Beavor Webb's outputs, entered.

Besides periodical regattas, the club was able to take in hand a good many matches, which were made up whenever a sufficient number of racing yachts to create sport happened to be lying off Southsea or about the port, and good prizes were always forthcoming, for, as is the case in the Royal Alfred Yacht Club of Kingstown, all money was devoted at this time to racing purposes. The match held on the 14th of August, 1880, is a very fair example of what these extemporaneous races were like. It was for yachts of 20 tons and under. The entries included: *Madge*, 10 tons, Mr. J. Coats; *Louise*, 20 tons; *Euterpe*, 20 tons, Mr. Bayley; *Freda*, 20 tons, Mr. Freke; *Maggie*, 15 tons, Mr. Taylor; *Viola*, 20 tons, Mr. Kelly; *Sayonara*, 20 tons, Mr. G. W. Richardson.

By the end of the first season the club had advanced to such a strong position in the eyes of yachting men and in the public estimation, that Her Majesty was pleased to accede to the request of the commodore, Prince Edward of Saxe-Weimar, to have it made a Royal club, and accordingly commanded that from May 27, 1880, the club should be styled the Royal Portsmouth Corinthian Yacht Club. Except perhaps in the cases of the Royal Cork, the Royal Yacht Squad-

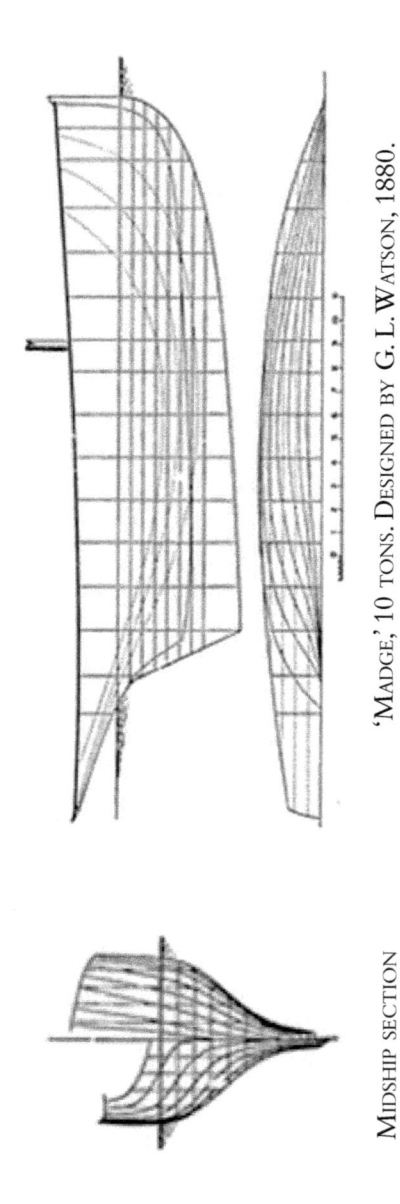

'Madge,' 10 tons. Designed by G. L. Watson, 1880.

Midship section

ron and Royal Highland, no yachting club has ever been known to grow so rapidly into popularity as to obtain the Royal warrant within the space of less than six months.

The season of 1881 began on April 6 with a yacht tonnage of 3,569 tons and 220 members belonging to the club. The year was an important one in its annals, for some of the best known of yachtsmen became members of the community. Captain Garrett gave up the Vice-Commodoreship, and was succeeded by Captain F. Sutton, late 11th Hussars, whilst Admiral Byng undertook the office vacated by Captain Sutton.

The greater number of those who had up to this time joined the Royal Portsmouth Corinthian Yacht Club were yachting members, and lived in all parts of the United Kingdom. The opening regatta was held on the glorious 4th of June, so dear to Eton and other memories. It witnessed the entry, in the race for yachts of 11 to 25 tons, of that favourite old 20-ton clipper the *Vanessa*, and the old Fairlie 25-tonner *Santry*. The courses this year finished between a mark-boat and the Southsea Pier.

At the third regatta another famous old ship threw down the glove to the *Gadfly* and Mr. Arthur Glennie's *Sonata*, *viz.* the 16-ton *Satanella*. On August 13, by the special command of Her Majesty, the club had the honour of holding its Annual Royal Regatta in Osborne Bay. The entries were large for all the items of the programme, no fewer than twelve boats starting in a class for 30 ft. and under, and thirty-one for the race for centre-boarders.

In this last race the Prince of Wales sailed his little crack *Belle Lurette*, and won the second prize. In the race for yachts of 40 tons and upwards the *Samœna*, *Annasona*, and *Sleuthhound* started. It may be stated here, that on the day of the regatta the club had 400 names on its list of members, the greater number of whom claimed some pretensions to being yachtsmen.

This was a rapid increase of 180 in less than four months, and distinctly proved that the club was already satisfactorily filling the much-desired need on the Solent, and it was most gratifying to those who had given their time and their energy towards the success of the venture that nothing but praise poured in from all quarters, because of the perfect organisation with which all regattas, matches, and general arrangements were carried out. Perhaps it is not too much to say here that the club owed much at this period of its existence to its honorary secretary, the late Mr. Charles McCheane, whose unflagging zeal and well-known gift of organisation helped to a very considerable extent to bring about the prestige which it was beginning to enjoy.

One great feature of the season of 1881 was the addition of a rule allowing any boat that had been hired by a member for a space of over three months to enter for the club races, in order to give every encouragement to the sport of yacht-racing. Many have been the times that such a rule has been begged for by yachtsmen, especially tiros at the game; but the Yacht Racing Association, and, in fact, all Royal Yacht Clubs with the exception of the Royal Portsmouth Corinthian, have placed a veto on any proposition which included in any way its introduction.

With the Royal Portsmouth Corinthian the rule proved in the early days of the club a great success, but latterly, as yacht tonnage was added to the club and members became provided with their own ships, the rule gradually died out, till at last it has disappeared altogether from the Book of Rules and Regulations.

The year 1882 was notable chiefly for the introduction of a new class in the regatta programmes, *viz.* that for 3-tonners. Four of these little vessels did battle in all kinds of weather and proved most successfully how much power and what fine sea-going qualities can be obtained by length and depth with almost a minimum of beam. Mr. Wynne Eyton and Mr. Quilter designed and raced the composite built *Mascotte*, Mr. A. W. Courtney the *Naiad*, the late Lord Francis Cecil the *Chittywee*, and Lord Ailsa and Mr. Baden-Powell the *Snarley Yow*. Of these the *Chittywee* was the best all-round boat, though the *Mascotte* gave her all she could do to beat her.

In the small length classes, the 20-ft. *Kate*, which had become the property of the Honorary Secretary during the winter of 1881, came to the fore in a remarkable manner, saving her time when necessary, and giving all comers a fair beating. The next year, however, witnessed her total defeat by Mr. Popham's little *Bird of Freedom*, a boat that is still to the fore.

The Annual Royal Regatta of 1883 was held as before at Osborne Bay, and proved a complete success, and the club could now boast of a patronage second only to that of the Royal Yacht Squadron. The programme on August 11, the day of the regatta, exhibited a great advance on those of the two previous years, as the classes ranged more after the fashionable formulæ, *viz.* for yachts of 40 tons and under, 20 and over 14, 14 and over 9 tons. The race for 40-ton yachts fell through, but was afterwards sailed on August 22, when the *Annasona*,

Tara, Sleuthhound, Phryne, and *Silver Star* crossed the line, and *Tara* and *Silver Star* (their first appearance under the flag of the Royal Portsmouth Club) came in first and second.

Among the twenties, which showed up for the first time, were the *Freda* and two well-known old warriors from St. George's Channel, the *Quickstep* and *Challenge*. In the race for 10-tonners the *Ulidia*, designed by Mr. W. Fife, jun., was the new addition to the club, and she fought it out with the *Buttercup*, this latter favourite being thoroughly beaten on all points of sailing.

During the year of 1884 the prosperity of the club was decidedly on the increase. In the first place, during the winter, the premises in the High Street, Portsmouth, which had up to this time formed the Prince of Wales's Club House, had been bought, altered and improved to suit the club's requirements. As it stands now, it is one of the most comfortable club-houses in the South of England.

The club also opened on Southsea Beach a Station House of its own, which has telephonic communications with the house in High Street, and all parts of the towns of Portsmouth and Southampton. It consists of a railed-off space, sufficient to allow of a fair frontage, besides room for the flagstaff, guns, and all such necessary fittings. The building is a very comfortable cabin, with all modern conveniences. The telephonic communication with Southampton is of the greatest possible service, as most of the small raters make the Itchen and its precincts their home.

On June 7 in this year, the custom (which has now died out) of having an opening cruise under the club officers was originated. Nothing can make up for the teaching which manoeuvring under sail affords, and it is a great pity more of such cruises do not take place, and that at regular intervals.

The officers of the club had remained the same up to this year, when Admiral Byng gave up the Rear-Commodoreship in favour of Mr. J. R. West. One of the great features of the season was the recognition of the foot classes, which became so popular during the following four years. The first and second regattas introduced races for boats or yachts of 25 feet and 30 feet on the load water-line. In the latter class the *Eclipse* and *Keepsake* were competitors, the *Eclipse* being the better of the two boats; and in the former the *Daphne, Wave,* and *Lil* were the three to race, the *Lil* being the principal winner. The Annual Royal Regatta, owing to the sad bereavement that had visited the Court, took place by royal command off Bembridge, instead of in Osborne

Bay as heretofore.

No fewer than fourteen items constituted the programme, of which the most interesting was the ten-ton match between the *Ulidia* and *Ulerin*, representatives of Messrs. Fife and Watson, the great Scotch yacht designers. On August 16 a fine match was brought off, and the amateurs' powers put to the test, when 'A Corinthian Plate,' a very handsome piece of silver work, weighing 134 ozs., was sailed for by the *Genesta*, *Marguerite*, and *Irex*.

Perhaps the most sporting matches that have been sailed under the red burgee with crown, star, and half-moon in centre, were three that sprang out of a race for yachts of 20 tons and under, and took place at the last regatta of the season. On this occasion the *Enriqueta*, 20-ton (cutter that was, but at this time a) yawl, snatched, by some few seconds on time allowance, first honours from the old *Quickstep*.

On the Monday following the regatta a friendly match was sailed between the two vessels, ending with the same result as on the Saturday. Two matches were then arranged to be sailed on the next and following days, the conditions of which were that amateurs alone were to man one yacht, while professionals were to take charge of the other. No pilot was to be allowed, and the prize was to be 1*l*. from each amateur should the professionals win, and a sixpenny pipe from each professional should the amateurs be successful. Lots to be drawn for the choice of yacht in the first race, yachts to be exchanged for the second.

The result of the lots on the Tuesday gave the amateurs the choice of ships, and they took the *Enriqueta*. The course was across an imaginary line from the Signal Station flagstaff to the mark-boat, round the Spit buoy, Warner Lightship and East Sturbridge buoy, leaving all on the starboard hand, thence round the Spit buoy and mark-boat on port hand, to finish between the mark-boat on port hand and Signal Station. Twice round, 20 miles.

The wind was light from the south-east. The professionals in the *Quickstep* were the first over the line, but it was before the gun fired, and they had to recross it. This was not taken advantage of by the *Enriqueta*, for the yacht, just as the gun fired, was, for some unaccountable reason, kept in irons quite two minutes by her helmsman. The *Enriqueta* was steered by her owner and Major Urquhart. The *Quickstep* won by 12 mins. 13 secs.

On the following day the conditions were identical, except that the yachts were exchanged. The tide, wind, and weather were the

'IREX'
64 TONS (JOHN JAMESON, ESQ.) DESIGNED BY ALEX. RICHARDSON, 1884.

same as on the Tuesday. Both yachts crossed the line at the same time. *Enriqueta* held the weather berth, and, hugging the mark-boat, went about at once; but *Quickstep*, by a very pretty piece of steering on the part of Mr. Maxwell Heron, was put about and brought on *Enriqueta's* weather. *Enriqueta* got away again under *Quickstep's* lee, owing to the latter having her sails too closely pinned in.

This error was fortunately rectified, and the *Quickstep*, with sheets slightly checked, at once sprang ahead and forereached on the yawl, but not sufficiently to prevent the *Enriqueta*, when off Southsea Castle, from going about and crossing *Quickstep's* bow, a proceeding which, had it not been for the fine helmsmanship displayed, must have ended in a collision. When the yawl tacked the next time, however, the *Quickstep* was to windward once more, and led round the Warner Lightship by 4 mins. The mark-boat was rounded at the end of the first round by the *Quickstep* 14 mins. 15 secs. ahead of the *Enriqueta*. On the second round the wind fell light, shifting and flukey, and, except that the *Quickstep* won, offered no very interesting points of sailing worth noting. Such matches as the foregoing are worth repeating; for it is when acting in competition with men who make fore-and-aft sailing their business that amateurs find out the value of their seafaring knowledge, and can accordingly gauge their strength and learn to amend their weak points.

In 1885 the first regatta—and regattas now took place once a fortnight regularly—was memorable for the maiden races of the *Elma* among the service boats, and the *Syren* in the 25-ft. class. The *Elma* had been an open whale-shaped admiral's barge. She was rigged with dipping lugs, and manned by sub-lieutenants from H.M.S. *Excellent*. The writer had the privilege of seeing her work her way to Bembridge late in the season, and the smart manner in which the boat was handled, and the lugs lowered, dipped, and hoisted, was one of the prettiest sights of the season.

The second regatta witnessed the *début* of the two latest additions to the 30-ft. class—the *Curtsey* and *Yum Yum*. The *Curtsey* proved herself the best boat of her year.

It was during this year that the new A, B, C classes were, for the first time, given a prominent place in the regatta programmes. These severally were supposed to include the full-blown racer, the out-of-date racer, and the ordinary cruiser. The idea was to try to create a method by which all yacht-owners might have an opportunity of joining in yacht racing. The system proved only a partial success, and the real gainers by the innovation, if there were any, were the sailmakers, who were kept employed, owing to many an 'old box' requiring spinnakers and other light muslin quite foreign to their original sail-plan.

The fourth regatta of the season took place away from the port, and off the new watering-place, Lee-on-Solent. The principal course started from over an imaginary line lying between the committee vessel and a flagstaff at Lee-on-Solent, round the north-east and east Middle buoy, the west Middle buoy, round the Bramble buoys, omitting the Thorn, Calshot Lightship, and Hill Head buoy, to pass between the committee vessel and shore, leaving all marks on the starboard hand; three times round.

On July 25, the first club match round the Isle of Wight took place. It was open to all yachts of 9 tons and upwards in the B and C classes. Two of Fairlie's old clippers came out in new feathers for this race, the *Neptune* and *Fiona*; and the former not only in this, but in many another thrash round a course during this and the following seasons, kept well in the van and showed that age had in no way been detrimental to her speed. The Royal Regatta was again held off Bembridge on August 8, when for the 10-tonners' prize the *Queen Mab*, and in the 5-ton class the pretty *Cyprus*, showed their wonderful weatherly qualities.

The day is one that will long be remembered by those who took part in the trips round the Nab. The course, for all the classes from 5 tons and upwards, was from an imaginary line between the committee boat and H.M.S. *Speedy*, round the Warner Lightship, the Dean Tail buoy and Nab Lightship, leaving all to starboard, to finish between the committee vessel on the port hand and the *Speedy*; twice round. The weather was boisterous, with half a gale of wind blowing from the southward and westward. There was a nasty cross sea off the Nab, which frightened more than one hardy salt from making a start, and the owners of the 30-ft. yachts did their best to have their course shortened. The only accident, which might have turned out disastrous, was the capsizing of the *Elma*, when making a board off the Nab Lightship. She was, however, righted, bailed out, and one by one all her crew got on board.

The next year (1886) exhibited a still further advance in the well-being of the club. The number of regattas during the season was increased from eight to ten, exclusive of matches and the annual Royal Regatta, which this year took place at Stokes Bay. Numerous new and old yachts were added to the club tonnage, for the B and C classes

'Neptune,' cutter, 50 tons. Built by Fife, 1875.

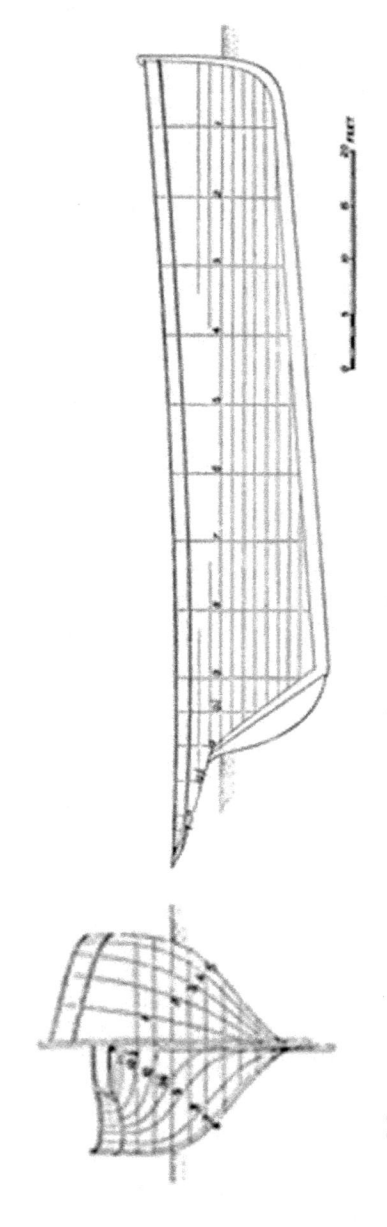

Midship section

began to fill, and many a forgotten old heroine was made to come out and don her long-left-off racing suits. Of those which thus appeared all spick and span were the *May*, 40 tons; *Foxhound*, 35 tons; *Veronica*, 92 tons; *Terpsichore*, 38 tons; *Leander* and *Nadejola*, twenties; and *Naiad* and *Lily*, old Mersey tens. Of the new yachts the *Hyacinth* was the fruit of the new classification, as she was designed and built by Mr. Arthur Payne, to race in the B class. This was the last year that any yachts were built to the 25-ft. and 21-ft. classes, the *Verena*, 25 ft., and the *Minima*, and *Volador*, 21 ft., being the last that were laid down on the stocks.

The number of members up to this date had been steadily on the increase, so that by the end of the year the list had reached over 600. Since the club had started in 1880, over 73 regattas and matches had been held, and more than 2,600*l.* given in prizes—a past history such as few, if any, of the older clubs can show.

In 1887 the Yacht Racing Association rating rule came into force, and though some races were provided for the 25-ft. class, still the main racing was among the A, B, and C and rater classes. The *Thalassa* and *Stella* were the first representatives of the 2½-raters, the *Sybil*, 26 tons, and *Mary*, 25 tons, coming out to wrest the prizes from the *Hyacinth*.

The next year it was found quite impossible to suit all owners so as to fill every event on a programme. This was owing to there still being a tonnage class, A, B and C, the new rating and the length classes. The consequence was that only seven regattas came off during the season, exclusive of the Royal Regatta, which was again held at Bembridge. During the season of 1888, the question of shifting keels was brought before the club committee, and a hard fight was made to have them abolished. There was the same curious assortment of classes as in the preceding year, because the rating rule had not as yet taken hold of the yacht-racing public.

By 1889 so great had become the popularity of the club and the demand for membership that it was decided to raise the annual subscription to 2*l.* 2*s.*, with an entrance fee of 5*l.* 5*s.* for non-yacht-owners, and 2*l.* 2*s.* for yacht-owners. The rating classes had now come into full swing, and the season started with a match for 20-raters, unique, in that it brought together no fewer than five newly launched competitors, *viz.*: the *Chiqueta, Dragon, Ghost, Siola,* and *Velzie*. By the third regatta eight 2½-raters were ready for the fray, seven of which were new boats that season—*Cock-a-whoop, Cosette, Humming Bird, Madcap, Nadador, Heathen Chinee,*' and *Musume*. Among the 10-raters were the old 5-ton flyer *Doris*, now swelled out to meet the more modern school, *Fantan, Dis, Decima,* and *Ethel.* The new *Blue Belle, Tar Baby,* and sometimes the *Thief,* formed the 5-rating class.

The event of the season was the handicap race for the cup given by the queen, which took place on August 10. It was open to yachts of 20 tons and over, and 17 started. The course chosen lay to the eastward, from an imaginary line between the flagstaff on the Spit Fort, and the committee boat, round the Nab Lightship, west buoy of the middle and committee vessel, leaving all on the starboard hand, to finish between the committee vessel and the Spit buoy. There was a strong south-westerly breeze blowing all day, which suited the large yachts well, and some of the finest sailing of the year was witnessed by those who were fortunate enough to follow the race.

Nothing of note occurred during the 1890 period of the club's history. The match which took place on August 2, for yachts rated at 40 tons and over, was the most successful of the season, for it brought together all the large cracks of the year, *viz.* the *Iverna,* 119, *Thistle,* 120, *Valkyrie,* 76, and *Yarana,* 72. The 5-rater class proved a very full one, the leading yacht architects sending out as representatives of their skill the *Valentine, Glycera, Quinque, Alwida, Archee,* and *Fair Geraldine.* The 2½-rater class received as new additions the *Troublesome, Babe, Janetta, Dolphin, Camilla,* and *G. G.* A class, however, which gave a fund of amusement, and was allowed a place in the club's programmes for the first time this year, was the ½-rater. No fewer than ten little boats formed its racing fleet, and were always ready to cross the line whenever a prize and race were offered them.

In 1891 these mosquitoes had a Champion Cup presented to them by Mr. Blair Cochrane, and eleven started at the third regatta of the season for this trophy, which was won by the little *Kittiwake,* the *Coquette* coming in second. Another new class, for 1-raters, was started this year, but only four competitors composed it, among them being the *Kelpie, Samœna,* and *Unit.* The Royal Regatta was held at Wootton Creek on August 8, and the annual race round the Island was perhaps the best race of the season. It will be seen that, after the rating rule came into force, racing among old cast-offs found no further favour in the eyes of the community, and as an example of the modern programme, the following on the next page, which is that of the Royal Regatta, is a very good specimen.

Of the sailing committee, which has done so much good work, there are names that have appeared on its list as serving members almost from the time a sailing committee was first formed. Capt. Sutton,

'YARANA' (NOW 'MAID MARION').
72 TONS. DESIGNED BY G. L. WATSON, 1883.

the honoured Vice-Commodore, and Mr. Gilman, the Hon. Treasurer, deserve first mention, as they have been office-holders from the foundation of the club, and Mr. Gilman's name appears in the earliest committee list. Admiral Hallowes and Major Bulkeley are next in order of seniority. Capt. Hayes, R.N., Messrs. Crampton and A. H. Glennie (the latter is the present Rear-Commodore) follow in order, while Capt. Nottage, Messrs. Flemmich, Laity, Walford, and Wildy bring up the rear. The membership of a sailing committee of such a club as the Royal Portsmouth Corinthian is no sinecure, and a man must be a keen yachtsman who will undertake the duties entailed.

ROYAL PORTSMOUTH CORINTHIAN YACHT CLUB
1891.

Commodore—General H.S.H. Prince Edward of Saxe-Weimar, G.C.B.

Vice-Commodore—Captain F. Sutton (*Gadfly*, 20 tons).

Rear-Commodore—J. R. West, Esq. (*Goshawk*, 239 tons).

THE ANNUAL REGATTA

Under the Patronage of their Royal Highnesses

THE PRINCE AND PRINCESS OF WALES

Will take place (weather permitting)

OFF WOOTTON CREEK,

On Saturday, August 8th.

FIRST RACE—YACHTS of 40-rating.

Prize, Cup value Sixty Guineas, presented by A. H. Glennie, Esq. Helmsman, value 5*l*. 5*s*. Entrance fee, 3*l*.

SECOND RACE—HANDICAP—YACHTS
of 60-rating and upwards.

First, value 50*l*. prizes presented by A. H. Glennie, Esq. Second, value 25*l*.

Entrance fee, 50*s*. Helmsman, value 5*l*. 5*s*., presented by F. C. Hill, Esq.

THIRD RACE—HANDICAP—YACHTS
under 60-rating.

First Prize, value 25*l*., presented by Julian Senior, Esq. Second Prize, value 10*l*. Entrance fee, 25*s*.

FOURTH RACE—YACHTS of 20-rating.

First Prize, value 20*l*., presented by S. M. Richards, Esq. Second Prize, value 5*l*., presented by Lt.-Col. A. D. MacGregor. Entrance fee, 20*s*.

FIFTH RACE—YACHTS over 2½, but not exceeding 5-rating.
First Prize, a Silver Cup, presented by Captain A. K. Wilson R.N.,V.C., C.B., and Officers H.M.S. *Vernon*.
Second Prize, value 5*l*. 5*s*., presented by W. A. Beauclerk, Esq. Entrance fee, 15*s*.

SIXTH RACE—YACHTS not exceeding 2½-rating.
First Prize, the 'Fernie' Cup, value 10*l*. 10*s*. (presented by Mrs. Fernie in memory of the late Robertson Fernie, Esq.)
Second Prize, value 5*l*. 5*s*., presented by the Vice-Commodore, Captain F. Sutton. Entrance fee, 10*s*. 6*d*.

SEVENTH RACE—YACHTS of 1-rating.
First Prize, value 6*l*. 6*s*., presented by Rear-Admiral Hallowes.
Second Prize, value 2*l*. 2*s*., presented by Colonel F. J. Smith, R.E. Entrance fee, 6*s*.

EIGHTH RACE—YACHTS of ½-rating, belonging to any recognised Yacht Club.
First, value 3*l*. 3*s*. Prizes presented by Paul A. Ralli, Esq.
Second, value 2*l*. 2*s*. Entrance fee, 3*s*.

NINTH RACE—SERVICE YACHTS.
First Prize, value 5*l*. 5*s*., presented by A. G. Wildy, Esq.
Second Prize, value 2*l*. 2*s*. Entrance fee, 5*s*.

All yachts must belong to the club, eighth and ninth races excepted. Yachts in all the races must be steered by amateur members of any recognised Yacht Club. The races will be sailed according to Y.R.A. Rules. Exceptions, time of entry, *two* to compete or no race; *four*, or no second prize.

The second and third races will be handicapped by the committee without appeal.

That the naval officers who are honorary members have been valued friends to the club goes without saying. Nothing could exceed the interest that has been taken in the club's welfare by the Commodore, H.S.H. General Prince Edward of Saxe-Weimar, especially whilst in command at Portsmouth. Neither must the club's mainstay, the honorary secretary, Mr. John Main, be forgotten. Almost from the beginning Mr. Main had acted as under-secretary to the then honorary secretary, Mr. C. McCheane, and it is not too much to say that when acting in that capacity he was the kedge anchor to the club, and frequently on occasions was called upon to play the part of best bower. When Mr. McCheane resigned his office on July 14, 1887, after an interregnum of three months, during which Captain Haldane was made acting secretary, Mr. Main was chosen unanimously to fill the vacant office, and not only those connected with the club, but all who have had to hold communication with him, know how well its arduous duties have been performed. It is to this gentleman that the writer is indebted for help in compiling this notice.

With a commodious house, a signal station to keep up, and prizes to be provided (nearly 6,000*l*. have been given to be sailed for up to 1893), the expenses, it is needless to say, are great and tax the funds considerably. Money, however, is always forthcoming through the liberality displayed by many of the members. Among those who have come forward to help the club with gifts of cups and prize-money are the following gentlemen, whose names are rarely absent from any notice or list calling for an extra supply towards the prize fund: Captain Sutton, Vice-Commodore; Mr. J. R. West, late Rear-Commodore; Mr. A. H. Glennie, Rear-Commodore; and Messrs. Julian Senior, S. Richards, and B. Paget. Mrs. Robertson Fernie makes an annual present of a purse in memory of her late husband, who was always a contributor up to the time of his death.

The club has certainly done more for amateur seamanship than any other inside the Isle of Wight; it was the first to start a system of fortnightly regattas, and has always been chosen by outside clubs to time the arrivals of their ocean races to the port of Portsmouth.

The usual annual regatta was held last year, 1893, somewhat unfortunately, during the squadron week at Cowes, whither the big cutters of the season had attracted so many lovers of yacht racing as well as general sight-seers. A very varied programme was provided, including all classes from the 100-tonner to the ½-rater, in all about five different races. The first was a handicap for yachts exceeding 19-rating, the course being from between the committee-vessel and the Spit Fort, round the N.E. middle buoy, Warner lightship, and Boyne buoy, all marks to be left on the port hand. This afforded a great opportunity for the spectators on Southsea beach to see the racing thoroughly well, as the competitors had to accomplish three rounds, making about a 40-mile course.

The object of handicaps is to get sport amongst craft of varied tonnage, class, and build, by giving time allowance. In the present case the largest vessel was *Mabel*, late *Irex*, 100-rating; the smallest, *Marigold*, 22-rating; *Mabel* allowing *Marigold* 39 minutes. Six started. A good

race ensued, as the following time of the finish will corroborate:—
Columbine, winner, 4 hrs. 32 mins. 41 secs.; *Castanet*, 2nd prize, 4 hrs. 36 mins. 15 secs.; *Creole*, 3rd prize, 4 hrs. 33 mins. 43 secs.; *Mabel*, 4 hrs. 38 mins. 14 secs.

Yacht	Rig	Rating	Handicap	Owner
Mabel	cutter	100	scratch	Mr. Muir |
Creole	"	40	10 minutes	Lieut.-Col. Bagot
Columbine	yawl	50	12 "	Mr. W. B. Paget
Castanet	cutter	40	14 "	Mr. W. R. Cookson
Hyacinth	yawl	50	27 "	Mr. T. C. Garth
Marigold	cutter	22	39 "	Mr. W. R. Martin

The 20-raters were represented by *Dragon*, *Deirdré*, and *Molly*.

The 2½-raters brought together were in number eight—*Elf*, *Gareth*, *Gavotte*, *Kismet*, *Meneen*, *Papoose*, *Faugh-a-Ballagh*, and *Undine*.

This race was for the Fernie Cup, value 10 guineas, won by *Kismet*, Miss Mabel Cox.

Four 1-raters started over a 12-mile course, and the ½-raters finished a very successful regatta by having a match over an 8-mile course; the *Mosquito*, belonging to Admiral Hallowes, beating the *Coquette* by half a minute.

ROYAL CINQUE PORTS YACHT CLUB, DOVER ESTABLISHED 1872

Commodore: H.R.H. Duke of Connaught, K.G.

Vice-Commodore: Earl of Pembroke

The leading feature in the regatta of the Royal Cinque Ports Yacht Club is the race to Boulogne and back, which really is the Channel match of the season; and in the year 1877, which was remarkable for hard winds and even gales on racing days, such as that when the Weymouth, as well as other regattas, was hopelessly stopped, the grandest race of the series was sailed June 14. The following fine fleet started:—

Yacht	Tonnage	Description	Builder	Owner
Australia	207	Schooner	Inman	W. W. Hughes, Esq.
Phantom	172	"	Hoad	A. O. Wilkinson, Esq.
Corinne	160	"	Ratsey	N. Wood, Esq.
Sea Belle	142	"	Harvey	H. Taylor, Esq.
Miranda	135	"	Harvey	G. C. Lampson, Esq.
Lufra	208	Yawl	Ratsey	J. Houldsworth, Esq.
Florinda	138	"	Nicholson	W. Jessop, Esq.

Yacht	Tonnage	Description	Builder	Owner
Jullanar	127	Yawl	Bentall	A. D. Macleay, Esq.
Vol au Vent	103	Cutter	Ratsey	Col. Markham

With a very hard E.N.E. wind blowing all reefed mainsails and jib-headers, 1877 was a great season for carrying away spars, and June 14 added its share. The arrival time round Boulogne mark-boat is worth recording.

	h.	m.	s.
Phantom	2	17	0
Australia	2	21	30
Corinne	2	29	0
Lufra	2	29	30
Miranda	2	32	0
Florinda	2	32	19
Sea Belle	2	35	15
Jullanar	2	36	0
Vol au Vent	3	0	15

The E.N.E. was now a little before their beam; with flattened sheets they all began to dive a little more than on the voyage out. At last, some five miles or so after rounding the Boulogne mark-boat, the leading schooner, *Phantom*, took a dive that was too much for her bowsprit, which snapped off short. Poor *Phantom*, in the prime of life, leading grandly and full of promise! After this there were no more accidents. The *Australia* had the lead, and finished, winning the 100*l*. prize, and establishing a record, 4 hrs. 12 mins. 40 secs. for the course, which has not been beaten up to the present.

The other racers came in as follows:—

	h.	m.	s.
Australia	4	12	40
Corinne	4	26	18
Florinda	4	30	38
Phantom	4	33	3
Miranda	4	34	32
Jullanar	4	36	30
Sea Belle	4	37	48
Lufra	4	38	38
Vol au Vent	5	24	0

Another good race over the same course, on June 28, 1880, was

'Arrow', Royal Cinque Ports Yacht Club.
117 tons (Tankerville Chamberlayne, Esq.). June 24, 1876.

won by *Latona*, 160 tons, built by J. White; A. B. Rowley, Esq.; duration of race, 4 hrs. 14 mins. 4 secs. Started 10.30 a.m., arrived at Dover 2 hrs. 44 min. 4 secs.

On July 22, 1889, the *Wendur*, yawl, 124-rating, 43 tons, built by and belonging to Thos. B. C. West, Esq., ran this time very close, starting 10 a.m., arrived at Dover 2 hrs. 14 mins. 28 secs. Duration of race, 4 hrs. 14 mins. 28 secs., being 24 seconds longer than *Latona*.

A race on Tuesday, June 14, 1892, was a very remarkable one, and showed what a 40-tonner is capable of in bad weather and hard wind in the Channel, which is not the smoothest water in a strong North-easter. The finish was as follows:—

	Arrived at Dover		
	h.	m.	s.
Lethe, yawl	3	17	11
Queen Mab, cutter (winner, 70*l*.)	3	34	9
Iverna, cutter	3	38	1
Thalia, cutter (2nd prize, 5*l*.)	3	47	28
Creole, cutter	3	57	32
Varuna, dismasted			

Duration of race, 4 hrs. 32 mins. 11 secs. Wind north-east, strong and squally.

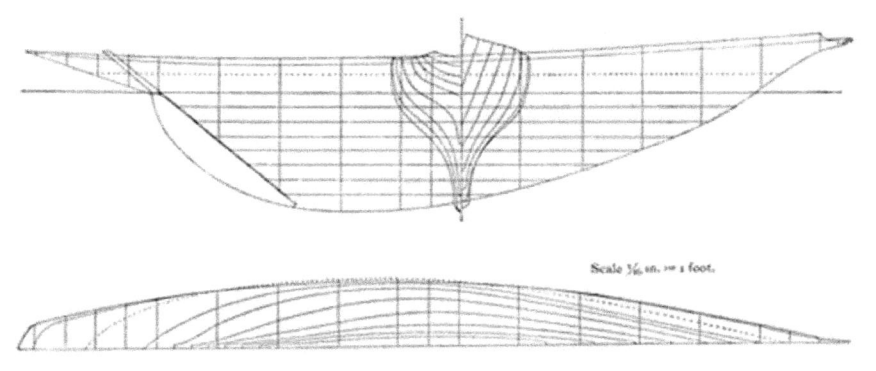

'Reverie,' 40-rater. Built for A. D. Clarke, Esq., 1891, by Messrs. Fay. Designed by J. M. Soper.

'Reverie.'
40-rater, by Fay & Co. Designed by J. M. Soper, 1891.
Hauled up at Fay's Yard.

CHAPTER 2

Scottish Clubs

THE ROYAL NORTHERN YACHT CLUB, ROTHESAY
By R. T. Pritchett

The Clyde is, and always has been, the great yachting nursery and centre of the North. The very mention of the name arouses all who have pleasurable recollections of the great waters which lead up to the narrow Clutha, whence emerged those monsters of the deep, *Lucanias*, and other triumphs of modern science. As recently as 1886 the steamer *Industry*, built by Fife of Fairlie in 1814, was lying in the mud at Haulbowline, after running some sixty years between Greenock and Glasgow. Yacht-building has always been vigorously carried on in the Great Estuary for three generations. The Fifes of Fairlie have designed and built grand vessels there, though the flat shore presents immense difficulties, which are greatly added to by the present increase of draught and lead ballast in yachts of all classes.

1824. NORTHERN YACHT
CLUB SEAL.

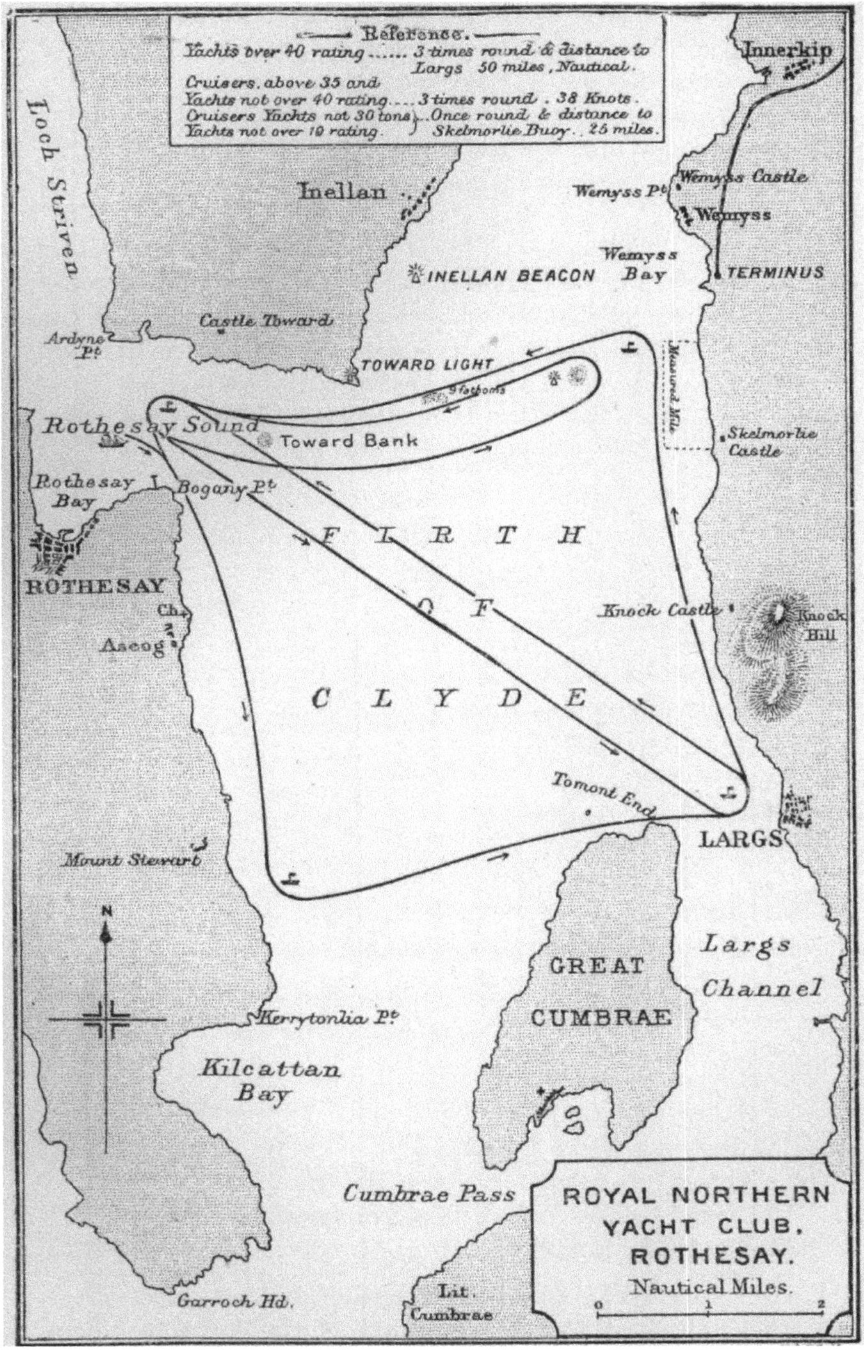
Reference.
Yachts over 40 rating ...... 3 times round & distance to Largs 50 miles, Nautical.
Cruisers, above 35 and Yachts not over 40 rating.... 3 times round. 38 Knots.
Cruisers Yachts not 30 tons Yachts not over 19 rating. ..Once round & distance to Skelmorlie Buoy.. 25 miles.
Loch Striven
Inellan
Innerkip
Wemyss Castle
Wemyss Pt
Wemyss
Wemyss Bay
TERMINUS
INELLAN BEACON
Castle Toward
Ardyne Pt
TOWARD LIGHT
9 fathoms
Measured Mile
Rothesay Sound
Toward Bank
Skelmorlie Castle
Rothesay Bay
Bogany Pt
ROTHESAY
F I R T H
O F
C L Y D E
Knock Castle
Knock Hill
Ch.
Ascog
Tomont End
LARGS
Mount Stewart
N
Largs Channel
GREAT CUMBRAE
Kerrytonlia Pt
Kilcattan Bay
Cumbrae Pass
ROYAL NORTHERN YACHT CLUB, ROTHESAY.
Nautical Miles.
0 1 2
Garroch Hd.
Lit. Cumbrae

The Royal Northern Yacht Club is installed at that delightful spot, Rothesay, noted for its fine bay; and though Clyde weather is known to yachting men as being somewhat impulsive and petulant, whipping out spars, destructive to balloon canvas unless the skipper is very weatherwise indeed, still for real sailing the Clyde affords some of the best courses in the world and the grandest sport from 23-footers to 200-tonners.

The Royal Northern Club had a very interesting origin. It dates from 1824, when it was founded by some gentlemen in the north of Ireland and west of Scotland who were devotees of yachting. A few years later the club was separated into two branches, an Irish and Scotch division, as will be perceived by the flags given here in illustration. One has the shamrock wreath, the other the thistles, each division having its own committee and officials.

Original Members, A.D. 1824

No.
1. Thomas Pottinger (Admiral 1825)
2. John Turnley
3. J. E. Matthews
4. R. Kennedy
5. Robert Thomson (first secretary) 1824, and admiral, 1827
6. Gordon Thomson
7. G. Matthews
8. Henry J. McCracken
9. Edward S. Ruthven
10. Thos. Ch. Stewart Corry
11. George Russell
12, 13, 14. McCrackens, junrs.
15. J. Smyth, Helensburgh (for many years Commodore of R.N.Y.C.)
16. J. Carrick, Greenock
17. Robert Langtry
18. Robert Christian, Sligo
19. Claudius Armstrong, Dublin
20. Robert F. Gordon
21. Edward Forbes Orson, Balyreggan House, Stranraer
22. John Kennedy, Cuttra

The records of the Scotch division prior to 1846 were unfortunately destroyed by an accident some years ago. The minute-book

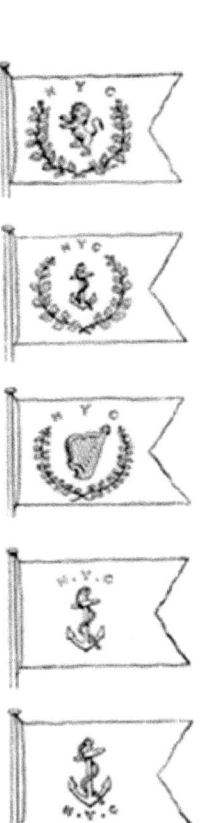

Royal Northern flags.

of the Irish division has, however, survived. From it we find that at a meeting of gentlemen interested in the foundation of the Northern Yacht Club, held at Belfast on November 5, 1824, it was resolved 'that the establishment of a yacht club is a highly desirable object.' A committee was accordingly appointed to that end, Mr. Robert Thomson being requested to act as secretary, and at a general meeting held April 8, 1825, Mr. John Allan of Glasgow accepted the post of secretary for the Clyde. At a general meeting at Belfast May 2, 1825, the secretary was instructed to write to Mr. Allan, to consult with the Scotch members and fix with them the place of rendezvous for the first general meeting of the boats of the club. The date arranged was the first Monday in June, and the Irish members declared that they were ready to meet the Scotch members 'in any part of the Clyde' on that day.

The club was known as the Northern Yacht Club. There is no record in the minute-book of the burgee adopted, but in an old picture, now in the club-house at Rothesay, the yachts are shown cruising off Garroch Head, in the Clyde, with red ensigns, the burgee also red, with the letters N.Y.C. in white. The present secretary has courteously sent a photograph of this picture, also of the flags, as an historical contribution. The first prizes offered were for pulling (rowing) matches to take place in Ireland.

The Marquis of Donegall was the first President of the club, and Mr. Thos. Pottinger, Admiral for 1825.

The full dress of the club consisted of a blue coat with crimson silk lining, with 'Marall's' vest, white or black pantaloons or breeches, and silk stockings to correspond. Members who appeared at the dinners of the club without this dress were fined 10s. At a general meeting held at Greenock, on August 3, 1825, Mr. James Hamilton, of Holmhead, was appointed Admiral for the ensuing year.

In May 1826, at Belfast, the yachts were divided into three classes:—

```
1st class over 30 tons register
2nd   "     "   15   "       "
3rd   "   under 15   "       "
```

The first regatta took place at Belfast, June 20, 21, 22, and on June 23 pulling races were rowed by members and their friends. On June 24 the yachts were to sail together 'in a fleet,' and 'manoeuvre under the directions of the Admiral.' This is quite an echo of the Cork Water 1720 Club.

A proposal of the Scottish members to separate the Club into two distinct branches was agreed to on May 16, 1827. It was probably after this date that each division had a distinguishing burgee; from an old print of these flags now in the club-house at Rothesay, the Irish division seems to have flown a red burgee with a harp, the Scottish division being distinguished by a lion in white.

H.M. King William IV. became Patron of the club in September 1830, and from that time it was known as the Royal Northern Yacht Club.

In 1831 the yachts of the Club were arranged in classes as under:—

```
1st class over 75 tons register
2nd   "     "   50 tons and under 75 tons
3rd   "     "   30   "     "     "   50  "
4th   "     "   20   "     "     "   30  "
```

5th " " 15 " " " 20 "
6th " under 15 tons

A two days' regatta was held at Belfast in 1836. The different classes just described were started at an interval of half an hour between each, beginning at 10.30 a.m., the prize for each class being ten sovereigns. On the second day a very important event took place, the race for the Belfast Cup, value 100*l.*, a time race for all sizes. Eight vessels to start, or no race. Entry 3*l.*; the second yacht to save her stake. It is to be regretted that the details of this race cannot be given. On May 21, 1838, at a meeting held of the few remaining members of the Irish division, it was resolved to dissolve that half of the Club and hand over any funds (they amounted to 14*l.* 17*s.* 2*d.*) to the secretary of the Scottish division.

It is unfortunate that the records of the Scottish division and of the Royal Northern Club, after the dissolution and prior to 1846, have been lost. It had prospered much. The Clyde was developing rapidly and with great energy, as is shown by their four days' Regatta in 1835, the first day at Helensburgh, the second at Greenock, the third at Dunoon, the fourth at Largs, which is without doubt one of the most enthusiastic of yachting stations.

It would be well to record here the cracks of the Clyde in 1835. The *Gleam* (see illustration over the page), *Falcon*, *Nymph* and *Clarence*, were very leading craft.

Tartar	30 tons		A. Morris
Sylph	30	"	J. Crooks
Dream	66	"	A. Ranken
Gleam (Fife)[1]	30	"	H. Gore Booth
Clarence	15	"	R. Sinclair
Amethyst	20	"	J. Smith
Wave	15	"	T. C. Buchanan
Emma	15	"	Jas. Bogle
Falcon	15	"	Jas. Kerr
Nymph	15	"	H. F. Campbell

Clyde yachting was now firmly established; Largs, Gourock, Greenock, Dunoon, Helensburgh, Rothesay, were the stations most frequented, and each successive season brings them forward more prominently, with well-sustained reputation.

---

1. The first celebrated cutter by Fife of Fairlie was *Lamlash*, 1814.

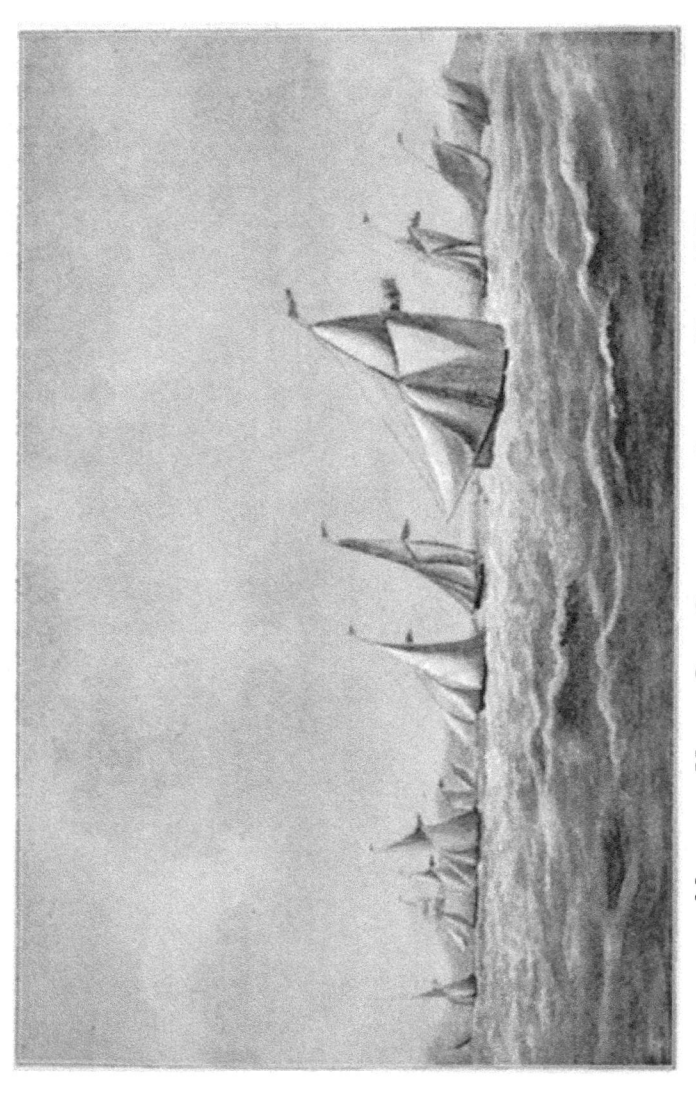

Northern Yacht Club Cruising off Garroch Head, 1825.
From a Painting by Hutcheson at R.N.Y. Club, Rothesay.

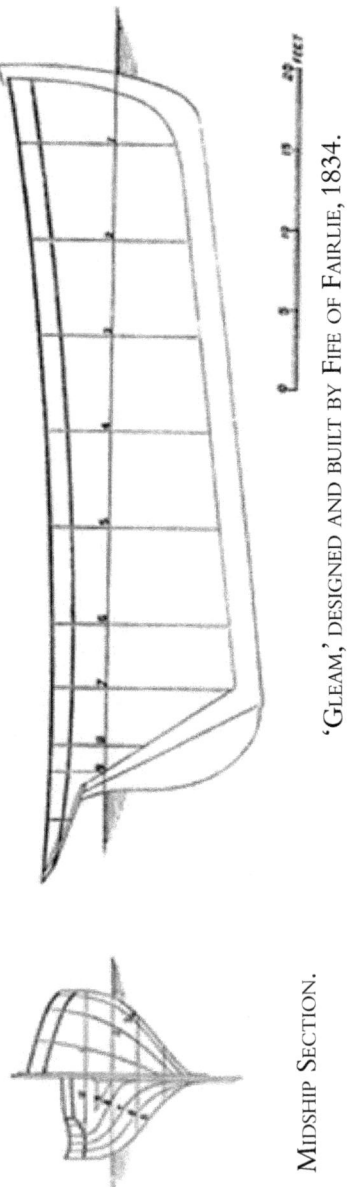

'Gleam,' designed and built by Fife of Fairlie, 1834.

Midship Section.

The present club-house at Rothesay was built in 1878, and the Royal Northern Yacht Club regattas are naturally always now held at that place, started from the commodore's yacht which is moored off Craigmore for that purpose. A chart of the course is given, showing the whole set of different distances.

The prominent feature of this club is that it has from a very early period of its history had a club yacht, which is open to hire by members for periods not exceeding a fortnight, and fine vessels they have from time to time chosen. The first was the well-known *Orion*, then came *Mosquito*, a grand iron boat built in 1848, designed by Waterman, and now a pilot boat doing good work. *Æolus* came next. In 1885 the club had their present vessel, the *Ailsa*, 66 tons, built by Fife of Fairlie; and who better could have been chosen?

It has already been mentioned that Mr. John Allan, of Glasgow, was the first secretary for the Clyde, 1825. Mr. E. F. Donald is the present secretary.

There is no doubt that, if variety be really charming, very charming weather can be found in the Clyde waters, even within the six-hour limit: dead calm, Zephyr, good sailing breeze, rain squalls, white squalls, and the rest.

Royal Clyde Yacht Club
By G. L. Blake

The history of the Royal Clyde Yacht Club affords one more proof of the old belief that slow and steady progress is the most enduring.

It is now nearly forty years since the following very modest announcement, under the heading 'Clyde Model Yacht Club,' appeared in the *Glasgow Herald*, of August 28, 1856:—

A number of gentlemen connected with yachting propose to form a club under the above designation, with the view of furthering a greater amount of emulation amongst the proprietors of small yachts. It is proposed to take in yachts under 8 tons only, being the smallest acknowledged by the Royal Northern Yacht Club, and to have an annual regatta, to be held in rotation at the various watering-places along the coast.

In answer to this call a meeting was held shortly after at the Globe Hotel, Glasgow, on which occasion about thirty-one gentlemen entered their names on the club's list as members. Messrs. Jas. Gilchrist, Archibald Kennedy, Richard Ferguson, Jas. Mum, J. Gibson, Jas. Spencer, Jas. Sutherland, and W. Kennedy were chosen to form the first

ROYAL NORTHERN YACHT CLUB, ROTHESAY.

committee and draw up a code of rules, Mr. W. Kennedy acting as secretary and treasurer.

At a general meeting held the following month, September, the late Mr. Jas. Smith, of Jordan Hill, was elected first Commodore, and Mr. Tom Holdsworth Vice-Commodore, and before the end of the year the little club boasted some fifty members.

On January 27, 1857, the Admiralty warrant was granted, allowing the club to fly the blue ensign with their burgee: blue with a red lion on a yellow shield in centre. Measuring officers were told off, who had to deal with the old Thames Rule of measurement, excepting in the method of taking the length, the club rule being that 'the length must be taken from outside of the stem to the outside of the sternpost at half the depth of each from the load water-line.' A curious provision was made, too, with regard to racing flags. The club had a series of flags numbered from 1 to 10, and each yacht was provided with a number according to priority of entry for a race, but this kindly thoughtfulness on the part of the ruling powers did not continue beyond a couple of seasons, and members had to provide racing flags for themselves, as they have done ever since.

Though an opening and other cruises had been held, together with a small meeting at Largs, the first great event of the Clyde Model Yacht Club took place on August 29, 1857, off Helensburgh, when four items made up the programme, and Captain Small, Messrs. James Rowan, James Gilchrist, Robert Hart, Dan Buchanon and Thomas Falconer did duty as the sailing committee. The commodore's yacht *Wave* was moored off the baths for the occasion, and the course chosen was from the commodore round the Shoal buoy—thence round a flag boat moored off Ardmore Point and back round the commodore's yacht, leaving all on the port hand; twice round for the first and second races, and once round for the third and fourth.

The first race was for yachts of 8 tons and under, and for this the *Fairy Queen*, 8 tons, Mr. Grant, junior; *Armada*, 7½ tons, Mr. Dickie; *Bella*, 8 tons, Mr. Walker; and *Maud*, 8 tons, Mr. St. Clair Byrne, sailed, and finished in the order given.

In the second face for yachts of 6 tons and under, the *Pearl*, 4½ tons, Mr. Ferguson; *Maria*, 5 tons, Mr. R. Lyall; *Leda*, 6 tons, Mr. Alexander Finlay; *Comet*, 5 tons, Mr. Steven; and *Clutha*, 5 tons, Mr. Spencer, entered, the three first coming in as named.

The third race, for yachts of 4 tons and under, brought four competitors together—the *Francis*, 3½ tons, Mr. Miller; *Lily*, 3½ tons, Mr.

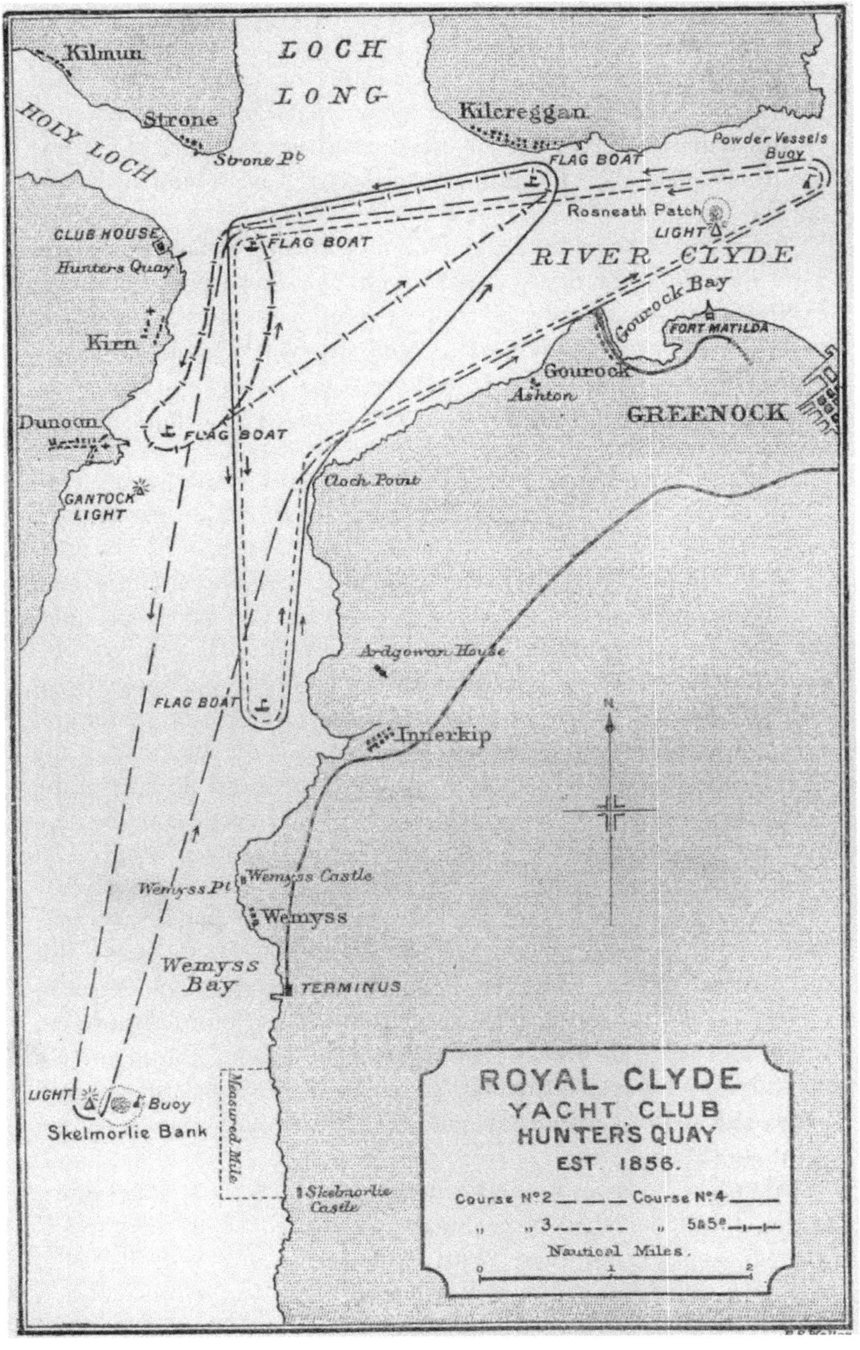

LOCH LONG
Kilmun
HOLY LOCH
Strone
Strone Pt
Kilcreggan
FLAG BOAT
Powder Vessels Buoy
Rosneath Patch
LIGHT
RIVER CLYDE
CLUB HOUSE
Hunters Quay
FLAG BOAT
Gourock Bay
FORT MATILDA
Kirn
Gourock
Ashton
GREENOCK
Dunoon
FLAG BOAT
GANTOCK LIGHT
Cloch Point
Ardgowan House
FLAG BOAT
Innerkip
N
Wemyss Pt
Wemyss Castle
Wemyss
Wemyss Bay
TERMINUS
Measured Mile
LIGHT
Buoy
Skelmorlie Bank
Skelmorlie Castle
ROYAL CLYDE
YACHT CLUB
HUNTER'S QUAY
EST. 1856.
Course No 2
Course No 4
" 3
" 5&5a
Nautical Miles.
0
1
2

Ure; *Echo*, 2½ tons, Mr. Sutherland; and the *Banshee*, 4 tons, Mr. Taylor. The *'Francis'* won, followed home in the order as above. The fourth item was for boats of 19 ft. over all, a class which, though developed almost out of recognition, has always remained a firm favourite.

It may here be noted that an attempt made at the close of the season to introduce the American 'sail area' rule of measurement signally failed.

Between the years 1857 and 1862 little of importance took place.

During 1863 the first symptoms of a break out from bounds was exhibited, and prizes were given for a race for yachts of 25 tons and under, besides one for yachts of 10 tons and under. A stipulation was made with regard to the latter race—*viz.* that each yacht was to be manned by one hand only, a dangerous though sporting condition which had previously brought disaster and proved fatal in Irish waters, and has never been permitted since. Both races filled, Mr. Fulton's *Glide*, 14 tons, won the first, and Mr. McIver's *Brenda*, 8 tons, the second.

With this divergence from the original scheme on which the club was founded the society threw off its old name and came out under the more independent title of the Clyde Yacht Club. To celebrate this era the annual regatta was lengthened out to a two days' programme, and the *Lesbia*, 37, cutter; *Reverie*, 41, schooner; *Kilmeny*, 30, cutter, and *Dawn*, yawl, met to do battle with the 15-ton *Torch*, the crack of the year. Besides the annual regatta, at which yachts from all parts of the kingdom were invited to compete, the Corinthian regatta of the club must not be lost sight of or hidden away behind the lustre of the great event of the season. It had formed part of each season's programme of events for some years, and had been the means of cultivating a true taste for amateur seamanship. Many a member can look back to his first Corinthian race as the beginning of his practical experience in yacht racing. The races at these regattas have been mostly handicaps, and two or three are always open to yachts in cruising trim. The only conditions of the regatta are that 'Yachts may carry their ordinary paid hands, but no extra paid hands, and must be steered by members of a yacht club.'

It is always pleasant to meet with names which are as well known as the club to which they belong, to whom their club owes much, and whose pride and interests are centred in its prosperity. It was in 1863 that two such members' names were added to the official list— the late Mr. J. A. Lockett as Rear-Commodore and Mr. William York as treasurer. Both these gentlemen have for the last thirty years been busily engaged in furthering the welfare of the club, the one in his capacity as secretary or treasurer, or both, the other in several offices, but principally as one of the house committee.

When the year 1867 closed the Clyde Yacht Club's first racing decade, the club was well under way and able to hold its own with any existing yacht-racing community, both as a provider of sport and for the attractions offered to the lovers of yachts and yachting, when with their friends they were brought together on the waters of the *Bonny Clyde*. This was noticeable in 1863, but it became much more so in 1865, when the well-known clippers *Mosquito*, 59 tons; *Glance*, 35 tons; *Fiona*, 78 tons; and the *Vindex*, 44 tons, came round to the Firth to sail under the Clyde Club's auspices.

Though opening and closing cruises had always been in vogue since the foundation of the club, it was left for the tenth year to start the long series of these expeditions, which last from a Thursday to the Monday morning following, and, with the combined attractions of racing, cruising and social gatherings, have proved such pleasant features in each season's yachting. The list of members had now reached over 100, while the yacht tonnage had risen to 1,200 gross, comprising 87 yachts of 5 to 103 tons. Among these were included the three most successful yachts of the year in the United Kingdom, and, to the praise of the Clyde shores it may be said, all built and designed by Mr. W. Fife of Fairlie—the *Fiona* in the 1st, the *Kilmeny* in the 2nd, and the *Torc'* in the 3rd class.

The season of 1868 would have passed without note or comment had it not been that the club founded an annual Corinthian match, in which two paid hands were to be allowed for yachts of 15 tons and over, and one paid hand to all the smaller yachts. The helmsman was to be an amateur, and no *shot-bag or shifting ballast* of any kind was to be permitted. Besides proving that the club possessed amateur seamen capable of handling a racing yacht of any size, the fact that that unseaworthy equipment shifting ballast, which had been in use in the Clyde foot classes and in most racing yachts during the early Fifties, was to be abolished, at all events in this race, was a move in the right direction.

1869 is a year of real historical importance, for it not only gives the date when the 40-, 20-, and 10-ton classes became generally acknowledged, but it brings credit to the Clyde Yacht Club where credit is due, as being the founder of these classes, which held sway for so many years. A year later the club was the first to introduce the smaller

THE START FOR ARDRISHAIG CUP.

class of 5 tons as a standing dish in its regatta programmes, and to the Clyde Yacht Club belongs the honour of being the first in the field to recognise that this diminutive class of flyers was well worthy on its own merits of being encouraged.

Channel matches had been long ere this time a matter of annual interest with some of the clubs in the south of England, as well as the Royal Alfred Yacht Club at Kingstown, and Royal Northern in Scotland; but the sport of Channel racing and open-sea work had either not been thought of, or had met with no favour, for the first Channel match held in connection with the Clyde Club did not take place till 1871. The race came off after the regatta held that year at Barrow and before the Clyde regattas, the course being from Barrow to the Clyde, so that the yachts about to visit and race in the Firth might find it worth their while to put on a spurt and make the best of their way to their destination. No better course could be chosen for trying a vessel on all points of sailing, to say nothing of her sea-going powers, including as it does the passage between the Isle of Man and the Mull of Galloway. For this race the *Enid*, 57 tons; *Livonia*, 280; *Glance*, 35; and *Coralie*, 35, started, all yachts at that date as racers. The *Glance* saved her time and carried off the trophy.

If 1871 opened up Channel groping under racing trim, '*progress*' must truly be held the motto for 1872. Not only was the club made a Royal club, and allowed the privilege of placing a crown over the lion's head in the burgee crest, but early in the spring of this year the Royal Clyde opened to its members the house which Mr. Hunter, of Hafton, had built for them at Hunter's Quay adjoining the hotel.

Of course with a settled headquarters, Hunter's Quay became the future rendezvous for all club fixtures, such as opening and closing cruises, regattas, matches and the like; and as the opening cruise this year may be considered the first general meeting of members afloat off the new house, it will not be amiss to give a short description of it. The meeting took place on Thursday, May 30, and began at 2 p.m. with a lunch at the club-house, after which at 4 p.m. the yachts weighed anchor under the Commodore, and sailed under his orders till the signal was made from the flagship for them to make the best of their way to Rothesay. On arrival there, those who were not required on board their vessels to stow sails and clear up for the night took their dinghies ashore, or were taken in their gigs, for a stroll through the old town. In the meantime on board the yachts, as soon as the decks had been cleared up and ropes coiled down in their places, the galley fires were lighted, so that by 7 p.m. the men had had their tea, and the cooks and stewards were ready with goodly repasts awaiting the coming on board again of the hungry masters and their friends.

Dinner over, the pleasures of the evening began with what is known as 'ship-visiting'—that is, the yacht-owner starts off, and either rows himself and friends in his dinghy, or is rowed in correct form, to some friend's yacht where he may remain, or, after a short visit, proceed, taking with him his host and as many of his friends as he can pack away in the gig's stern-sheets, to some other yacht, and so on *ad infinitum*. To row himself is much the better plan, since it means independence of the crew (which perhaps may consist only of one hand), and avoidance of a troubled conscience, that the man or men are being kept up and prevented from turning in.

The following morning only a few burgees were visible, most of the yachts having donned their silken racing flags, for an early start had to be made in a handicap race to be sailed *viâ* the Garroch Head (the most south-westerly extremity of the Isle of Bute) to Tignabruich. More than half the yachts were started in this race, for which four cups were provided as prizes. The contingent of small non-racers made Tignabruich by way of the Kyles of Bute, as did also some of the larger sailing yachts, which preferred calm and untroubled travelling to a dusting round the Garroch Head. The gathering at the head of the Kyles is, if anything, more enjoyable than that spent at Rothesay. The anchorage is more land-locked, and therefore less liable to disturbance from winds or sweeping seas, and ship-visiting can be carried on without any fear of a ducking or other unpleasantness.

On the Saturday morning, the members of the club and their friends breakfasted together at 9.30 at the Royal Hotel, when the prizes were presented to the winners; after which a few returned to their yachts, got under way, and dispersed with the object of extending their cruise, while those left behind remained to enjoy the beautiful scenery and walks with which the locality abounds, and on Sunday attend church parade on board Lord Glasgow's yacht.

Beyond the adoption by the club of the Royal Alfred Yacht Club rules and regulations, nothing of any moment worth chronicling took place till 1875, in which year the purchase was completed by the club of the whole of the grounds and buildings, including the hotel and club-house, and early in 1876 the members enjoyed the privilege of not only having a club-house, but also an establishment worked on the principle of a private hotel, where they could provide themselves

'Marjorie.'
BLUE, WITH WHITE CROSS. 68 TONS (J. COATS, JUN., ESQ.).
BUILT BY STEELE & CO., 1883.

'May'
42 TONS (W. CHRYSTAL, ESQ., VICE-COM. ROYAL CLYDE).
BUILT BY STEELE & CO., 1881.

and their families or friends with comfortable quarters on very reasonable club terms.

In this matter the Royal Clyde Yacht Club is specially fortunate, as also in one other, *viz.* the magnificent scenic setting by which their possession is surrounded. Nothing can equal the Holy Loch for beauty and charm of colour, on a summer's evening, particularly about sunset, or an early winter's morning, with its sunrise lowering and accompanied by ever-changing tints lending their enchantments to the rugged grandeur of the hills which bound it. This, with the distant view up the Clyde, obtained from the club-house windows or frontage, is not to be surpassed in any country in the world.

At the opening of the season of 1877, and the close of the second decade, the club numbered no fewer than 643 members, with a fleet of yachts computed at 195, and as the Club Regatta now occupied two days, the three Clyde clubs—*viz.* the Royal Clyde, the Royal Northern, and the four-year-old Mudhook Yacht Club—considered it necessary to work together for the furtherance of sport, and held their first meeting to arrange a suitable date for celebrating a 'Clyde Week.' A change was also made this season in the several courses at the regattas, a change which had been for some time considered desirable, and which turned out a welcome improvement.

The new courses were as follows: For First-Class Yachts, from Hunter's Quay to Toward buoy, thence to Skelmorlie buoy, thence to the Powder Vessel's buoy, and thence to Hunter's Quay, leaving all on the port hand; twice round, distance 50 miles.

The Second-Class Course lay from Hunter's Quay to Skelmorlie buoy, thence to the Powder Vessel's buoy, and thence to Hunter's Quay, leaving all on the port hand; twice round, distance 40 miles.

The Third-Class Course was from Hunter's Quay to a flagboat moored in Inverkip Bay, thence to the Powder Vessel's buoy and back to Hunter's Quay; twice round, distance 30 miles.

The Fourth-Class Course was from Hunter's Quay to the Inverkip flagboat, and back to Hunter's Quay; twice round, distance 24 miles.

The Fifth-Class Course lay from Hunter's Quay to a flagboat moored off Dunoon Pier, thence to a flagboat moored off Kilcreggan and back to Hunter's Quay; twice round, distance 11 miles.

Another new feature this season was the introduction of the Yacht Racing Association's scale of time allowances, based originally on that drawn up for the Royal Alfred Yacht Club by their late secretary, Mr. James A. Lyle. This scale had been in general use by the R.A.Y.C. for many years.

In 1878, not only the club, but all those who had partaken of its hospitality, had to lament their loss in the death of Mr. Samuel King, one of the most kind and genial of its members. This year was remarkable for the entry in the race for first-class yachts on the second day of the regatta. Five yachts crossed the line for the 60*l.* prize, not one of which was less than 100 tons measurement, *viz.*, the *Lufra*, 222 tons, yawl; *Jullanar*, yawl, 130 tons; *Condor*, 190 tons; *Cythera*, cutter, 116 tons; and *Formosa*, cutter, 103 tons. From that day to this there has never been such a meeting of so many first-class large racing yachts, showing so great a tonnage. It may be said also of the useful little 5-ton class, at this time at its zenith of popularity, that the entries this season were the largest that have ever been known. No fewer than eight of these mosquitoes, including Mr. York's pretty little 6-ton yawl *Rocket*, came to the fore on all the great occasions provided for their sport.

During the years 1879, 1880, and 1881, there was a satisfactory increase in the number of members, and a consequent augmentation of the club funds. The annual amount given away at this period in prizes had reached something over 450*l.* The entries at the regattas during the seasons of 1880 and 1881 were splendid in the 20-ton class; no fewer than seven 20-tonners and the 15-tonner *Maggie* crossed the line in 1880, and in 1881 the same number, less the *Maggie*, did likewise. A new class of 2½-tonners was started in 1880 with seven yachts to its name, and in 1881 still another class had to be catered for, consisting of 3½-tonners. The entries, too, this year, in the first class must not be forgotten; for in these days of fashionable small yacht racing it almost reads like a fairy tale when it is said that, out of nine entries, seven yachts were of 89 tons and over, the other two being about 60 tons each.

If the above two years are notable in the annals of the club, in the following year, 1882, its prosperity was evinced in a marked degree by the addition to its possessions of a club yacht; and as there are only one or two clubs which provide such a luxury for their members, it may not be amiss to give a short account of the *modus operandi* employed in connection with it. Among the 600 to 700 members of the club there were many who did not care to keep yachts of their own, but enjoyed an occasional cruise. It was in answer to a proposition made by one of these gentlemen that funds were procured by means of shares, which were bought by individual members, and by the club itself. In this way the necessary amount of purchase money was speedily collected, and a committee was told off to superintend the choice, purchase, and fitting out of a yacht, with all arrangements connected with manning, and the carrying out of the regulations in regard to hire, &c. The yacht thus secured by the club was the *Alcyone*, 35-ton cutter, which had been built by Mr. D. Hatcher, and had proved herself no mean performer in the 40-ton class. She is a good wholesome vessel, and a fast and able sea-boat. Her accommodation is excellent, and includes berths for five passengers at least. There is capital headroom between decks, and any amount of space for stowage of baggage, &c.

The *Alcyone* is manned by a captain and four hands, and when a member hires the yacht he has no expenses whatever to provide for beyond the hire and the keep of himself and friends while on board. Four rules were framed by the committee in charge, as being necessary for the working of the scheme, *viz*:

First.—The limit of time for hire is 14 days. Second.—The cost of hire is 3*l*. 10*s. per diem*, including cruet stores. Third.—The club is to keep a supply of liquors on board, to be supplied at a small profit. Fourth.—Hirers are bound, if called upon, to deliver up the yacht in the Holy Loch, or at any other anchorage inside the Cumbrae Head.

If it is desired to keep the yacht for a month, then it must be done by two members joining together in the hire, the one putting his name down for the first fortnight, and the other for the second. The cost of hire may seem at first sight somewhat heavy, but the *Alcyone* is kept up like a private yacht, and no money has been spared to provide every possible contrivance which might be conducive to comfort. The success of the venture is proved by the fact that she has rarely been disengaged or unlet for more than a day or two during any one season since her purchase.

Another sign of prosperity was the institution of an annual club ball, which is held at the St. Andrews Hall, Glasgow, during the winter months, and acknowledged to be one of the principal balls of the year and one of the great events of the winter season.

The next year—1883—showed a still further advancement in the club's popularity, for it was the chosen recipient of a Queen's Cup. This prize was sailed for on July 14, during the 'Clyde Week,' in a race for all yachts over 40 tons, and no fewer than eleven yachts started.

If, however, 1883 has been rendered famous for being a Queen's Cup year, 1884 will be noted for the success of its closing cruise, and the sport it provided. This season surpassed itself in the number of entries for the closing cruise handicap, and never have so many yachts

'THISTLE'
WINNING THE QUEEN'S CUP IN THE CLYDE.

come forward to race for the handsome cups, the gifts of members of the club, as on this occasion. In the first match for yachts over 40 tons, ten entered, including five over 90 tons, three 60-tonners, and two of 40 tons. It was the race for 20-tonners, however, that gave real character to the meeting, and there can be no mistake in saying that no other club in the kingdom has ever had to start so many as nine 20- and two 15-tonners in one race, all clever fast yachts, and no third or fourth rate cruisers, as will be seen from their names: *Clara*, *Lenore*, *Amathea*, *Louise*, *Sayonara*, *Irene*, *Thyra*, *Maggie*, *Calypso*, *Rival*, and *Gem*. In the race for 10-tonners seven started, among them the old *Helen* schooner, 17 tons, a yacht which saw more hard sailing than perhaps any other belonging to the club. She was built at Cowes, and was one of Halliday's pretty creations, a few of which are still to be met with. In 1892 she was unfortunately driven on the rocks off Hafton in the Holy Loch, during a severe gale, and was soon smashed into matchwood. For the prize in the 5-ton class three put in an appearance, all the fastest racing yachts of the year.

The courses for yachts of 40 tons and upwards were altered in 1885; instead of rounding the Powder buoy a mark buoy anchored off Kilcreggan became the furthest point. In 1886 the club forwarded a challenge to the New York Yacht Club, in the name of Mr. Jas. Bell, and this ended in the yacht *Thistle*, now known as the *Meteor* and owned by H.I.M. the German Emperor, being built, and sent across the Atlantic, to contend for the Cup won by the *America*. The *Thistle* and *Volunteer* matches were the consequence, and they are so well known that it would be superfluous here to furnish an account of them; suffice it to say that, though the Scotch yacht did not win the great event, her performances with the *Volunteer* not only taught British yachtsmen many a lesson, but afforded not a few hints to their American rivals.

At the beginning of 1887, the end of the club's third decade, the finances of the club consisted of a capital of 6,990*l*., and the amount at this time annually expended on yacht racing was 487*l*., exclusive of gifts of money made by individual members. During the ten years the numbers on the list of members fluctuated from 610 to 640: in this particular year only 610 names appeared on the list. With regard to the number of yachts sailing under the club flag, there had been the same variation, for though always between 180 and 197, this year the yachts numbered only 189, or 11 fewer than the previous year, the gross tonnage amounting to 12,302 tons.

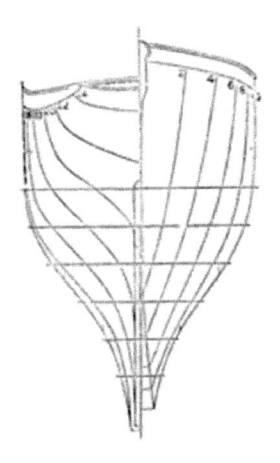

'CLARA,' 10 TONS, MIDSHIP SECTION

'LENORE'
FIFE OF FAIRLIE, 1882.

During the winter of 1886 many matters were discussed which brought forth fruit in the season of 1887, and made that year more important than it otherwise would have been. First of all, the club had to regret the loss of their Commodore, Lord Glasgow, who, after acting for over a quarter of a century in that office, was compelled to give up the appointment owing to failing health. Mr. John Clark was elected to take his place, and Messrs. Jas. Bell and H. Lamont became Vice- and Rear-Commodores. Mr. York, to whom the writer is much indebted for assistance given him in compiling this notice, held the office of secretary and treasurer, which he had so ably filled for over twenty years. During the winter the club had acquired three boats, of 19 ft. length on the load water-line, for the benefit of those members who wished to go out for a day's sail; the three boats being made, as far as the designer, builder, and sailmaker were concerned, as nearly equal in merits as it was possible for them to be, in order that they might show good sport when taken out racing together. Prizes for a race for these boats have since been regularly given at the regattas, to encourage members to take them out match sailing. In this way they have proved very useful in initiating many a tiro into the secrets and mysteries of yacht racing.

This year, too, witnessed another change in yacht measurement. The Yacht Racing Association had formulated and passed a rule of measurement by length and sail area, the length to be taken along the load water-line. This rule was adopted by the club, and at the regattas all yachts were rated according to it, with the exception of the 3½-tonners; these, as they happened to be the class of the year, were allowed to race under the old rule for which they were built. As many as six of these little vessels made the Clyde their headquarters and sailed at the regattas.

Through the club's agency, it must not be forgotten, telegraphic communication was opened up between Hunter's Quay, Glasgow, and the outer world. The club provided an office and guaranteed the sum required by the Post Office authorities, and by so doing conferred a benefit not only on themselves but on the whole surrounding neighbourhood.

Early in 1888 the club was engaged in determining the several classes under which yachts built to the 'rating rule,' as it was called, should sail. For this purpose, Messrs. R. Wylie and J. B. Hilliard, the two well-known representative Clyde yachtsmen, were chosen delegates to consult with the other leading yacht clubs in the North regarding the adjustment of a classification for the smaller yachts and sailing boats racing on the Clyde, and full powers were given them to carry out any decision that might be arrived at. Those adopted were the 10, 6 and 3 rating classes with two length classes, one of 17 ft. on the water-line and 19 ft. over all, with a sail area limited to 530 ft.; the mainsail or lugsail not to exceed .75 of the total sail area; the other class to be for boats 15 ft. on the water-line. The 6-rating class was chosen that it might form one in which the 3-tonners of the preceding year would be able to enter, as they ranged over 5 and under 6 as raters. At the time these changes were taking place a rule was introduced that there were to be no 'restrictions on the use of centreboards.'

The great feature of this year's regatta was the 'Queen's Cup,' the second presented to the club within five years, an event of which the members may justly be proud. In the interim between the Corinthian and annual regattas a channel match round Arran was inaugurated, for yachts not exceeding 9 tons Thames measurement and belonging to any recognised yacht club, for 50*l.*, given in two prizes of 35*l.* and 15*l.*, and presented by two members of the club. The course lay from Hunter's Quay down the Firth, through the Kyles of Bute, down Kilbrennan Sound between Arran and Cantyre, rounding Pladda Island, and home by any route. The yachts were to be *bona fide* cruisers, and only jib-topsails were prohibited. No restrictions were made as to crew or helmsman. No fewer than eight small yachts sailed in the race, and it proved a far greater success than was at first expected.

If this is to be known as the second Queen's Cup year, it will also have to be remembered for the terrible fire and loss of the club-house and hotel on July 12, nothing of which was saved, with the exception of some furniture, one or two models, and a few odds and ends. A club could be called upon to face no greater calamity, especially at a time when the season is at its height. Craigend Villa, within a short distance of the old house, was promptly rented as a makeshift for a year, and fitted up to meet all immediate necessities, while steps were taken at once to make arrangements for the building of a new house on the old site. To forward this the sum of 10,000*l.* was voted, which with another 8,000*l.* did not cover all the expenses. At the present moment there does not exist a more beautiful or conveniently arranged yacht club-house in the kingdom.

Notwithstanding the liberal sums devoted by the club to match sailing, there have always been at each regatta meeting a plentiful supply of cups and purses forthcoming to swell the list of prizes, the gifts of

'Verve'
23-footer (*Robert Wylie, Esq.*)

individual members. To enumerate all the donors would be out of place here, but it is impossible to overlook such names as Bell, Buchanon, Clark, Coates, Falconer, Ferguson, Forrester, Lockett, Ure, Wylie, and York, names which will ever be linked with the club's successful past.

The year 1890 was remarkable principally for the number of 10-raters belonging to members, and entered for races in that class. It seemed like a resuscitation of the old 10-tonner days. On the other hand, the Clyde, the home of the 5-tonner, had not a single 5-rater to its name, and a 6-rating class had to be formed to take in the Irish contingent, which with Mr. Inglis's little *Darthula* raced for the prizes provided for them. The 2½-rater class made its entry in the club programmes, and started with a small fleet of seven yachts, including four belonging to the Royal Ulster Yacht Club; but in 1891 this class became the fashionable class of the year, and the club of itself could boast of no fewer than eight of these small fry.

The fleet belonging to the club in the year 1857 numbered 56 yachts, mostly of very small tonnage. By 1867 the number had risen to 87 only, but then the gross tonnage was very much greater, viz. 1,200 tons. In 1877 there were 194 yachts, including a few screw steamers. In the year 1887, 189 names appeared on the club yacht list, i.e. five fewer than in 1877, but the total tonnage on the other hand amounted to 12,302 tons. The last half-decade, however, has quite eclipsed all preceding years, for the yachts now flying the Royal Clyde Yacht Club burgee number 267, which represent a gross tonnage of no less than 14,407 tons. Last year not far short of 1,000*l.* was given in prizes.

The club at the present time numbers 951 members, which will be seen to be an increase of over 300 within the last five years. It is a pleasure seldom accorded to writers of club histories to have to record such an exceptional advance, and in bidding farewell to the society, it may be firmly hoped and prophesied that long ere the close of its fourth decade the R.C.Y.C. will have increased its list of members to over four figures and its yachts and yacht-tonnage in proportion.

The Royal Forth Yacht Club
By R. T. Pritchett

The Forth Club was established in 1848 under the name of the 'Granton Yacht Club,' and received permission from the queen to assume the title of 'Royal Forth' in 1883. The flag of the club is the blue ensign of Her Majesty's fleet, with a gold crown and Maltese cross. The club is now well supported, having as patron the Duke of Buccleuch, K.T. Sir Donald Currie, K.C.M.G., is Commodore, backed by a very influential staff. The Hon. Secretary is Mr. Bruce Fenwick. The number of members amounts to nearly 2,000, with a total tonnage of about 4,600; but the Firth of Forth has serious disadvantages as a yachting centre, being favoured neither by nature nor circumstances as is the Firth of Clyde, which absorbs all yachting interests. Mr. T. B. C. West, who carried off the Queen's Cup at the Regatta in 1892 with his well-known 40-rater *Queen Mab*, presented a challenge cup of 100 guineas, to be sailed for annually in the month of June. That, however, was not sufficient inducement to get a large entry. The fact is there are so many regattas now that the tendency is to concentration, and consequently outlying stations suffer.

The Royal Forth Yacht Club had a match in June 1893, at the beginning of their water sports, from Hartlepool to Granton, for a prize of 30*l*. The starters were

The *Creole*	Cutter	40-rater	Lieut.-Col. Bagot.
Daydream	Yawl	89- "	Mr. James Shepherd.

The wind was very light at the start, which took place at 10.50 a.m. on Thursday, June 22. Later on light airs from east-north-east helped them; but off the Farne Islands—without any notice or disturbed appearance in the sky—a tremendous squall struck *Creole*; she, however, behaved splendidly, and was specially well handled. By Saturday morning the weather had moderated and they got the mainsail on her and ran up past Inch Keith, getting the gun at 11.34 a.m. from the *Iolanthe*.

The larger vessel, the yawl of 89-rating, had her troubles too, and finally got into the Tyne on Saturday morning, under storm canvas.

On the last day of the racing—June 26—there was a match for yachts belonging to the Royal Forth Yacht Club, for the T. B. C. West Challenge Cup, the entries confined to members of the club. Five yachts entered for the race, over a course of forty miles. The tonnage was very small, and the handicap one of large range; it will be noted that *Ida*, at scratch, allowed *Lintie* 1 hr. 23 mins. 48 secs.

Yacht	Rig	Rating	Handicap	Owners
Ida	Cutter	12	Scratch	Messrs. Park & Wilson
Nora	"	8	12 m. 24 s.	Dr. W. S. Armitage
Uranus	"	3.9	36 m. 47 s.	Mr. F. A. Robertson
Glance	"	3.7	40 m. 42 s.	Mr. W. A. Bell
Lintie	Lug	—	1 hr. 23 m. 48 s.	Mr. G. W. Mitchell

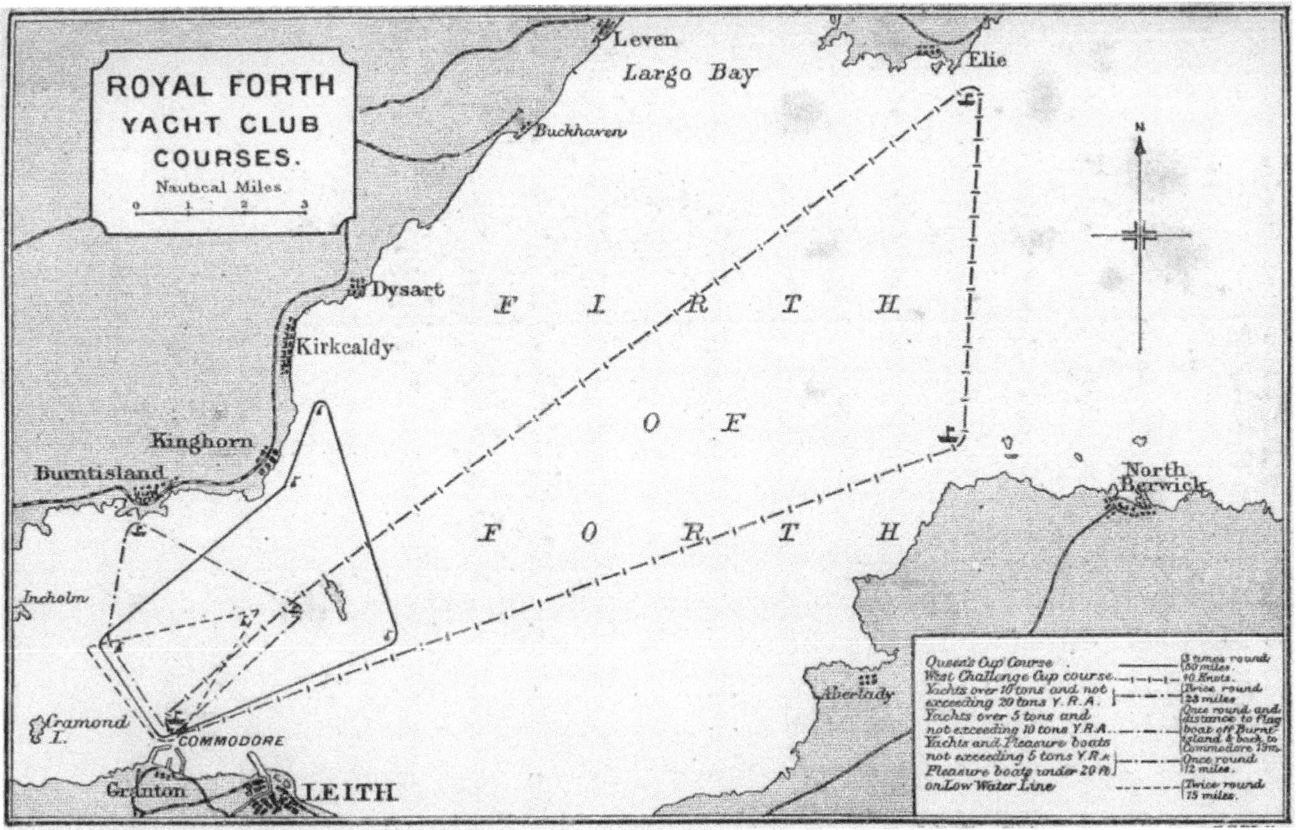
ROYAL FORTH
YACHT CLUB
COURSES.
Nautical Miles
0 1 2 3
Leven
Largo Bay
Elie
Buckhaven
N
Dysart
Kirkcaldy
F I R T H
O F
F O R T H
Kinghorn
Burntisland
North Berwick
Incholm
Cramond I.
COMMODORE
Granton
LEITH
Aberlady
Queen's Cup Course
3 times round 50 miles.
West Challenge Cup course
10 Knots.
Yachts over 10 tons and not exceeding 20 tons Y.R.A.
Twice round 23 miles
Yachts over 5 tons and not exceeding 10 tons Y.R.A.
Once round and distance to flag boat off Burntisland & back to Commodore 13m.
Yachts and Pleasure boats not exceeding 5 tons Y.R.A.
Pleasure boats under 20 ft
Once round 12 miles.
on Low Water Line
Twice round 15 miles.

The start took place at 10.37 a.m., with a nice breeze from the north-west. *Lintie* led off, but *Nora* soon took up the running and led all the way home, finishing at Granton:—

	h.	m.	s.
Nora (winner)	6	21	32
Ida	6	29	30
Uranus	6	47	0
Glance	7	42	32
Lintie	7	58	0

This will give some idea of the application of time allowance.

The Royal Eastern, established 1835, is a small Scottish Club whose existence may be noted; but yachting does not flourish much on the East Coast.

Chapter 3

Irish Clubs

The Royal Cork Yacht Club
By R. T. Pritchett

The ancestral origin of this club, which has its station at Queenstown, was the Water Club of the Harbour of Cork, established in 1720. It is therefore the *doyen par excellence*, and its rules and orders as carried out in its early days are original and entertaining. A few of the rules may be quoted:

1. Ordered that the Water Club be held once every spring tide, from the first spring tide in April to the last in September inclusive.

2. That no admiral do bring more than two dishes of meat for the entertainment of the club.

3. Resolved that no admiral presume to bring more than two dozen of wine to his treat, for it has always been deemed a breach of the ancient rules and constitutions of the club, except when my Lords the Judges are invited.

5. Ordered that the secretary do prepare an Union flag, with the Royal Irish harp and crown on a green field in the centre.
Ordered that the Water Club flag be hoisted on club days early in the morning on the Castle of Haulbowline.

9. Ordered that no long tail wigs, large sleeves or ruffles be worn by any member at the club.
Ordered that when any of the fleet join the admiral, if they have not guns to salute they are to give three cheers, which are to be returned by the admiral, and one cheer to be returned by the captain so saluting.

13. Resolved that twenty-five be the whole number of the members that this club may consist of.

14. Resolved that such members of the club or others as shall talk of sailing after dinner be fined a bumper.

20. Ordered that the Knight of the Island for the time being do suffer no person or persons whatsoever to go into the club room, unless brought by a member, or by an order of five members at the least, under their hands, on pain of being cashiered.

21. That the admiral singly, or any three captains whom he shall appoint, do decide all controversies and disputes that may arise in the club, and any captain that shall refuse to abide by such decision is to be expelled. *N.B.* This order to extend to the chaplain, or any other inferior officer.

April 21, 1737.—Ordered that for the future, unless the company exceed the number of fifteen, no man be allowed more than one bottle to his share, and a peremptory.(What a 'peremptory' was remains a mystery.)

OLD MEMBERS, 1720

Lord Inchiquin
Hon. James O'Bryen
Charles O'Neal
Henry Mitchell
Rich. Bullen, Chaplain
John Rogers

NEW MEMBERS, 1760

★ Thomas Newenham
Morough O'Bryen
George Connor
Rich. Longfield
James Nash
William Hodder
★ Philip Lavallin
John Newenham
Walter Fitzsimonds
★ Samuel Hoare
William Hays
Michael Parker

* Abraham Devonshere
John Bullen
* Robert Rogers
* James Devonshere
John Walcot
Thomas Parsons
Henry Puxly
Robert Newenham, Sec.

1760.—Members whose names are marked thus * subsequently died or left the club; the following were elected in their room, and are added in MS. in the old copy:—

Edward Roche
Edmund Roche
Richard Dunscombe
John Atkins
John Baldwin
Robert Baldwin
Sampson Stawell

The fleet to rendezvous at Spithead on club days by the first quarter ebb, any boat not being in sight by the time the admiral is abreast of the castle in Spike Island, to forfeit a British half-crown for gunpowder for the fleet.

When the admiral hoists his foresail half up, it is for the fleet to have a peak upon their anchor, and when the foresail is hoisted up and a gun fired, the whole fleet is to weigh.

Observe that if the admiral wants to speak with any of the fleet he will make the following signals.

If with the vice-admiral he will hoist a white flag at the end of the gaff or derrick, and fire two guns.

If with any private captain he will hoist a pendant at his derrick, and fire as many guns as the captain is distanced from him and from the same side.

When he would have the fleet come to an anchor, he will show double Dutch colours at the end of his gaff and fire a gun.

When the admiral will have the whole fleet to chase he will hoist Dutch colours under his flag, and fire a gun from each quarter; if a single boat he will hoist a pendant and fire as many guns from the side as a boat is distanced from him. When he would have the chase given over, he will haul in his flag and fire a gun.

YACHTS OF CORK WATER CLUB, 1720. FROM AN OLD PICTURE AT THE R.C.Y.C., QUEENSTOWN.
SAILING ORDERS FOR THE WATER CLUB FLEET, 1720

CORK WATER CLUB PUTTING OUT TO SEA, 1720.

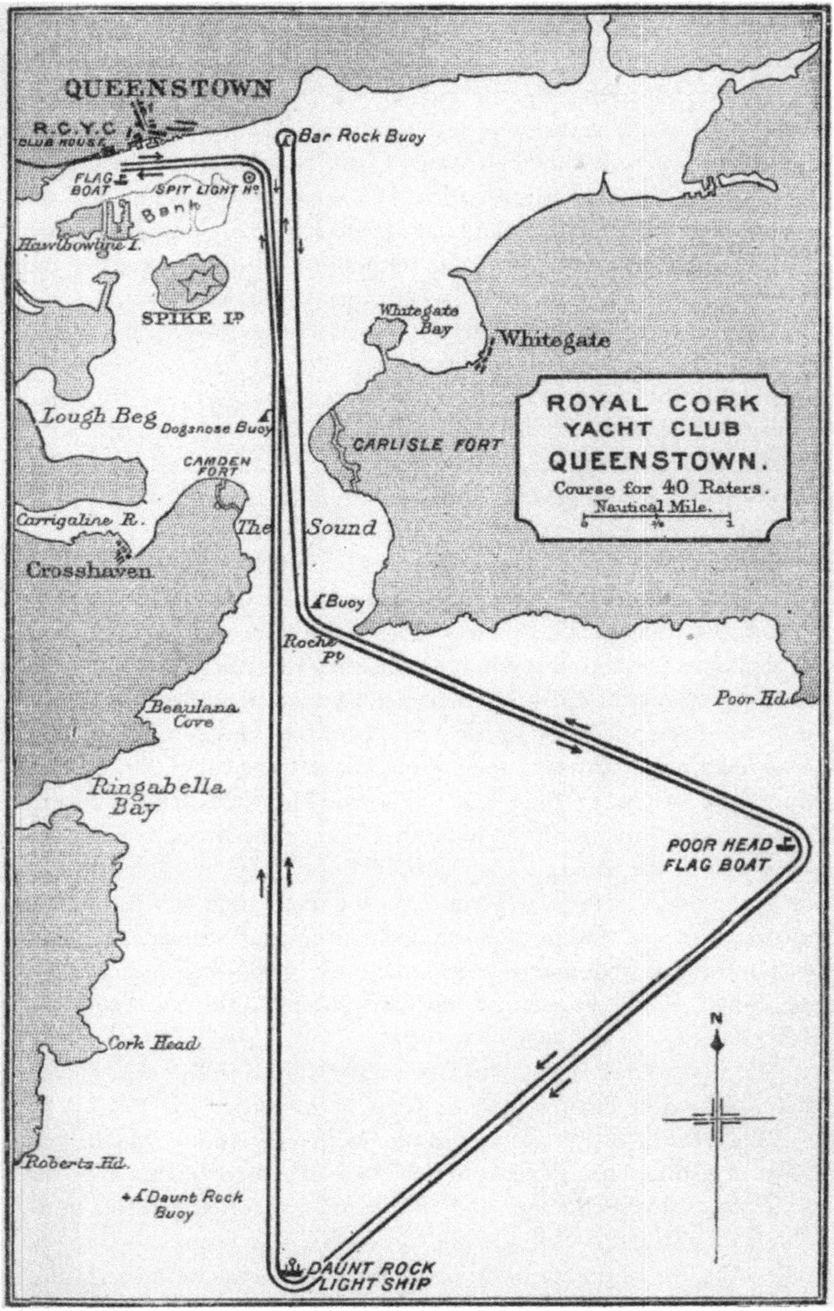
ROYAL CORK
YACHT CLUB
QUEENSTOWN.
Course for 40 Raters.
Nautical Mile.
QUEENSTOWN
R.C.Y.C
CLUB HOUSE
FLAG BOAT
SPIT LIGHT Ho
Bank
Hawlbowline I.
SPIKE Id
Bar Rock Buoy
Whitegate Bay
Whitegate
Lough Beg
Dogsnose Buoy
CAMDEN FORT
CARLISLE FORT
Carrigaline R.
The Sound
Crosshaven
Buoy
Roche Pt
Poor Hd.
Beaulana Cove
Ringabella Bay
POOR HEAD FLAG BOAT
N
Cork Head
Roberts Hd.
Daunt Rock Buoy
DAUNT ROCK LIGHT SHIP

Some storm seems suddenly to have burst upon the gay fleet, for after the year 1765 there is a long vacuum in the records. The club journal sets forth, however, that on July 1, 1806, the Marquis of Thomond, Lord Kingsale, the Fitzgeralds, the Penroses, the Newenhams, the Drurys, and others, styled therein 'original members,' met, and agreed to revive the old Water Club; but there is no reason to suppose that the club was set afloat in its ancient splendour, and the attention of the members would appear to have been chiefly directed to the useful purpose of exciting competition among the fishing and rowing boats in the harbour, to which they gave annual prizes.

Towards the end of the year 1821, the yachting spirit of both sexes in Cork Harbour declined, and the Water Club was but feebly kept up; indeed, Lords Thomond and Kingsale, Messrs. Savage, French, Cooper Penrose, Thomas Roland, John Marragh, William Harrington, John Roche, with a few others, were its sole representatives; and the club as a body at this period may be almost said to have become extinct, as no meetings were held, or proceedings recorded.

But the next year a party of youngsters, higher up the river, took possession of the vacant territory, and in 1822 a little fleet was again seen in the harbour. This society, originating in a picnic club, having its rendezvous at Monkstown, and consisting of small craft, did not assume the title of the Cork Harbour Club, but contented itself with the more humble appellation of the 'Little Monkstown Club.' From these small beginnings, however, the present Royal Cork Yacht Club had its immediate origin, in 1828, when Thomas Hewitt, Caulfield Beamish, and a few other enterprising individuals of the Monkstown Club, supported by the patriotic proprietor of 'Footy,' John Smith-Barry, and the greater part of the old Water Club members then living, met and resolved to revive and re-establish it on a solid and permanent basis.

The new arrangements were judiciously made, and the club, re-established under the title of the Cork Yacht Club, rose rapidly to eminence.

The Water Club is ably and favourably noticed in the *Tour through Ireland.* (London. Printed for J. Roberts, in Warwick Lane, 1748.)

I shall now acquaint your Lordships with a ceremony they have at Cork. It is somewhat like that of the Doge of Venice wedding the sea. A set of worthy gentlemen who have formed themselves into a body, which they call the 'Water Club,' proceed a few leagues out to sea once a year, in a number of little vessels, which for painting and gilding exceed the King's yacht at Greenwich and Deptford. Their Admi-

YACHT CLUB FLAGS.
THE DATES SHOW WHEN THE CLUBS WERE ESTABLISHED.

ral, who is elected annually, and hoists his flag on board his little vessel, leads the van and receives the honours of the flag. The rest of the fleet fall in their proper stations and keep their line in the same manner as the King's ships. This fleet is attended with a prodigious number of boats, which, with their colours flying, drums beating, and trumpets sounding, forms one of the most agreeable and splendid sights your Lordships can conceive.

The Union with harp and crown in the centre on a green field, was granted by the Lords of the Admiralty to William, Earl of Inchiquin, for the Cork Harbour Yacht Club, in 1759.

The present club-house is delightfully situated at Queenstown; though old association clings rather to Haulbowline, with its quaint history. The old pictures in the club-rooms of the Water Club yachts are valuable as showing what the craft were in those days. Age has sombred them down so much that many details are unfortunately lost. We are indebted to Major H. H. Newman, the Hon. Secretary, for his assistance, and also to Major Lysaght, who kindly photographed these paintings.

The Clubs at Kingstown, Dublin Co.

Kingstown Harbour, so admirably adapted for sailing, has long been a favourite spot with yachtsmen. Formerly Kingstown was a small creek called Dunleary, but King George IV. embarked there on September 3, 1821, and promised a grant for a new harbour, which was finished in 1859 at a cost of 825,000*l*. This harbour encloses a clear sheet of water 250 acres in extent, of depth from 15 ft. to 27 ft. at low water, with a rise of 8 ft. or 9 ft. It affords good holding ground and shelter from all winds, and, being a harbour of refuge, there are no harbour fees. As a yachting station, in addition to being a safe anchorage, it has the advantage of enabling a yacht to get in or out to the open sea in a few minutes at any tide. The East Pier is a mile long, and forms one of the most perfect marine promenades in the world. Yachting took root here when the St. George's Yacht Club was established in 1838, though perhaps it should more strictly be dated from 1845 as it was in the latter year it obtained its Admiralty warrant.

It has now become Royal, with Her Majesty the Queen as Patroness; Lord Dunleath (formerly John Mulholland, Esq.,) Vice-Commodore. A remarkably fine class of yachts is brought together in this club, and when the regatta is held Kingstown Harbour presents one of the finest aquatic spectacles in the world, embracing yachts and sailing

'ERYCINA'
96 TONS (F. B. JAMESON. ESQ., R. ST. GEORGE'S YACHT CLUB). BUILT BY FIFE, 1881.

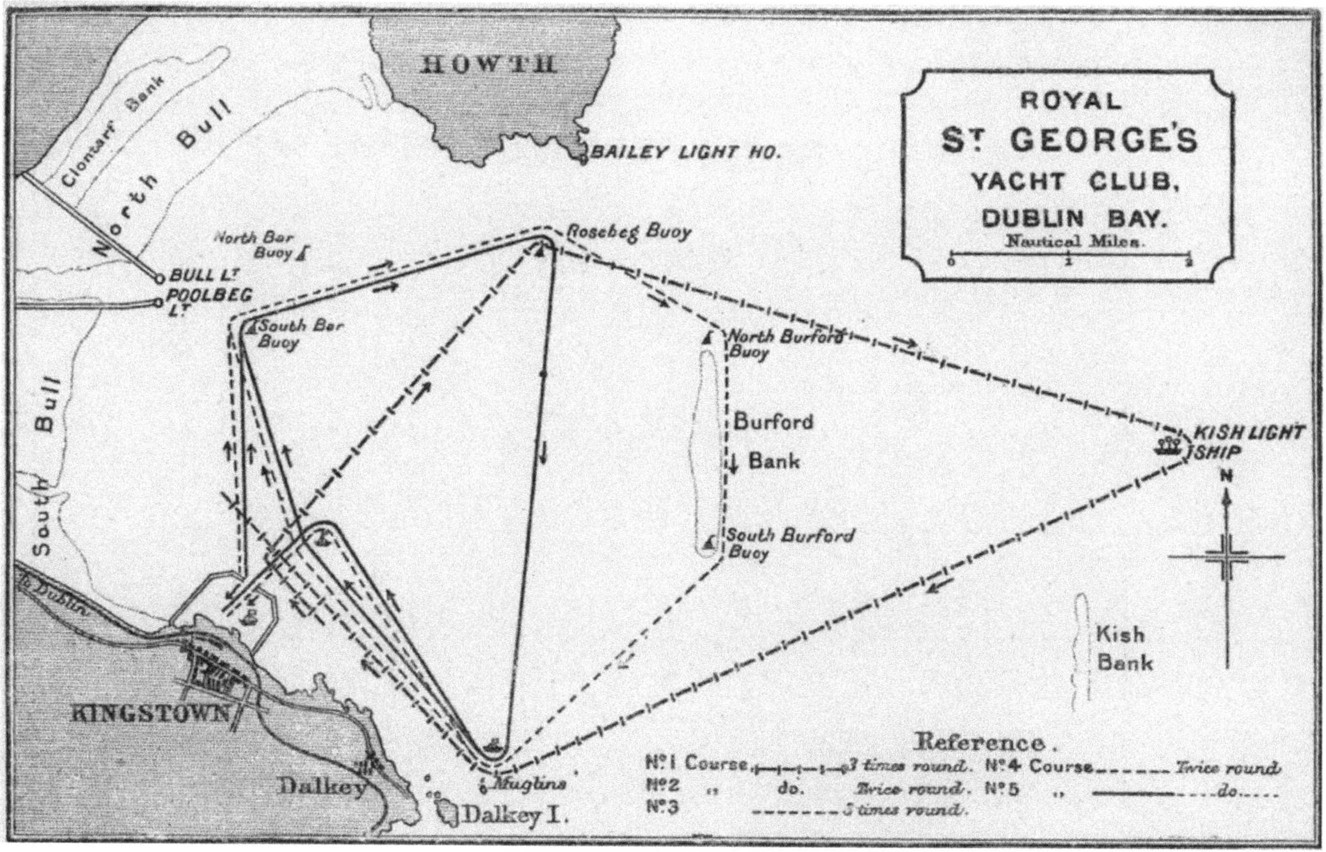
ROYAL
ST. GEORGE'S
YACHT CLUB,
DUBLIN BAY.
Nautical Miles.
0
1
2
HOWTH
BAILEY LIGHT HO.
Clontarf Bank
North Bull
North Bar Buoy
BULL LT.
POOLBEG LT.
South Bar Buoy
Rosebeg Buoy
North Burford Buoy
Burford Bank
South Burford Buoy
KISH LIGHT SHIP
N
Kish Bank
South Bull
To Dublin
KINGSTOWN
Dalkey
Muglins
Dalkey I.
Reference.
No. 1 Course 3 times round. No. 4 Course Twice round
No. 2 ,, do. Twice round. No. 5 ,, do.
No. 3 3 times round.

boats of all classes. The 'Mermaids' and the 'Water Wags,' which give annually great sport in the Bay, are described in a following chapter. The Royal Irish Club has its club-house in a fine and convenient situation; established as it was in 1846, there will soon be two yachting jubilee regattas in Dublin Bay. July is the month when aquatic revelry is in full swing. Many is the hard race sailed from the harbour round The Kish, and many the spar carried away when the high-spirited Corinthians have been cracking on. The Royal Ulster meets at Bangor, Co. Down, having the Marquis of Dufferin as Commodore; Lord Dunleath as Vice-Commodore; Captain Sharman-Crawford, of *Red Lancer* fame, as Rear-Commodore.

ROYAL ALFRED YACHT CLUB
By G. L. Blake

No sporting society in the whole of the three kingdoms has done more to encourage seamanship than that which has its station in Dublin Bay, and has been known for so many years past as the Royal Alfred Yacht Club. Worked on a basis somewhat different from that of most clubs, whose object is the encouragement of amateur sailing, this community sprang into being on March 19, 1857, at a meeting held in Gilbert's Hotel, Westland Row, Dublin, under the chairmanship of that fine practical yachtsman the late Mr. William Cooper, so well known to all patrons of the sport by his valuable works on the pastime he loved so well, written under the pseudonym 'Vanderdecken.'

'*Smartness*' might have been the motto of the newly launched club, for within a few weeks of the above date the Irish Model Yacht Club—thus it was christened while yet on the ways—had taken on board all the essentials necessary for a lengthened and prosperous voyage. Acker's signals were its code, and words of wisdom in the form of club rules had been duly got out and printed. A captain of the fleet, secretary, and treasurer, backed up by a very able committee of thirteen, constituted the 'powers that be'; and under their auspices, on May 21, the yachts of the club made their *début* in company in Ireland's Bay of Naples.

It was during the following year that one of those rules was framed which proved for so many years such a notable club feature. It ran as follows:

'Every Saturday shall be a Fleet day unless there be notice to the contrary, and all yachts on the station, under a fine of 5*s*., shall be bound to join the fleet at a given hour, unless a satisfactory reason for

'Oimara' 'Flying Could' 'Iona' 'Fiona' 'Arethusa' 'Pantomine' 'Gwendoline'
169 tons 75 tons 63 tons 78 tons 58 tons 'Flag Boat' 142 tons 197 tons 'Garrion'
Royal Irish Yacht Club Cup, Kingstown, July 24, 1873 (from a picture by Admiral Beechy).

the yacht's absence be given to the Sailing Committee. No yacht is to join unless the owner, or a member of a Yacht Club, be on board.'

Of course this regulation has had to be rescinded in order to allow of club matches taking place, and the cruises in company have become less frequent; but it is impossible to estimate the value to seamanship of fleet sailing, because there is no method by which the sailor can more readily attain to the complete command of his vessel, and make her answer to his bidding. Sailing as he will be on such occasions in company with yachts of various sizes, sail-carrying power and speed, the yachtsman who can keep station will have learnt not only to have a confidence in himself and his vessel, but also how to vary her degrees of sailing from the reeling off of knots to an up and down log line.

In 1859 the club was practically reorganised. A new book of amended rules and regulations was printed, and a book of signals produced and compiled by Mr. Jas. A. Lyle, who had been appointed honorary secretary. Among these new rules was this very useful and simple one: 'Each owner is to lodge with the secretary a duplicate of his racing flag, and this flag is to be carried on board the commodore's yacht of the day, to facilitate signalling and avoidance of mistakes.'

Towards the end of the season Lord Otho Fitzgerald, who had up to this time acted as captain of the fleet, gave up the office, and till it was eventually done away with, a Challenge Cup was instituted, open to all yachts of 15 tons (the largest size among the racing fleet) and under, to be sailed for annually. It was ruled that in future the holder of this cup should fill the office of captain of the fleet for the ensuing year.

So far the club matches had been few and somewhat irregular. Three classes had been formed, consisting of yachts of 10 and not exceeding 15 tons, of 6 and not over 10, and of others under 6 tons. This year, however, was started the annual series of racing matches, which have for over thirty years been so popular with the racing fraternity of St. George's Channel and the Clyde; and each season's programme has only undergone such alterations as have been necessitated by the increased tonnage of the competing yachts, or as may further racing according to the fashionable sizes of the yachts of the period. About this date, too, it was found necessary to obviate the difficulty which was being felt with regard to manning and sailing yachts, owing to the number of large yachts, which already flew the club burgee; the original rule, that permitted members only to be employed, was therefore stretched, in order to admit of any member of a Royal Yacht Club, who had paid his subscription, or any gentleman amateur not a seafaring man, being entered as a racing hand.

In 1864 the club advanced another step safely, and emerging from its chrysalis stage of a model yacht club, butterflied it in public as the Prince Alfred Yacht Club, keeping the same objects in view as hitherto, viz., the encouragement of match sailing and the acquisition of practical knowledge amongst its members of how to steer and handle their own vessels, especially while sailing. Commodores were appointed in place of a captain of the fleet, to carry on the more extended duties of the club; and Messrs. Putland, Scovell, and Bolton, whose names are household words throughout the yachting world, were the first officers to hold the appointments. No fewer than five classes had now to be created to take in the racing fleet; the class for yachts of 40 tons and over included all the big ones, that for 7 tons and under was open to the small fry.

Two years later (1866) the Duke of Edinburgh identified himself more closely than heretofore with the club that bore his name, by becoming its patron, and presenting a cup to be sailed for; and it was during this season that prizes were instituted, in the shape of gold pins bearing the club burgee, to especially encourage the art of helmsmanship. 1866 is also worthy of being remembered as having witnessed the introduction of the annual Kingstown and Holyhead matches, with which, since that time, the racing programme of the season has nearly always started.

The standing rule which specially distinguishes this club is that all money received shall go towards racing expenses and prize funds. The consequence follows that, limited though the club is to 300 members (there were 200 in 1864), it is able to provide good prizes for all classes, and can show more sport for its money than many another richer club which is hampered with a house. The proof of the pudding is in the eating, and the success of this homeless club, as many have called it, should read a really useful lesson to the committees of all young yachting or other sporting communities, not to be too anxious about bricks and mortar or entering on the responsibilities of housekeeping.

In 1868 another new feature, which at once became popular and is so to the present day, was started by Mr. G. B. Thompson. This was a series of matches to be held each year for yachts manned by amateurs only; and it is in some of these races, which have taken place during the past quarter of a century, that the capabilities of the members have prominently appeared as first-class able seamen. This season, however, will always be remembered for the race that was sailed on June 1 by the 2nd class yachts—*viz.* those over 25 and under 40 tons, in which the 3rd class yachts were allowed to enter at 26 tons. The *Xema*, 35; *Vampire*, 20 (rated at 26); *Echo*, yawl, 37; *Secret*, 31; *Kilmeny*, 30; *Wavecrest*, yawl, 35; and *Amberwitch*, yawl, 52 tons, started. Three paid hands were allowed to each yacht. The course lay from Kingstown Harbour, round the North Bar buoy, Kish Lightship, and the Hauling buoy in Kingstown Harbour—twice round, to start from moorings. Though the weather was anything but satisfactory, all the morning had been fine, and there had been scarcely any wind, so that light muslin, in the shape of large topsails, balloon foresails, and big No. 1 jibs, was donned by all the competitors, at all events for the reach out to the Bar buoy.

The old *Bat* was the first to get away, but she was soon overhauled by the 'Echo,' the rest following in line abreast. As the day grew on, the wind, from being shifty and all over the place, gradually settled down from the eastward, and the *Wavecrest* being the first to feel the true wind, she very naturally made use of it, and went through her vessels as if they had been at anchor. She was not allowed, however, to have the game all to herself for many moments, as the *Amberwitch* and *Xema* were soon on her track, while the *Kilmeny* and *Vampire* indulged in a luffing match, and almost allowed the *Secret* and *Echo*, which were doing rearguard, to overtake them.

The buoy was rounded in the order given above, and as the wind had been increasing rapidly the crews were now called on to show their smartness in handing in the wind persuaders and substituting second jibs and working foresails for the close-haul out to the Kish. Those who know what the face of the waters is like off the Kish Bank when a hard easterly wind has set in will have some idea of the kind of business that was being transacted on this occasion, on the outward journey. Soon it became evident that topsails were altogether out of place, and those who had shifted ballooners for small square-headers had to take them in again and house their topmasts. The *Xema* alone held on, though it could easily be seen that her topsail was not helping her at all. She had quite trouble enough too, as it turned out, without having useless top-hamper aloft, for her weather bowsprit shrouds began to show such signs of distress that it became necessary for her to hand in her head-sail and set a small jib.

The *Amberwitch* was heeling and toeing it to such an extent that, by sagging away to leeward, it became quite clear she was by no means having things her own way. The *Xema*, on the other hand, notwithstanding her sail-plan, coming up under the *Kilmeny's* lee, was forereaching well on her, when a further trouble overtook her in the parting of the main outhaul, and the traveller coming in as far as the reef battens—there were no outhaul horses in 1868—left the mainsail in a bag, a misfortune which was at once taken advantage of by the *Kilmeny*, who promptly gave her the go-by.

The *Vampire* had quite as much as she liked with the broken sea she had to drive through, but it would have rejoiced the heart of the late Mr. Dan Hatcher, her builder, had he seen the way in which his little vessel stepped it out to windward and held her own with her larger sisters. The Kish was passed by the *Kilmen* as leader of the van, and she was followed by the *Xema*, *Amberwitch*, *Echo*, and little *Bat* in the order named. Now that they had rounded the lightship topmasts were sent on end again by all, with the exception of the *Echo*, whose crosstrees had come to grief; square-headers were once more seen aloft, and sheets were checked well off for the run to the harbour. On nearing the piers the wind lightened as quickly as it had got up; it left the leading yachts almost becalmed, and only just able to gybe round the mark.

Starting away again for the second round, the *Xema* made use of the lack of wind to set up her headgear and secure her bowsprit shroud, but she had barely set things to rights before the wind came on with double vigour. It was a reach this time out to the Kish, and weight naturally telling, *Kilmeny* was outpaced by the *Xema*, which led round the lightship, followed closely by the *Amberwitch*, *Kilmeny*, *Echo*, and *Vampire*, with *Wavecrest* to bring up the rear. The *Secret* had got into difficulties about a mile from the lightship by her bowsprit snapping off close at the gammon iron, and with the sea that was running its crew had their work cut out for them in clearing the wreckage and sending out a jury spar. With the rest of the fleet it was a case once more of up topmasts and topsails for the run home, and a most exciting race was being sailed by the *Xema* and *Amberwitch* for the first place (the latter had to allow *Xema* 2 mins. 12 secs., as she was a 51-ton yawl), when the wind, drawing off the shore as before on nearing their destination, brought it to an end.

The sheets had accordingly to be hardened in, and a board to be made into Scotsman's Bay to get the benefit of the young flood, which was running in shore. A couple of short tacks now brought the

Xema clear out on the weather of the *Amberwitch* and *Kilmeny*, so that, gaining inch by inch, she managed to win at last. Nothing could have exceeded the smart manner in which the shifting of sails and the work aloft was carried out on board all the yachts.

In 1869, the honorary secretary, Mr. Lyle, to whom the club will ever be indebted for the care and interest he has shown in furthering its welfare, gave a tankard as a prize for a one-handed race, the conditions of which were

'Only one man, and he a member of the club, shall be on board, and all others must leave before any canvas is set or station taken.'

Flying starts had not yet come into fashion, and therefore buoys had to be picked up. No fewer than ten yachts started for this race, five of which were over 10, and three over 5 tons. The *Queen*, 15 tons, was the winner, but the season will be best known by the introduction of the celebrated Champion Cups, which have ever since shared the honours with the Corinthian matches in the club programmes. To secure the necessary funds for providing these luxuries, members were permitted to commute their annual subscriptions by the payment down of 10*l*. By this means the greater portion of the handsome pieces of plate, for which so many flyers of their day have competed, were obtained.

The Duke of Edinburgh, who, as already remarked, had been patron, assumed in 1871 the duties of commodore, a post he is still holding; the club had become Royal in the previous winter. The limit in the number of members was increased from 200 to 300, and the club burgee also underwent a change. Up to this date the club had sailed under no fewer than four different burgees. The original flag consisted of a red anchor on a blue field, but this only enjoyed a short life, as the anchor was changed into an Irish crown before the first season was over. In 1859, the flag appeared with a white ground, a blue cross with four points at the intersection of the cross forming the design, and in 1861 the field was changed again from white to red, with the new device of a yellow foul anchor. Now for the last time the device was altered from the ordinary foul anchor to that of a foul patent Trotman under an Imperial crown. The patent improved anchor represents the club's leading position as a Corinthian yacht racing society.

Besides five champion cups of the several values of 120*l*., 60*l*., 35*l*., 25*l*., and 15*l*., one in fact for each class, the Duke of Edinburgh presented a 50*l*. cup. A gale of wind sprang up during the race for this prize, which was won by Mr. George Putland in the *Enid*. She was the only one of all the yachts that crossed the line—flying starts were instituted this year—to finish the course, and it was the rounding of the Kish Lightship in this race by the *Enid* that Admiral Beechy took as the subject of one of his most celebrated sea pictures. The *Egeria*, schooner, was disabled very early in the race by the carrying away of the iron strop round her boom.

During the season of 1872 the club was presented with the first of the three Queen's Cups of which it has been a recipient. Matches during the summer alternated each Saturday with cruises in fleet under one of the club officers, with regard to which one great point should be noticed, *viz.*, that it has been the custom to sail only one match as a rule on each of the racing Saturdays. There are many other clubs which would do well to follow this example, as it is not infrequently next to impossible with some clubs for outport members and yacht-owners, when wishing to join in Corinthian matches, to obtain competent hands.

1872 was the last year in which single-handed racing received club support. A single-handed match had been sailed each season since their inauguration by Mr. Lyle, Mr. Alec Richardson winning twice (in 1870 and 1871) in the *Naiad*, 10-tonner; but the sad loss of Mr. O'Connell, one of the most popular and sporting members of the club, together with his yacht, and the narrow escape from foundering of another, emphasised the advisability to stop such races for the future. The race in which this disaster occurred took place on June 1. The day was a peculiar one. A double-handed match had been sailed during the fore and early afternoon, when a nice S.E. breeze favoured the competitors, which had one and all carried large topsails aloft. This race was finished, however, in a heavy downpour of rain, and was won by the vice-commodore, Mr. George Thompson, in the *Madcap*, 20 tons.

After the race was over the rain came down in such torrents that there was some hesitation about allowing the single-handed match to start, though there was no appearance of any heavy weather setting in. This fact, and there being no sea to speak of, settled the question, and accordingly the *Petrel*, 10 tons, Mr. W. G. Jamieson; *Mocassin*, 10, Mr. Corrigan; *Madcap*, 20, the vice-commodore; *Torment*, 5, Mr. Miller; and *Peri*, 5 tons, Mr. O'Connell, most of them with reefed mainsails, made a start at 3 hrs. 5 mins. in the order named. The weather soon afterwards became very thick, and nothing was seen of the yachts till 6 hrs. 34 mins., when the *Petrel* was discovered making for home. A number of yachts were out all the afternoon, and some of them on coming into harbour had passed the word that things were not going on as sweetly as they might outside. The wind had shifted to the S.W., and a considerable sea was running, increased or rather broken by the flood-tide. The *Mocassin*, who had given up, corroborated the statement that was flying about, and soon after the *Heroine*, 60-ton cutter, arrived with her topmast gone, followed by the *Whirlwind* yawl, with the loss of her gig washed away from her davits.

The danger was now clearly apparent, and a tug was immediately sent out to look for the yachts, as it was feared the small ones would be unable to beat up against the sea and make their port. The *Pleione*, schooner, had fortunately fallen in with the *Madcap*, and put a hand on board her just in the nick of time, for she had shipped a heavy cargo of water below owing to her fore hatch having been washed overboard, and her head-sheets had gone. The *Torment* ran for Howth, whence she was helped back to her moorings by a friendly tug, which was sent later on to her assistance.

The *Pleione*, however, reported that the unfortunate *Peri* had been pooped, and that she had immediately foundered, taking with her her plucky crew. The schooner had sailed on and about the spot for some time, hoping against hope to recover some memento of the catastrophe to carry back to Kingstown, and the tug was also employed in cruising round the locality, but to no purpose, as nothing was seen after she went down of either the *Peri* or her owner. Though it is now more than ten years since this sorrowful occurrence, the name of Mr. D. O'Connell, beloved by all who knew him as a keen sportsman and a most genial friend, still remains green in the memory of Irish yachtsmen.

Useful as the single-handed matches were for bringing out a display of seamanship, confidence and independence, it was as well under the circumstances that at this time they should end; but it seems a pity that the two-handed matches should have received their death-blow as well. The extra hand means all the difference between danger and safety.

Of the work carried out by the club perhaps the programme for 1874 gives as fair a sample as it is possible to choose, taking one year with another. The list of matches was as follows:—

Nos. 1 and 2. Matches to and from Douglas, Isle of Man.

No. 3. Match for yachts not exceeding 7 tons. No. 5 Champion

Cup, with 7*l*. added.

No. 4. Match for yachts not exceeding 20 tons. Corinthian Race. 25*l*. Helmsman 5*l*., with tankards for the crew.

No. 5. For yachts not exceeding 25 tons. No. 3 Champion Cup; with 25*l*. added.

No. 6. Open to all yachts. Corinthian Race, 50*l*. Helmsman 5*l*., and tankards for crew.

No. 7. For all yachts not exceeding 7 tons; 15*l*. given by Mr. Macartney.

No. 8. Match open to all yachts. No. 1 Champion Cup, 50*l*. added; two helmsmen's prizes of 4*l*. each.

No. 9. For all yachts not exceeding 15 tons; 1st prize 15*l*., 2nd prize 10*l*., given by Mr. Fulton. Helmsman 5*l*.

No. 10. For all yachts not exceeding 40 tons. 2nd Champion Cup, with 35*l*. added.

No. 11. For all yachts not exceeding 15 tons. 4th Champion Cup, with 15*l*. added.

One more race, which was promoted this year, must not be forgotten, as it would prove a very advantageous item in all yacht-club programmes, *viz.* a swimming match in clothes. The conditions were as follows: 'Each member must wear woollen socks, a pair of slippers, shoes or boots, woollen or canvas trousers, a flannel shirt, with a guernsey or yachting jacket; the distance to be covered 200 yards.'

In the Corinthian matches it may be noticed that the club not only gives the customary helmsman's prize, and that a good one, but each member of the winning crew receives a tankard with the yacht's complement or the club burgee engraved on it, a principle again worthy of adoption by all Corinthian yacht clubs in races where no paid hands are permitted.

At this period the club had the fine total of 163 yachts to a list of fewer than 300 members; and to show how admirably everything was carried on to the furtherance of sport, prizes were given to the amount of 364*l*. out of an income of 521*l*., the club expenditure being more than covered by 78*l*. These statistics are of interest as showing what can be done by a club when not fettered by club premises.

The entry in the season of 1875 for the No. 1 Champion Cup is worthy of a notice here, since no fewer than seven of the large cracks of the year put in an appearance—*Fiona*, 75 tons; *Cuckoo*, 92; *Neva*, 62;

Speranza, yawl, 85; *Latona*, yawl, 165; *Egeria*, schooner, 147; and *Gwendolin*, schooner, 197 tons; and as an example of a R.A.Y.C. Corinthian match, that which took place on July 17, 1876, for 'Twenty Tonners' will long be remembered, not so much for its record of spar-breaking, as for the seamanlike way in which difficulties were overcome. The description of the race is here given almost in the words of an account for which the writer is indebted to Mr. James Drury, who was himself an active witness on the occasion. The weather was far from favourable owing to a strong gale during the previous night having raised a nasty tumbling sea on the banks, while the wind, though moderate in the early part of the afternoon, at times blew in fierce squalls, rendering it necessary to reduce canvas at awkward moments.

The entries were:—

Hinda	18 tons		Mr. G. B. Thompson.
Sheilah	20	"	Mr. Pascoe French.
Challenge	20	"	Mr. Fred Thompson.
Sunshine	20	"	Mr. D. MacIvor.

Prizes: Owner, 25*l*.; helmsman, 5*l*.; crew, tankards. Course No. 3 (24 miles), no paid hands allowed. Though the number of competitors was smaller than usual, the quality was extremely good, all four being well known as about the best of their class. A nice southerly breeze was blowing, making it an easy reach to the South Bar buoy, and the tide was just beginning to flow to the northward. The *Hinda* was the first away, steered by her owner, followed close astern by the *Sunshine*, which had won so many prizes in 1874, with Mr. Henry Dudgeon at her helm. *Sheilah* was third, with the late Mr. Pascoe French as pilot, and last, though only some 45 seconds behind the leader, came the *Challenge*, with a crew who had come over from Liverpool in her or by steamer, and comprised the cream of the Mersey and Cheshire yacht clubs, among them Mr. Richardson, her designer, who now handled the lines. The *Hinda* and *Sunshine* each carried a crew of eight hands all told, while the *Sheilah* and *Challenge* had a complement each of ten hands, including the helmsman.

All the yachts had whole lower canvas and jibheaded topsails set, except the *Sheilah*, who had a small square header aloft, and *Sunshine*, who had prudently reefed her mainsail and foresail, although they still looked big enough for a 30 even thus reduced. The *Sheilah* soon showed her speed off the wind, as, going through *Sunshine's* lee like a dart, she led the fleet and placed herself some 50 seconds ahead of any other by the time she had made the first turning point, where it was 'gybe ho,' and she increased this lead to 2¼ minutes at the Rosebeg, the others having played at luffing and thus impeded each other.

Sheets were now hardened in for a close haul to the North and South Burford buoys, and *Sheilah* soon found her topsail too much for her in the jumpy sea; but unfortunately it had been set with the tack to leeward, and was not therefore handy for shifting, while, worse than this, her big No. 1 jib was pulling her head off, and with a single sheet only it was more than her foremast hands could manage to get it properly aft. The *Challenge* held a beautiful wind, and getting clear of the other two, weathered fast on *Sheilah*, though she did not head-reach on her. Mr. French, wishing to shift his topsail, went about on the port tack before he could weather the South Burford, but meeting the *Challenge* on the starboard tack, and fearing he would not be able to clear her, stayed under her lee, with the effect of being dead covered for four or five minutes, when the first bitter puff that came clear of the after leach of *Challenge's* mainsail whipped *Sheilah's* topmast over her side. She was immediately hove about, and her crew set to work to clear away the wreck, Messrs. Drury and Dunne running aloft and casting off the topsail lacing; but before they could get the sail down or the rigging secured, it was found necessary to go about again in order to pass the mark on the proper hand, and four or five minutes banging about of the wreck to leeward laced everything up into such a horrible state of confusion that it took the crew all they knew to get the topsail below, the broken mast on deck, and the rigging secured.

The *Challenge* in the meantime, capitally sailed and handled, crept away steadily, and the *Hinda* drew up on the *Sheilah*, while the *Sunshine* still kept the rear, not seeming to like the rough water. At 2 hrs. 27 mins. 35 secs. the *Challenge* stayed round the buoy in Kingstown Harbour, followed by the *Sheilah* 2 hrs. 33 mins. 10 secs., having her tricolour flag flying from her crosstree. The *Hinda* rounded at 2 hrs. 34 mins. 55 secs., and the *Sunshine* at 2 hrs. 37 mins. 30 secs. The wind was now much more westerly, and the squalls stronger. The *Sheilah* set her balloon foresail for the reach out, in hopes of lessening the distance between her and the leader, and certainly gained a little. After the gybe Mr. French determined to shift his jib, especially as the starboard whisker had begun to buckle, and for this purpose gybed back and ran in under Howth—a great loss of time, for when the boom came over again the *Hinda* was ahead.

The *Sunshine*, after reaching Rosebeg, carried away her mast bodily, some 17 ft. from the deck, and the whole top-hamper fell overboard, leaving her helpless, and in anything but a pleasant predicament with so heavy a sea running, and the rocks of Howth under her lee. However, several yachts and a tug went off to her assistance, and after drifting round the Bailey, the tug got hold of her and brought her back, a sad wreck, to Kingstown Harbour. Meanwhile the squalls were becoming sharper, and the sea heavier and more broken, threatening destruction to bowsprits and bobstays, as the little vessels wallowed in the trough. The *Sheilah*, showing her power, drew up abreast and close to the *Hinda* between the Burfords, and all hands were admiring the way she was carrying her canvas, having her jib-topsail still aloft, and going like a bird, when *crash!* away went her mast, just under the hounds, leaving her quite as helpless as the *Sunshine*, but in clearer and more open water.

No one was hurt, and the *Sheilah* at once triced up her tack, lowered her foresail, and hove to alongside her disabled consort in order to give help if required. Her crew employed themselves, while waiting, in hauling down a reef. This *Challenge* perceived, and having matters quite safe, she at once followed suit, and made all snug for the thrash home of four miles; a happy matter for her, as her mast was badly sprung and might have gone at any moment. By the time the reefs were down, the *Whirlwind*, 77-ton yawl, belonging to Mr. J. Townsend, had hastened to the assistance of her disabled little sister, and sending a warp to her, took her in tow. The *Challenge*, on resuming her course, was well ahead, and eventually the race ended by her rounding the flagships at 4 hrs. 37 mins. 10 secs., winning the prize for her owner, the helmsman's prize for Mr. Alec Richardson, and tankards for her crew, who deserved them well for their pluck in coming from Liverpool and for the way they sailed and handled their vessel. In addition to other damages, it was discovered on reaching the harbour that the *Sheilah's* mast, with the rigging and all, had settled down 2 inches, having badly torn the wood of the mast, while *Challenge's* mast was also reported 'queer' aloft.

The No. 1 Corinthian Match, which took place in 1879, would also give subject for much interesting reading and reflection did space permit, for smarter seamanship or a more exciting finish could not have been seen anywhere, not even in the bonny Clyde. It is only right to say that the members of this little club spare no energy or pains in order to become efficient racing yachtsmen; and to go out on a dirty afternoon to practise under difficulties shifting sail, reefing down, sending up and housing topmast, reefing in bowsprit and seamanship in general, is one of the means that have been before now employed to bring about the state of perfection which is exhibited by its leading hands, and for which the club is and always has been so famous.

At the beginning of the eighties the courses underwent some slight alterations, and as these hold good at the present day it may be found useful information if they are given here.

No. 1 Course.—From outside Kingstown Harbour to the South Bar buoy, thence to Rosebeg Bank buoy, the Kish Lightship, to a flagship moored off the East Pier End; three times round—48 miles.

No. 2 Course.—The same as No. 1; only twice round—32 miles.

No. 3 Course.—Kingstown Harbour to South Bar buoy, thence to Rosebeg Bank buoy, North Burford buoy, South Burford buoy, to flagship moored off the East Pier End; twice round—24 miles.

No. 4 Course.—Same as No. 3, only once round, thence to South Bar buoy and the flagship off the Pier—16 miles.

No. 5 Course.—Kingstown to South Bar buoy, thence to a flagboat moored two miles S.E. half-E., and to the flagship; twice round—4 miles.

Of the various new classes that have sprung up within the last ten years, perhaps that in which the 3-tonners *Rival, Duchess, Senta, Currytush*, and *Mimmie* are chiefly prominent has given about the most sport. Of these little ships, the *Currytush*, one of the late Mr. Payton's greatest successes, could not only show her tail to the flyers of her class wherever she presented herself, but she gave the Solent 30-ft. class a good dressing in a thrash to windward against a nasty head sea and in a hard blow. The small class for yachts of seven or six tons and under has always been a great favourite in Dublin Bay, but for two or three years a regular 5-ton class held sway, and the season of 1885 witnessed its dying kick in the coming together of the *Shona, Luath, Delvin,* and *Doris*. The *Luath* and *Doris* were new this season. The 18-ft. and 25-ft. open-boat classes, however, both have run these very fine in public favour, especially the latter. The rule of measurement adopted, and the conditions of sailing, are as follows:—

The extreme draft is not to exceed one-sixth of the load-water-line.

The counter, if any, is not to exceed one-sixth of load-water-line, nor is the rabbit, where it intersects the afterside of the sternpost, to come nearer the surface of the water than 4 in.

The overhang of the bow, if any, is not to exceed one-sixth of the load-water-line. Any excess of overhang beyond these limits must be added to the length of the load-water-line, and the result taken for class and time-allowance.

The whole overhang of any counter, whose rabbit, where it crosses the afterside of the sternpost, is less than 4 in. above the surface of the water, must be added to the length of the load-water-line, and the result taken as the length for class and time-allowance.

The crew, including helmsman, is not to exceed one man for every 7 ft. or fraction of 7 ft. One of these may be a paid hand.

Centreboard boats are allowed to compete, but the plates are never to be lowered beyond the limit of one-sixth of their load-water-line and must be kept down at a fixed draught during the whole race. (If the latter part of this rule has been altered, it is only lately that the alteration has been made.)

The Royal Alfred Yacht Club is still houseless, and keeps to its original purpose of devoting all its available funds to the encouragement of match-sailing. It has lost within the last few years the valuable assistance of its late secretary, Mr. James A. Lyle, who might almost be said to have fathered the club from its earliest infancy; but with a foundation so ably laid, a working team of thoroughly practical seamen to officer and steady the helm (and to whom I am greatly indebted for the help given me in compiling this paper), the members have every reason to be proud of the position their association holds as a representative racing yacht club.

"Graphic Cruisers" of Dublin Bay
Notes By the Hon. Skipper

A lovely night, a gentle breeze, a glassy, heaving ebb, all sail set, the boat coaxingly pulling at her moorings, her port and starboard eyes bright and glistening, her punts (choked with artists' sketchings, gear, and a gun-case or two) safe at the davits; her deck rather littered with Gladstones and canvas bags; a murmuring sound from below, accompanied by a light clatter of coffee cups: on deck are only 'Billy' (our cook), 'Jack,' the 'boy' (general fag and washer-up), and the 'skipper'

OUTWARD BOUND.

(one of the party selected by ballot for the cruise).

The buoy is overboard, 'Jack' hauls the stays'l to windward, Billy lowers the chain silently through the hawse, the *Iris* gently glides from among the surrounding boats, and is off for a week or two, heavily laden with an artistic, musical, medical, legal, and other 'crew' seeking relaxation, and a recovery from that dyspepsia which sooner or later overtakes every hard worker in this so-called temperate climate.

In this boat the passengers are converted into 'crew'; all must work, all obey the lawful commands of the skipper for the time being, though perchance he may not be the best sailor; and although some of the members are crack yachtsmen, all loyally avoid offering nautical advice *unasked*. Each is allotted some particular duty. One is medical officer, another is second in command, and the most onerous task is that accepted by the 'steward.' He is generously assisted by the advice of such of the crew as have had experience, and has 'Billy' and 'the boy' to carry out his behests; neither of the latter appearing much on deck, for the boat is worked in easy watches by the 'crew.'

It would almost appear that some insidious apology should prelude a description of such a homely and slow craft as that selected for this occasion; but, as she fills a space in the different classes of yachts, and has proved an unspeakable comfort for the purposes intended, these, and the means adopted, may have an interest for many who enjoy quiet pursuits. The crew was a typical one. There were several artists, several ardent naturalists, and a photographer (a lawyer, who could prove to demonstration that a photographer *might* also be an artist), and all practised music.

The cruise was limited to Dublin Bay and a few harbours north and south.

Some of the most beautiful spots, from an artist's point of view, cannot be reached in a deep boat, and so our draught was limited to less than 3 ft. 6 in., a condition complied with by the *Iris*. She is 60 ft. long over all, with a beam of 12 ft. 6 in., diagonally built of mahogany, with a metal keel, as well as internal ballast cast to fit her. Her mid-transverse section shows a rather barrelled bottom, but her form forward and aft is such that she rolls very little; and, for this reason, and also from the fact that her saloon table is not far from the plane of her centre of rolling motion, the swinging apparatus of the dining-table has been removed, and it is now a satisfactory fixture.

As it was intended to frequent shallow waters and dry harbours like Howth, Lambay, Rush, Skerries, Wicklow, &c., provision had to

Section of 'Iris.'

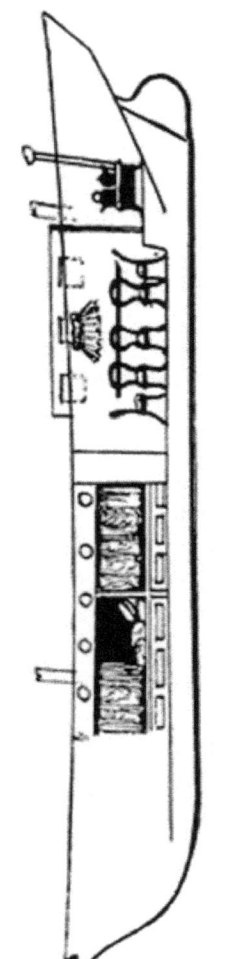

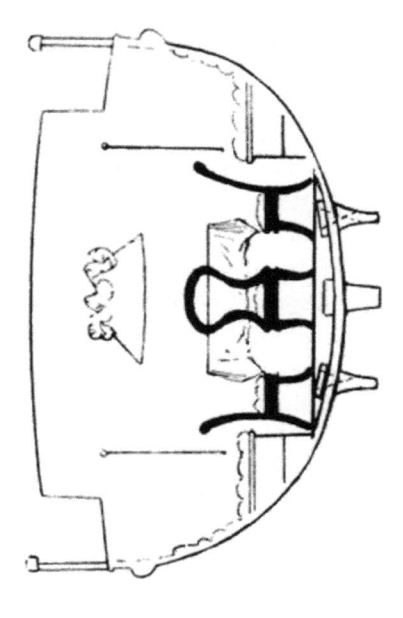

Section of 'Iris,' showing permanent legs.

be made for taking the ground comfortably. It is not possible to do this with 'legs.' There is always a doubt on the mind of the responsible officer as to which side she is likely to cant, and whilst on one side of the boat there may be good hard sandy ground, on the other may be a patch of soft mud, into which the leg may gently subside if she unfortunately happen to cant in that direction. Again, the time when the tide will leave her may be some hours hence, and a weary waiting ensues, perhaps after a stiff passage, when all hands long to 'turn in.' Of course, when you have a paid crew, they do the waiting; but a paid crew in this cruise would in great measure defeat the main object of the expedition.

To obviate the necessity for 'legs,' a simple and efficient substitute is shown in the transverse section. Two deep bilge pieces 10 feet long are bolted to broad stringers above the timbers, and extend fore and aft some 5 feet longer than the bilge pieces, thus distributing the strain over a large portion of the boat. They are wide at the skin, and taper downwards. The bolts are inserted diagonally, and the bilge pieces are shod with keel bands; they are modelled on the outsides, but the inner faces are flat and *almost* parallel, being further apart aft than forward by one inch, for reasons that need not here be mentioned. Such a contrivance helps to improve the leeway of so shallow a boat, although not proportionately to the area immersed. It is objectionable on grounds set forth by Kemp and others, as offering a larger surface for friction than is the coefficient for the lateral gain; but it is a great comfort when you have to take the ground and wish to have dinner with ease of mind (a necessity with a dyspeptic), and a joyful exchange for the sloppy, and lumbering, and inconvenient and unsteady 'legs.'

The boat is 'ketch' rigged—probably the safest of all rigs, and certainly the simplest and least laborious to be worked by few hands; indeed, this boat has been worked to windward in a narrow tideway, single-handed, over and over again. This comfortable rig was determined upon after many experiments. The boat was originally schooner-rigged, with sails by Lapthorn; but she would not wear, at least quickly enough for safety, in narrow waters and crooked channels, especially in strong winds. This difficulty in 'wearing' is common to many good-sized boats. Quite recently I saw a revenue cutter charging away towards a bank with several hands at the tiller, and the main sheet eased off without affecting her mad career until the officer scandalised her mainsail; then she slowly yielded the point, and just cleared the bank by tearing up the sand and mud, leaving a yellow track behind her.

Again, during the recent racing season, the pilot-boat (about sixty tons) started from Kingstown Harbour for her cruising ground. The old pilot at the helm sucked his pipe with confident air as she slipped; you could almost imagine his saying, 'This old boat and I are old chums; I know her. See how, with one finger on the tiller, I make her gracefully fall off to avoid that group of yachts ahead!' Suddenly the smile disappears; the pipe is chucked from his mouth. She won't fall off! she is charging bang into the yachts! The old man's legs are toughened out, and both hands grasp the tiller, as a shout from the man forward, who is hauling the jib to windward, calls the attention of the other pilots aboard, and one who grasps the situation rushes to the peak-halliards and scandalises the mainsail; then she tears away showing her copper as she fills, while skippers around fire a volley of muttered blanks at the 'old tub' as she makes for the harbour's mouth.

But with the ketch-rig the helmsman of the *Iris*, by manipulating the mizzen-sheet, threads her in safety to or from the wind along a shallow tortuous gut left by the fallen tide. Remember she is 60 ft. by 12 ft. 6 in., and with *a draught of less than 3 ft. 6 in*. Her ability to take the ground upright is a source of gratification to the artistic members of her crew; neither flowing nor ebbing tide, nor a shift of wind, makes it necessary to alter the positions of the sketching-seats, easels are a convenience that may be comfortably indulged in, and then the operations of the steward are not disturbed. But there is another great advantage in being able to take the ground in this manner when you have to stop in harbours that are nearly half dry at low water—an advantage having a large element of safety, and best illustrated by a case in point, an incident in our recent cruise.

We had spent the night on the beach at Ireland's Eye, an island north of Howth, rich in geological, archaeological, and botanic interest. On one side a shingle and a silver strand, a ruined abbey, and a charming view. On the other, wild and romantic cliffs, thousands of sea birds, a smuggler's cave, a seal cave, and a very remarkable profile rock. Here in the summer you may see a Lord Justice picnicking with his family, a Bankruptcy Judge, a gallant and skilful yachtsman, prowling after rabbits, a Churchill gazing at profile rock and smoking like a furnace, an Academician describing the hermit's cell, a citizen from Dublin dining with his friends, an excursion of the Dublin Sketching Club working in platoons, and, should lovely harmony startle the night air, perhaps some members of an opera company have come

THE BAILEY, DUBLIN BAY.

'GRAPHIC' ARTISTS AT WORK DURING THE GALE OF
OCTOBER 5, 1892.

down by the last train after the performance to breathe the fresh air and sleep aboard the *Iris*.

Well, as I said, we spent the night at Ireland's Eye, and in the morning found the barometer dropping rapidly far away at the harbour on the mainland. The coastguards had hoisted the one point downwards, indicating a gale from the south'ard. We were in perfect shelter, but as we had arranged to help the Tennis Club Entertainment that afternoon by playing some stringed instruments, we hoisted sail and made for Howth Harbour, coming to anchor in nice time to escape the preliminary bursts of the truthfully predicted 'blow.' The wind blew off shore, and so there was no send or swell in the harbour. We were free to anchor in very shallow water, careless whether we were left high and dry or not, and herein lay our safety, not from wind nor wave, but from vessels rushing for shelter into the small and crowded portion of the harbour where the water is deep, and also from craft dragging.

Last year, during a gale off shore, eleven boats of different sizes, one an iron steamer, dragged into a corner of the harbour and crunched one another into matchwood. There was no 'sea,' only a disordered and irregular 'chop.' The *Iris*, drawing only a few feet of water and anchored within an inch or two of the bottom, could not be approached by any dragging or sailing boat of greater draught; long before reaching her they would be fast aground.

In the evening, after our labours for our friends ashore had been satisfactorily completed, we pulled aboard fairly dry, and in a few moments were seated at dinner, the boat perfectly upright and immovable, with about 2 ft. 6 in. of water around us. The lamps gave a rich glow of colour and glitter to our table, all the more comfortable from the contrast with the sudden cold without and the howling and moaning of the gale. After coffee we lounged on deck, well wrapped up, to enjoy a cigar and observe the storm. The lighthouse lamps burned brilliantly, and the anchor lights of the craft in harbour flickered and struggled for a feeble existence, their movements showing that over there at any rate there was rolling and uneasiness. Here, our steadiness was enjoyable, as was also our dry deck, due to our bulwarks of over 2 ft. high.

Suddenly above the breakwater appeared a black pyramid, growing bigger every moment; then another, then many. They were fishing-vessels beating for the harbour for shelter, but they slowly disappeared one by one; they had gone about on the other tack; we might shortly expect them in. Soon there struggled in the narrow mouth the shadow of a close-reefed trawler of sixty tons or so. Why does she stop? Is she on the rocks at the light? No, she has missed stays; there is not room to do more than drift astern, and she disappears in the darkness. And in less than half an hour she will try again, for the harbour has a difficult entrance. A few minutes afterwards there rushes in a more fortunate vessel; then comes another, and another—each in turn makes straight for us, but we smoke quietly; we know they cannot approach. Still they are near enough to enable us to hear, above the fighting winds, the shrill cries of the men to 'Let draw,' or 'Hold on, Pat,' the rattling of blocks, the vicious flap of the canvas and shock of the heavy boom as each vessel goes about, and soon the rattling of cables as anchors are dropped, followed by such silence as the gale permits, while the men seek some rest after a heavy battle with nature.

In the meantime the occupants of the other boats at anchor have had serious moments; dangerously near came some of the fishing vessels, and even when anchors had been let go anxious eyes blinkingly peered against the salt, blinding wind to see if the trawlers' anchors held, and that the boats were not drifting down upon them with inevitable result. Skippers also watched their own holding gear with some concern; for if one of these crafts dragged, she would be broken up against the breakwater, and should she be fortunate enough to ground she would be down at the ebb, but, especially if she were a racer, she would not rise again with the next flow. Here we leave them and go below to our comparatively calm and safe berths, knowing that even should it calm down by morning we shall see tired and worn faces around us, and that we, thanks to our substitute for 'legs,' shall have slept in ease and peace, and awakened refreshed in body and in mind.

In order to get headroom there is 'trunk' 'rise' on the deck, as shown on the cross-section drawing, 18 in. high (in one place higher) and some 40 ft. long, leaving a conveniently wide gangway on the deck at either side; this rise has a number of dead lights at the sides, as well as skylights above; and during its infancy the boat was severely criticised. She was called the *Tramcar*, and had other more opprobrious compliments paid her. As to her speed, there were sundry allusions to crabs and their propensities for walking backwards. It was therefore excusable, taking into account the windage due to the superstructures and high bulwarks, and to the general form of the boat and also to the bilge pieces, if we had very humble notions as to the speed of the *Iris*; and although we all believed in 'the craft you sail in,' it was with some amazement that we found her unexpectedly fast in reaching, and therefore fast with the wind aft. This particularly struck us one

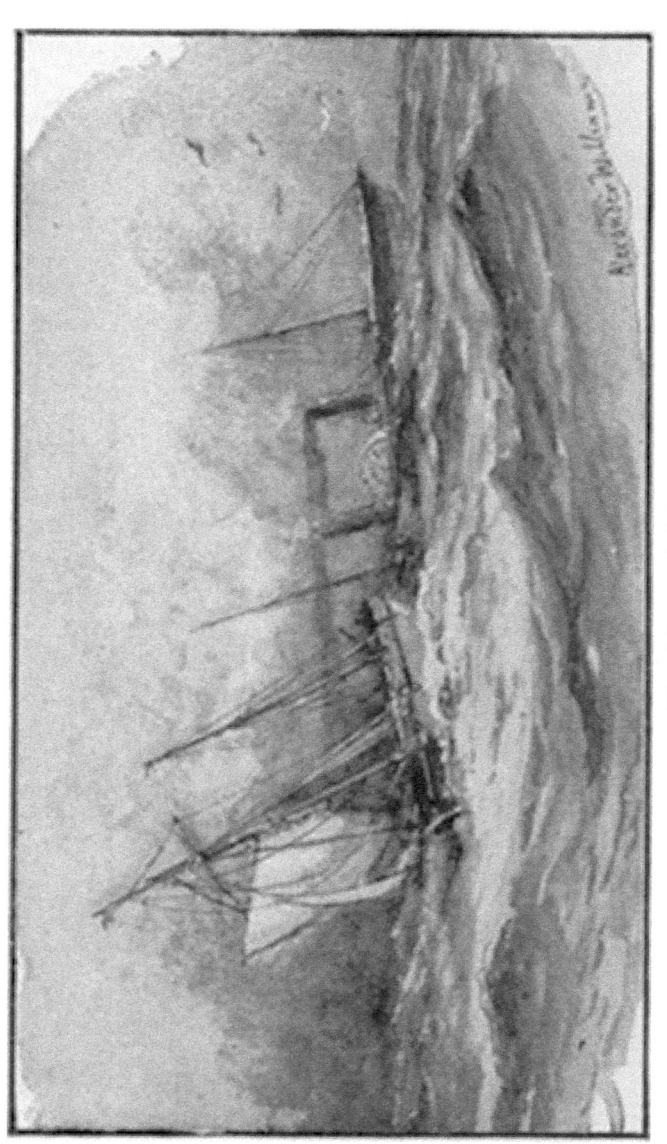

HER MAJESTY'S MAILS.

morning when we saw a fine racing-cruiser rounding the Bailey. The wind was fresh and free; someone said, 'Here comes Charlie. Watch how he will swoop past us in his triumph.' But Charlie didn't triumph, neither did he swoop; we watched carefully until we saw that *Charlie was going astern!*—a fact that surprised us as much as it did Charlie.

Again, many said that a boat with such a high freeboard and so little draught would not claw off a lee-shore in a bad sea; but as she was designed for artist's work chiefly in local waters, where there is protection every four or five miles, it was not intended that she should be submitted to heavy weather. We always had a lurking suspicion that she would not do very well in a seaway, but here we were again agreeably surprised; for, seizing a favourable opportunity, we brought her round the nose of Howth (as nasty a spot as anyone could wish in dirty weather), and there we put her through her facings, with the result that we found her an able vessel, safe to stay even when much knocked about, and when we purposely allowed her to make a stern board, with the aid of the mizzen, we could put her head in which direction we chose. Several steamers passed us during the trials, and these were shipping tons of water, while we did not take a cupful.

Around the boat, six inches below the covering board, is a very wide 'rubbing-piece,' a ribband of 'thumb' moulding, whose form will be understood by reference to the cross-section drawing. This projects some inches from the side of the boat, and the effect of this small bead in throwing off seas is most remarkable. Often have we watched green lumps of water lapping up her sides with a rush that threatened to bring them over the bulwarks in the next instant, especially at her bows, but on reaching this 'stroke' the whole mass seemed diverted outward, and to drop back into the sea. True it is that action and reaction are equal and opposite, and the momentum of the wave must have been communicated to the boat in some way (likely to be detrimental to her speed and affecting her leeway), but we were unable to realise practically any injurious effect to at all balance the pleasure of a dry boat.

Such, indeed, is the general success of the boat as a quiet, safe cruiser, that it is intended to have a new one designed by some crack authority with better lines, built of steel, with the important existing features adhered to, but doubtless with much improvement in the speed. As to the rigging, the stays'l carries a boom and the sheet travels on a 'horse,' the jibsheets run aft, and the mizzen-sheet is made fast to a cleat on the under side of the mizzen-boom; thus the helmsman can put her about single-handed if he please. In smooth water he puts the helm down, and, when she fills on the other tack, shifts the jib. In a short sea, if she is likely to lose way in stays, he puts the helm down, slips a loop over it, then hauls on the mizzen-sheet till the sail is fore and aft, when she goes about with certainty. He then shifts jib; he does not take the sheet from the cleat, but simply hauls on the fall; consequently the sail does not require adjustment when the vessel fills. In smooth water, such as the Broads or Windermere, or the Liffey Estuary, no particular tactics are needed in going about, but in the frequently troubled water of Dublin Bay these matters are noteworthy when we remember that she is 60 feet long, has a beam of 12 ft. 6 in., and draws only 3 ft. 6 in. of water.

Report of the Hon. Medical Officer

In one of the steamers of which I had medical charge it was a common saying that all that was medicinally required by the crew and passengers was a weekly dose of 'one pint of sulphur wash and 2 oz. bilge nails,' and that teeth might be drawn by the 'key of the kelson.' No such drastic treatment should be required on a yachting cruise, but a few medicines and surgical appliances should always be on board, and the sanitary condition of the boat should be rigorously and minutely inspected, not only before starting, but daily during the cruise, be it long or short. To begin with, before stores or passengers come aboard I have the carpet or other covering taken up and some of the flooring lifted along the entire length of the boat, and I carefully see that no fragments of food, animal or vegetable, have accidentally got about the ballast, that no pieces of paper, however small, nor sawdust, nor shavings, nor 'matter out of its proper place' of any kind whatever, is left below the flooring.

I personally see that the limbers are cleared, and that a copious flush of water redolent of calcium chloride or 'Sanitas' is poured in forward and pumped out of the well aft. Next, I inspect the sail lockers, and if there be any musty smell, I have the sails, &c., removed on deck and hung up to thoroughly dry; in the meantime the locker beams and ceiling are washed over with a solution of chloride of lime and thoroughly aired. The steward's store lockers and cooking utensils are carefully examined, a solution of potassic permanganate being freely used; the mattresses are turned over and searched for the slightest mouldiness, and, if any be detected, are sent ashore to be taken asunder and stoved; the lockers under the berths are aired, and

STORM WITHOUT, CALM WITHIN.

KINGSTOWN, DUBLIN BAY.

the Indian matting with which the bunks are lined taken down and examined, and, should there be any mustiness, which will surely be the case if it has not been kept dry, I condemn it and get fresh—fortunately it is a cheap material. The w.c.'s are of the underline type and consequently require rigorous examination, as that kind is subject to leakage, and they should always be provided with simple means for tightening up the joints, and so devised that all the strains due to pumping, &c., are self-contained. There should also be an automatic supply of a strong solution of permanganate of potash every time the w.c. pump is used.

Besides this, however, I always make the boy pour in a pint of strong permanganate solution night and morning, and with a good air-draught, secured by having the door made so that there are several inches above and below between it and its frame, I have never had the slightest reason to doubt the efficiency of the apparatus as a sanitary appliance. Earth-closets are a delusion; you cannot get earth, nor even sand, when on a cruise, and there are other serious objections. Carpets should be examined for mould in the interstices of the material, and should any be detected, however slight, the carpets should be taken ashore—they cannot be properly treated in a small boat. In short, fungoid life of any kind must be stamped out, and it is to be observed that yachts of every kind, and especially small ones, are peculiarly subject to this kind of parasite, for it frequently happens that boats are not inhabited, or only partially so, for some weeks, or even months. Without fires in the cabins, or other means adopted to withstand the moist air inseparable from the conditions, then it is that the microscopic fungoid plants flourish.

Anon, fires are lighted, the air becomes dried, people move about, currents of air sweep through the cabins, and the spores, invisible to the naked eye, are wafted in myriads about the saloon, sleeping-cabins, and galley, until they come to rest on some moist place, there to propagate again if not checked. Fortunately, when the moist place happens to be the mucous membrane of our nostrils, the spores betray their presence, for the motion produced by the impact due to such shape and weight and composition produce the sensations which we term 'a musty smell.' I have frequently noticed objectionable odours of this class about many fine yachts, and most small ones, but they are never absent from short-voyage cross-Channel steamers; these almost invariably reek with them to such an extent that often strong, good sailors feel ill before the vessel leaves the wharf.

With such precautions as I have outlined, almost any boat may be made 'sweet.'

Accidents of a serious nature involving surgical aid seldom occur in yachts; and if the cruise be a short one, a couple of needles, a scalpel, a forceps for extracting splinters, a stronger one for fish-hooks, a thermometer, and a long strip, two inches wide, of india-rubber sticking-plaster rolled up in an air-tight tin-box, will enable one to meet any case likely to arise. And for medicine I carry a mild aperient, magnesia cit., in bottles with air-tight covers, a supply of compound zymine (a most valuable ferment), and Burroughs's pocket-case. Phosphates I administer by selecting the food of the person under treatment. And I see that there is an abundant supply of fruits on board. Often I have noticed individuals in a yachting party come aboard for a cruise of a few weeks, all life and gaiety, and next day be quite depressed by the reaction from the excitement and novelty of the change. Such a person requires a little immediate treatment, or several days may elapse before he or she will be fit to enjoy the pleasures of the situation. It is necessary that there should be agreeable amusements to occupy the minds of the party, when lamps are lighted and all assembled in the saloon; and the function of providing these in some measure falls within the doctor's duty.

The food should be carefully considered by the medical officer. When a party of very young men embark on a yachting excursion they seldom pay much attention to the quality of this necessary fuel; quantity appears to be with them the important consideration. But when the party consists mainly of men who have already embarked upon the responsibilities of life, men whose brain power is severely taxed, the *cuisine* must be such that, although they be not persons who 'live to eat,' they can regard the table as an additional attraction to the company surrounding it.

One of the most important elements towards the smooth working of the whole party is the presence of a lady, wife or mother or daughter of a member; her advent has a humanizing influence on the male members, however diverging their temperaments may be. If she be an artist or a musician (every lady should be a musician in its best sense) and does not object to smoking—if she be an artist she *won't*—in a properly ventilated, not draughty, cabin, her presence will be still more appreciated; and whether she be ashore or afloat, the fact that a gentlewoman is a member of the party helps to give a peaceful restful glamour to the whole cruise. These remarks are intended to apply chiefly to small vessels. In large steamers, Transatlantic or others, the duties of the medical officer are rather directed to restoring people when they have become ill. On a yachting cruise his great aim should be to keep people well.

Notes by the Hon. Steward

When I first accepted this post I felt rather inclined to resign at once, for when the party came on board I was saluted with what were intended to be facetious orders. It was nothing but, 'Steward! take care of this ammunition.' 'Steward! let me have some soap and hot water; get my bag down from deck and let me have a brandy and soda, and, look here! be quick about it, like a good fellow.' But having often benefited by the efforts of predecessors, I endured the good-natured badinage, which died off after the first day. My first duty was to see that the cooking appliances, cutlery, and table furniture were in good serviceable condition; and I found that 'Billy' had the entire service present on parade. The stove was a cast-iron one, a 'Fortress,' Smith & Wellstood, of Glasgow. It is a remarkable success. Though perhaps a little large for a small boat, as a great piece of the trunk deck was removable in fine weather, and the galley was otherwise well ventilated in cold, the heat was never objected to—at any rate 'Billy' never mentioned it.

Catering for a cruise lasting a day or two, however large the party, does not call for any special remark, as it is easily done; but a cruise of more than four or five days in a yacht of limited accommodation involves some forethought as regards a *menu* offering a sufficient and agreeable variety. If you can calculate on making harbour periodically, arrangements may be made to have provisions sent from town to the railway station, to be called for. But in that case you are tied to call, and this fixity of programme is objected to by 'Graphics.' It follows that the provisions for the whole cruise must be carried. Now, as regards meats, flies are great enemies to the satisfactory hanging of meat in a boat. It is surprising the number one comes across on a coasting trip. I have often met three or four bees or wasps far away from shore, and big bluebottles turn up in the galley, unexpected and unwelcome guests. One of these is sufficient to make several joints of meat very objectionable in forty-eight hours.

A perfect corrective for this state of things is a CO_2 box—that is, a box like a refrigerator, fairly air-tight, and with a communication from a small steel cylinder of compressed carbonic-acid gas; this gas is in a liquid state, and a little is allowed to expand into the box occasionally. So long as there is carbonic-acid gas in the box, the lamb, or mutton, or beef, or other food, will not be troubled with insect life, larvæ or otherwise. If it be desired to cool the contents of the box, a good gush of the liquid gas is admitted. As it expands into the gaseous state it absorbs heat, and a temperature of -20° C. has thus been produced. The carbonic acid used a by-product, hitherto wasted, from the fermenting tuns of breweries. It is now collected and pumped into steel cylinders. I am informed that before long it will be sold for 1*d.* per pound liquid: at present the price is 3*d.* in Dublin.

In practice we do not use so low a temperature as that above mentioned, which would blister some hands, and leaves a hoar frost over the contents of the box. We simply fill the box with gas at ordinary temperature, taking advantage only of its antiseptic properties. We have kept lobsters under a little pressure for six months. At the end of that time they had not parted with the delicate flavour of fresh lobster, and were totally unlike the tinned lobster one buys, which, with nearly all the tinned meats I know of, will keep you from starvation, and that is all that can be said in their behalf. The prolonged high temperature to which they must be subjected in order to kill the bacillic spores practically destroys the best qualities of the natural juices.

Some of the tinned vegetables are good and nutritious. Apples, French peas, French beans, pineapples, sweet corn, potatoes, pears, peaches, and tomatoes, arranged in order of merit as I have found them, are invaluable in a boat; but before using them examine the tins inside, especially those containing acid fruits. If the tins display a beautiful crystalline pattern inside, the contents should be dropped into cold water and rinsed for a few minutes before using. In any case the peas and beans and apples should invariably be rinsed in an abundant supply of cold water, and the fluid contents of the tins thrown away. It often surprises me that the makers of tins for 'canning' purposes do not invariably use those that are enamelled or 'glazed' inside; then there would be no fear of metallic oxides.

At present, for what reason I will not state positively, the soups sold in tins do not agree with people. The flavours and the different kinds certainly afford variety enough, and would be unspeakably convenient aboard; but any experimenter, who has not a stomach like an ostrich, will find that if he uses these for a few days he will be ill. I make the statement without qualification. You cannot make any kind of soup in an ordinary way that will keep in bottle. The 'extracts of meat' do

RINGSEND, DUBLIN.

MONKSTOWN, DUBLIN BAY.

IRELAND'S EYE.

not contain any nourishing property; in fact, if you take any two animals, human or otherwise, feed one on water only, and the other on 'extracts of meat' only, the latter will be *sure* to die first (proven). As a consequence of all this we find it desirable to make our soups aboard, and for that purpose carry meats, &c., in the carbonic-acid box I have described.

But the 'extracts of meat' *are* of great use in making rich and delicious gravies. They may not be very economical, but that cannot be perfectly studied in a boat, and it is possible to dress up the not too stewed contents of the stewpot, after the soup has been poured off, with a few capers, a little salt, a suspicion of pepper, and a thickened gravy made of 'extract of beef,' just thick enough to make a coating around each piece of meat—call it 'stewed beef,' or a more elaborate name if you like—and you will find that not only will none of it be left, but also no one will suspect it to be the remains of the soup at table a quarter of an hour before. The fish we have had meantime, it goes without saying, considering we are in Dublin Bay, is abundant and delicious. I do not know why Dublin Bay herrings should have such a delicate and inimitable flavour. The fish are much smaller than the Scotch herrings and are beautifully marked, and require only a drop or two of Harvey's sauce (Lazenby's) to bring out the proper flavour—they are of course grilled.

With the small stores I have found it economical and convenient to set aside portions for each day. Thus, if the cruise is to be for ten days, I wrap up ten portions of cheese, for example, in air-tight paper, and there is not a moment's loss of time when cheese is required for dinner. Butter for each day is similarly kept in jars; that which is over after each day is not wasted. Bread is kept in glazed earthen crocks with covers; salt in glazed earthenware jars; tea and coffee in bottles with air-tight screw covers; everything that can be put into an air-tight case is so protected, and each case has a particular fitting in a particular locker, so that no time is lost looking for it, no room is wasted, and if the boat gives a lurch or two nothing falls about nor is spilled.

In a coasting cruise you can always send a boat ashore for plenty of fresh vegetables; but, except fish, eggs, and crustacea, you cannot get any other good provisions at any provincial place of call.

'Billy,' our cook, had been to sea on a coaster, where he filled a similar berth. His ideas of the perfection of cooking took the direction of 'plum duff,' of course taking especial care that most of the plums were at one end, the end the skipper would be sure to select. We had no 'plum duff' in the *Iris*, but Billy's training was of such use that little instruction was needed to enable him to make a very respectable orange pudding, and to deftly and lightly make a paste suitable as a cover for any baked dish. In utilising food that is always at hand in a cruising boat, as crabs, scollops, oysters, &c., few can excel a sailor cook after he has been carefully shown how to dress them; and to this end it is necessary that the hon. steward should be able to perform each operation himself. It is not sufficient to have a cookery book aboard; as a general rule some little petty detail is omitted, it may be a quantity, or a matter of *modus operandi*, which perplexes the operator at the critical moment and makes the dish a solemn doubt.

On the other hand, if the hon. steward selects such recipes as he thinks will be useful from some good cookery books, and practically tests them ashore, he will be able to find out the weak points and amend them, and will have the gratification to know that the crew is not doing violence to itself by tasting his dishes in commiseration for his feelings. In small craft it too often, indeed nearly always, happens, that the feeding department is very crudely dealt with, and the material aliment itself is adequately described by the half-raw, half-boiled, stale, tough, naked generic term of 'grub.'

'Water Wags' and 'Mermaids' of Dublin Bay
By Thomas B. Middleton

Kingstown is the headquarters of the Royal Alfred Yacht Club, the Royal Irish Yacht Club, the Royal St. George Yacht Club, and several minor sailing clubs, including the Water Wags.

The pleasantest part of a coast to reside on is, perhaps, that which has a sandy beach shelving gently down into deep water. Along such a beach in fine weather boating, bathing, and fishing are easy and enjoyable occupations; the wavelets ripple, making soft music with the pebbles, and the little skiff lies half in the water waiting to be stepped into and pushed off. But such halcyon weather cannot always be counted on in this climate. The waves are not always ripples; they quickly turn first to breakers and then to a heavy surf, that surges up to the highest water mark if the weather becomes at all broken or the wind comes in from the sea, and consequently the boatman must be prepared to deal with such a change when it occurs, and overcome the many difficulties then presented.

First, the boat cannot be left anchored in the open, as she will surely be lost or damaged in a gale. She must therefore be able 'to

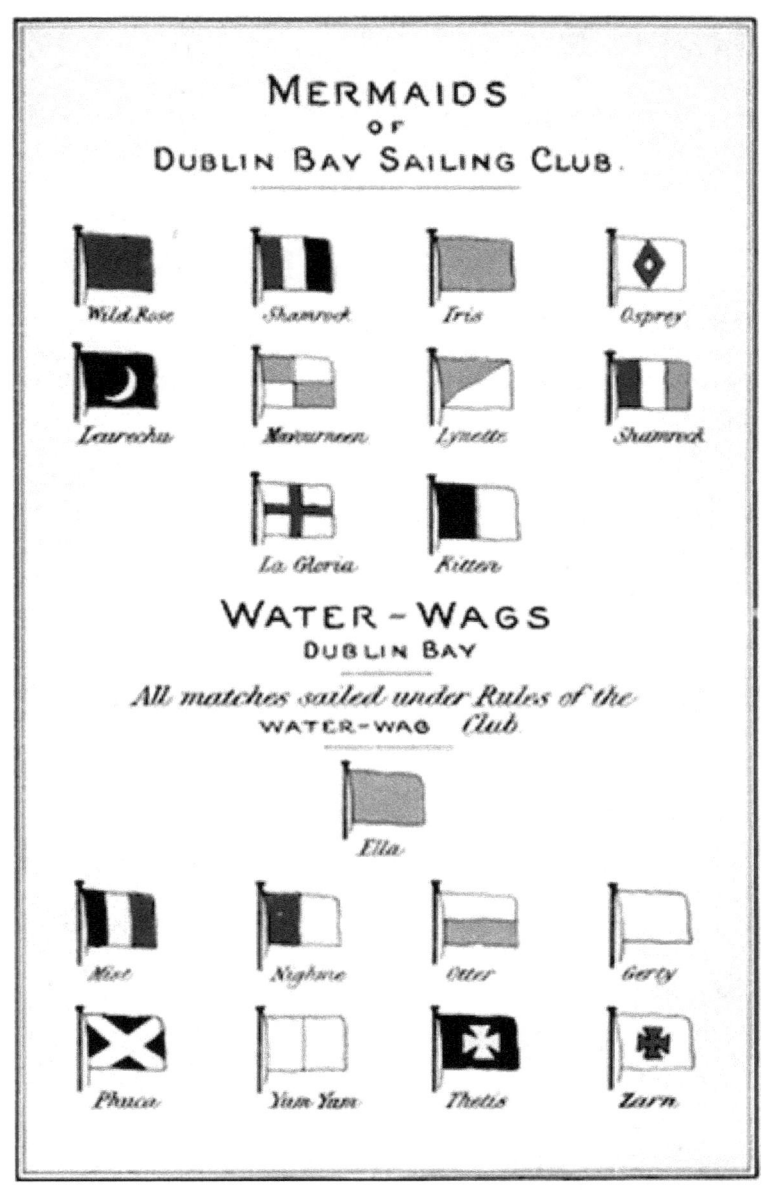

MERMAIDS
OF
DUBLIN BAY SAILING CLUB.

Wild Rose	Shamrock	Iris	Osprey
Laurecha	Mavourneen	Lynette	Shamrock
La Gloria	Kitten		

WATER-WAGS
DUBLIN BAY

All matches sailed under Rules of the WATER-WAG *Club*

	Ella		
Mist	Nightne	Otter	Gerty
Phuca	Yum-Yum	Thetis	Zarn

MERMAIDS OF DUBLIN BAY SAILING CLUB. WATER-WAG DUBLIN BAY.
ALL MATCHES SAILED UNDER RULES OF THE WATER-WAG CLUB

take the ground handsomely'; that is, she cannot have a deep keel, for her bottom must be broad and flat; and, secondly, she cannot have any weight of ballast in her, as it would fatally strain her when she stranded, and make her too heavy to draw out of the reach of the waves. Now, a boat with no keel and no ballast makes, as everyone knows, a bad sailor; in fact, she will only run dead before the wind like a duck's feather on the water: so a little keel of 3 in. or 4 in. is generally used, and the boat ballasted with sandbags filled on the beach, or stones, which are emptied or thrown overboard before landing again. This plan has the objections of being very laborious and making the boat very heavy to launch. If she ships two or three seas in the operation she becomes hopelessly submerged, and the advantages gained are very slight, as such a boat will scarcely sail closer to the wind than a broad reach—even then making considerable leeway and being very slow and uncertain in stays.

It was to improve on this state of affairs on the beach of this description that is to be found at Shankill, in the county of Dublin, that the 'Water Wag' was evolved from a Norwegian *pram*, into which a boiler-plate was fitted for a centreboard as an experiment. This novel craft was called the *Cemiostama*. She was built in the year 1878, and was a great success; she sailed like a witch, carried a large sail with ease without any ballast save the iron-plate, worked well to windward without making any leeway, spun round like a top when the tiller was put down, and when the boiler-plate was raised she ran in on the surf, floated in a few inches of water, and eventually sat on the strand on her flat bottom. The plate (which weighed nearly 1 cwt.) was then lifted out of her, and she became as light to haul up as an ordinary shore skiff.

It was accordingly decided to build seven or eight centreboard double-ended 13-ft. punts with great beam (4 ft. 10 in.), full lines, and a flat floor. The 13 ft. was chosen as the best size that two persons could haul up without help, a larger boat being too heavy for two, and consequently liable to damage by being left in the surf while help was being obtained; and the round stern was to divide the surf when the forepart stranded, and prevent it jumping into the boat as it does in the case of a square stern.

In order that these boats might have an occasional race between themselves, to preserve the type and to save the expense of outbuilding and the trouble of handicapping and time allowance, it was further arranged that all the boats should be built on the same lines, and the canvas limited to a cruising amount. This was accordingly done, and they proved themselves to be such good seaboats, and so generally useful for two or three amateurs to amuse themselves along the shore in, that 'The Water Wag Association' was started in 1887, to further develop and preserve the principles of the class. Though it was started by boys, several older Wags joined, and as the boat was never designed for speed, the racing was not originally intended to be hard-down serious sport, but more a sort of friendly sail round a course in boats all alike, and that consequently should be all together; but of course skill in working would bring one to the front and make her harder to catch. Hence the rollicking title 'Water Wag,' and the institution of a king and queen, bishops, knights, and rooks, to manage the affairs of the club, their chief duties being to get up as much fun and as many jolly water excursions as possible.

The first two or three seasons saw this idea carried out with great success; but gradually the racing grew more keen and serious, until it eventually became the sole object for which the boats assembled, so much so that it is now nothing but racing from early in April till late in September. The Water Wags' own races are held round Kingstown Harbour (the head quarters having migrated there when the generation which formed the Shankill Corinthian Sailing Club grew up and disintegrated over the world); others are got up for them by the Dublin Bay Sailing Club in Scotchman's Bay, outside the harbour, and there are races at the local regattas at Kingstown, Dalkey Bray, Greystones, Wicklow, Clontarf, Howth, and Malahide; so that since the class was started they have had nearly 300 competitions.

They have greatly increased in numbers, and have become quite a local type of small boats in Kingstown, as they work in and out through the yachts and shipping, and are very handy to take four or five persons in to listen to the bands from the water.

They are not confined to Kingstown Harbour, however, as they have sent representatives to the River Plate, Hong Kong, the Persian Gulf, Australia, and many foreign ports. Their principle has been largely adopted in the B division of the Dublin Bay Sailing Club, which consists of 18-ft. boats called 'Mermaids,' which are practically large Water Wags, being entirely open, with 6-feet beam, fitted with centreboard and carrying no ballast. These have a limited racing sail-area of 180 feet, but they are not further confined as to shape, and some have the rounded stern and some the square. They are very fast, lively boats, requiring a crew of three or four nimble hands, principally to be employed in shifting ballast, and they give a great deal of sport, as many as twelve or fourteen starting in a race every Saturday afternoon.

The 'Water Wag' costs complete between 15*l*. and 20*l*., a silk racing lug from Lapthorn and Ratsey alone coming to 2*l*. 15*s*. McAllister, of Dumbarton, built most of them; but Atkinson, of Bullock, Co. Dublin, and Doyle, of Kingstown, have built many more.

In handling, the skipper—especially if he is a tiro at the art—must be very careful, as 75 sq. ft. of canvas, and a 13-ft. mast in a 13-ft. boat, without ballast, require attention and caution if there are any puffs knocking round; so that the mainsheet must never be made fast, no matter how fine and calm the weather is; the halliards should also run very free, and the oars should always be carried, in case it becomes judicious to lower the sail in a squall. But a little practice will enable the skipper to sail his boat without danger during weather that any small open boat can be out in; and it is really marvellous what weather and seas the Water Wags have gone through.

Sailing out of sight of help in any small open boat is to be deprecated, and no exception to this rule is to be made with Water Wags, as they unquestionably run a risk of filling in unskilful hands; but, in that event, the absence of ballast is an advantage, for they do not go to the bottom as a ballasted boat will, but will actually support their crew if no attempt is made to climb up on them.

A lug of 60 sq. ft. is ample to begin with; and for most days when not racing, and for single-handed sailing, a reef should be taken in, or two kegs of water-ballast carried, unless on a very fine day.

The following sailing regulations are carefully enforced during racing:—

Only the boats of members shall compete in the races, and as it is one of the fundamental principles of the Water Wags that the boats shall be similar in every respect save sail-plan, it shall be in the power of the officer of the day to disqualify any boat that, in his opinion, is trying to gain an unfair advantage by infringing the above principle.

Each boat shall not carry more than three or less than two persons during a race, all of whom shall be amateurs, and shall be steered by either a member or a lady. And no money shall be awarded to a boat for a walk-over, but she may fly a flag therefor.

Each boat shall carry on all proceedings of the Water Wags, all her platforms, floorings, thwarts, and stern sheets, also a pair of oars not less than 9 ft. long, with spurs or rowlocks for same; also, either one solid cork ring-shaped life-buoy, not less than 30 in. in external diameter, and capable of floating for three hours 21 lbs. of iron suspended therefrom, or two smaller ones of the same material and shape, which shall each float for the same time 14 lbs. of iron; or they may substitute a cork life-belt that will float 10 lbs. for three hours for each of the small life-buoys, providing each life-belt is worn the entire time the boat is afloat. Before taking a prize the owner of the boat shall declare to the party awarding it that the spirit of this rule has been carried out. And it shall also be the duty of every other competitor to protest against a boat without a life-buoy. The life-buoys shall rest unattached to anything in the boat, with nothing over or resting on them, so that they will immediately float out in the event of a capsize.

All persons on board who cannot swim 100 yards are requested to *wear* life-jackets.

The following are the limitations of a 'Water Wag' 13-footer:

Length over all, 13 ft.; beam, 4 ft. 10 in.; depth and lines, that of model A.

Centreboard to be of iron and pivoted at forward end of casing. Length shall not exceed 4 ft. When hauled up flush with top of casing, no portion shall project below keel. Immersed surface below keel shall not exceed 2½ sq. ft. Thickness at any point shall not exceed $3/8$ of an inch.

Keel outside garboard strake, inclusive of thickness of keelband, if any, shall not exceed in depth 1½ in. Keelband of iron, brass, or copper, not to exceed in thickness ¼ in.

Stem and stern post.—Moulded depth of, to be clear of hood by not less than 2 in.

Kedge not to exceed 15 lbs. No metal cable allowed. No ballast of any description save water.

Mast not to exceed over all 13 ft., measured from top of keel to truck, and not to be stepped above keel more than 3 in.

Fore and aft sails not to exceed 75 sq. ft. in area.

Spinnaker not to exceed 60 sq. ft. in area, and is only to be used before the wind, and in no case as a jib.

A full-sized tracing of the builder's moulds can be obtained by sending 2s. to the Society for Employment of Women 21 Kildare Street, Dublin, (as at time of first publication).

'KING'S FISHER,' 1776.

COMMODORE THOMAS TAYLOR, OF THE
CUMBERLAND FLEET, 1780.

Chapter 4

The Thames Clubs and Windermere

The Royal Thames Yacht Club
By Edward Walter Castle and Robert Castle

In the year 1775 was founded the 'Cumberland Fleet,' and as the Royal Thames Yacht Club is its lineal descendant, the latter may with all justice claim the title of the 'Mother of Yacht-racing,' at least in Great Britain.

The year 1770 was a most important epoch in Thames yachting, and we think the lines and drawing of our first cup-winning yacht should be given here. The *King's Fisher*, as the sketch shows, was clinker built. Her owner, Commodore Thomas Taylor of the Cumberland Fleet, was so thoroughly the practical founder of yacht racing on the Thames that his statue should be placed on the Thames Embankment—with a bronze plaque of his yacht and the cups he won—and if times are too bad to go that length, a medallion portrait plaque could go on the Temple Embankment Arch, for the *King's Fisher* was built close by. Her dimensions, as shown in her lines, were, length 20 ft., beam 7 ft.

The Cumberland Fleet, or, as it is often called, the Cumberland Sailing Society, was founded under the following circumstances.

In the year of grace 1775 the first rowing regatta that was ever held in England took place upon the Thames—on June 23. Previously to this, however, a meeting of 'several very respectable gentlemen, proprietors of sailing vessels and pleasure boats on the river,'[1] held their annual meeting at Battersea, and resolved that on the regatta day they would draw up in a line opposite Ranelagh Gardens, so as not to be in the way of the competing rowing boats. On July 6 of the same year

---

1. *Public Advertiser*, June 1, 1775.

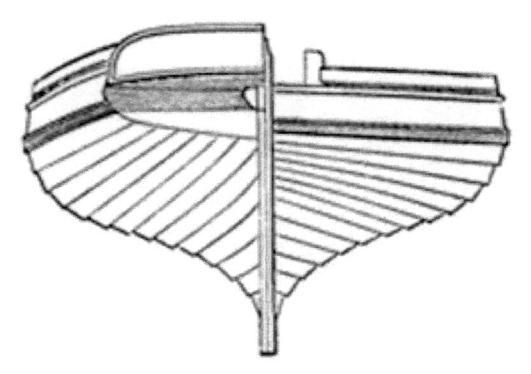

The 'King's Fisher,' 1776,
midship section.

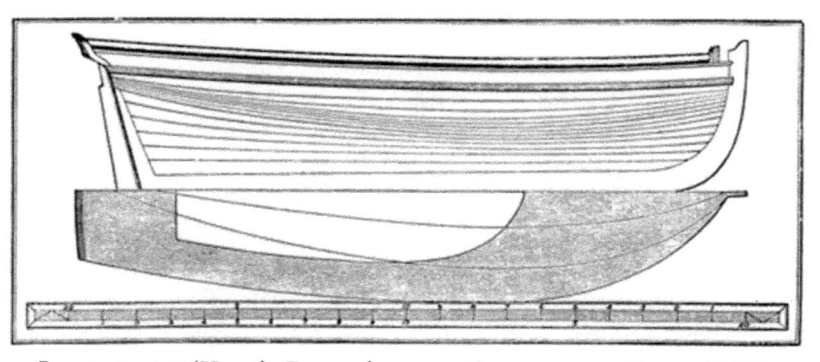

Lines of the 'King's Fisher,' of the Cumberland Fleet, 1776.
Commodore Thomas Taylor's yacht.
Winner of Silver Cup, 1776.

Button, 1776.

an advertisement appears in the *Advertiser*, that his Royal Highness Henry Frederick, Duke of Cumberland (a brother of George III., and an admiral in the British Navy) was about to give a silver cup[2] to be sailed for on July 11. The advertisement is as follows:—

A Silver Cup, the gift of His Royal Highness the Duke of Cumberland, is to be sailed for on Tuesday, the 11th instant, from Westminster Bridge to Putney Bridge and back, by Pleasure Sailing Boats, from two to five tons burthen, and constantly lying above London Bridge. Any gentleman inclined to enter his Boat may be informed of particulars by applying to Mr. Roberts, Boat-builder, Lambeth, any time before Saturday noon next.

On account of the weather, however, the race was postponed until July 13, when it came off with great success, and the *Aurora*, owned by a Mr. Parkes, described as 'late of Ludgate Hill,' won the cup. The second boat in was named the *Fly*, but who owned her the newspapers of the day forgot to mention. From the *Morning Post*[3] we get the information that only those boats 'which were never let out to hire' would be allowed to enter, and also that 'the gentlemen, about 18 or 20 in number, who sail for the prize have come to a resolution to be dressed in aquatic uniforms.' This seems to prove that the club had already been formed before the match, and was probably an outcome of the club at Battersea mentioned above. We also find from the old newspapers that the owners (who, by the way, were always styled 'captain') had to steer their respective vessels, and in the case of this first match were allowed two assistants; so it would seem that what nowadays are called 'Corinthian rules' were in the early period of yacht-racing a *sine quâ non*.

There were very solemn ceremonies attending all these early races. The duke embarked on board his state barge from one of the stairs, and the royal standard was immediately hoisted at the bow. Another barge was in company with a band of music, and they then proceeded to the place of starting. The racing boats were anchored in line, with their sails furled; their places having beforehand been determined by lot. Each vessel, when racing, carried at her gaff a white flag with a red St. George's Cross upon it, and with one, two, three, or more blue balls, according to her position at starting. The captains were stationed in wherries, and on the arrival of the duke's barge were by signal ordered on board their respective vessels. Then, on the firing of a gun, the

---

2. The cup of 1775 was destroyed in a fire. *Morning Herald*, June 23, 1781.
3. *Morning Post*, July 10, 1775.

race was started. Time allowance was an unknown quantity in those primitive days, and the boat which succeeded in passing the winning-post first claimed the cup. The victorious captain was then taken on board the commodore's barge, and with great ceremony introduced to his Royal Highness. In the meantime the duke's butler had filled the cup with claret and handed it to his Royal Highness, who thereupon drank the health of the winner, and then presented him with the cup. The captain then drank to the duke and duchess, with three cheers; the whole ceremony having been performed amidst the strains of martial music, salvos of artillery, and the huzzas of the crowd upon the river and its banks.

The fleet then proceeded up the stream to Smith's Tea Gardens, which lay where the gasworks now are, on the Surrey side of Vauxhall Bridge, and dined together. The duke himself was very often present at these festive gatherings, and later on in the evening they all visited Vauxhall Gardens and made a night of it. The first commodore of the club was a Mr. Smith, who, we believe, was the proprietor of Smith's Tea Gardens, and he probably held the office until 1779. That year the commodore's broad pennant was changed from red to blue, and the club dined at the Royal Oak, Vauxhall, which seems to show a change of officers. Anyhow, the following year, 1780, Mr. Thomas Taylor was commodore, as is shown by the cup he won,[4] and he held that office until the year 1816, when he gave up yachting.

The Cumberland Fleet had the white ensign, but without the St. George's Cross in the fly, and their burgee was a white one, with an equal armed red cross on it; *i.e.* the cross did not come out to the point of the flag. At the Royal Thames Club House they have several relics of the ancient fleet; there is the chairman's ivory gavel with the inscription 'Cumberland Fleet,' which is still used at every annual meeting; there are also (besides some curious prints and pictures) a cap of one of the rowers of the commodore's barge, and a club button, though it is not known whether it belonged to one of the rowers or to a member of the club. The Cumberland course originally was, as we have already shown, from Westminster Bridge to Putney and back, but in 1776 it was altered to Blackfriars Bridge, Putney, and back. Later on, the winning-post was at Smith's Tea Gardens, by that time called Cumberland Gardens.

The fleet evidently used to sail together and manoeuvre as well

---

4. This cup is, (at time of first publication), in the possession of the Taylor family, as are those won in 1776 and 1782.

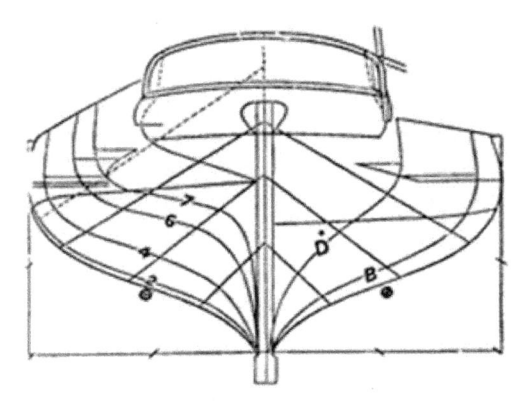

First 'Cumberland,' 1780,
midship section.

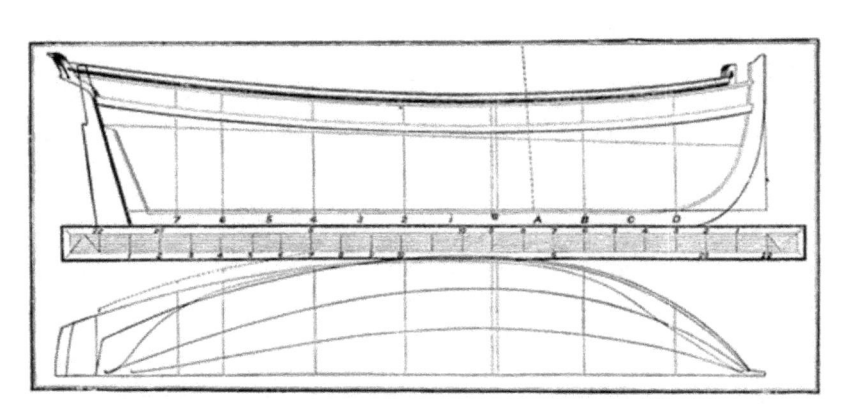

Lines of Commodore Taylor's yacht,
first 'Cumberland,' of Cumberland Fleet (Thames), 1780.
Winner of Gold Cup, 1780.

as race, for in 1776, in honour of His Majesty's birthday, 'they went up the river with colours flying and music playing'; and in 1793 a set of signals were printed (a copy of which may be seen framed at the Royal Thames Club House) whereby the commodore could manoeuvre the sailing boats like a fleet of men-o' war; indeed there is a print extant, dated 1778, wherein the fleet are being so manoeuvred off Sheerness.

The first private match, under the auspices of the club, seems to have come off, between two of the sailing boats, on April 20, 1776, but no mention is made of their names. Some of the expressions used in the newspapers about the different matches are very curious; in one paper it is called 'Fluviatic and Fresh Water Frolics,' and in another 'Thamesian Pleasantry,' and again, 'Water-racing Galloways,' but the best of the lot is in the *Morning Post*[5] of 1782, where the race is described as 'a Fluviatic Cavalcade.'

The yachts belonging to the Cumberland Fleet did not confine themselves to river sailing, for in one of the papers of 1777 it is stated that the *Hawke* had been cruising about the Channel, and had been chased into Calais by an American privateer. The Duke of Cumberland gave a silver cup each year, of the value of twenty guineas; but in 1781, when the seventh became due, a silver-gilt cup of the value of fifty guineas was presented to the club by His Royal Highness. This was to be sailed for by the boats that had won the former prizes, and the advertisement goes on to say, 'The members of the Society do hereby, with the permission of His Royal Highness, challenge and invite all gentlemen, proprietors of pleasure sailing boats, within the British dominions, to join with them in the contention.'[6]

The first attempt at this race on June 25 failed for want of wind, and the match had to be re-sailed on July 9, when the cup was won by the *Cumberland*, belonging to Commodore Taylor. This race, the first open match ever sailed, seems to have caused a good deal of excitement, and the river and its banks were densely crowded. The papers of the day speak of the many thousands present, of all sorts, 'from the peerless "Perdita" to the Princess "Ran."'[7]

For some unexplained reason, 1782 was the last year that the duke gave a cup to the 'Fleet.'[8] He certainly remained its patron up to his

---

5. *Morning Post*, July 26, 1782.
6. *Morning Chronicle*, May 5, 1781.
7. *Morning Herald*, June 27, 1781.~
8. There is a print of the start for the 1782 match at the R.T.Y.C.

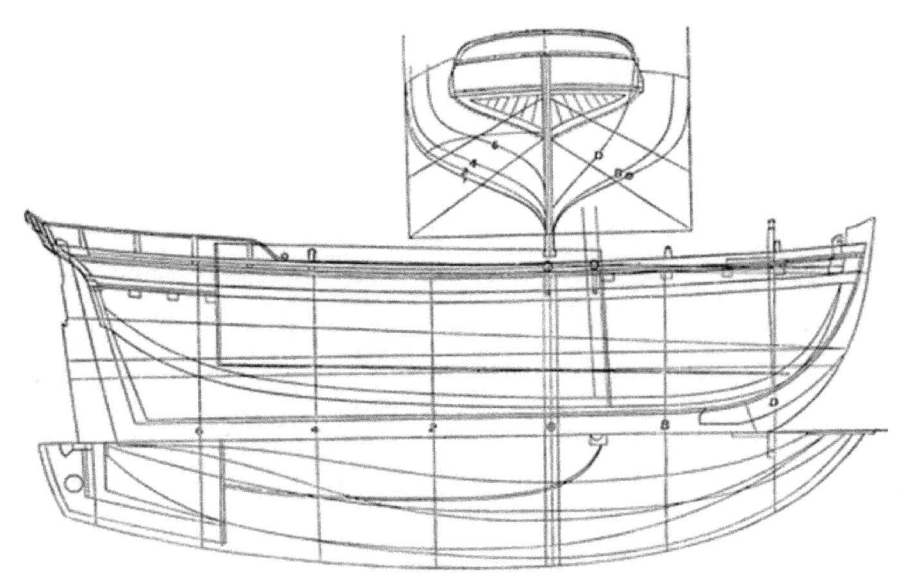

LINES OF COMMODORE TAYLOR'S YACHT,
SECOND 'CUMBERLAND,' LAUNCHED FEBRUARY 14, 1790.

YACHT OF CUMBERLAND FLEET, 1781.

death in 1790, but he ceased to take any personal interest in the affairs of the club. This cup was won by the *Caroline*,[9] belonging to Captain Coffin, and seems to have had a curious history, as in 1886 it was discovered in a pawnshop at San Francisco, and, it is said, was bought and raced for by some yacht club in America. On August 10, 1782, the first below-bridge match of the Cumberland Fleet took place. It was between the *Caroline*, Captain Coffin, and the *Eagle*, Captain Grubb, for a wager of 40*l*.: the course being from Cuckolds Point to the Lower Hope, and back again. The *Caroline* won easily.

The years 1783 to 1785 have no matches recorded against the club. On August 21, 1784, the commodore's boat the *Cumberland* went badly ashore on the rocks off Margate.[10] She must, however, have been afterwards saved, as she was commodore's boat at the match of 1786. A new era opened to the 'Cumberland Fleet' in the year 1786.[11] Jonathan Tyars became proprietor of Vauxhall Gardens, and to celebrate the jubilee of the Gardens (which had been open just fifty years), and also the new management, he gave an annual silver cup and cover, to be sailed for by the Cumberland Fleet, and a wherry to be rowed for by the watermen on the Thames.

The one thing curious about this match is that the *Prince of Wales* sailing boat was advertised for sale, and it goes on to say, 'which no doubt will have the best chance to win the Jubilee Silver Cup which will be sailed for on the 17th inst.' She won that cup!

The proprietors of Vauxhall Gardens continued giving an annual cup to the club until the year 1810, when the last prize offered by them was sailed for on August 6, and won by the *St. George*, 7 tons, Captain James Gunston. The ceremonies attached to the giving of the Vauxhall Cup differed but slightly from those attending the Duke of Cumberland's prize. The race started, as before, from Blackfriars Bridge and sailed round a boat stationed near Putney Bridge and back past a boat moored off Vauxhall Stairs, next door to Cumberland Gardens.

The gardens in the evening were magnificently illuminated; a wonderful transparency of the sailing match was on show, and the former prize cups won by the club were arranged on pedestals in front of it. There are many incidents connected with the Cumberland Fleet during all these years. The *Morning Chronicle*[12] says: 'There was

---

9. *Times*, August 9, 1886.
10. *Public Advertiser*, August 25, 1784.
11. *Morning Post*, July 5, 1786.
12. *Morning Chronicle*, July 19, 1786.

an attempt of foul play against the *Prince of Wales*, the winning vessel of 1786, by other boats getting in her way, but she got all clear by a liberal use of handspikes.' In 1787 the match on July 19 was ordered by the club to be re-sailed August 3, on account of some mistakes in the sailing directions made by the competing yachts; this was eventually won by the *Nancy*, Captain Dore, but the *Blue Dragon* was disqualified for booming out her jib.

There must have been some form of Admiralty warrant extant in those days, as we find that the members of the club are requested (in an advertisement) to meet at the Crown and Anchor Tavern in the Strand, and it goes on to say,[13] 'The gentlemen who enter their boats are to attend at the same time to draw lots for situation at starting; and are hereby informed that they are expected either to produce their licence from the Admiralty, or other proofs of being owners of the vessels they intend to sail.'

In 1791,[14] Commodore Taylor, with a party of friends, started in the *Cumberland* for Bordeaux, but we have found no reference to his having arrived there. This year there was a dreadful accident at the race for the Vauxhall Cup, by the bursting of a cannon at Cumberland Gardens, at the moment that the *Mercury*, Captain Astley, was winning; by this two persons lost their lives. This is also the first year in which a second prize was given, *viz*. a silver goblet. The year 1793 was kept as a septennial one, and a handsome silver-gilt cup was presented to be raced for; the club thereupon challenged the world.

On July 27, 1793, the *Cumberland*, Commodore Taylor, and the *Eclipse*, Captain Astley, had a match for a turtle, which the commodore won, and the members of the club had a turtle feast on the strength of it. In 1794 the proprietors of Vauxhall put a wonderful car upon the river, on the match day. It was drawn by tritons and was moved by invisible oars. It contained, besides bands of music, Father Thames attended by his river gods; and for several years this appeared, but with different devices.

A curious light is let in by the newspapers of 1795 [15] on the way they managed matters when racing. The *Mercury*, which was the leading boat, somehow got foul of the *Vixen*; whereupon the captain of the *Vixen* cut away the rigging of the *Mercury* with a cutlass and fairly well dismantled her, another boat, the *Mermaid*, winning the cup. We

---

13. *Public Advertiser*, June 7, 1788.
14. *Star*, June 13, 1791.
15. *Times*, July 23, 1795.

CIRCULAR OF CUMBERLAND FLEET, 1775.

have failed entirely to find any sort of protest against such high-handed proceedings. There was another cup presented to the Club besides the Vauxhall one in 1796; it was given by the proprietor of Cumberland Gardens. A match for a wager of forty guineas took place on August 11, 1797,[16] between the *Mercury* and the *Providence*, from the Gun Wharf at Blackwall round the Nore Light and back; this was won easily by the *Mercury*, which did the distance in 12 hrs. 5 mins., beating the *Providence* by twenty miles.

The year 1800 was again kept as a septennial one, or, as the papers prefer to call it, a 'Jubilee,' and there is in existence a print of the *Cumberland*, Captain Byrne, winning the cup. Mr. E. Smith, owner of the *Atalanta*, which won the Vauxhall Cup in 1801, presented the same year a cup to be raced for, and it was won by the *Mercury*, Captain Astley. Another septennial (or Jubilee) cup was given by the proprietors of Vauxhall Gardens in 1807, and this fell to the *Bellissima*, owned by Captain Farebrother. This year the contractors for the State Lottery gave a cup to be raced for on the Thames, and all the boats entered for it belonged to the Cumberland Fleet. A new public Garden was started in 1809, called the Minor Vauxhall, and Mr. Sheppard, its proprietor, gave a silver cup to be sailed for on the river. The first two attempts failed to come off, but at the third and final one the *St. George*, Captain Gunston, won the prize.

The last cup given by the proprietors of Vauxhall Gardens, in 1810, was won by the *St. George*, and the same year Mr. Sheppard (who had changed the name of his Gardens to 'The New Ranelagh') again gave a cup, which was won by the *Sally*, belonging to Captain Hammond. The proprietor of the New Ranelagh Gardens also gave cups in the years 1811 and 1812, and although the club is not mentioned in connection with them, none but vessels belonging to the Cumberland Fleet were entered. On July 16, 1812, the club gave two cups, by subscription, to be raced for from Blackwall to Gravesend and back, which were won respectively by the *Mercury* and the *Vixen*. As the years roll on the newspapers get rather confused about the sailing matches, and the name of the old club very rarely occurs, although we have seen an account book where the subscription of one guinea is mentioned as having been paid to the secretary of the Cumberland Fleet, in the year 1818.

The years 1814, 1821, and 1822 have no sailing matches recorded against them, but these, with 1783 to 1785, are the only ones in which

---

16. *Star*, August 15, 1797.

we have failed to find a race of some sort or other. After Commodore Taylor's retirement it is believed that Mr. Edward Nettlefold was elected in his place, but there is, great confusion on the subject, for in 1817 he is called commodore of the 'London Yacht Club,' which in another number of the same paper is called the 'New Cumberland Fleet.' Most probably there had been some dissensions among the members of the club, but whatever had happened, there is no getting over the fact that in the year 1823 the Cumberland Fleet had a below-bridge race, and that it was under the direction of Commodore Edward Nettlefold.

The year 1823 is a most important one in the history of the club. On July 17 there was a race for a silver cup in honour of the king's coronation,[17] and the newspapers [18] go on to say:—

The *Favourite* steam packet, soon after ten o'clock, came down from the Tower. This boat was elegantly decorated, and was crowded with ladies. The gentlemen of the 'Old Cumberland Fleet' were on board, under the direction of their respected Commodore, Edward Nettlefold, Esquire, under whose direction the match took place.

The cup was won by the *Venus*, belonging to Captain George Keen. In the *Public Ledger* of July 17, 1823, is the following advertisement:—

> His Majesty's Coronation
>
> The Subscribers and Members of the Old Cumberland Fleet will dine together at the Ship Tavern, Water Lane, Tower Street, this day at four o'clock precisely to celebrate the coronation of His Most Gracious Majesty King George IV.; when the superb silver cup, sailed for in honour of that event, on Thursday last, from Blackwall to Coal House Point, below Gravesend and back, by gentlemen's pleasure vessels, will be presented to Captain George Keen, the winner of the prize; and to arrange the articles for the sailing match to take place on Wednesday afternoon, the 30th instant, and to start at three o'clock from Blackfriars Bridge, and sail to Putney and back to Cumberland Gardens, under the especial patronage of the proprietors of the Royal Gardens, Vauxhall.

At this dinner the club must have decided to change their name, as appears from the following extract from a Vauxhall programme of July

---

17. George IV.
18. *Morning Advertiser*, July 18, 1823; *Sporting Magazine*, July, 1823; *Morning Chronicle*, July 19, 1823; *Globe*, July 18, 1823; *Public Ledger*, July 19, 1823.

30, 1823, announcing the match 'given by His Majesty's Coronation Sailing Society, entered into for celebrating annually the Coronation, and formed by new subscribers and members of the old Cumberland Fleet'; the last three words being printed right across the page in large type. They also changed their flag, adopting a white one with a crown in the upper corner next the staff, with the letters 'G.R. IV.' underneath, and the words 'Coronation Fleet' in the fly. This flag had a crimson border all round, with lettering of the same colour.

OFFICERS' BADGE, R.T.Y.C.

This match of July 30, 1823, is a very important one, as, owing to a dispute over the prize, the present Royal Thames Yacht Club was formed. The facts are as follows:—In the race the *St. George*, Captain Brocklebank, came in first, and the *Spitfire*, Captain Bettsworth, was the second boat. Captain Bettsworth, however, protested against the *St. George* being given the prize, for the following reasons:—'That the *St. George* during the match was steered by two persons, which was contrary to the sailing articles signed by all the competitors previously to starting. The articles alluded to state that "the vessels must be sailed by their respective owners, or by any person they may think proper to appoint." The appellant states the breach of articles to have been committed between Blackfriars and Waterloo Bridges.' [19]

On August 6 the club met to consider the question at the Ship Tavern, Water Lane; and after Capt. Bettsworth had produced witnesses and the matter had been argued out, it was determined by ballot, and by a majority of one, that the race should be re-sailed on

---
19. Globe, August 5, 1823.

Monday, August 11. On August 7, however, a protest was sent to the commodore, signed by seven members of the club (none of whom, by the way, had a boat in the match), asking him to call another meeting of the society, to either confirm or rescind the vote on August 6, and mentioning the fact that Captain Brocklebank had not been present at the ballot. On August 8 another meeting was held, at the Ship Tavern, of the captains and owners of the pleasure boats that had been in the race of July 30; they resolved to send in a protest to Commodore Nettlefold, in which they stated 'that if such resolution be rescinded, we have unanimously determined never to enter any of our boats for any cup to be given on any future occasion by the "Coronation" Fleet,' as they considered the merits of the question had been fully and fairly discussed.

This protest was signed by eight of the captains who sailed in the match. On August 9 a further meeting of the club was held, and the resolution of the 6th instant rescinded, in spite of the protest, the cup being handed over to Captain Brocklebank as the victor. On this decision the captains held another conference (probably on the evening of August 9), decided to form a new club, and to call a special meeting on the question. On August 14, 1823, at the White Horse Tavern, Friday Street, it was decided to form such new club, and to call it the 'Thames Yacht Club.' Most of the old members of the 'Cumberland' Fleet are supposed to have joined it. The 'Coronation' Fleet went on with varying fortunes until the year 1827, when it seems to have fallen into abeyance; but it was revived again in 1830 with a great flourish of trumpets, only to be absolutely dissolved on January 3, 1831, at a meeting of the club, held at the British Coffee House, Charing Cross; and that very same year their commodore, Lord Henry Cholmondeley, was racing as an ordinary member of the Thames Yacht Club. So that those members of the 'Coronation' Fleet who did not join in 1823 were finally absorbed in the Thames Yacht Club in 1831.

Since that period the life of the club has flowed along pretty evenly, with a few ups and downs, like the noble river from which it takes its name. The first match of the Thames Yacht Club was held on September 9, 1823, for a cup valued at 25 guineas, when ten boats entered. They sailed the old course from Blackfriars Bridge, and finished at Cumberland Gardens; but in this case, for want of wind, the match had to be re-sailed on the 10th, when the cup was won by the *Spitfire*, Mr. T. Bettsworth. The following year they had an above- and a below-bridge match, and this was regularly continued until 1840, after which the above-bridge match was given up. The *Don Giovanni*, owned by Mr. J. M. Davey, won cups in 1824 and 1826; she was considered the crack boat of her day, and there is a song in existence which ends as follows:—

Now toast the Don Giovanni's crew, who bear the prize away,
And may they always sail as well as they have sail'd today!
Then fill each glass with sparkling wine, and bumpers let them be,
And drink to Captain Davey's health—his health with three times three:

For the cup is won, the match is done,
And settl'd is the rub;
Let mirth abound, and glee go round.
In this—the Thames Yacht Club.

In 1827 a 50-guinea cup was given to be raced for, from Blackwall to Gravesend and back, to celebrate the event of His Royal Highness the Duke of Clarence becoming patron of the Thames Yacht Club. This was won by the *Lady Louisa,* belonging to Mr. T. Smith.

The following year there was a split off from the club, caused by their refusal to give prizes for very small boats, so the seceders formed the Clarence Yacht Club, which existed for several years. On August 28, 1830, two cups were given to be raced for below bridge, in honour of the Duke of Clarence coming to the throne as William IV. The yachts sailed in two classes, the first of which was won by the *Matchless*, 19 tons, Mr. J. Hyatt; and the second by the *Brilliant*, 8 tons, Mr. W. Bucknall. On October 7 of the same year, at a meeting of the club, it was resolved 'that the uniform button should be altered from T.Y.C. to R.T.Y.C.'; in other words, they had become the 'Royal Thames Yacht Club.' This year the fleet of the club consisted of forty-three vessels.

The burgee of the Thames Yacht Club was probably a red one, with the letters T.Y.C., as we find that on February 3, 1831, a red burgee was agreed to having the letters R.T.Y.C. under a crown. There were two cups given by the club, on September 15, 1831, to celebrate the coronation of their Majesties William IV. and his queen. The first was won by the *Lady Louisa*, and the second by the *Water Witch*. In December 1834 a white burgee was adopted with a crown and the letters R.T.Y.C. in red; and on February 19, 1835, an Admiralty warrant was granted to the club authorising their vessels to carry a white ensign without a red cross, but with the union-jack in the upper corner, and bearing in the fly a crown over the letters R.T.Y.C. in red. William IV. died on June 20, 1837, and on July 27 of the same year Her Majesty

LORD ALFRED PAGET'S 'MYSTERY' PASSING 'BLUE BELLE' MAY 23, 1843.

'CYGNET,' 35 TONS, BUILT BY WANHILL, 1846. WINNER OF QUEEN'S CUP, R.Y.S., 1849; OF QUEEN'S CUP, R.T.Y.C., 1851.

Queen Victoria became patroness of the club. The following year special prizes were given in honour of the queen's coronation, and there is in possession of the club a portrait of Commodore Harrison holding the cup in his hand.

In 1840 a challenge cup of the value of 100 guineas was given, to be won twice consecutively by the same yacht, without reference to ownership. It was eventually secured by the 'Secret,' Mr. J. W. Smith, on June 8, 1847. The Admiralty took away the white ensign from the Royal Thames Yacht Club in 1842 (as well as from several other clubs that had the right of flying it), and only allowed the Royal Yacht Squadron to continue its use. In July of the same year, however, the Admiralty granted to the Royal Thames a blue ensign with a crown in the fly. On June 30, 1845, a cup of the value of 60*l.* was presented by Earl Fitzhardinge, and the yachts had to be manned, steered, and handled by members of the club only. The *Belvidere*, 25 tons; the *Prima Donna*, 25 tons; the *Phantom*, 20 tons; and the *Widgeon*, 24 tons, were entered, the cup being won by the *Belvidere*, belonging to Vice-Commodore Lord Alfred Paget.

In the year 1848 the Admiralty granted to the club a further warrant, dated July 24, giving them the plain 'blue ensign of Her Majesty's Fleet,' and of this they still enjoy the use. Time allowance first appears in the matches of the Royal Thames on June 29, 1849, in a race from Erith to the Nore and back, when half a minute per ton for difference of tonnage was allowed. July 8, 1851, the queen for the first time gave a cup to be raced for by the club, the course being from Erith, round the Nore and back; it was won by the *Cygnet*, 35 tons, owned by Mr. H. Lambton, M.P. The club established an annual schooner match, which was held regularly for several years, the first having been on June 1, 1853. In 1855 the club had 170 yachts in its fleet, but in 1861 they had reached to 241 vessels; at the present date they are some 350 strong. In 1862 the *Marina*, on rounding the Nore lightship, ran into the club steamer, the *Prince of Wales*, damaging herself considerably, and had to be towed back.

As she was leading vessel at the time, and it was the fault of the steamer getting in the way, she received a special prize. On May 21, 1866, the first Nore to Dover race of the club took place, although they had one or two matches to Harwich and the Isle of Wight before that date. At the beginning of 1868 there was another split in the Royal Thames, and those who left established the 'New Thames Yacht Club,' which is still in existence. The same year the club was

Start of 25-Tonners, Royal Thames Yacht Club, from Greenwich, 1848.

'Phantom,' 25 tons, R.T.Y.C., 1853.

again honoured by the presentation of a Queen's Cup, which was raced for from Gravesend to the Mouse and back. In 1874 His Royal Highness the Prince of Wales became commodore, and for the first time in the history of the club a rear-commodore was elected, Mr. Thomas Brassey. Queen's Cups have also been given to the club in 1874, 1880, and 1885; but in the year 1887, on the occasion of Her Majesty's Jubilee, the club, to mark that event, gave a special prize of 1,000 guineas in an ocean match round Great Britain, the winning-post being at Dover. This was won by the *Genesta*, belonging to Sir Richard Sutton, Bart.

Such, in bare outline, is a rough history of the oldest yacht racing club in existence. It is epitomised from a larger work on the same subject, which has been our labour of love for some years, and we hope that the book will be published to the world at some future time.

Royal Corinthian Yacht Club, Erith
By R. T. Pritchett

Perhaps one of the most sporting clubs on the Thames or elsewhere is the Royal Corinthian Yacht Club, which has its headquarters at Erith. This, the original Corinthian Club, was formed in May 1872; but several other clubs have since been started at various ports, and have copied the title with the affix of the place to which they belong.

During the first year some 200 members were enrolled, but the number rapidly increased, and the club has now close upon 500 members, and possesses a valuable freehold club-house standing in an acre of ground on the banks of the Thames at Erith. The house includes a large club-room, nearly 70 feet long, a committee room, and a bunk-room for the use of members wishing to sleep there. Underneath are extensive stores, with twenty large sail lockers, each capable of holding the gear of a 20-tonner. These are let to members at 30s. *per annum*. There is room in the grounds for any number of the smaller fry which are not too heavy to be hauled over the wall, and they have a good snug berth here for the winter.

The classification of the yachts for racing purposes does not extend to anything exceeding 20-rating, and for this size of vessel only one paid hand is allowed. The remainder of the crew, including the helmsman, must be members of the club.

In the first year or so of the club's existence the racing was mostly confined to the smaller classes, and the 5-ton *Arrow*, at that time head of her class, was a frequent competitor. About this period the *Adèle* and the *Ada* were in the Thames. These gave way in turn to the *Virago*, 6 tons, *May*, 6 tons, and the *Alouette* and *Freda*, each 5 tons. The 10-ton *Zephy'*then came up into the river, and had some hard tussles to save her time from the smaller vessels; and Major Lenon's *L'Erie*, 10 tons, also competed occasionally with success. In the larger class *Dudu*, *Torch*, *Ildegonda*, *Surge*, *Aveyron*, *Sweetheart*, *Dione*, and *Nadejda*, gave some good racing, and one memorable day, when all the above but *Ildegonda* and *Torch* sailed a race in a gale of wind, in company with the yawl *Dryad*, nearly every yacht in the race had some mishap to gear, *Dryad* and *Dione* being dismasted.

From 1875 to 1880 the racing was kept alive by the 10-ton class, the meeting of the *Lily*, *Florence*, *Merle*, *Mildred*, *Chip*, *Preciosa*, *Juliet*, *Elaine*, and *Robinson* being looked forward to with eagerness by the amateur crews. *Florence* was the pick of this bunch, but the arrival of the *Maharanee*, and then of the celebrated *Buttercup*, soon altered the state of affairs. *Buttercup* swept the board for some time until Mr. W. Cory brought *Ulidia* into the club, and she in turn scored off *Buttercup*. This virtually closed the 10-ton racing in the Thames.

In 1881 some excitement was caused by the starting of the 3-ton class on the Thames, and as no paid hands were allowed in these little vessels, the Corinthians were in request in club matches. The *Muriel* was brought over from Ireland by the Messrs. Fox, and had for competitors the *Maramah*, *Mascotte*, *Naida*, *Primrose*, *Venilia*, and *Snarley Yow*, of which the latter was probably the fastest. The excitement culminated in a race for a 50*l*. cup, subscribed for by several enthusiastic members, and sailed for under the auspices of the Corinthian Yachting Club on June 13, 1882, *Muriel* winning the cup after a splendid finish with *Snarley Yow*.

The next year saw the advent of *Chittywee*, who spread-eagled the old fleet, and was in turn knocked out by the redoubtable *Currytush*. This killed the 3-ton class in the Thames, and for some time class racing was at a discount. The Corinthian Yacht Club, however, by arranging a system of handicaps and other races to suit the vessels belonging to the club, nearly always succeeded in getting good entries for its matches, an annual handicap race from Erith to Ramsgate, open to all yachts in the club, being still one of the most popular events of the season.

The 20-rating class has not been patronised for some time in the Thames, but *Decima*, *Fan Tan*, *Dis*, and *Corona* have had some good

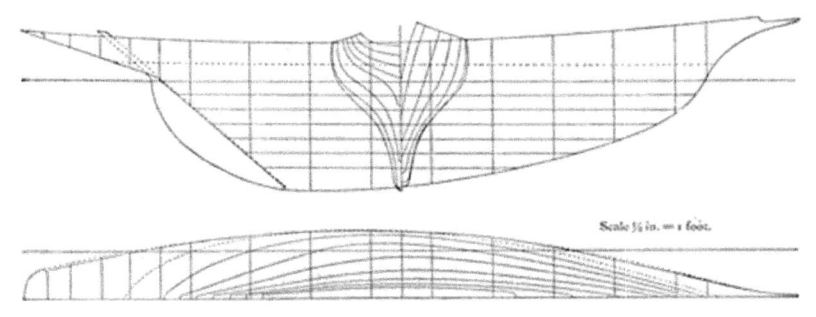

LINES AND MIDSHIP SECTION OF THE 'DIS,' 10-RATER, BUILT FOR A. D. CLARKE, ESQ., 1888. DESIGNED BY J. M. SOPER.

'DECIMA' *A. E. PAYNE*, 1889.

'TOTTIE,' ROYAL CORINTHIAN YACHT CLUB, 21-FT. CLASS.

racing between 1890 and 1892 in the 10-rating matches. The entries in the numerous handicap matches have included the above four yachts and such vessels as *Gardenia, Neaira, Terpsichore, Norman, Mimosa, Wenonah, Cyclone, Ildegonda, Œnanthe, Nadejda, Alpha Beta*.

In 1888 an attempt was made by the club to encourage a class of small cruising yachts by limiting the length and sail-area, and seven or eight were built from the designs of Messrs. G. L. Watson, Fife, Dixon Kemp, J. T. Howard, Douglas Stone, A. E. Payne, A. Watkins, and others. This class, known as the Thames 21-foot class, has since then furnished extremely close racing, and it is worthy of note that the first boat built, the *Tottie*, designed by Mr. Watson, successfully held her own for five seasons. The season of 1892, however, showed that the *Eva*, designed and built by Mr. Stone, of Erith, was quite as good as, if not better than, *Tottie*, her new owner, Mr. Wyllie, sailing her in first-class form. Much of the *Tottie's* success must be put down to her extremely skilful handling by the brothers Simpson, who rank among the best amateurs of the day.

While the 21-foot class has undoubtedly been a most popular one in the Thames, it is unfortunately the fact that the original idea of encouraging a good useful cruising boat was not fulfilled, the ingenuity of the designers being too much for the few restrictions imposed. We believe that three of the original boats which were not so successful in racing are now being used as cruisers, but the faster or deep-keeled boats are hardly of the type that would be chosen for this purpose.

The names of the 21-footers are *Tottie, Eva, Diskos, Haze, Dorothy, Fancy, Mehalah, Genie, Magnolia, Saivnara, March Hare, Narwhal, Nyleptha,* and *Macnab*.

During the last two or three years prizes have been offered for 2½-raters, but the class has not as yet taken any hold on the Thames men, the only entries having been *Camilla* and *Cock-a-whoop*. This club now offers a challenge cup for 1-raters, *viz*. the cup won by the 3-ton *Muriel*, and presented to the club by Captain H. C. Fox.

The Club received the Admiralty warrant to fly the Blue Ensign in 1884, and in 1893 Her Majesty the Queen was graciously pleased to command that the club should be called the Royal Corinthian Yacht Club.

The present officers of the club are: Robert Hewett, Esq., Commodore, and Rear-Commodore of Royal Thames, and of *Buttercup* celebrity; J. Weston Clayton, Esq., Vice-Commodore; Frank C. Capel, Esq., Rear-Commodore; H. Neville Custance, Esq., Hon. Treasurer;

and T. G. F. Winser, Esq., Secretary.

In order to extend the usefulness of the club to its members, the committee last year secured a club-room at Burnham on the Crouch, a most charming piece of water for small craft. With the greatly improved state of the Thames at Erith, however, it is probable that most of the yachts will come back to the headquarters of the club as of old. It is many years since fish were caught at Erith, but of late they have returned, and the Thames is now in as good condition as could be desired. This river and its estuary form a perfect cruising ground for the amateur yachtsman, and with a snug anchorage and comfortable quarters at the end of a cruise, such as the Royal Corinthian Yacht Club affords, he must be a glutton who is not satisfied.

The number of yachts belonging to the club is 220, ranging from 1 to 500 tons.

Royal London Yacht Club

The Royal London was established in 1838, and takes the lead in the Victorian period. It began its career in May 1838 as the Arundel Yacht Club, when the majority of the yachts were probably kept on the foreshore at the foot of Arundel Street, Strand. Its flag at that time was a red field, white border, and white letters.

In 1845 the name was changed to the London Yacht Club, and the flag adopted was a white field with a blue cross, the union in the upper corner, a gold star in the lower. In 1846 the star was changed for the City arms, on receipt of a grant of this privilege from the Corporation of the City of London. 1849 was an important year in its history. The club received the patronage of Queen Adelaide, whereby it became Royal (a privilege not so easily obtained in those days), and also the recognition of the Admiralty by which the possession of an Admiralty warrant was secured to its members.

In early days the races were sailed above bridge, with an occasional bold venture as far down the river as Erith or Gravesend; but, finding by experience that no serious dangers existed in such then comparatively unknown waters, the above-bridge races were in a few years abandoned, and the time-honoured course from Erith round the Nore and back adopted. After many years, owing to the increase in the size of the yachts, and in both the number and size of the vessels navigating the Thames, another change was made. The Royal London always showed energy where yachting progress was concerned, and was the first to adopt flying starts on the Thames. A small class raced thus May 14, 1878, and it may be noted that the club was one of the first clubs in the United Kingdom, if not actually the first, to adopt the Y.R.A. rules, October 20, 1892. The office of Admiral was filled by the election of H.R.H. the Duke of York to that post. A striking illustration, not only of the progress of the club, but also of the development of yachting, is shown in the following table:—

Year	Number of Yachts	Aggregate Tonnage	Average Tonnage
1848	15	161	11
1892	248	17,000	69

On the social side its advance has been equally striking. After wandering about for many years, in 1857 rooms were engaged at the Caledonian Hotel, Adelphi. In 1882 the prosperity of the club justified the opening of a branch club-house at Cowes, and three years later the London headquarters were moved to their present position in Savile Row. These changes were attended by the most satisfactory results. The numbers, instead of fluctuating between 200 and 300 as they had done for a series of years, at once began to increase, and now there are over 700 names on the books. The yachts have increased correspondingly.

The London Sailing Club, Hammersmith

The London Sailing Club is a vigorous and practical association which has to be specially commended for two features lately introduced. The first of these was an exhibition in its rooms of 1-rater half-models, scale 1 inch to the foot, each to carry a centre-plate—the design to show shear plan, body plan, and half-breadth plan. Each design was accompanied by a sealed envelope containing the designer's name. These envelopes were not opened until after the designs and models had been judged, and the prizes, three in number, awarded by Mr. Dixon Kemp. The whole arrangements were most satisfactorily carried out. The exhibition opened February 21, 1893, the models remaining on view until March 6. These models, from the hands of professionals as well as amateurs, were in some cases very beautiful. The first prize was awarded to Mr. David Weir, of Partick. The second ran Mr. Weir very close indeed, and when the envelope was opened the name of J. M. Soper was discovered, a name associated with many leading Solent small raters. The awarding of prizes is always a responsibility, but with Mr. Dixon Kemp's experience and scientific knowledge he had little difficulty.

The second feature referred to was the reading of papers by leading authorities on practical subjects connected with construction and sailing. The first paper, on centreboards, was read by Mr. Dixon Kemp, and illustrated with diagrams on the blackboard, and a discussion opened by Mr. Warrington Baden-Powell, of canoe fame, followed. The reading of these papers has a good influence in bringing members and their friends together. For special subjects experts and specialists are invited, and much valuable information is often afforded. About it as a club there is nothing very particular to be said. It is popular with its members, and very successfully carries out the objects of the foundation.

The Upper Thames Sailing Clubs

In the year 1893 the queen graciously extended her patronage to the small raters, now so much in vogue, inland and on the coast, by presenting a 50-guinea Challenge Cup, to be annually sailed for by the Upper Thames Sailing Clubs during the Bourne End week, when the Upper Thames Club hold their fresh-water festival opposite the club-house which was constructed in 1889 at Bourne End, Bucks. The spot is well selected, and affords a commanding view of the long clear reach in which the matches are sailed over a course of nine miles. The Duke of Connaught is their President, the commodore, Colonel FitzRoy Clayton, a practical enthusiast of great experience, one day thrashing a 1-rater through bad weather inland, and the day after perhaps hauling on to the mainsheet of one of our big racers out in the open, equally enjoying both.

The secretary is most practical and does much to assist the club with his large fleet of divers kind, from Norwegian punt and American sneakie built by himself, to his steam launch *Leopard*. He has yet another craft of considerable interest, a Dutch yacht, a perfect marvel of the Hollander's handicraft and beauty of finish; she was built in Friesland about 1830, and is as sound now as when first launched. The Challenge Cup, which is in the form of a bold flagon, pilgrim bottle shape, height 17 in., weight 99 oz., was first sailed for at Bourne End on Jubilee Day, June 21, 1893, by the following clubs, Thames, Thames Valley, Upper Thames, Tamesis, Thames United, and Oxford University. The morning of the 21st was bright with a strong sailing breeze.

The race was set for 1.30, and soon after noon all the crews were carefully overhauling their gear and studying the barometer. The weather suggested then having to reef down at the last minute. It must

Upper Thames Sailing Club and Club-house, Bourne End, Bucks, 1893.

Upper Thames steam yacht 'Cintra.'

be remembered that the river is not wide at Bourne End, and that it was a flying start. Ten boats were under weigh, all trying and manœuvring for position, and yet all was done without a foul or a protest; the handling was admirable, it was really a sight to see. A little water might have been shipped, but that was soon baled out, and the curious acrobatic performances of the shifting ballast, stretching out to windward, was also a prominent feature.

The *Challenge*, 1.1-rater, O.U.S.C., led at first for three or four rounds, *Mona*, .85, close up, *Mirage*, 1.0, going well and looking very handsome. At the finish there was capital racing. In the last round but one *Mona*, .85, leading, caught a hard gust and took in a reef in a very workmanlike way to make sure of saving her mast. It was admirably done and elicited great praise, as she came in running neck and neck with *Challenge*, 1.1-rater, both on different gybes, *Challenge* with her little spinnaker on the port hand and *Mona*, .85, on the starboard. The spinnaker must be the same size as the jibs in these races. The secretary had handed over his steam launch *Leopard* to Captain Bell of the Thames Conservancy, whilst he and the commodore sailed the *Kitten*, which came in fourth. The six-day festival of the six Thames Sailing Clubs, so happily and pleasantly blended, promises well for small-rater sport in the future.

THE ROYAL WINDERMERE YACHT CLUB

The beautiful Lake district is provided with an excellent yacht club, well organised, with workmanlike system and detail; and, as a fresh-water club, it is here described after the Thames associations. It was founded in 1860 and possesses a Royal Warrant dated 1887. The headquarters are at Bowness, adjoining the Old England Hotel, and consist of club-house, reading-rooms, billiard and committee room, and boat landings; and the club has a very hospitable arrangement, like the Bombay Club, by which gentlemen not residing within ten miles of Bowness, on being proposed and seconded by two members, can be admitted as temporary members, for a week, fortnight, or month, for a moderate fee. The sailing committee request owners to see that professional crews of yachts engaged in races wear white or blue jerseys, yachting or man-of-war caps, or straw hats. The ensign is red with crown in fly.

The leading feature of the Royal Windermere Lake Yacht Club is well shown in the illustration on p. 185, as, out of comparatively few members, fourteen are at the starting line, a proportion very seldom

'Feeling it' off the Ferry.

Royal Windermere Yacht Club. A fair start.

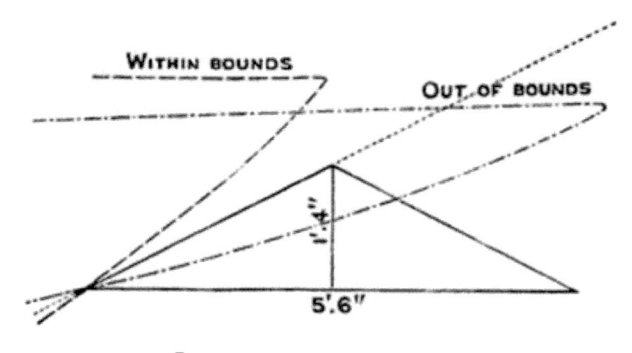

Limit angle of counter.

met with in any club, and certainly suggesting great unanimity and good feeling. The beautiful surroundings of the lake constitute a great charm, though crews in racing craft have not much time to admire picturesque landscape.

The Windermere Club takes precautions to ensure as much as possible real, well-contested races, and like the 'Water Wags' at Dublin has definite club measurements, thus:—

(*a*) Length of yacht on load-water-line, from fore side of stern to after side of rudder post, shall not exceed 20 ft., and the total length from fore side of stern to extreme end of counter shall not exceed 25 ft. 6 in., and no part of stern above or below water shall or sternpost below water shall project beyond the 20-ft. gauge. A yacht shall be considered to be on her load-line when she lies adrift from her moorings in smooth water, without crew, with all sails set and racing gear on board.

(*b*) Beam (extreme outside measurement) shall not be less than 6 ft. 6 in. without beading or moulding.

(*c*) The draught of water shall not exceed 5 ft. 6 in. when the yacht is on her load-water-line.

(*d*) The yacht shall show at least one-quarter of an inch of her rudder-post clear of the water when on her load-water-line.

(*e*) No part of the counter shall intersect a triangle or the produced perpendicular thereof shown on p. 186. Base 5 ft. 6 in. on load-water-line produced perpendicular 1 ft. 4 in. from water.

(*f*) The length of mast from deck to trunk or end of pole shall not exceed 26 ft. 8 in. Bowsprit from fore side of mast to extreme end shall not exceed 19 ft. in length. The boom from aft side of mast to the end shall not exceed 18 ft. 6 in. and the gaff (measured parallel to the boom) shall not exceed 16 ft. 8 in. in length. It shall, however, be optional to have a boom 22 feet in length from aft side of mast to the end, provided that the gaff does not exceed 15 ft. in length. Topsail yard shall not exceed 18 ft. 9 in. in length.

(*g*) Hoist of mainsail from thimble to thimble 16 feet.

(*h*) From deck to pin of jib halliard sheave or pin of block shall not exceed 23 ft. 9 in.

(*i*) Mast from deck to pin of topsail sheave shall not exceed 25 feet 9 inches.

(*j*) No yacht shall have less than 32 cwt. of ballast, and no ballast shall be carried inside of yacht.

These restrictions certainly tend to uniformity and good sport.

SMART BREEZE FOR RACING, WINDERMERE.

FAIR WIND ROUND THE BUOY.

CALM WEATHER.

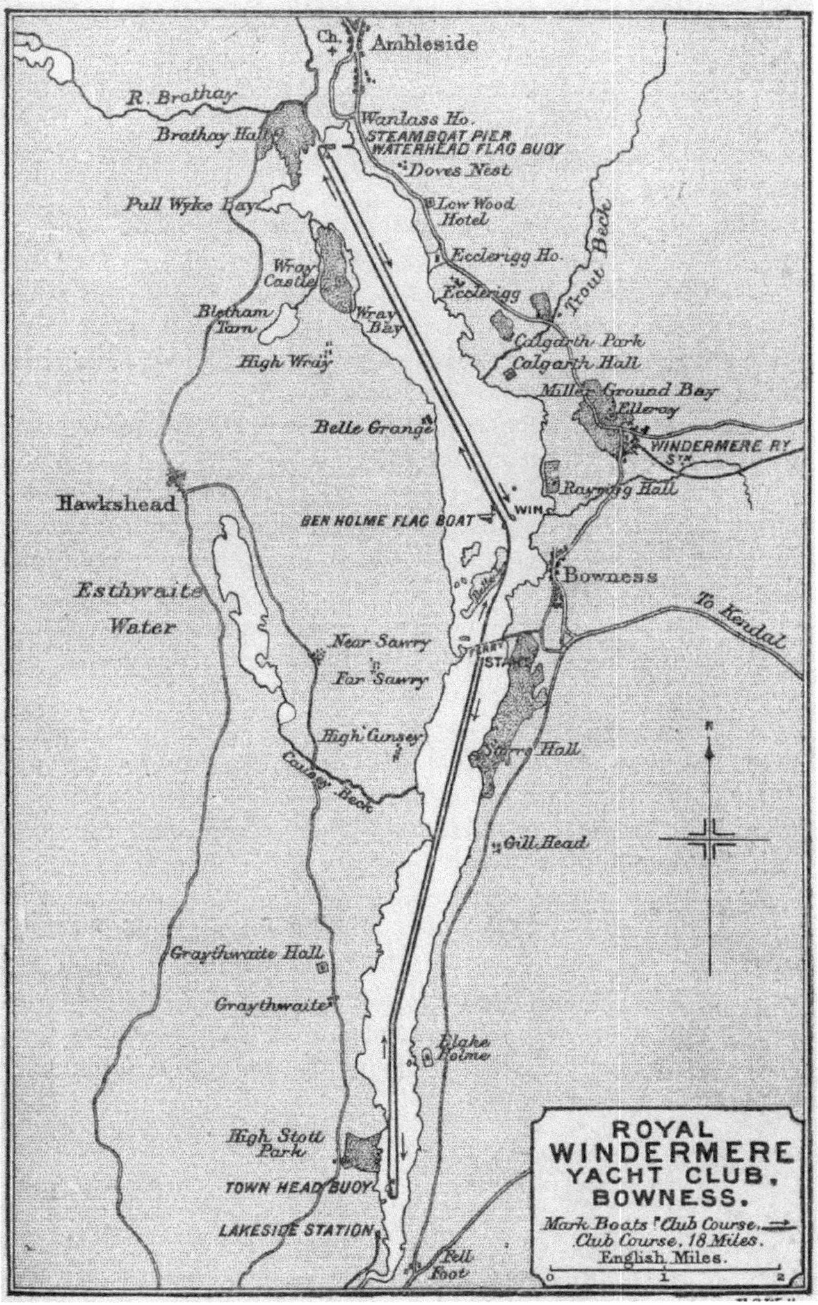
ROYAL WINDERMERE YACHT CLUB, BOWNESS.
Mark Boats Club Course.
Club Course, 18 Miles.
English Miles.
0
1
2
Ambleside
Ch.
R. Brathay
Brathay Hall
Wanlass Ho.
STEAMBOAT PIER
WATERHEAD FLAG BUOY
Doves Nest
Pull Wyke Bay
Low Wood Hotel
Wray Castle
Ecclerigg Ho.
Ecclerigg
Trout Beck
Blelham Tarn
Wray Bay
Calgarth Park
Calgarth Hall
High Wray
Miller Ground Bay
Elleray
WINDERMERE RY. STN.
Belle Grange
Rayrigg Hall
Hawkshead
BEN HOLME FLAG BOAT
WIN.
Bowness
Esthwaite Water
To Kendal
Near Sawry
FERRY STAGE
Far Sawry
High Cunsey
Storrs Hall
Cunsey Beck
Gill Head
N
Graythwaite Hall
Graythwaite
Blake Holme
High Stott Park
TOWN HEAD BUOY
LAKESIDE STATION
Fell Foot

The yachts have to be constructed with *natural frames*, spaced not more than two feet apart with steamed timbers, between with single pine, larch, oak, pitch pine, American elm, English elm, bay wood or teak planking, and decks. Iron floors are allowed, but no iron or steel frames.

The size of racing flag at the main peak during a match to be 2 ft. 6 in. by 1 ft. 6 in.

Fore and aft sails—namely, mainsail jib and topsail only, and no square sails or other sails set as square sails—must be used at Club matches. No footsticks or jackyards are allowed to gaff topsails; no booming out of the sails is permitted even by hand, except by sheets hauled aft of the fairleader. Every yacht sailing in a race must carry at least two life buoys ready for immediate use.

The general and sailing rules published by the Royal Windermere Yacht Club are practical and ably drawn up.

As will be seen by the chart, Bowness is situated about a little north of the half length of the Lake. The Ben Holme flag boat opposite, at the north end, is the Waterhead flag buoy, and at the south end of the lake is the Town Head buoy.

The club course is from the ferry round a flag buoy off Town Head at the south extremity of the Lake and back to the Ben Holme flag boat, opposite Bowness. The distance is 18 miles.

The Waterhead course is from Waterhead, N. extremity of the Lake, round flag buoy, off Ben Holme (Bowness), thence round flag buoy in Lowood Bay, thence round flag buoy in Pull Wyke Bay, thence round Waterhead flag buoy, sailing the same course again and turning off Waterhead. The natural formation of the surrounding district explains the special necessity for the two life buoys ready for immediate use, as squalls and stormy weather are characteristics of the Lake district, although the regattas are sailed in the finest season, during the month of July. The secretary, Lieut.-Col. Arthur L. Reade, has courteously furnished details of this interesting inland club. The photographs of the 'Beauties of the Lake' of Windermere are by Mr. Bronskill, of Bowness.

CHAPTER 5

Yachting on the Norfolk Broads
By G. Christopher Davies

The sailing of small yachts and boats is vigorously indulged in upon the rivers and lakes of Norfolk and Suffolk, in what is popularly known as the Broad District. There is, indeed, every temptation to the sport in this favoured region. No *mal de mer* can haunt its smooth waters; there is no tossing about in exposed anchorages, but instead the mooring by grassy banks odorous with flowers. Gales lose their terrors and zephyrs gain additional charm on these placid and sinuous waterways and toy lakes. Yet there is room enough and to spare for all the evolutions the boat-sailer delights in, and the exploring cruises dear to the owners of small yachts, while life on sailing houseboats is sufficiently tempting to the laziest lotus-eater. The adventurous can make adventure, the explorer can lose himself in mazy reed-beds, the lounger can lounge with the minimum of trouble, the young can picnic in the most luxurious fashion, ladies can 'yacht' in the most lady-like way, and complexions will not pale (what is so piteous as a seasick woman?) upon these favoured streams.

Even the sturdiest sea cruiser acknowledges the charm of the quiet gliding between their verdant banks, and the quiet sleep dependent upon neither watch nor riding light. No one enjoys a sail at sea in fair summer weather more than I do; but upon the many occasions upon which the sea has been rougher than I approved of, I have said in my haste: 'What a fool I must be to desert the safety and surety of the Broads for this, which is neither safe nor sure!' At the same time it is only fair to say that, after a quick and pleasant passage to some foreign port, I have also said: 'Better one such sail than many on the Broads.' My boating life has been spent in a vacillation between the quiet pleasures of the Broads and the excitement of the sea; and I have

THE 'GREYHOUND.'

THE FISHER'S HOME, THE BROADS.

made many attempts to procure craft in which to enjoy either at will. This is a difficult matter, inasmuch as the draught necessary for able work at sea is too great for the rivers.

Although many thousands know well the district of the Broads, yet to the bulk of people it is still a *terra incognita*. It is therefore necessary to give at least a brief description of the *locus in quo*. Taking one's stand at Great Yarmouth, with one's back to the sea and facing inland, one sees—or could in truth see if one ascended the lofty Nelson Monument—first the narrow and busy harbour which conveys the waters of all the rivers to the sea, then a great tidal lake known as Breydon Water, four or five miles long. From this one can ascend by vessel the greater River Yare, which for twenty miles of broad and sinuous course threads the marshes to Norwich. On the right is the Bure, commonly called the North River, which twists and turns for twenty-seven miles to Wroxham, and is navigable further yet to Coltishall and Aylsham. Tributary to this river are the Ant and the Thurne, giving access to the largest of the Broads. Southward of Breydon is the deep and clear Waveney, with Beccles twenty-three miles from the sea at Yarmouth, and a short cut to the sea by Oulton Broad and Lowestoft.

Broadenings of these waterways at many points have become, by the growth of reeds and accumulations of soil, lakes or Broads, more or less separate from the rivers, but in most cases having navigable access to them. The characteristic of the district is its extreme flatness and the consequent slight fall of the river-beds, the current being mainly tidal, with not much difference of level at that. Yet this flatness is not monotonous; for, in addition to the ever-varying and ever-pleasing cloudscapes seen to best advantage in flat regions, there are beauties on the marshes and river borders of no common order. The luxuriant growth of reeds around the lakes gives the feeling of utter seclusion from the madding crowd.

The gay hues of flowering plants, altering with sunshine and shadow of clouds on the wind-swept marsh, the deep shades of groves, the clear and winding rivers, the dark-brown and high-peaked sails of the wherries with their graceful curve of leach, and the white sails of the yachts scattered here and there, now reflected in a glassy reach, and again seeming to thread the verdant marshes where no water is visible from one's standpoint; the kestrel hovering over the 'rand,' a jay hunting a reed-bed for nests and eggs, waterfowl of many kinds, the splash of fish in a quiet bay, a heron by a lilied dyke, and innumerable noticeable incidents of bird and insect life, make the hours too short which are spent on these singular waterways.

In order to fully understand the peculiarities of the craft navigating the Broads and rivers both for trade and pleasure it is desirable to appreciate the necessities of the district; and for this purpose it would be well to step on board some kind of craft on which one can be independent of hotels as well as railways. For it is quite clear that journeys by rail cannot show one the life of the Broads. It is singular what a difference the point of view makes. Thus there are reaches where the rail and river run near each other. From the rail there is nothing to see but a flat marsh and a winding river. But from a boat on the river the view assumes an altogether different aspect. If one pleases, the tall and swaying reeds, brown topped and feathery, may bound the scene, hide the rail, and provide one with the loneliness of nought but water and sky—a veritable solitude; or from a higher standpoint the eye may travel with a keen interest over the reed-beds and the brilliant-hued marsh, past windmill and dwarf tree to the undulating and wooded higher lands which are the shores of the marsh.

For choice for a mere cruising holiday, I would take, if middle-aged, a real Norfolk wherry converted into a roomy houseboat as presently to be described. The Norfolk wherry is a craft quite unlike those of any other district, and eminently suited to the shallow and somewhat narrow waters of its birthplace. The limit of suitability seems to have been reached by perfection, since of late years no alteration whatever has taken place in the design of the wherry or its sail. As it is the aboriginal craft, so to say, of these waters, and its graceful sail forms a constant object of interest upon the waterways, it merits the pride of place in a description of Norfolk craft. It has greater interest also in that it is suitable for cruising in other waters, notably in those of Holland and Friesland, where Mr. Doughty found that a Norfolk wherry was even more suitable for Dutch waters than the Dutch vessels, so far as pleasure purposes go.[1]

The draught of an unladen wherry is from 2 ft. 4 in. to 2 ft. 6 in., with a beam of 13 ft. and a length of 52 ft. It has a short hollow bow, with the greatest beam well forward and a fine run aft. It has only a few inches outside keel, yet in fairly smooth water it lies remarkably close to the wind, going fast through the water all the time. The mast is stepped 12 ft. 6 in. from the stem, and is a splendid spar of spruce fir or pitch pine 37 ft. deck to hounds, without any stay other than a forestay, and supports a single sail of the following dimensions: luff, 27

---

1. See *Friesland Meres in a Norfolk Wherry.*

ft.; foot, 28 ft.; head, 29 ft.; and leach, 44 ft. 6 in. There is no boom, and the gaff has a high peak. The sail is hoisted by a single halliard set up by a winch on the mast.

A drawing and lines of a wherry accompany an article by myself which was published in the *Field* of March 20, 1880, to which the reader who may be interested can refer. The mast swings in a tabernacle, and the heel is weighted with lead and iron to the extent of 1½ ton, and is so well balanced that a boy can lower and raise it. It will be seen that the rig has the extreme of simplicity to recommend it. One man can sail a 30-ton wherry, although he generally has the assistance of his wife or a mate. When within a few yards of a fixed bridge the sail is rapidly lowered, the forestay tackle cast off and windlass unhitched from the mast, and down comes the mast as gently as possible; the wherry shoots through the bridge, and up go mast and sail the other side. The mainsheet works on a horse on the cabin-top in front of the steersman, and with his back against the tiller he controls the great craft with ease. The stern is pointed, and the rudder is no less than 5 ft. in breadth. Of course the tonnage of the craft varies; the above measurements are those of a medium-sized one. A cabin about 6 ft. long in front of the small steering-well accommodates the crew, and there is a long hold, reaching to the mast and protected by movable hatches, for the cargo.

A few years ago some ingenious person hit upon the idea of converting a trading wherry into a pleasure one by raising and permanently fixing the hatches, placing windows at the sides (there is no bulwark, and but a narrow plankway between the edge and the cabin sides), dividing the roomy interior into saloon and bedrooms, and so producing a commodious and comfortable sailing houseboat, which has become exceedingly popular. There are numbers of them about now, and they are always in demand for hire by parties visiting the Broads.

The large sail carries a sort of flounce laced on to the bottom of it called a bonnet, and the removal of this is equivalent to lowering a topsail. The trading wherries carry no ballast when empty of cargo, but the pleasure wherries have a sufficient quantity of scrap iron. They move in the lightest of airs, and in strong winds are marvellously stiff. They will tack in channels no wider than their own length, but in narrow waters they are helped round by the man giving the bows a set off each bank with a 'quant' or long pole (Latin *contus*); they are capable of high speeds, and the easy way in which they get about the nar-

REGATTA TIME.

WROXHAM PLEASURE CRAFT.

row and shallow waters is surprising. Occasionally they essay the sea passage from Yarmouth to Lowestoft, instead of going round by the rivers, and even race at sea; but it cannot be doubted that in doing so they go beyond the margin of safety. Although Mr. Doughty successfully towed a wherry behind a steam tug from Yarmouth to Stavoren, another wherry essaying the same feat was lost. The low, long, flat hull cannot stand rough water, and the heavy mast with its weighted heel is a dangerous lever in the wrong position.

Many yachts have been built after the plan of the wherry, but with yacht-like hulls above water. At first the simple wherry rig was retained, but soon there came a boom to the sail, and then a bowsprit and jib, additions which, no doubt, make the vessel faster, but mean more help in handling—two men instead of one, and so on. These barges, as they are called, have increased greatly in number during the last few years. The other day I counted no fewer than twelve lying moored on Oulton Broad, where five years ago one such would have attracted attention. The immense influx of visitors to the Broads is, of course, responsible for this increase. The latest of these barges, the *Waveney*, is no less than 58 ft. long, but it is believed that there is considerable difficulty in getting her about.

The barge yacht is more seaworthy than the wherry, and one—the *Ianthe*—has twice crossed the North Sea to Holland for cruising in Dutch waterways. She was fortunately favoured with fine weather, and it would, no doubt, be needful to make as sure as possible that the weather was set fair for a day or two before venturing. The draught is but 5 ft. or less, and the heavy pole mast is set far forward, while there is an open well, so it would not be the best kind of craft for bad weather. Still, for modest sails out of the harbour, for Dutch waters, and for Norfolk rivers, these barges possess every advantage, while they are most comfortable to live upon.

The barges look smarter than the wherries, inasmuch as they have white sails instead of brown or black, and yacht-like decks and fittings; but I must say that for pure river cruising I prefer the plain wherry. It is more picturesque in appearance, and, size for size, easier to handle, although, no doubt, the latest types of barges are faster.

Taking one's departure from Wroxham, one finds a narrow river crowded with boats. Only a few years ago, (at first publication), the arrival of a single yacht at Wroxham was an event. Now both banks of the river are lined with wharves, yachts, and boats, and boat-builders' sheds are springing up on every side. A striking tribute to the favour in which the Broads are held is the boat-letting establishment of Mr. Loynes, who at the first Fishery Exhibition exhibited models of small open centreboard boats, to be converted at night into sleeping cabins by most ingeniously contrived awnings. In consequence of this he desires, and very properly, to divide with the writer the honour of first drawing the public attention to these favourite cruising grounds.

From the small beginning he then made he has come to own many yachts, large (20 tons) and small (3 or 4 tons), mostly built by himself, capable of navigating the shallowest of the Broads, comfortably fitted with all essentials of comfort, and attended by most civil and capable men. He is now introducing his boats to the Friesland meres, and it is probable that many of his Norfolk customers will follow him to that larger lake-land. His vessels are mostly centreboard and of light draught, the latter, by the way, being of more vital necessity than ever. The tourist steamers which now rush up and down the Bure draw down the soft mud from the sides and deposit it in the channel, so decreasing the depth. A few days before writing this I had a 25-ton cutter towed up from Yarmouth to Wroxham, for the purpose of laying up, by a steam-launch. By taking out ballast her draught was reduced to 5 ft. 6 in., yet she grounded at least twenty times in the upper reaches, right in the middle of the channel.

The river below Wroxham is very narrow and very sinuous; its banks lined with groves of trees which intercept the wind. The lofty peak of our wherry's sail holds the air over the bushes, and we keep slowly moving along, while smaller boats are either becalmed or, catching sudden puffs, lay over at alarming angles. It is a Saturday evening, and very many little yachts, from the open lugsail sailing boat on which a high-roofed cabin-top has been placed to the 4- or 8-ton yachts of smarter build, are making their way down to more open waters for the happy and healthy week end, most blessed to the person whose occupations are sedentary. A mile or two of charming river reaches brings us to Wroxham Broad—a lovely sheet of water surrounded by an inner circle of tall green and feathery topped reeds and an outer circle of bushes and trees. It is entered by a narrow gateway from the river, and boating is freely permitted, subject to certain wise regulations which are as much to the interest of the public as to that of the riparian owners.

The reeds have a golden belt where the rise and fall of the water has left its yellow mark, shining brightly in the westering sun. In the smooth patches under the lee of the reeds one may see the sparkle of bait flying out from pursuing pike or perch, and in the still bays the coots and water-hens dive and splash. Across and across the Broad skim the white sails of boats and canoes making the most of the dying breeze, and the wavelets sink to ripples, and the ripples are shot with streaks and patches of cloud-reflecting calm. We leave this, the most beautiful and deepest of the Broads, to make the most of the evening air down the river.

On the occasion of the annual regatta there is a prodigious water frolic at Wroxham, which is attended by perhaps a hundred sailing craft of all kinds, and much merriment results.

Gliding quietly down stream we pass on the left Hoveton Broads, Great and Little—nurseries of wildfowl and kept strictly private, with chains across the entrance; on the right Salhouse Broads, Great and Little, on which boating is permitted under protest; and further still on the right Woodbastwick Broad, also strictly private. Hoveton little Broad is a breeding-place of the black-headed gull, which nest here in great numbers.

So by wood and mere and sighing reed we pass with many a twist and turn until we reach the hostelry of Horning Ferry. Here, as night draws on, many vessels arrive. Strolling along the bank we can note what is after all the great fun of Broad yachting—the camping and living on board a floating house, however small. The big wherries and barges are of course floating houseboats, comparatively luxurious; but at the other extreme here are three or four open boats covered in with canvas tents or awnings luminous with the lamps within, and with myriads of dazzled night insects pattering against the shining canvas. The evening meal is being discussed, then there is the clatter of washing-up, the cleaning of knives by thrusting them into the soft bank, the washing of plates with tufts of paper, and the general tidying-up which is part of the fun to young men, but which ceases to possess any charm to older ones. These rivers are capital places for the man fond of single-handed sailing. One well-known and elderly amateur sails a lugsail boat alone, but at a proper distance behind him comes his man in another single-handed boat. The latter pitches his master's tent and relieves him of household troubles, and retires to his own boat tent when not wanted. This is really a capital arrangement.

When the stars come out, the herons settle in the shallow pools; the wild duck fly from the sheltered decoys and preserved sanctuaries to more open feeding-grounds; a shot rings out on the August night from some reed-hidden gunner who has been patiently awaiting the

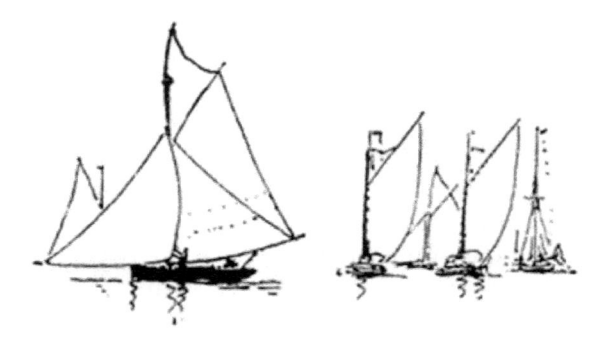

Wroxham Broad.

Smooth-water bowsprit.

River Waveney craft.

evening flight. In contrast come the notes of a piano and song from a barge; along the bank is a row of lights from cosy cabins; the inn is thronged with boat-sailers eagerly discussing their common sport; then the last cheery goodnights, and silence falls over the lone marsh and winding river.

In the morning there is the splash of swimmers, blankets and bedding are put out to air on the cabin-tops, spirit and paraffin stoves mingle their scent with that of frying bacon and the wild thyme on the banks. About ten o'clock the little yachts spread their sails to the freshening breeze, and off they go. If we have ladies on board, they will probably wish to go to Horning Church in the morning, and can then sail in the afternoon with a clear conscience—a compromise approved by the strictest sabbatarian, who finds in the peace and quiet of Norfolk waters an assurance that neither the wind nor he is a sinner in the gentle movement.

After lunch the wind has freshened so that we take our bonnet off (off the sail, that is) and smaller vessels reef. The wind, too, is ahead, and we have to tack a great deal as we continue our course down stream. Still the river course is so tortuous that every reach is not a head one; sometimes, indeed, we can lay one reach on one tack and the next reach on the other tack. It is pretty to watch the yachts shooting from side to side of the river (which widens as we proceed); they lay over, with the water bubbling over the lee deck and the foot of the great balloon jib deep in the water. The long bowsprit sweeps over the grass of the margin as the helm is let go; the boat shoots up into the wind, is upright with fluttering jib for a moment, then off she goes on the other tack to repeat the manœuvre at the opposite shore.

If the mainsheet is well handled the mainsail never shakes. As it loses the wind on one side it catches it on the other, the jib being kept slightly aback until the boat's head is well off the wind. It is no joke to handle the jibsheets of an 8- or 10-ton boat. In spite of soft cotton rope being employed, the chafe will try the horniest hand. In sailing the jib is worked to every puff, eased off or drawn in at every variation in direction or strength of wind. The man in charge watches the wind pressing down the grasses and reeds and darkening the water in advance, and trims his sheet to every puff or lull. If he does not, why, the boat is not sailing her best—that is all. The mainsheet man, too, is almost as particular.

When there are hands enough to work the sheets no one thinks of making a sheet fast. The bends of the river are too frequent for that.

Again, there is almost always another yacht ahead or astern, and you strive to overtake the one or sail away from the other, so that every day's sail is more or less of a race. In passing or meeting other craft the rules of the road are well observed, and the steering is usually so excellent that a space of six inches is considered an ample margin of distance from the other vessel. These narrow rivers soon develop considerable skill in this direction, and accidents do not often happen. The least rare is that of misjudging the rate at which a wherry is coming, and getting athwart her bows while tacking; but a direct collision is averted, and the yacht's bowsprit or mainsheet is the only thing which suffers.

On the right we pass Ranworth Broad, a fine lake in two sections, the larger of which is now in process of being closed to the tourist; on the left the mouth of the narrow River Ant, which, after twisting like an eel for some five miles, opens into the navigable but shallow Barton Broad, of considerable size. There is a bridge over the Ant so narrow that the larger kind of vessels cannot get through.

The tract of marsh widens out and the view broadens. On our right is a mile-long channel leading to South Walsham Broad, part of which is navigable and part private. As an instance of how vibrations of movement are carried along water, a gentleman residing at South Walsham tells me that when the water near the staith is covered with a thin veneer of ice he can tell when a wherry entered the mouth of South Walsham Dyke from the river, a mile and a half away, by the ice rippling and cracking.

Passing the ruins of St. Benedict's Abbey on the left, we presently come to the mouth of the river Thurne, up which we sail for a few miles to Potter Heigham Bridge, where in company with several barges and yachts we moor, with the intention of visiting Hickling Broad and Horsey Mere on the morrow. The night falls dark and lowering, with flashes of summer lightning in the south lighting up the great distance of flat and treeless marsh; but no rain falls, and a quiet night and sound sleep bring us to the dewy morn of another glorious summer day.

Most of the larger yachts and pleasure wherries have centreboard sailing dinghies, and it is more convenient to take ours through the narrow arch where the tide-impelled current sweeps upward to diffuse itself over the terminal lakes, twenty-five miles from the sea by river, three miles by land. Here, save in the tourist-crowded month of August, may be found true solitude. The river runs through far-reaching marshes, a branch leads through a wilderness of water and tall reeds, the brown tops of the latter trembling against the clouds from our low point of view. Water, reeds, clouds; a kestrel hovering overhead, our boat gliding on clear, shallow water over trailing weeds and shoals of startled rudd; then the wider channel of Heigham Sounds, and at last the expanse of Hickling Broad. Four hundred acres it is said to be, but the reedy margins absorb a great part of this. Still, there is water enough to make the scene imposing, and the first thought of a boating-man is—What a splendid place for sailing!

But looking down through the clear water one sees that the bottom is almost within reach of one's arm, and even in the channels there is only sufficient water for a wherry. It is obvious, therefore, that the shallow centreboard boat is the only type fit for Hickling. It maybe useful to mention that a recent judicial decision gives as the law that the public have the rights of navigation and passage over Hickling Broad, but that those of fishing and shooting are vested in the riparian owners.

Not far from Hickling, and connected with it by Heigham Sounds and a narrow dyke, is Horsey Mere, so near the sea that the sea-water at times wells into it in the shape of salt springs. At the entrance of the mere a small cruising yacht is lying, the men having gone ashore for a walk over the sand dunes to the sea. The mooring rope is fast to a deck scrub thrust into the bank, and a heifer, having found out the roughness of the scrub, is leisurely rubbing herself all over and most thoroughly against the bristles. A wherry sweeping down the dyke with peak lowered leaves us but scant room to pass as we sail back to Heigham Sounds.

From Potter Heigham we sail in the wherry down the Thurne, into the Bure, and so on to Acle Bridge, where the mast has to be lowered. From Acle to Yarmouth the sail is not so interesting. The tide runs strongly and the banks are shoal. This part of the passage is undertaken of necessity, and not for pleasure. At Yarmouth we enter Breydon Water, where the greater space and depth of channel brings us into contact with larger yachts. Still, it is yachting in miniature, and the man accustomed to Cowes must think it rather ridiculous of us to call our small craft yachts. I much prefer the old and truly descriptive term of pleasure boats. When the Broad sailor comes to Breydon he feels that, comparatively speaking, he is in the open sea, and a beat across it with a smart breeze against tide means wet plankways and an exciting sail.

At the top of Breydon to the left is the entrance of the river Waveney, so shallow and dangerous as to be avoided. The River Yare, to the right, is wide and deep, and gives good sailing ground up by Reedham to Cantley, where the chief river regattas are held, and higher still to Norwich. From Reedham a narrow and straight canal, called Haddiscoe Cut, leads into the Waveney at a point above its shallows and a fixed bridge. The bridges on the Yare and the Upper Waveney from Haddiscoe to Beccles are railway bridges, opening save when a red flag or lamp denotes the arrival of a train. The scenery on both rivers seaward of Reedham is flat and uninteresting, and it is above Reedham, on the Yare, and St. Olave's, on the Waveney, that the beauty of the landscape adds interest to the sailing.

As one proceeds up the Waveney and through the narrow dyke which connects the Mid-Waveney with Oulton Broad, Lake Lothing, and the sea at Lowestoft, one meets great numbers of yachts and sailing boats, and we may now dwell more closely upon the characteristics of these.

The old term in existence before the more ambitious title of yacht was *pleasure boat*. This was applied to the decked sailing boats we now call yachts, and is perpetuated in the sign of the Pleasure-boat Inn, Hickling. A favourite type, of which but few examples exist, was the lateener, first, I believe, consisting of two lateen-shaped sails, but afterwards of a lateen-shaped foresail and a gaff-mizen. The foresail was set upon a short mast right in the bows and raking well forward, and the yard was often twice the length of the vessel. Such a rig was very close-winded, and handy enough to handle once the sail was up; but the long yard was a great nuisance in raising and lowering the sail, and the reefing had to be done along the long yard instead of the short boom. The boats also were dangerous in running before the wind, being apt to run under head first. This may have been partly owing to the short and full bow which was deemed necessary to support the weight of the mast and sail, and which at high speed created a great hollow in the water.

Possibly a lateen-rigged, sharper-bowed boat would even now be found to be a very fast and handy type for our rivers. The balance lug so much in vogue is but a lateen sail with the fore-angle cut off. I only know of two lateeners of late on our waters—the *Ariel* of Beccles, a boat of about 10 tons, and the *Black Maria* of Barton Broad. The owner of the latter died recently, and it is possible the yacht is not now in commission; but she looked picturesque threading the narrow and sinuous reaches of the Ant on her way to and from Barton Broad.

A light-displacement boat is a necessity upon Norfolk waters. It is not only that the depth is small and that the draught of a boat should not exceed 4 ft. 6 in. if she is to get about comfortably, but the water displaced by her movement has but little room to disperse in the narrower channels. It is sufficient to watch the light-displacement sailing wherry going fast through the water with scarcely a ripple, and making but slight difference in the level of the water at the grassy margins, and then to see a heavy-displacement steam wherry going not so fast, yet piling up the water in front of her, filling and emptying the dykes and runlets as she passes, to understand that the one thing essential for speed is light displacement. Again, in a heavy-displacement craft of my own which is sometimes brought upon the rivers, whenever the waterway is constricted she moves slowly and the river craft gain upon her. When the channel suddenly broadens she seems to leap forward and away in a striking manner.

Many yachts have come to try their speed with the Norfolk boats, but generally having greater displacement have come off second-best, although possibly better craft in more open waters. The old type is a flat-bottomed boat with a deep keel spiked on to it; the angle between the keel and the hull is filled in with more or less graceful curves, but the principle is the same in the most successful of the modern racing yachts, as it was in the older craft: a beamy, flat hull and a comparatively deep keel. Practically there is no change in the midship sections other than that which more skilled workmanship and more artistic design have evolved. The principle is only the same, however, so far as the midship section is concerned. Great advances, or at all events alterations, have gradually been made in the longitudinal design of the boats.

Quick turning has always been a necessity with the yachts of the Broads, and this has been attained by the help of three peculiarities—a keel short for the length of the boat, a rudder so large as to be in reality a movable keel or leeboard, and an enormous jib, which is the only head-sail. The size of the jib is also influenced by the fact that it has to balance the equally enormous mainsail. In order partly to carry as much sail as is required for these smooth waters the mast is always well forward, and with a large mainsail and boom projecting far over the counter great head-sail is a necessity.

The old measurement of racing craft used simply to be length on the 'ram' or keel, which as long as all boats were of the same type in other respects was fair enough. But a boat, say, 20 ft. over all would have a counter of 9 ft. or 9 ft. 6 in.; practically half her length would be counter. I do not think this great counter was altogether the result of an attempt to cheat the tonnage measurement, although no doubt this may have had some influence. It was more the result of circumstances; the yacht with a short keel, well forward, and great rudder, turned more quickly than a boat of similar size with longer keel and smaller rudder. About half this great counter was permanently immersed, and when a boat laid over, almost the whole of it came into bearing.

It was popularly supposed that the broad, flat counter peculiar to the old boats bore the weight of the boom; the yachts, though very quick and handy, carried tremendous weather helm and were very hard to steer, sometimes taking the strength of two men to prevent them shooting into the wind. When the helm is let go, the little vessel shoots so quickly into the wind that she might be put about on the other tack by backing the jib, without further touch of the tiller. In fact, so powerful is the great overhang of mainsail and jib in controlling the balance pivoted on the short keel that I have many times tacked a 4-ton boat up a narrow reach without touching the tiller at all, simply by manipulating the sheets, and this, too, while sailing single-handed. This was by way of experiment only.

The usual way of sailing a 4-ton, or, for the matter of that, a 10-ton yacht single-handed, is while going to windward to make the mainsheet fast, steer with your back, and work the jibsheet with your hands. Reaching or going free you work the mainsheet and jibsheet alternately as best you can. All the boats have large open wells, the jibsheets lead aft through a couple of blocks shackled to the clew of the sail, with the standing part fast to eyes on each plankway, and leading blocks further aft. Thus there is just sufficient purchase to enable a strong man to control the jibsheet of a 10-ton boat. In sailing these boats there is no making the jibsheet fast if you wish to get the best speed out of the vessel. They are trimmed to an inch, and every bend of the river means a careful and anxious adjustment of the jibsheet. The same remarks apply to the mainsheet, and where two or three equally capable amateurs are engaged in sailing there will be keen differences of opinion as to the proper quantity of sheet to be allowed out, and hot arguments as to the advisability of an inch more or less, when to the man accustomed to sailing in more open water the difference would appear immaterial.

In tacking, the stern of the boat swings upon the pivot of the forefoot, and it frequently happens that in sailing close to the bank of the river before putting about, although the bowsprit bends the grasses, and the stem is clear of the bank, yet the counter cannons against the bank or shaves the mud.

Whether it was found that advantage was taken of the keel measurement to get larger boats by means of immersed counters, or whether it was simply to give more scope to designers, is a matter of controversy; but it was ordained that half the length of the counter had to be added to the length of keel to form the factor of length, the rest of the measurement being according to the Thames rule. This rule of measurement prevailed for many years without any particular alteration in the type of boat supervening. Then, and only recently, length on the load-water-line was taken, and presently the Y.R.A. rules of measurement and rating were adopted.

The effect of the alteration has been to lengthen the keel, and perhaps to round up the forefoot a little. It has been suggested that it would be as easy to attain the quick turning by rounding the forefoot and having the greatest draught aft as it is by the present method of keeping the draught well forward and shortening the keel; but there is this objection—the shores next the banks are frequently shoal and muddy. When the boat swings round on her deep forefoot, if that is free from mud the lighter draught stern is sure to follow; but when a light draught forefoot is still free from the mud, the deeper draught stern swings on to it and is caught, and the boat's head pays off to leeward before she releases herself.

Experience goes to show that in the larger classes the boat with much drag aft is not suitable for these shallow-margined rivers, and that to succeed in racing it is necessary to be able to perform the feat of waltzing a boat round and round in little more than her own extreme length, as the writer has done by way of experiment. A boat which will only handle when she has steerage way does not stand much chance.

The yachts used generally to be built by that rule-of-thumb method, the result of long and slow experience, which has often proved more sure than the experiments of science; but of late years two boat-builders have studied intelligently the principles of design, and have applied them with great success to the building of the most successful craft yet seen upon these waters. These two are Mr. Brighton of Yarmouth, and Mr. Mollett of Brundall. The former has confined his attention to the larger class of craft in use here, and the latter to the smaller vessels. First of Mr. Brighton's boats to attract attention was the 3-tonner *Trixie*, then the 9-tonner *Wanderer*, and then the 4-tonner *Greyhound*, all in their time the best boats of their class, although run hard by those of other designers. The *Trixie* is a boat 27 ft. 6 in. over all, 20 ft. 6 in. stem to sternpost, 24 ft. on the water-line, 6 ft. 6 in. beam, and 3 ft. 9 in. draught of water; boom 25 ft., gaff 20 ft., bowsprit outboard 22 ft. She carried about 4 tons of lead ballast. The *Greyhound* was designed by William Brighton, but built by workmen of the owner, Mr. John Hall, of Yarmouth. In design she is undoubtedly the best produced by Brighton, and therefore the best boat of her size on the rivers. Proportionately to size, she is a better boat than the *Wanderer*. Since she was built, in 1889, she has won 175 first prizes and 30 second, in addition to several challenge cups, and is also a good little boat at sea, thinking nothing of making the 'outside' passage direct from Lowestoft to Dover in fair weather. The design we give is traced from the moulds off which the yacht was built. The dimensions are as follows:—

Length L.W.L.	25.27 feet
" over all	34.45 "
Beam	6 feet 8 inches
Overhang forward	3.30 "
" aft	5.88 "
Rudder-head from taffrail	6.0 "
Draught amidships	5.0 "
Lead on keel 3 tons	
No inside ballast.	

For sea-work her rating is 3.9 tons.

Boom	22.55 feet
Gaff	17.15 "
Foresail	359.3 square feet
Topsail	110.0 " "
Mainsail	452.2 " "
	921.5 " "

For river-work she spreads 1,014 sq. ft. sail-area, and her rating is about 4.5.

The boat is built entirely without caulking, with not a single butt in deck or hull. The keel is Memel oak; skin of yellow pine $1^{1}/_{8}$ inch;

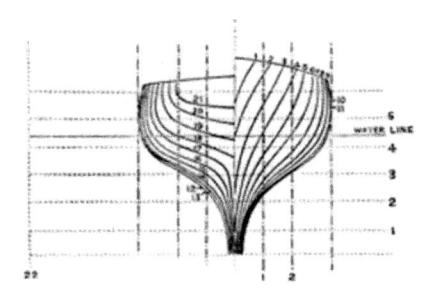

'Greyhound,' midship section.

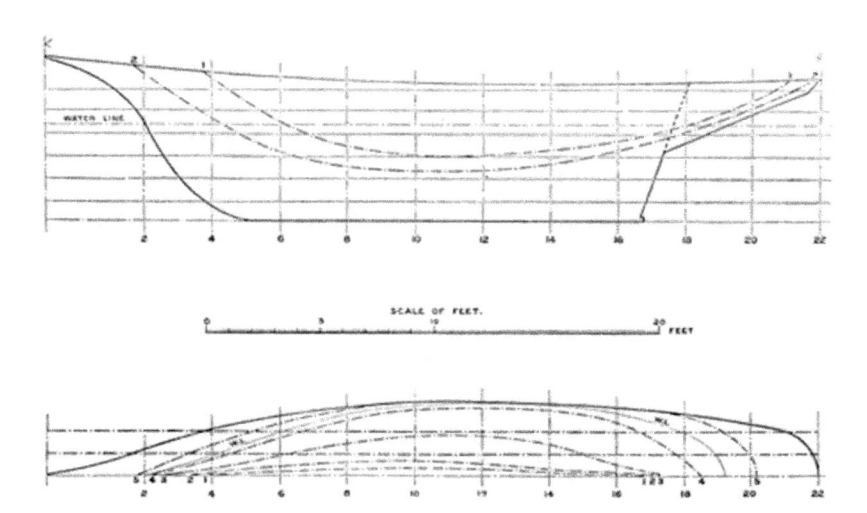

Lines of the 'Greyhound,' 1892, Norfolk Broads yacht.

sawn timbers 2 inches square, with steamed timbers 1½ inch square. She is in every respect beautifully finished, and some of her success may be attributable to the excellence of her workmanship.

The designer has refused us any dimensions of the *Wanderer*, but we believe that practically she is an enlarged edition of the *Greyhound*. She has been run close, if not excelled, by the *Corona*, a boat designed for both sea and river, and fairly good on each. She has greater draught and more rise of floor, with greater displacement. At first she was fitted with a centreboard, which, however, was found as useless as it generally is in a boat of comparatively deep draught. Its province is in shoal boats. I tried a centreboard in the 4-tonner *Swan*, but discarded it after one season. None of the racing yachts over 3 tons have centreboards, and experience has shown that on these waters the centreboard is only of use for the smaller and flatter boats. It is true that Loynes, the boat-letter, has many yachts up to about 20 tons fitted with centreboards, but then his vessels are designed to navigate the shallowest Broads, and centreboards are a necessity in his case. He is, by the way, an adept at fitting centreboards with various devices to facilitate handling them, and his cranks and automatic brakes and other mechanical contrivances are most ingenious and effective.

The *Corona* was designed and built by Peed of Oulton, who had built several fast-sailing boats. She is supposed to be a better boat in rough water than the *Wanderer*, running her close also in the river reaches at Cantley, where the regattas are frequently held. She is also a comfortable cruising boat, having two cabins with good accommodation. Her chief measurements are:—

Length over all	50 feet
" W. L.	33 feet 6 inches
Beam	9 "
Draught	6 "
Ballast	6 tons

Mr. Mollett's boats have chiefly been of the open and half-decked class. His first great success was the *Cigarette*, a centreboard lugsail boat, which won a great number of prizes and was a perfect witch in going to windward. He followed this up by several similar boats, all fairly successful and betraying advances in cleverness of design and experiments upon well-thought-out principles.

In 1890 Mr. Mollett startled the boating fraternity by producing a kind of double-hulled boat called the *Gossip*, which, to use his own words, is 'curious though fast.' Her deck appearance is that of an oblong raft, and the section of her hull is that of a flattened **W**. There is no actual division between the hulls, but a hollow runs along the middle so that when the boat is on an even keel the top of the hollow is upon the water-line. When she heels over the windward hull is raised more or less out of the water, and the vessel sails on the support of the leeward portion, the windward portion acting as a kind of outrigger or windward ballast. The buttock lines are, roughly speaking, segments of a circle of long radius with only the middle and lower part of the segment immersed. She had no keel, but a centreboard dropping between the hulls, and a deep rudder. Her dimensions are: Length over all, 28 ft.; length on L.W.L., 17½ ft.; beam, 7¼ ft.; depth, 2¼ ft.; draught of hull, 10 in.; draught with plate down, 3¾ ft.; area of sail in foresail and lug mainsail, 460 ft.

The *Gossip* was extremely fast running and when sailed full, and won several races. Her mode of going to windward looked peculiar, as she was sailed broad full and rattled from side to side of the river at a rare pace, so that although neither sailing so close as the other competing craft nor shooting so far in stays, being so light, yet she would often make a point to windward quicker than any of them by reason of her speed; and, after all, as Mollett says, the object is to get to windward as quickly as possible, no matter how you do it.

The *Gossip* had, however, one grave defect. She would turn turtle with astonishing suddenness. Her vanishing point was soon reached. She had to be sailed with the utmost skill and caution, and it is only by good luck that she has not yet drowned anyone. The only time I sailed in her, being unaware of this peculiarity, I as nearly as possible had her over in a sudden puff; which, as I had my children on board, might have been a serious matter. Her owner tells me that she has capsized five times, and has very frequently been on the verge of capsizing.

A design of this remarkable craft, and an interesting article upon her by Mr. Mollett, appears in the *Field* of January 10, 1891. Mollett took the centreboard out and substituted a fixed keel with 5 cwt. of lead on it, which he was sanguine enough to say rendered the boat practically uncapsizable. She has, however, capsized several times since then. He afterwards removed the keel and returned to the centreboard, with which he thought the boat was faster and handier. Since then a succeeding owner has reverted to a sort of heavy fin-keel, but the boat has not done so well in racing as formerly. Her canvas is, however, worn and stretched, which may have something to do with

'Castanet.'

Hull of the 'Castanet.'

'Mystery,' Thames boat ('foreign' boat).

it. We hope, for the sake of her owner and his companions, that she will disappear somehow or another before any fatal accident results from her use.

Noticing how cleanly our flat counters leave the water, Mollett thought—What is the use of having a sharp bow to divide the water? Why not have a double-sterned boat, and let the bow slide over the water instead of through it? Something of this idea was present in the building of the *Gossip*, but in the *Castanet*, lately built for Mr. Russell Colman, the idea has had full sway. There is a broad, flat, spoon bow, differing very slightly on deck from the stern, and not differing at all on the water-line, so that it is practically immaterial which end is selected to go first. There are the same segments of large circles for buttock lines. The load-water-line is 17 ft. 3 in., and on deck 29 ft., the overhang being very nearly equal at each end. The beam is 7 ft., and the extreme draught of the short fixed keel, which is spiked to the bottom of the spoon, is 3 ft. 2 in., with 23 cwt. of lead. The latter is disposed at the bottom of the keel in a triangular bulb.

If you take an ordinary tablespoon and press it into a soft substance at different inclinations, the water-lines which it will mark are much the same. The principle is the same in the *Castanet*. The water-lines lengthen and narrow as she heels over, and the length at which she is measured when upright is considerably exceeded at both ends. The spoon comparison is only to a certain extent applicable, as one end of a spoon is smaller than the other, while in the case of the *Castanet* both ends are large ends. There is no deadwood except what is necessary for the keel, and the rudder is a projecting one. Mollett's theory is that it is better to cut away every inch of deadwood which is not absolutely necessary for preventing leeway. He finds the boats so constructed sail faster in every way. As to whether a fin-keel or a weighted centreboard is the better, he has not yet made up his mind.

The *Castanet*, although beaten in her first race by the *Gladys*, a boat of conventional design, has subsequently proved herself the fastest of her class. When sailing fast she lifts herself out of the water forward and slides very easily over it, although her flat bow makes a noisy brabble of the surface water, which is, however, not detrimental to her speed. Of course she would not do in rough water, but in smooth she is stiff, fast, and remarkably handy. In spite of her square ends, which are but little narrower than the rest of the boat, she is, owing to excellence of workmanship, rather a handsome boat than otherwise. It is not likely that another *Gossip* will be built, but the *Castanet* is a taking precedent which may be followed up with advantage.

There are other designers and builders of fast boats, which have, however, nothing peculiar in build or rig to justify especial notice. They are simply well-designed boats of light displacement and large sail-area, very fast and very handy.

There are two boating clubs in existence which provide regattas for the encouragement of sailing. The senior and more select club is the Norfolk and Suffolk Yacht Club, which professedly holds races for the 9-and 10-tonners—the 'large yachts' of the Norfolk rivers. It has a club-house at Lowestoft which is a great convenience to yachtsmen using the harbour, but as a river club it has not much vitality. The junior club is the Yare Sailing Club, which welcomes all amateurs as members who can pay a 5s. subscription. It professedly encourages the sailing of open and half-decked boats, and the smaller class of yachts of 4 tons or thereabouts. It has a large number of members, most of them keen boat-sailers, and its regattas are well attended and the races numerously and keenly contested.

The classes in the Norfolk and Suffolk Club are: Not exceeding 2-rating, exceeding 2 and under 5-rating, and exceeding 5-rating; and those in the Yare Sailing Club as follows:—Class 1.—Exceeding 2-rating and not exceeding 5-rating. Class II.—Exceeding 1-rating and not exceeding 2-rating. Class III.—Not exceeding 1-rating. Any 'foreign' boats (all persons not natives of Norfolk are foreigners) which can sail in these classes are welcome, and any wrinkle they can teach will be quickly taken up.

The *Mystery*, a Thames open boat, is almost the only strange boat which has succeeded in showing the way to the local racers, and I think she would not be second to either *Castanet* or *Gladys*. It would be most interesting to see a match between the well-known Thames *Ruby* and our Y.S.C. boats. Regattas are held at various points on the river, and there are, in addition, local regattas unconnected with clubs.

Once a year there is what is called an Ocean Match—that is, a match from Lowestoft to Harwich—on the Saturday before the regatta of the Royal Harwich Yacht Club. This is looked upon as a great adventure by the river boats, which tackle the sea under the cloud of canvas which is enough on the rivers. The trip to Harwich and back, and the excitement of bringing up in wide water, after the safety of a grassy margin, furnish food for many tales for the rest of the year. The *crux* of the thing is the passage round the bleak Orfordness, where the tidal race raises a cruel sea if there is any wind; the great mainsails with their long booms cannot easily be reefed under way.

One necessary rule upon these rivers sometimes causes trouble to strangers who are unaware of it. In the narrow reaches it is almost impossible to pass a boat to leeward, so if the overtaking boat can but get a few inches of her bowsprit overlapping to windward of the slower boat, the latter must give way and let the other pass to windward of her.

Visitors often get nervous when they see a wherry bearing down upon them, but there is no occasion for them to do so. If the boat-sailer observes the rule of the road, he may be sure that the wherryman will do so. The latter are a very civil and obliging class of men, taking a keen interest in the doings of smaller craft and yachts. It is usual, however, for the yachtsman to remember that he is on pleasure bent and the wherryman on business, and he therefore gives way sometimes when not compelled to do so, to save the wherryman from having to put his craft about. In return the wherryman will often, when tacking, keep his craft shooting in stays to let a yacht beat past him. The wherries are so long and take up so much of the river when beating to windward that it is often very difficult to pass them at all unless they make this concession.

The rowing boats which are hired by inexperienced people in great numbers at Oulton Broad are great sources of danger. The occupants generally go the wrong side of a sailing boat, and it is a wonder that accidents do not more often occur. Another source of difficulty are the anglers, who are very fond of mooring off the windward bank (where there is a quiet 'lee') well out in the channel, and perhaps at a 'scant' corner—that is, where the next reach being to windward the sailing vessels hug the corner as closely as possible in order to get a good shoot into the next reach and so save a tack. It does not do, however, to hug the corner too closely, as if it is at all shallow the way of the boat is deadened, though she may not actually touch the mud.

The 'putty,' as the black soft mud of the river bottom is locally termed, plays an important part in sailing on Norfolk rivers. It serves sometimes to help a vessel to windward. Thus a wherry might not be able to hug the weather shore or to lay close enough to sail along the middle of a reach, but if she drops to the leeward shore the pressure of water between her bows and the mud will 'shoulder' her off and stop her leeway, so that she can drag round a corner and save a tack. Some of the wherrymen will say that they could not put their craft aground if they would while sailing sideways along the mud. The deeper-draught yachts do not reap this advantage to any extent.

One of the things which make a yachtsman ask if life is worth living is to run hard on the putty. He gets out his quants and shoves; but the poles sink deep into the mud, and require more force to withdraw them than to drive them in. Those who know the river best seem to me to get oftenest aground, because they cut it too fine, and if their calculations are out by an inch or two they stick fast. The desperate struggles to get free are more amusing to other people than to the chief actors in the scene.

How blessed is the sight under such circumstances of a friendly steam-launch! I remember well one heart-breaking experience of my own in a 4-ton yacht which I was sailing single-handed. I got aground in the Bure at Yarmouth in the awful place known as the North End, and with a falling tide. I got off at last, after exerting myself until my heart beat frantically, my mouth was parched, and my eyes dim; then seizing a bottle I supposed to contain beer, I tossed half a tumblerful down my throat ere I found it was *vinegar*!

A good half of Oulton Broad is taken up by yachts lying at their moorings, which are buoys at a sufficient distance apart to give the boats room to swing. There appears to be some doubt as to what authority has the right to interfere, and so nothing is done; but a better plan would be to have proper mooring-places along the shore where yachts might moor in tier, a small charge being made for the privilege.

Below Oulton Broad is Lake Lothing, a tidal lake communicating with Lowestoft Harbour. A lock gives access to it. Lowestoft Harbour is a most convenient one, easily entered at all states of the tide. A large basin is reserved for the use of yachts during the summer months, and from its easy facilities for a day's sail at sea or a run up the Broads in the dinghy or steam-launch it is yearly becoming more popular with yachtsmen.

Leaving Oulton Broad and re-entering the Waveney, we find deep water right up to Beccles, which some sea-going trading vessels use as their port; but in the upper reaches the river is very narrow. It is, however, extremely pretty. Almost the last of the lateeners—the old *Ariel*—hails from Beccles.

On every Whit Monday there are great goings-on at Oulton. There is for one thing a regatta, and the Broad is literally crowded with boats; and for another it is the smacksman's yearly holiday, and he is very much in evidence both ashore and afloat. It is, however, but fair to say that the disgraceful scenes of drunkenness and fighting which formerly characterised Whit Monday are not so marked. The smacks' crews are now so well looked after by mission-ships afloat and Salvation Armies ashore that a most gratifying improvement has taken place in their manners and customs.

On a Sunday morning it is interesting to stroll round by the fish wharves in Lowestoft and listen to the outdoor services and services on smacks, and note the intense earnestness animating the rough-looking seamen who are the speakers, and the respect with which they are listened to even by well-known rowdies.

We leave Oulton Broad in company with several barges, and it is a race between us to get to Cantley, on the Yare, in time for a regatta of the Yare Sailing Club. Our wherry is gradually left behind by all the barges, but they have to wait at Herringfleet Bridge on account of a train, and as we come up just as the bridge is opened we are again on even terms with them, and are third out of six as the procession files along the narrow Haddiscoe Cut. At Reedham we meet the contingent of trading wherries which have started from Yarmouth with the flood, and several yachts on their way to Cantley, so that as we pass the picturesque village of Reedham and turn to windward up the broad reaches of the Yare the scene is a very animated one. At Cantley it is difficult to find a mooring-place, and the northward bank is lined with yachts for half a mile.

After the regatta we can sail up a most interesting part of the river, by the pretty ferries of Buckenham, Coldham Hall, and Surlingham, exploring Rockland and Surlingham Broads in the dinghy, and so on up to Norwich, just below which city the riverside scenery is most beautiful.

The rapidly increasing popularity of the Broads has given a great impetus to the trade of boat-letting, and the agencies are too numerous to mention. It may be useful, however, to say that, just as Loynes has made Wroxham a well-known starting point, so Bullen, of Oulton Broad, has done the same by the latter water. He owns or has the command of a large number of yachts and barges, some of which are suitable for Holland. At Norwich Messrs. Hart & Son, of Thorpe, have a similar agency, and the fishing-tackle makers and secretaries of yacht and sailing clubs keep lists of yachts to let. An advertisement in the *Eastern Daily Press* will elicit replies. Also, if any reader of this article chooses to write to me at Norwich, stating what kind of craft he

A START.

IN THE GLOAMING.

BIRDS OF A FEATHER.

wants, *and enclosing a stamp*, I will forward the letter to a suitable yacht agent. I will not, however, undertake to reply to any letter, because in one or two of my boys' books I promised to do so, and the consequence is I get a recurring crop of letters from boys in many parts of the world, which are excessively inconvenient to a busy man, although it would be unkind not to reply to them.

To sum up, the rivers of Norfolk and Suffolk, with Oulton, Wroxham, Barton, and Hickling Broads, are most excellent cruising grounds for small yachts and sailing boats; and as for racing, I really think that 'foreign' boats, if their owners would remember that light displacement and a gigantic spread of canvas are essentials, would have an excellent chance of lowering the pride of the local men. The power of quick turning is, of course, a *sine quâ non*.

Practically the chief interest of the Broads to visitors lies in their cruising advantages rather than the yacht racing to be obtained or seen; and it may serve a useful purpose to go more into detail as to the nature and cost of the craft to be hired for cruising, and to give itineraries of short cruises. While yachts can be hired at Norwich, Wroxham, Yarmouth, and Oulton Broad, the business is more scientifically carried on at Wroxham and Oulton than elsewhere, and the convenience of visitors more thoroughly consulted by the persons already named as catering for the public there. The class of craft is also rather different. At Oulton there are for comfort the usual barges and wherries, and for fast sailing the usual four to ten tonners of the smart type already described.

At Wroxham a fleet has been built consisting of vessels chiefly designed for ease of handling and comfort of camping and cruising, without any pretensions to racing speed. They are also of shallower draught than the Oulton boats, and have as a rule centreboards instead of the deep fixed keels of the others. It is, therefore, a matter of individual taste, and further comparisons would be invidious and perhaps unjust. With the deeper yachts it is customary to explore the shallower Broads in the jolly, while the smaller centreboards can be taken there. Those who chiefly love the science of sailing will prefer one sort, and those who delight most in exploring every lilied pool and in camping will prefer the other.

It is unfortunate, perhaps, to have to mention names in a book not intended to advertise persons whom it will probably survive, and it may seem unjust to other meritorious traders in the same line; but in the interest of the reader it has to be admitted that Bullen of Oulton and Loynes of Wroxham have taken too prominent a part in the exploration of the Broads for us to shirk mentioning them, any more than we can avoid naming the chief builders and designers.

None of Loynes' craft draw more than 3 ft. 6 in., and they range from twenty-three tons downwards. The largest will sleep four ladies and four gentlemen. The cost of hire is from 10*l.* to 12*l.* 10*s.* per week, according to the season, the height of the season being July and August. The hire includes two men, who are boarded by the hirers. This boarding of the men is rather a nuisance, but it is so much the custom that attempts to make the men board themselves, paying them increased wages, do not answer on the rivers. The 4-ton boats will sleep three, and the hire per week with attendant is 4*l.* 10*s.*, and without an attendant 3*l.* 15*s.* All household necessaries are supplied, and visitors need only bring rugs, towels, and provisions.

At Oulton, Bullen has a number of craft, ranging from a large pleasure wherry accommodating twelve persons, and let at 12*l.* per week, to the typical 10- and 5-tonners. He has also several of the barge yachts, now so fashionable. One of them, the *Ianthe*, has been twice to Holland, crossing the North Sea with safety, notwithstanding the shallow draught and large sail, with heavy mast set well forward. Bullen says that, for gentlemen who wish to get plenty of sailing, his 10-tonners are the best, but for ladies who require comfort and real pleasure the barge yachts or wherries are preferable.

A fortnight is required to do all the rivers and Broads properly, although much may be done in a week if the winds and weather are favourable.

With only a week to spare, it would be best to stick to the North river, or Bure. Thus, if starting from Oulton, Norwich, or Yarmouth, sail straight away to Wroxham, say two days' journey; on the third day back to Horning and up the coast to Barton Broad; fourth and fifth days up the Thurne to Potter Heigham, and do Hickling and Horsey Mere; sixth and seventh back to the starting point. Much depends, however, whether the object of the cruise is to loiter about and fish, or to sail and cover the ground. In the latter case the following is an itinerary I have carried out in a week.

Starting from Wroxham, Yarmouth can be reached the first day; second day up the Yare to Norwich; third day Norwich to Oulton Broad; fourth day up the Waveney to Beccles; fifth day Beccles to Yarmouth; sixth day Yarmouth to Potter Heigham; seventh day do Hickling Broad in the morning, and sail up to Wroxham in the evening.

A dead calm, or a combination of head wind and adverse tide, might, however, upset the plan by a day. It would be well, therefore, to stipulate in the hire that the yacht might be left short of its destination, to be taken back by the man.

Most people will take fishing tackle with them on a cruise on the Broads, but I hope everybody will leave their guns at home. The incessant popping away with shot-guns and pea-rifles is quite useless in results, very annoying to riparian owners, and very dangerous to the public. A camera is a much better weapon. Few districts offer better or more artistic subjects for the photographer's skill. A dark room is provided upon some of the pleasure wherries, and the tripod is almost as common an object on the marshes as the windmills.

COMMODORE STEVENS, FOUNDER OF THE
NEW YORK YACHT CLUB, 1844.

CHAPTER 6

Yachting in America
By Lewis Herreshoff

The degree of leisure and wealth, so essential to the development of yachting, was not realised by the citizens of the American seaboard until nearly one-third of this century had passed, and even then only a mere handful of nautically inclined sportsmen could spare time from the stern duties of country settling and fortune-hunting to follow in any measure their tastes in seeking pleasure on the alluring waters that flowed at their very feet.

It must not be supposed, however, that our ancestors took absolutely no pleasure in sailing; they had their pirogues and other small craft which were kept ostensibly for trade, but which served the double purpose of affording gain and pleasure.

In the traditions of my ancestry I learn of a small boat kept by one

R.Y.S. Cup,
won by the 'America,' 1851.

who used her to visit an island farm, whence he brought produce; and another would sail down the bay (Narragansett) for the love of it, but largely to meet and pilot up the tortuous channel his returning vessels from their coastwise trade.

No people were ever more advantageously situated for yachting, as to frequency of harbours and tempting conditions of water and weather, than are the dwellers on the eastern seaboard of North America. True that the season for yachting is from May to November only in the more northerly portions (north of Hampton Roads); but if a genuine yachtsman takes in five months of his beloved sport, it will be found that the remaining seven will be none too long to talk over the exploits of the past season, and prepare and plan for the coming.

As the character of water and weather that surround a locality has a direct bearing and influence on the form and rig of yacht, it is thought that a short sketch of the coast and its surrounding waters will be of interest.

The shores of Maine, as well as those of the British Provinces, present one of the most interesting fields for yachting that can be found in the whole continent of North America.

The deeply indented coastline and numerous outlying islands afford endless variety in scenery as well as in the surface of the water. Choice may be had between sheltered bays and the open sea.

The atmosphere during the first half of the yachting season is somewhat obscured by fogs, but after July the air is clear and bracing, with pleasant breezes from the sea during the day, and land winds during the night from north-west. Tidal currents are swift and the change of level is large, particularly on the shores of the provinces, ranging from 10 ft. or 12 ft. at Portland to far more as one sails eastward, whilst in the Bay of Fundy the rise and fall often reach 50 ft. Moving southerly, good yachting ground will be found from Cape Anne to Cape Cod; the waters thus included are fairly smooth in summer with harbours available every few miles, the shores being fully occupied by summer resorts where the visitors are, as a rule, yacht-owners, or deeply interested in aquatic sports.

In fact, this locality, embracing Massachusetts and Cape Cod Bays, with their many inlets and harbours (the chief being Boston Harbour), is the scene of more yacht racing and boat racing than any other sheet of water in America, as evidence of which some of the open regattas often start no fewer than 130 yachts and boats varying from 15 ft. to 50 ft. in length.

The winds off the coast of Massachusetts are moderate, twelve to fifteen miles an hour, easterly in the early part of the season, and south-west during the summer, with north-west in the autumn. Tidal currents are moderately strong, with range of level from 6 ft. to 10 ft., fogs are infrequent and short in duration. After rounding Cape Cod, Nantucket Sound is entered, a large semi-enclosed sheet of water full of sand shoals, amongst which the tide rushes to and fro with great speed, and whilst it is always traversed by yachts and trading vessels, it cannot be said to be strictly a favourable yachting ground, although sail-boats of shoal draught may be seen sailing for pleasure or fishing, which pastimes are enjoyed by the visitors that flock to the island of Nantucket and the adjacent mainland during the summer season. Fogs are very dense and frequent during nearly, the whole of the yachting season; the winds are more fresh than in Massachusetts Bay, and usually are from south to south-west, except in autumn when north or north-west may be expected.

From the foregoing we sail directly into Martha's Vineyard Sound, where strong winds and tidal currents are found, with fewer obstructions in way of shoals than in Nantucket Sound.

On the right of Martha's Vineyard Sound lie the Elizabeth Islands, some of which are picturesque. The nearest one to the mainland at Wood's Holl, called Naushon, is owned by several of the Forbes family, who for many years have been—and still are—most interested and intelligent patrons of yachting; and in one of the most beautiful little harbours on the north side of Naushon may be seen their fleet of yachts, lying at the safest of anchorages, often a dozen, some sailing vessels, and others steam.

Through many of the passages between the Elizabeth Islands access may be had to Buzzard's Bay, whose shores are everywhere dotted with the houses of summer dwellers, singly and in small villages; so it goes without saying that yachting; or more correctly boating, is the chief pastime, and no more agreeable field can be found for it, save perhaps the adjoining Bay of Narragansett, which without doubt is the paradise of yachtsmen.

The winds of Buzzard's Bay are fresh, even strong, and seeing that its expanse is unbroken by islands, it is often rough—perhaps too rough for pleasure-sailing in boats of the size usually seen; but in Narragansett Bay, though the winds are fresh its waters are not so rough, as its many islands prevent in a great measure the formation of waves uncomfortably large. Here, as in Buzzard's Bay, the tidal currents are moderate and change of level from 4 ft. to 6 ft.; fogs are less frequent than in Buzzard's Bay, and are never long in duration.

In the ocean, directly south from the mouth of Narragansett Bay, lies the most favoured spot on the entire coast for yacht racing, and for the last forty-five years it has been the scene of the most interesting races held away from the racing grounds at the approach to New York Bay; but for the best results of racing no place on the coast is equal to it, its winds are fresh and constant, its tidal currents are moderate and regular in their time and direction, so that little advantage can be had by one familiar with the locality over those who are not.

Few 'flukey' days can be remembered off Newport, and year after year the races there are becoming more and more important, as the waters in New York Harbour and its approaches become crowded, and as yachtsmen seek more open water than exists in the vicinity of New York. Twenty miles west of Narragansett Bay, Long Island Sound is entered; it is a glorious expanse of water, more than one hundred miles long and having an average width of fifteen miles; it is a thoroughfare for an enormous traffic, and in the season yachting and boating are most successfully and agreeably followed. Its tidal currents are generally moderate; in a few places they are swift; fogs are infrequent.

South of Long Island, and protected from the sea by a narrow spit of sand, are several shallow bays on which boating is largely followed; proximity to New York makes this shore sought for as a summer resort, and as boating is the only thing to be done in way of pastime, it is small wonder that so many boats are to be seen.

The harbour of New York with its approaches, and surrounding waters of the East and Hudson Rivers, are all splendid ground for sailing; but, seeing that traffic has so taken possession of nearly every available spot, yachting is forced into the more distant waters of the lower bay, and those parts of the Hudson less frequented by trading vessels. That part of the sea east and south of the Sandy Hook Lightship is a famous racing ground, and is destined to become even more so as competing yachts find the crowded waters of even the lower bay unsuitable for a just comparison of the speed of their vessels. The seacoast of New Jersey, like that of Long Island, has many inlets leading to sheltered, shallow bays, where may be seen numberless small yachts and sail-boats from 40 ft. in length downward to the most unpretentious cat-boat.

Delaware Bay and River are well adapted for yachting, but few large yachts are to be seen there, the dwellers in that section being content with boats and small sloop yachts.

Chesapeake Bay is a noble stretch of water that is almost unknown to the yachtsman. Its advantages are many, and in the near future it is to be hoped that the inhabitants along its shores will avail themselves of so fortunate an opportunity for sailing with more agreeable conditions than exist anywhere south of New York Bay.

Fogs are rare and tidal currents slight, except when induced by a constant high wind either up or down the bay; the rise and fall also from purely tidal causes are very small.

Hampton Roads and tributary waters are all well adapted for yachting and boating, but all their reputation as a yachting centre has yet to be made. For boats or small yachts there exists an inland watercourse through the Canal of the Dismal Swamp from Hampton Roads to the chain of sounds that skirt the sea-coast of the Carolinas, the waters of which are for the most part shallow, but well suited for small sailing craft, and more particularly for small steam yachts drawing less than 6 ft. of water. Albemarle, the most southerly of these sounds, is broad and deep, and well adapted for the navigation of yachts of the largest tonnage. Access to the ocean may be had at Hatteras Inlet, or still farther south for smaller vessels at Morehead City, where the navigator must take to the open sea if he would continue his voyage still farther to the south.

More than 200 miles of open ocean must be passed before Charleston, South Carolina, is reached, which port is well suited for small yachts and sail-boats, many of both classes being already in use as purely pleasure craft. Southward from Charleston is good ground for sail-boats and small steam yachts, numerous islands forming protected channels through which one may pass as far south as Savannah in Georgia. At Brunswick, in the same state, is a bay with a large area of protected water formed by the shelter of islands in which yachts of modest size thrive, but apart from convenience for shooting and fishing little use is made of any craft unless by the more venturesome tourists from the Northern States.

Florida is more the home of the steam yacht than of the sailing craft; you may ascend St. John's River for a distance of 260 miles in a steam yacht; at a few places where this beautiful stream swells into a lake boating may be pursued with no small degree of satisfaction. In the Bay of St. Augustine one finds many small yachts and a very agreeable place to sail them, a yacht club, and many evidences of civilisation in the way of opportunities for sport and pleasure-seeking.

There is also in Florida an extended system of inland navigation, which at present is but partly developed; soon, however, the entire length from north to south may be traversed in a vessel of moderate draught. Of course steam-yachting in such situations is by far the most satisfactory. The Gulf Coast in general does not present a very favourable field for yachting except under steam; in summer it is too hot, and in winter the winds are not steady nor well suited to the taste of the average yachtsman.

There is a deal of semi-protected water along the shores of Mississippi and Louisiana, and also some at widely separated bays in Texas, so that, with a few exceptions, yachting has not been established; at New Orleans, however, there is a yacht club that has for its field some of the large inland lakes where yachts of moderate size can be used with satisfaction.

The Pacific coast is not well designed for yachting on account of the extreme infrequency of harbours, and the generally rough sea found off the coast from Puget's Sound as far south as Point Conception. Puget's Sound is said to be a most favourable place for all marine sports, fishing and shooting as well as yachting; it is surely large enough, and also there is no lack of depth of water, but some time must elapse before the dwellers along its shores will find sufficient time and money to indulge in any pastime. The Bay of San Francisco is well adapted for yachting with vessels of moderate size, the winds are mostly from seaward and are strong, even more so in summer than in winter. There is a yacht club in San Francisco with a large membership and a goodly number of yachts, but most of their sailing is done inside. The scarcity of coal, and consequent large cost, seems to hinder the introduction of steam yachts, but a large number of naphtha launches are used with evident satisfaction.

South of Point Conception the conditions are far more favourable for yachting than in the north; but the want of good harbours, well distributed, will always serve as a block to the sport. It is true that, owing to the wonderfully quiet waters, a shelter is not essential, for a gale of dangerous force is a rarity from a direction that would render anchorage unsafe; but it is the unceasing swell of the ocean that renders landing difficult, and makes felt the absence of a harbour over at least two-thirds of the coast from Santa Barbara to San Diego.

Santa Barbara channel is a charming expanse of water which in summer is admirably calculated to afford great pleasure to the lover of yachting. Fogs are rare, winds steady and moderate in force from

S.S.W.; but in winter there is such an entire absence of wind that sailing is wholly impracticable.

On the islands that form the southerly limit of Santa Barbara channel may be found several pretty harbours with most interesting surroundings in scenery, as well as fine fishing and shooting. Forty miles eastward of the Santa Barbara Islands lies the beautiful island of Santa Katalina, where there is a fine harbour for small yachts; and as this island is somewhat removed from the influences of the ocean it may become, in the near future, a favourite centre for all aquatic sports. San Pedro, the port of Los Angeles, has what passes for a harbour, in which may be seen a few yachts and smaller pleasure craft, the embryo squadron of the Los Angeles Yacht Club. San Diego boasts of the finest harbour in South California, and, taken in connection with the neighbouring islands, it is truly a very attractive spot for yachting, which, as yet, has not made much advancement; but by the recent organisation of a yacht club it is hoped that the sport will become well established, and afford pleasure to the many tourists who flock to that blessed climate, where sun and air invite one to spend one's days in comfort and in love with all nature. It will be years, however, before yachting on the Pacific coast will have reached anything like the proportion that it has assumed in the east.

It will be easily seen that the Atlantic coast of the United States and British Provinces offers the greatest facilities for both boating and yachting. In almost every situation there can be found large areas of sheltered and semi-sheltered water specially suitable for small yachts and boats; and it is at once seen that all these expanses of protected water are easily accessible from the open ocean, where those disposed and properly provided may find as large a range of sailing or cruising as their fancy or means will admit. The very favourable distribution of wind, the infrequency of fogs, and the rarity of storms during the yachting season, all combine to make the conditions for general yachting as advantageous as possible—in fact, nothing more perfect could be found even if we search the world over.

From June 1 to the middle of September only one storm of any importance may be expected; it is from the north-east, lasting two days, and occurs about August 20. About the middle of September a gale from the south-east is expected, but it is short in duration, not over eight hours, and if other storms come from the east or north-east, they are always foretold two or more days in advance by the Weather Bureau, prompt notice of them being published in every daily paper in the section threatened; north-east, east, north-west storms are always heralded by the same office; the south-east storms are the only ones that come unforetold. Thunderstorms and sudden squalls are becoming more and more infrequent on the northern and middle Atlantic coast. It is thought that the settling of the country, with its network of railways and telephonic wires, exerts a dispersing influence on all local electrical storms; but, be that as it may, they are now little felt where once they were of almost daily occurrence in the height of summer.

The generally quiet character of the water available for yachting, and the prevailing pleasant weather with moderate winds, combined to influence the form and rig of boats and yachts in use for the first half of this century, and if one carefully examines the situation, it will be found that the style of pleasure craft chiefly in vogue was well adapted to the requirements of the then yachtsman; but as years passed, new influences were at work and new requirements sought for, so that to-day the build and rig of boats and yachts used by our ancestry seem likely to disappear, save perhaps in certain localities where the shoal draught must be considered, as along the south shore of Long Island, the coast of New Jersey, and in much of the waters of the Southern States.

In illustration of the effect that winds and waters have on the form and rig of yachts, one need only compare the yachts in England with those in America. The conditions of weather and sea are as different in the two countries as are their vessels; but it must also be admitted that the rules of time allowance arranged to equalise yachts of different size in racing has also had large influence in separating so widely the form of yachts in the two countries, a difference which, under the newest order of rules and intercourse, is rapidly disappearing.

The history of yachting in America begins with the brilliant career of the Stevens brothers, notably the elder of the three, John C., whose life and labour seem to have been devoted to the development of the best type of vessel for pleasure. He may justly be called the father of yachting. The Stevenses lived in Hoboken, and in the early years of this century to cross the Hudson to New York by the established ferry boat was slow and uncertain, so naturally the Stevens brothers had each his own boat, and crossed the river by his own skill, either by sail or oar. Through ferrying themselves over the river, they became very skilful in the management of boats, and the love and talent thus awakened were held by them all their lives.

The first craft of any importance owned by John C. Stevens was

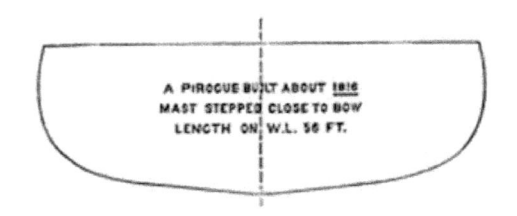

'Trouble,' midship section.

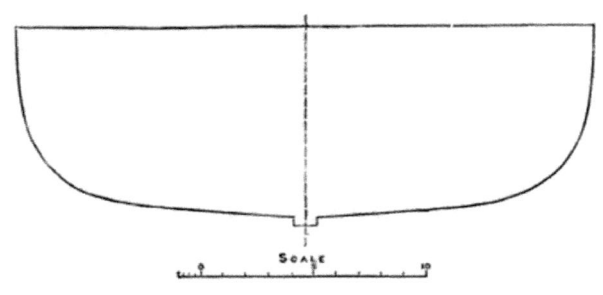

'Maria,' sloop, 1846, midship section.

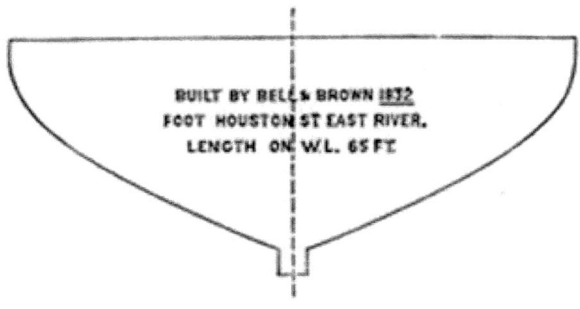

'Wave,' midship section.

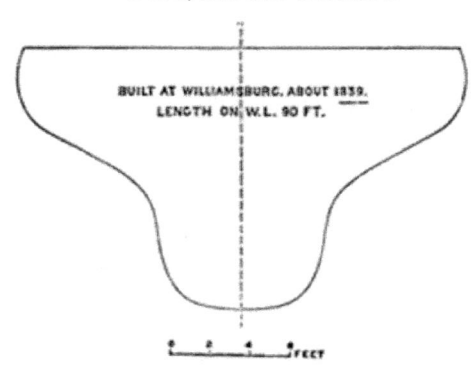

'Onkahya,' midship section.

Diver, built in 1809, but of her there exists no record, save the fact of her being 20 ft. long. He built *Trouble*, in 1816; she was a pirogue, a style of vessel much in vogue in those days, 56 ft. long, two masts, one in the extreme bow, the other a little aft of amidships, with no bowsprit or jib. Her mid-section is here shown; she was wide and flat, with a round, full bow, and was said to be very fast for that class of craft; she has the honour of being the first yacht in America, and without doubt was a comfortable seaworthy vessel, but was soon put aside by her progressive master, who in the following fifteen years built and owned several craft of various sizes and rig.

It seems to have been a passion of Mr. Stevens to experiment. Indeed, this striving for something better was the key-note of his life, and a boon to yachting, since the science of naval architecture made very rapid progress during his career; for he died having carried the form of vessels from their rude model in early times to the vastly improved *Maria*, which famous yacht stands as a monument to his skill and determination to improve.

One of the fancies of Mr. Stevens was a catamaran, or a boat with two hulls. She was built in 1820 and named *Double Trouble*. The sides of the hulls toward the centre were parallel. But the old *Trouble* beat her easily, and she was laid aside to make room for something new and better. In 1832 Mr. Stevens built the schooner *Wave*; she was 65 ft. water-line and proved to be fast. She visited Boston in 1835 and 1836, and beat all yachts she found there.

Wave was sold to the United States Government in 1838, and used in the Revenue Marine Service. Her section is here given.

About this same date other yachts began to appear. The schooner *Dream* was built in New York by Webb & Allen; her length was 47 ft. over all, and she was a well-known yacht, until 1855, when she was lost near Bridgeport, Connecticut. The schooner *Sylph* was built in Boston in 1833 by Wetmore & Holbrook, for John P. Cushing, and finally sold to R. B. Forbes. After he sold *Wave*, Mr. Stevens brought out *Onkahya*, a schooner, in 1839; her tonnage was 250, length on water-line 91 ft.

Onkahya was a departure from other craft in many respects, some of which may be seen in her mid-section here shown. Her keel was of iron, which gave her unusual stability, and her bow was long and fine to a degree. She was but a moderate success as a racer, but was a very good cruiser, having made a voyage to the West Indies. She was sold to the United States Government in 1843.

After five years' service under the Revenue Marine flag, *Onkahya* was lost on the Caicos Reefs, West Indies.

Mr. Stevens next appeared on board *Gimcrack*, a schooner built in June, 1844, by William Capes, of Hoboken, and designed by George Steers. She was about 51 ft. extreme length, and 49 ft. on water-line, 13 ft. 6 in. beam, 5 ft. 2 in. deep, and drew 7½ ft. of water. Her chief peculiarity was a sort of fixed centreboard of heavy plate-iron—in short, like the fin-keel of today, only without being loaded with lead at the lower edge. This fin was 4 ft. wide, and 12 ft. or 15 ft. long.

Gimcrack was not wholly satisfactory to her owner, but served for three years; several years later she was broken up at Oyster Bay, Long Island. No model or drawings of her now exist.

The little cabin of *Gimcrack* has the honour of being the birthplace of the New York Yacht Club, an organisation that has done vastly more than anything else to foster a love of yachting, and to promote progress in naval architecture.

On its roll is entered the name of every noted yachtsman in America, and every important yacht has at one time or another been the property of one or more of its members. The story of the formation of the New York Yacht Club is best told by reading the minutes of the first important meeting, and as it has such a direct bearing on the progress of yachting, it is here given in full:—

MINUTES OF THE NEW YORK YACHT CLUB

On board of the *Gimcrack*, off the Battery (New York Harbour), July 30, 1844, 5.30 p.m.

According to previous notice, the following gentlemen assembled for the purpose of organising a Yacht Club, *viz.*: John C. Stevens, Hamilton Wilkes, William Edgar, John C. Jay, George L. Schuyler, Louis A. Depaw, George B. Rollins, James M. Waterbury, James Rogers, and on motion it was resolved to form a Yacht Club. On motion it was resolved that the title of the club be The New York Yacht Club. On motion it was resolved that the gentlemen present be the original members of the club. On motion it was resolved that John C. Stevens be the commodore of the club.

On motion it was resolved that a committee of five be appointed by the commodore to report rules and regulations for the government of the club. The following gentlemen were appointed, *viz.*: John C. Stevens, George L. Schuyler, John C.

Jay, Hamilton Wilkes, and Captain Rogers. On motion it was resolved that the club make a cruise to Newport, Rhode Island, under command of the commodore. The following yachts were represented at this meeting, *viz.*: *Gimcrack*, John C. Stevens; *Spray*, Hamilton Wilkes; *Cygnet*, William Edgar; *La Coquille*, John C. Jay; *Dream*, George L. Schuyler; *Mist*, Louis A. Depaw; *Minna*, George B. Rollins; *Adda*, Captain Rogers. After appointing Friday, August 2, at 9 a.m., the time for sailing on the cruise, the meeting adjourned.

John C. Jay, Recording Secretary.

The New York Yacht Club soon showed vitality, energy, and power, as the following reports of the first matches will clearly show what amateur and Corinthian crews could do in those days. 'None but members to sail and handle their yachts' was the rule, and Commodore Stevens's big sloop *Maria*, a winner in 1848, was 160 tons.

First Amateur Corinthian Regatta of the New York Yacht Club
October 6, 1846

For a cup subscribed for by members of the New York Yacht Club. None but members to sail and handle their yachts. The allowance of time on this occasion was reduced to 45 seconds per ton Custom House measurement.

The course was from a stake boat (the *Gimcrack*) anchored off the Club House, Elysian Fields; thence to and around a stake boat anchored off Fort Washington Point; thence to and around a stake boat anchored in the Narrows (off Fort Hamilton), turning it from the eastward and return to the place of starting. Whole distance 40 miles.

Second Amateur Corinthian Regatta of the New York Yacht Club
October 12, 1847
Over The New York Yacht Club Course

By a resolution passed at the second general meeting, July 13, 1847, it was decided by members, not yacht-owners, that on the second Tuesday in October, a regatta should take place for a prize made by their subscription, the yachts to be manned and sailed exclusively by members, allowing each boat 'yacht' a pilot.

The following gentlemen were appointed a committee to regulate

'Gimcrack.'
Mr. J. Stevens, 1844.

OCTOBER 6, 1846.—
CORINTHIAN REGATTA OF NEW YORK YACHT CLUB—CLUB COURSE ENTRIES AND RECORD OF THE REGATTA

Rig	Name	Owner	Tonnage	Start	S. Island	L. Island	S.W. Spit	House Stake Boat
Schooner	Gimcrack	John C. Stevens	25	10.00.00	12.19.13	—	—	—
"	Dream	George L. Schuyler	28	10.02.00	—	—	—	—
"	Spray	Hamilton Wilkes	37	10.04.00	12.04.55	12.12.10	—	4.28.28
"	Cygnet	John R. Snydam	45	10.06.00	12.06.35	12.13.52	—	—
Sloop	Una	J. M. Waterbury	59	10.08.00	11.40.11	11.47.00	1.28.43	3.43.40
Schooner	Siren	W. E. Miller	72	10.10.00	12.07.02	12.14.22	2.02.05	4.23.00
"	Cornelia	William Edgar	94	10.12.00	12.21.11	—	—	—

The *Dream*, *Gimcrack*, *Cygnet*, and *Cornelia* did not finish. The *Una* won the prize—a Silver Cup. Wind fresh from the West during the race.

October 12, 1847.—
Corinthian Regatta of New York Yacht Club—Club Course Entries and Record of the Regatta

Rig	Name	Owner	Ton	Start	Fort Washington Point	Narrow	Finish	Actual Time
Sloop	Maria	John C. Stevens	160	10.58.20	11.54.00	2.38.10	4.02.45	5.04.25
"	Lancet	George B. Rollins	20	10.00.00	10.54.00	—	4.36.09	6.36.09
Schooner	Siren	W. E. Miller	72	10.21.40	11.17.00	2.48.55	4.24.20	6.02.40
"	Cygnet	D. L. Snydam	45	10.10.45	11.05.00	2.38.00	4.26.15	6.15.30
"	Spray	Hamilton Wilkes	37	10.07.05	11.01.00	2.40.00	4.28.31	6.21.26
"	La Coquille	John C. Jay	27	10.02.35	10.58.00	2.45.00	4.29.12	6.26.27

This was *Maria*'s first race.

The tide at starting was at the last of the flood, tide turning ebb at 12 m. Wind strong from S.W. The *Maria* won, beating the *Siren*.

the regatta, with full power to postpone if the weather should prove unfavourable.

 Edward Ceuter.
 Lewis M. Rutherfurd.
 Nathaniel P. Hossack.

SAILING COMMITTEE:
 George L. Schuyler
 Andrew Foster, Jun
 William E. Laight

 The formation of the New York Yacht Club was followed by a rapid augmentation of the yachting fleet, and general interest seemed to be suddenly awakened in the sport. The attention of designers and builders became centred on pleasure craft, so that in the first five years of the life of the club several new builders and designers came into public notice. Foremost among them was George Steers, who showed marked ability in designing; indeed, it is not too much to say that his ideas in naval architecture and construction were a guide in the art for many years. Some of his best known yachts of this period were *La Coquille*, schooner, 1842, length 44 ft. 6 in.; *Cygnet*, schooner, 53 ft. 2 in., 1844; *Cornelia*, schooner, 1847, length over all 74 ft.; *Gimcrack*, before mentioned.

 In 1846 Winde & Clinckard, of New York, built *Coquette*, schooner, length 66 ft.; she made the passage from Boston to New York in 29 hrs., and returned in 28 hrs. *Brenda*, schooner, was turned out by the same builders in 1845; she was 48 ft. over all. She visited Bermuda in May 1849, and on the 14th of that month sailed there a match with *Pearl*, beating her 55 secs., this being the first international race found in any American record.

 The schooner *Spray*, was built by Brown & Bell, of New York, in 1844; her length was 49 ft. 8 in. over all.

 Commodore Stevens contented himself with *Gimcrack* for three years, during which time he was evidently accumulating strength for a great stroke in yachting, which in the autumn of 1847 culminated in his last and by far the most famous yacht, the sloop *Maria*, the largest pleasure craft of her class ever built in this or any country. George Steers assisted the Commodore in designing, and during the winter of 1847 and 1848 she was built by William Capes in Hoboken. Sloop *Maria* was originally 92 ft. long on water-line, she had the full round entrance and gradually tapering after body, a style popularly known

Model Room of New York Yacht Club.

as the 'cod head and mackerel tail,' a form that prevailed generally in all vessels up to about this date. After two years Commodore Stevens became tired of the full round bow of *Maria*, and in 1850 she was lengthened forward, so that she became 110 ft. on water-line, and 116 ft. on deck.

Maria was such a departure from accepted rules, and became so well known in all yachting circles, that a full description of her is deemed worthy of record in these pages.

Her beam was 26 ft. 6 in., 8 ft. 3 in. depth of hold, 5 ft. 2 in., draught of water at stern, and 8 in. forward. She had two centreboards, a small one near the stern to aid in steering, and the large board 24 ft. long in the usual position; this main board was of iron and lead, weighing over seven tons. When first launched *Maria's* centreboard was not pivoted, but worked in a vertical line, both ends being dropped to the same depth.

The great weight of this board was partly balanced by two large spiral springs, one at either end, which were extended when the board was lowered. Length of mast 92 ft., 2 ft. 8 in. in diameter at deck, and 1 ft. 11 in. at hounds; it was a hollow spar, being bored out, for the first 20 ft. having a hole 12 in. in diameter; for the next 20 ft. 10 in., and above that the bore was 7 in. Her main boom was 95 ft. long, 2 ft. 7 in. in diameter and 2 ft. 4 in. at the slings; it was built up with staves like a barrel, inside it was a system of truss-work with long tension-rods reaching nearly to the ends. Length of main gaff 61 ft., with a diameter of 2 ft. 2 in. Her bowsprit had an extreme length of 38 ft., with a diameter of 2 ft.; it entered the hull of the yacht below deck, leaving the deck space above all free and clear; there was also a jibboom which materially lengthened the bowsprit, so that the point where the jib-stay was attached was 70 ft. from the mast.

Area of mainsail, 5,790 sq. ft.; the cloths of this were placed parallel to the boom, the bighting running fore and aft instead of vertically as usual. It was thought by the commodore and his brothers Robert and Edward, who were equally interested with him in the ownership of the yacht, that a sail thus constructed offered less opposition to the passage of wind than a sail made in the usual style; but the plan was open to objections, so that it never became popular. Her jib presented 2,100 ft. of surface, leach 69 ft.; its foot, 70 ft.; foot of mainsail, 94 ft.; hoist, 66 ft.; head, 60 ft.; and leach, 110 ft. *Maria* had a working topsail, but it was rarely set.

Commodore Stevens with his famous craft took part in many races and matches during the first six years of *Maria's* life; she usually beat all her competitors, the few failures she suffered being attributable to the failure of one or other of some new devices in her rigging or fittings; for her owners were for ever trying something new in way of experiment.

At one time the ballast of *Maria* was disposed in a layer on the outside of her planking, the lead being about 2 in. thick at the rabbit and tapering to a half-inch about half-way out to the turn of the bilge. *Maria* had several test matches with the schooner *America*, just before that vessel departed on her eventful voyage to England in 1851; *Maria* usually beat the schooner easily, particularly in smooth sea and moderate wind. It is related of *Maria* that on one day when conditions favoured her she sailed three times completely around *America* in a comparatively short distance, which performance forms the subject of a spirited picture here given.

After the death of Commodore Stevens, and when *Maria* was the property of his brother Edward, the yacht was lengthened about 6 ft. or 7 ft., and finally rigged as a schooner. She was then sold and used in the fruit trade, making voyages to the coast of Honduras; but in October 1870, as she was bound to New York with a load of cocoa-nuts, a storm overtook her when in the vicinity of Hatteras, in which she succumbed, and vessel and crew were never more heard of.

James Waterbury was also a prominent yachtsman in those early days. The sloop *Una* was built for him in 1847 by George Steers, 64 ft. long, lengthened in 1851 to 68 ft., and again in 1854 to 71 ft. 9 in.; tonnage, 70. The sloop *Julia* was built for Mr. Waterbury in 1854 by George Steers, and designed by Nelson Spratt; her length was 78 ft. 8 in. extreme, and 70 ft. on water-line. This wonderful vessel seems to have sprung into existence by chance; her designer was a quiet, obscure man, whose ideas of naval architecture appear to have been far in advance of his time.

Julia was one of the handsomest yachts of her day, and the fastest when proper allowance for difference of size was made. It is true that *Maria* nearly always beat her, but in those days the system of allowance favoured the larger vessel, which error exists in allowance tables in use at present. The sloop *Rebecca* was built in 1855 by William Tooker, a brother-in-law of George Steers, for J. G. van Pelt. Her length over all was 72 ft., 65 ft. on water-line, 19 ft. 2 in. beam, 5 ft. 8 in. deep, 6 ft. 3 in. draught, 3297.62 sq. ft. of sail spread, tonnage 77.6. The schooner '*America*,' the most famous yacht of her day, was built

'Black Maria,' Sloop, Beating 'America,' Schooner, in Test Race, New York, 1850. 132 tons. Built 1848. (Commodore Stevens, N.Y.Y.C.)

by George Steers and W. H. Brown, designed and superintended by George Steers, launched May 3, 1851, for John C. Stevens, Hamilton Wilkes, George L. Schuyler, James Hamilton, J. Beekman Finlay, and Edward A. Stevens, brother of Commodore Stevens.

The *America* was 94 ft. long on deck, 83 ft. water-line, 22 ft. 6 in. beam, 9 ft. 3 in. depth of hold, 11 ft. 6 in. draught; her mainmast was 81 ft. long, 76 ft. 6 in. foremast, her main topmast was 33 ft. 6 in. long, no foretopmast, 58 ft. main boom, no fore boom, 28 ft. main gaff, 24 ft. fore gaff, 17 ft. bowsprit outboard, 170 tonnage. After *America* finished her brilliant career in England in August 1851, she was sold there to Lord De Blaquiere and remained in foreign waters for ten years; she then fell into the hands of the Southern Confederacy, and when the U.S.S. *Ottawa* visited Florida in 1862 *America* was found sunk in St. John's River. She was raised, pumped out, and sent to Port Royal, thence to Annapolis, Maryland, where she remained in Government service for several years, and was finally sold to General B. F. Butler. She still remains in yachting service as staunch as ever, and by no means the least handsome nor slowest of the national pleasure fleet; in fact, she is to day a monument to the skill of her designer and excellent thoroughness of her builder.

The racing of the *America* in England 42 years ago has without doubt had more influence, directly and indirectly, on the yachting world than the performance of any other yacht, and both countries concerned owe to her designer and owners a debt of gratitude that will remain uncancelled for generations; for it has been the means of bringing the two yachting nations together in many friendly contests, resulting not only in marked modifications in the form and rig of the yachts of both countries, but the social intercourse begun so many years ago has continued and increased greatly to the benefit of yachting, and has led to a more complete union of all interested in the promotion of close international relations.

In 1845 Robert and Isaac Fish (brothers) established themselves in New York as builders and designers of yachts and other vessels. On the death of Isaac, 'Bob Fish' continued the business and turned out many well-known yachts, sloops at first and later schooners. His yachts were generally successful as racers, and next to Steers his designs were thought to be best; but whilst his yachts were fast and usually successful in other respects, their form was not destined to live, for the system of shoal draught and wide beam is now obsolete, except in waters where the conditions require special features. Fish showed no

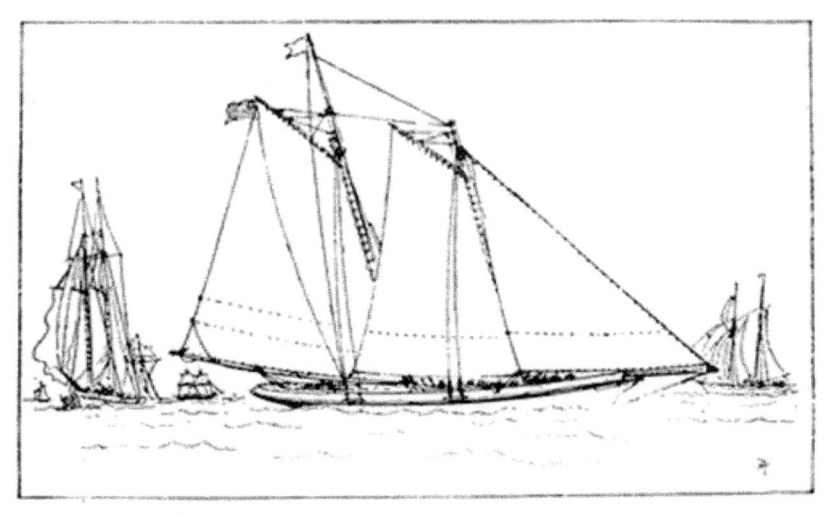

'AMERICA,' 170 TONS, 1851 (COMMODORE STEVENS, N.Y.Y.C.)

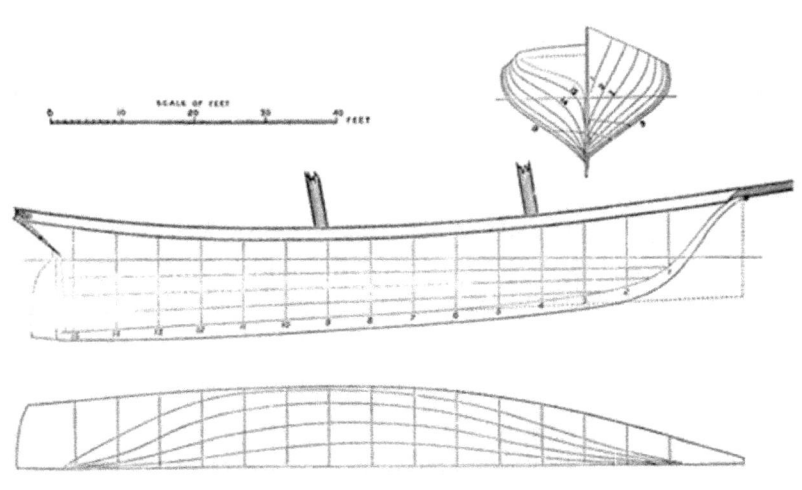

LINES AND MIDSHIP SECTION OF THE 'AMERICA,' LAUNCHED MAY 1, 1851.

tendency to change the model then in vogue, his last yacht being just like the earlier in form and in general proportions.

Mr. Fish had great skill in 'tuning up' a yacht for racing, and many craft owe their success to his ability.

A few of the best-known yachts by Mr. Fish were, sloop *Newburg*, 1845; sloop *Undine*, sloop *Gertrude*, 1852; *Victoria*, 1856—this last became a blockade-runner in 1863, was captured, sold, and afterwards wrecked. Sloop *Eva*, 1866, afterwards a schooner, was capsized and lost on Charleston Bar. *Meteor*, schooner, 1869, a large and fine vessel, was lost the same year on Cape Bonne, whilst cruising in the Mediterranean. Schooners *Wanderer* and *Enchantress* were both very successful vessels, and fast in their day. In 1869 Mr. Fish remodelled *Sappho*, giving her wholly new lines and changing essentially her proportions, vastly improving the sailing qualities of the yacht, as was afterward proved by her successes in foreign waters as a racer. Another designer and builder of about this period was D. D. Mallory, of Noank, Connecticut; he brought out many fast and otherwise successful sloops, but it can be said of him, as of Robert Fish, that his tendencies in designing were not in a direction toward improvement; the same wide, flat, shoal-draught vessels were adhered to from first to last.

Some of Mallory's best-known yachts were *Mystic*, 1856, *Richmond*, 1857, *Mallory*, 1858, *Haswell*, 1858, *Plover*, 1859, *Zouave*, 1861. In 1864 the Herreshoffs began yacht building and designing in Bristol, Rhode Island. They had inherited tendencies toward everything connected with marine affairs, and having been born and bred on the shore of Narragansett Bay, their attention was early turned to boating, and later to yachting. From the outset the Herreshoffs departed from old forms, and struck out for something better than the 'skimming-dish,' as the popular model was truly but irreverently called. Some of the best known yachts built in Bristol were *Kelpie*, 1864, *Qui Vive*, 1864, *Clytie*, 1865, *Sadie*, 1867, *Orion*, 1870, the schooners *Ianthe*, *Triton*, *Faustine*,' and a great number of smaller craft of either sloop or cat rig.

In 1872 Mr. N. G. Herreshoff, the younger of the two brothers connected in yacht-building, and the designer, brought out the *Shadow*, 37 ft. over all, a sloop whose fame is still fresh in the mind of every yachtsman in America. She has won more races than any American yacht, and even today can give the best of the new yachts a very hard pull. The *Shadow* has the honour of being the first yacht built on what was afterwards known as the 'compromise model'; that is, a design that combines the beam of the American with the depth of the English

'Shadow,' 1872.

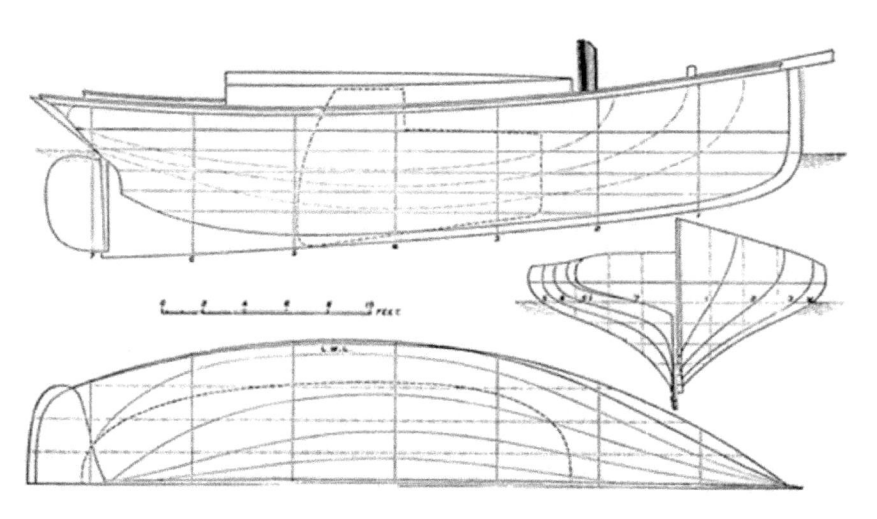

Lines and midship section of the 'Shadow,'
designed by N. Herreshoff, 1872.

yacht. From her earliest performance *Shadow* showed speed and admirable qualities, but strangely enough, her form was not reproduced nor copied for nearly fifteen years, which may be accounted for in a measure by her designer having deserted the yachting field and turned his attention to steam engineering and to the designing of steam yachts. Mr. Herreshoff, however, did not wholly abandon his interest in sailing vessels, and occasionally put forth a sailing yacht, or more properly boat, one of which, the cat-boat *Gleam*, was very famous for speed both in native and English waters.

Another well-known cat was *Alice*, 1879; she took twelve first prizes out of eleven starts during her first year, in one race there having been two prizes offered. During the ten years from 1860 to 1870, covering the period of the War of the Rebellion, yachting interests were at a low ebb, and comparatively few pleasure vessels of any kind were built.

A change presently came over the fancy of yachtsmen, which was shown by a feeling against large sloops, mostly on account of their being difficult in management. The long boom is always an element of danger and inconvenience, so that during the period alluded to many of the old sloops were rigged into schooners, and toward the latter part of the decade schooners became more successful and popular on account of their ease in handling, and their being far better adapted for ocean cruising, which at that time became more and more general with the owners of pleasure craft. The coming of *Cambria* in 1870, and later of *Livonia*, seemed to act as a stimulant in the construction of schooners, and many were built and found to be very satisfactory and successful.

A list of the best known and most successful schooners that existed about 1870 and 1871 would include:—*Phantom*, 123 tons; *Maggie*, 132 tons; *Sylvie*, 106 tons; *Tidal Wave*, 153 tons; *Madeleine*, 148 tons; *Rambler*, 160 tons; *Idler*, 133 tons; *Dauntless*, 268 tons; *Magic*, 97 tons; *Fleetwing*, 206 tons; *Palmer*, 194 tons; *Alice*, 83 tons; *Fleur de Lys*, 92 tons; *Eva*, 81 tons; *Restless*, 95 tons; *Josephine*, 143 tons; *Calypso*, 109 tons; *Widgeon*, 105 tons; *Halcyon*, 121 tons; *Tarolenta*, 204 tons; *Alarm*, 225 tons; *Vesta*, 201 tons; *Wanderer*, 187 tons; *Columbia*, 206 tons; *Sappho*, 310 tons; *Enchantress*, 277 tons; *Mohawk*, launched in June, 1875, 326 tons; *Ambassadress*, 1877, 431 tons; *Intrepid*, 1878, 276 tons; *Grayling*, 1883, 91 ft. long, 136 tons, designed by Philip Elsworth, remodelled by Burgess in 1888; *Montauk*, Elsworth designer, 1882, 193 tons; *Sea Fox*, 1888, designed and owned by A. Cass Canfield, 204 tons.

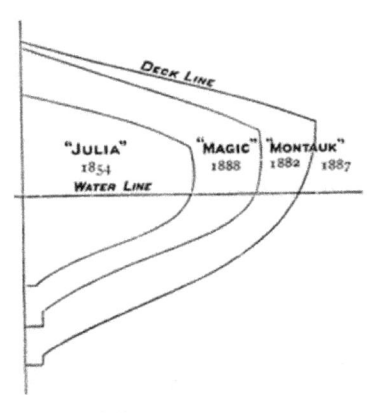

MIDSHIP SECTIONS.

Some very fast sloops appeared after 1860, but in less number than before that date. The following list covers those that were best known and noted for speed:—the *Mannersing*, built by David Kirby, Rye, New York, launched June 11, 1858, 58 ft. over all, 54 ft. 4 in. length on water-line, 18 ft. beam, 5 ft. 1 in. deep, and 4 ft. draught, centreboard, 24 tons; she was very fast, won three races out of five, was later owned in New Bedford, where she was wrecked. The *Mallory*, built by D. D. Mallory, 1858, 55 ft. over all, 51 ft. length on water-line, 18 ft. beam, 6 ft. deep, 5 ft. draught, a very handsome and fast vessel, 45 tons; she was lost at sea on a voyage from Havanna to New York, no survivors. The *Annie*, built by Albertson Brothers, Philadelphia, designed by Robert Fish, 1861, 53 ft. over all, 45 ft. 6 in. length on water-line, 18 ft. beam, 4 ft. 2 in. deep, 3 ft. 6 in. draught, centreboard.

Annie was first owned by Mr. Anson Livingston, who was the best amateur yachtsman of that day; he sailed *Annie* in five races and won them all; she was finally shipped to California on the deck of the vessel *Three Brothers*, and is now doing very satisfactory duty in the Bay of San Francisco. *Addie,* V. sloop, built by David Kirby for William Voorhis, 1867, 65 ft. 10 in. over all, 57 ft. length on water-line and 17 ft. beam, 5 ft. 4 in. deep, 4 ft. 4 in. draught, centreboard; she was but fairly fast, and underwent many changes. *Coming*, sloop, centreboard, designed by R. Fish, 1868, 62 ft. over all, 57 ft. length on water-line, 20 ft. 3 in. beam, 5 ft. 5 in. deep, 5 ft. draught, $53^{25}/_{95}$ tons; she was not at first fast, but later, when owned in Boston, she developed very good speed, and won several races.

Gracie, launched July 1868, was modelled and built by A. Polhemus

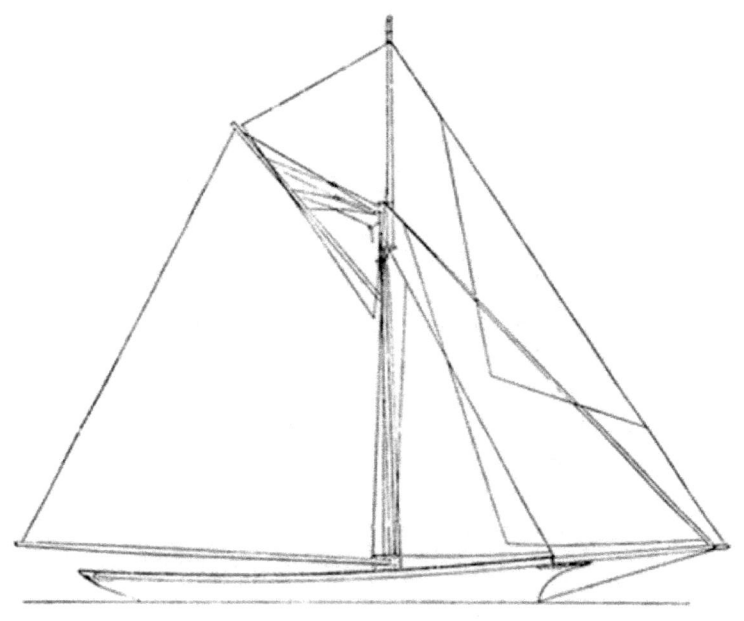

Sail plan of 'Gracie.'

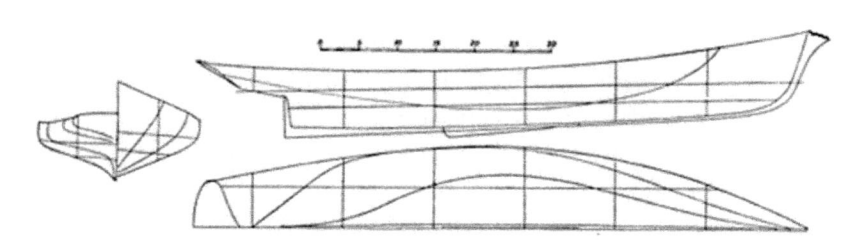

Lines and midship section of 'Gracie,' New York Yacht Club, launched July 1868.

at Nyack, New York. Her dimensions were then 60 ft. 3 in. over all, 58 ft. 6 in. water-line, 18 ft. 8 in. beam, 5 ft. 6 in. depth of hold, and 5 ft. draught, centreboard lengthened 2 ft. aft in 1869. In 1874 she was lengthened to 72 ft. 9 in. over all, 62 ft. water-line, 20 ft. 6 in. beam, 6 ft. 6 in. depth of hold, and 5 ft. 8 in. draught. In 1879 she was again rebuilt and altered by David Cool at City Island, and lengthened to about 80 ft. over all, with same water-line, a beam of 22 ft. 6 in., 7 ft. depth of hold, and 6 ft. 8 in. draught. Her mast was 74 ft. over all, topmast 36 ft., boom 63 ft., gaff 31 ft., whole length of bowsprit, of which 19 ft. is outboard. That was the dimension she had when she sailed with the *Bedouin*, the *Puritan*, and *Priscilla*. She was again altered in 1886, giving her 16 tons inside ballast, the rest on the keel.

When she was launched her tonnage, old measurement, was $54^{45}/_{95}$; today it is $102^{68}/_{95}$.

Such are the changes made in old yachts now-a-days. A new one every year is all the fashion; no alteration of originals, but new lines entirely.

The following were notable yachts:—

The sloop *Madeleine*, built by David Kirby, Rye, New York, and launched March, 1869, designed by J. Voorhis. Length over all 70 ft., 65 ft. length on water-line, 21 ft. beam, and 7 ft. 9 in. deep, 6 ft. 6 in. draught. In her original form she was a failure, but in 1870 was changed to a schooner. After alterations to her design of hull in 1871 and again in 1873, she became a fast yacht, and was chosen to defend the 'America' Cup against the *Countess of Dufferin* in 1876.

The cutter *Vindex*, built by Reanyson and Archibald in Chester, Pennsylvania, in 1871, designed jointly by A. Cary Smith and her owner, Robert Center. She is the first iron yacht built in this country, being a new departure in design as well as rig, though not famous for speed, and was not a racer; still she was an excellent vessel for cruising, and was particularly comfortable in beating to windward in strong weather. *Vindex* was 63 ft. overall, 56 ft. length on water-line, 17 ft. 4 in. beam, 7 ft. 6 in. deep, 8 ft. 10 in. draught, keel, 68 tons.

The sloop *Vixen*, centreboard, built by Albertson Bros., of Philadelphia, for Anson Livingston, designed by R. Fish, 1871, length over-all 52 ft., 44 ft. length on water-line, 16 ft. 6 in. beam, 6 ft. deep, 4 ft. 5 in. draught, 37 tons. Sailed thirty-seven races in the New York Yacht Club, and won eighteen first prizes.

The sloop *Fanny*, built by D. O. Richmond, in Mystic, Connecticut, 1873. Length over all 72 ft., 66 ft. length on water-line, 23 ft. 9

in. beam, 6 ft. 9 in. deep, 5 ft. draught, centreboard, 90 tons. She sailed twenty-six races in the New York Yacht Club, and won ten prizes. Sloop *Arrow*, built by David Kerby for Daniel Edgar, 1874, 66 ft. 6 in. over all, 61 ft. 8 in. length on water-line, 20 ft. 2 in. beam, 6 ft. 6 in. deep, 5 ft. 6 in. draught, $69^{64}/_{95}$ tons. Her career was short and creditable under the flag of the New York Yacht Club, she having, in her first year, entered five races and won four prizes. Sloop *Mischief*, designed by A. Cary Smith, built by the Harlan Hollingsworth Co., of Wilmington, Delaware, of iron, 1879; 67 ft. 6 in. over all, 61 ft. length on water-line, 19 ft. 11 in. beam, 7 ft. 9 in deep, 5 ft. 3 in. draught, $79^{27}/_{95}$ tons. *Mischief* was chosen to defend the 'America' Cup against *Atalanta* in 1881; she has sailed twenty-six races and won eleven prizes. The sloop *Pocahontas* was built by David Kirby for a syndicate. Launched in 1881, she was 71 ft. 11 in. She was intended to defend the 'America' Cup against *Atalanta*, but was badly beaten by *Mischief* and *Gracie*, and was retired, bearing the well-deserved sobriquet *Pokey*.

The sloop *Priscilla* was built of iron by the Harlan Hollingsworth Co., Wilmington, Delaware, and designed by A. Cary Smith for James G. Bennett and William Douglas, with a view to defend the 'America' Cup against *Genesta*, but the trial races showed '*Puritan*' to be the best yacht, 1885. She was sold in 1886 to A. Cass Canfield, who did all in his power to bring her into racing form, but improvements in designing set her hopelessly astern. *Priscilla* was 95 ft. 6 in. over all, 85 ft. 3 in. length on water-line, 22 ft. 6 in. beam, 8 ft. 9 in. deep, 8 ft. draught, centreboard. She was rigged into a schooner in 1888, but as a racer has never made a creditable record.

The sloop *Atlantic* was built by J. F. Mumm at Bay Ridge, Long Island, designed by Philip Elsworth for Latham A. Fish and others. She was built to defend the 'America' Cup against *Galatea*, but in the trial races she was beaten by both *Puritan* and *Mayflower*, and was retired. In 1887 she was sold, and changed into a schooner. Length over all 95 ft., 84 ft. 6 in. length on water-line, 23 ft. 2 in. beam, 9 ft. 6 in. deep, 9 ft. draught, centreboard, $159^{81}/_{95}$ tons.

Amongst designers of this period A. Cary Smith, whose name is mentioned above, stands unquestionably first in New York; his boats were and are to-day favourites amongst yachtsmen. It may be said of him that he displayed good sense in designing, and whilst his productions have not been famous as racers, still they are by no means the last to return; and when we consider qualities of staunchness, trustworthiness of working in stress of weather, and all except the extreme of speed, his yachts have not been excelled. In late years, beside yacht designing, Mr. Smith has taken up the modelling of fast screw and side-wheel steamers for special passenger coastwise traffic, in which line his skill has proved pre-eminent; vessels of his design are today, (as at time of first publication), the fastest afloat, and, like his other work, are marked by evidence of perfect understanding of the requirements; in short, he builds for the special use demanded, and therefore his labours are followed by success.

He first came before the public in 1871, when he jointly with Robert Center designed the iron cutter *Vindex*, at Chester, Pennsylvania. Then he built the schooner *Prospero*, and it was said that he laid down the lines from paper draughts without having a model, which was at that time a great fad. Then he designed and built the *Norna* and *Intrepid*, *Mina*, *Iroquois*, and *Zampa*; he has now designed and is superintending the building of two schooners, two ferry-boats, and one *Sound* steamer. He is also a fine marine artist, and has painted many noted yachts: the '*Sappho* for Commodore Douglas, and *Dauntless* for Commodore Bennett, the *Wanderer*, *Columbia*, the *Vindex*, and many other celebrated yachts.

About twenty years after the organisation of the New York Yacht Club, the Brooklyn Yacht Club was formed, and, soon following it, the Atlantic Yacht Club appeared. The new clubs were composed of men who owned generally a smaller class of yachts than that in the older club, but their members were interested and active, and races were held in early summer and in autumn, as well as a cruise to Newport in midsummer.

The desire for club formation was prevalent in Boston about the same time that the Brooklyn and Atlantic were started. The Boston Club was a promising institution, and called together a very respectable fleet of yachts; races and cruises were held, and much discussion on, and comparison of, designs were indulged in, to the decided advantage of the style of rig and general management of pleasure craft both in cruising and racing.

Early in the '70's there appeared a sudden disposition to form yachting clubs wherever a handful of boats could be found with owners living near each other. Club after club was started, many of which were short-lived, but in a little time the discordant elements were separated, and in all the clubs that now exist can be found a healthy social spirit, and a true disposition to advance the cause of yachting by the encouragement of Corinthian races and cruises. With the organi-

INTERNATIONAL RACE, 1886. 'GALATEA' (LIEUT. W. HENN, R.N.) PASSING SANDY HOOK LIGHTSHIP.

'PURITAN,' 1885 (GENERAL PAINE, N.Y.Y.C.)

sation of the Seawanhaka Yacht Club of New York, and the Eastern Yacht Club in Boston, the circle of really important clubs seems to be filled; but it is today easy to find as many as twenty-five or thirty clubs scattered from Maine to Florida, whose influence and example offer encouragement to the promotion of social intercourse and yacht designing.

About the year 1880 there began to arise amongst yachtsmen a feeling of uneasiness in respect of the design of yachts then in vogue, and for so many years in successful use.

It was the natural sequence of the gradual change that was being wrought in the surroundings of the class that seek pastimes, and with increase of leisure and wealth there came a desire for more seaworthy vessels; cruising had then become a settled thing, and a winter's cruise in southern waters was no unusual event. The ever-increasing communication with England, and consequent friendly intercourse, led directly to a desire on the part of many American yachtsmen to adopt a design—if not an exact copy—something more after the style of the English yacht.

The sad accident to the *Mohawk* also had its influence in unsettling our faith in the wide, flat model, and in 1881, when the *Madge* came in amongst us and showed what speed and weatherly qualities were present in the English design, and when also the cutter *Clara* drove home and clinched the work the *Madge* had begun, there then set in a regular *furore* amongst American designers and yachtsmen for something that was different from the then accepted forms of hull and styles of rig. In 1885, when it became necessary to defend the 'America' Cup against *Genesta*, it dawned on the yachting fraternity that a stroke must be made or the much-prized trophy would return to its native shores.

As usually happens in a country of progressive and intelligent people, the need calls forth its own means of cure, and Edward Burgess came to the front with a solution of the difficulty.

The new designer created nothing newer than a refinement of what existed in the sloop *Shadow*, built fourteen years before; but his clever combination of what is best in English and American designs gave us in the *Puritan* a vessel of which a designer might well be proud. The nation was satisfied with her performance, and grateful to her promulgator. The success of the cutter *Puritan* at once placed Mr. Burgess in advance of all American designers, and at the same time her form and rig were pronounced to be entirely successful, and from that moment the compromise model, as it was called, became established on what has proved most firm foundation; for it has not only revolutionised designing in America, but has had a very marked influence on the form of yachts in England, to their evident improvement—at least, it is natural to conclude that the best of two widely divergent results in yacht designing would lie in a middle position between the two.

In 1886 Burgess brought out the cutter *Mayflower* to meet *Galatea*, but the former yacht had small need of her superiority over *Puritan*, for *Mayflower* easily beat her opponent, and again the cup renewed its length of days on this side of the ocean.

In 1887 a most determined and well-planned movement was made by Scottish yachtsmen against the 'America' Cup. It was beyond question the most hard-fought battle in yachting that had occurred up to that date, but the hastily built *Volunteer*, also designed by Mr. Burgess, proved again that it was no easy task to carry off the cup that had then been fully naturalised by a residence in this land of thirty-six years.

The much-coveted cup now enjoyed a season of comparative rest, and year after year the new design became stronger and more securely established in the good opinion of American as well as English yachtsmen. The old question of centreboard *v.* keel still vexed the minds of those interested, and without doubt it will be long insoluble; but seeing that both have inalienable advantages, both types of construction will be used so long as a demand for yachts for varying conditions shall exist. Let it be admitted, however, that the newest design of keel yachts have their form below water so shaped as to very nearly resemble a centreboard, and the best shape of centreboard yachts have lateral resistance enough to do fairly good work to windward with their board drawn up; so in this particular, as in the general form of the hull, the best practice lies in combining both devices.

It must also be freely admitted that for the pure comfort and pleasure of sailing, for an appreciation of the inspiring motion, as well as for the comfort of increased deck and cabin room, nothing yet has exceeded the form of yacht now falling into disuse; and for the pleasure of sailing on the usually smooth waters of our sheltered bays, and wafted by the moderate breezes that are most frequently found, nothing can surpass for pure enjoyment the cat-boat of middle size, say about 25 ft. in length.

In 1888, the lovers of racing pinned their faith to the 30-foot class, and Burgess's fame rose higher and higher. He became the idol of his countrymen; a gift of 10,000 dollars indicated in some measure the

	Over all ft.	in.	W.L. ft.	in.	Beam ft.	in.	Draught ft.	in.	Tons	Date
Schooners:—										
Sachem, C.B.	105	0	86	6	23	5	8	5	—	1886
Marguerite, C.B.	97	0	79	9	21	0	11	0	65	1888
Quickstep, C.B.	83	0	65	0	20	0	7	0	54	1889
Cutters:—										
Volunteer, C.B.	104	0	85	9	23	2	10	0	—	1887
Mayflower, C.B.	96	9	85	7	23	5	10	0	—	1886
Puritan, C.B.	93	0	81	1	22	9	8	2	—	1885
Harpoon, C.B.	63	0	45	8	16	0	7	5	—	1891
Oweene, K.	62	0	45	8	13	3	11	0	23	1891
Gossoon, K.	53	0	39	6	12	0	9	2	—	1890
Hawk, C.B.	42	0	29	8	11	0	8	0	8	1890
Titania, C.B.	81	5	69	9	21	0	8	1	—	1887

C.B. Centreboard. K. Keel boats. W.L. Water-line.

'Volunteer'

'Gossoon,' keel boat, 1890. Designed by E. Burgess.

regard of his admiring friends, and really he deserved it: he was gentle and unassuming in manner, always courteous, and interested not only in his favourite profession, for unlike many gifted men he had more than one side. His love for and knowledge of natural history were scarcely less remarkable than his skill in the pursuit to which he devoted all his time during the last four years of his life. Mr. Burgess was for many years secretary of the Natural History Association of Boston, and resigned that position only when forced by pressure of business, consequent on the supervision of construction and fitting out of the many yachts that he yearly put forth. The appended list and dimensions of some of the best known and most successful of Mr. Edward Burgess's yachts is interesting as showing the change in chief proportions of the several yachts as compared with craft of the older design.

At this time the minds of our yachtsmen were sorely fretted by the performance of the cutter *Minerva* from Scotland. She laid all low who dared to wrestle with her, and not until the concentrated strength of our great designer was invoked could she be beaten. Even then the *Gossoon* could not always outstrip her, but the newly developed skill that she set in motion did not rest with the beating of *Minerva*, and today she would have no chance. Great strides were made in 1891, placing on an even footing the famous 46-foot class with yachts of 20 ft. superior length.

The year of 1891 was famous in bringing to a climax the development of the new idea; several new designers of merit appeared, notably Mr. William Gardiner of New York. His *Lyris* was a marvel of speed, and in her class she was well nigh invincible. 1891, indeed, opened with every nerve at the highest tension. One incident was the return of Mr. N. G. Herreshoff to the field of sail-yacht designing from which he had retired nineteen years before. To add to the interest and excitement, several designers contributed their skill in forming the famous class of 46-footers that rendered that season long remembered in yachting annals. Burgess had four, and Fife of Scotland, General Paine of Boston, Herreshoff of Bristol, and J. R. Maxwell of New York, each sent one yacht to the lists; so the new fleet represented, not only well-tried skill, but the work of several who were new in the field.

No one of the fleet of racers attracted so much interest and discussion as the cutter *Gloriana*, keel, the Herreshoff production; she was a decided departure from accepted forms, and destined to create a revolution in the science of naval architecture.

Criticism was poured upon *Gloriana* from every side—a very few thought she might sail moderately fast, but the majority who expressed their minds all united in declaring that nothing but abject failure could follow such an act of boldness as her model appeared to all but her designer, and perhaps her owner, Mr. E. D. Morgan.

Mr. Herreshoff, however, had built a small craft in the autumn of 1890 which was on much the same lines as *Gloriana*, except that the latter was a more complete representative of the new system; the trial boat of the previous autumn showed qualities in sailing and handling that gave the designer of *Gloriana* courage to proceed with a craft that called forth general condemnation before she was launched, a feeling which was quickly changed to astonishment and approval as soon as she was tried against other members of her class. The feature of *Gloriana* that marked her amongst all other yachts of that season was her abnormal overhang, showing a length over all of 70 ft. to that on water of 45 ft. 3 in.

This unusual degree of overhang gave an opportunity for the elongation of the body of the yacht, the fullness of the bilge being extended quite to the extreme point of the bow and stern.

The lines of *Gloriana's* entrance seemed almost bluff; but owing to the flare of that portion of the hull where contact is first made with the water, she appeared to roll it underneath her in a manner that disposed of the displacement more easily than by the nearly vertical sides of the usual wedge-shaped bow; at least if one could judge from the very slight and superficial character of the 'fuss' made around her bow, and also by the diminished effect of the wave under the lee bow to turn the yacht to windward (shown by her very easy helm), the inference is clear that this form of entrance does its work with less expended power than the old form. Another most advantageous result of the elongation of the body of *Gloriana* is the fact that when she plunges into rough water the part of the hull immersed by pitching presents lines that are just as long and easy as those shown when the yacht is sailing in smooth water.

This feature of *Gloriana's* performance gives her a higher rate of speed when compared with yachts of old type at times and conditions when the speed of all the old formed yachts suffer a marked diminution.

Besides the fact of a gain in speed with a given power, this form affords an increase of space below as well as on deck, and if the vastly increased buoyancy be considered, enabling the yacht to carry greater

'GLORIANA,' 1892. DESIGNED BY HERRESHOFF.

'WASP,' 1892. HERRESHOFF'S DESIGN.

spread of sail and carry it well, it will be seen what a really important improvement was demonstrated in *Gloriana*. She sailed during her maiden season eight races and took eight first prizes—a clean record—and with the exception of one race all were sailed with her largest club topsail set. Had she met with fairly rough water, as occurred on one of the races, her superior sailing qualities would have stood forth in even stronger contrast.

The yachting season of 1891 was clouded by the death of Mr. Burgess, which happened soon after the close of the June races, the result of which he never knew, as the defeat of his *Syanara* and *Mineola* was never told him. By his death, yachting received a blow from which it may not quickly recover; he enjoyed to the utmost the regard and gratitude of the public, the measure of which was shown by the voluntary creation of a fund for the education of his children.

As was predicted, the season of 1892 was not as exciting as the previous year; the 46-foot class received a new member in the cutter *Wasp*, from the Herreshoff hand; she was an advance on *Gloriana*—the same ideas more fully developed—the changes being in part suggested by or taken from the design of a new type of boat afterwards called 'fin-keel,' the first of which craft was launched and tried in the autumn of 1891; but of this more will be said later.

Wasp found as opponents her sister *Gloriana*, now passed from the hands of her original owner and from good management, and the reformed *Beatrix*, a centreboard cutter of 1891, now worked by the Adams Brothers, two of the most acute yachtsmen in the country, who so improved the *Harpoon*, as they renamed her, that for a time it was thought *Wasp* would be out-sailed; but except in the Goelet cup race off Newport, when *Wasp's* skipper made a capital blunder, the Herreshoff flyer made a record but little less clean than that of *Gloriana* in 1891. *Gloriana* took third place to the *Harpoon's* second, the result of poor handling, and in a degree to the constantly prevailing light winds in which all the races were sailed, light club topsails being carried in every instance.

A novel and interesting feature of the yachting season of 1892 was the 'fin-keel' boat, a production of N. G. Herreshoff. It will be seen from the cut below that some of the peculiarities of the *Gloriana* form are embodied in this singular craft—namely, the long overhang and the rounded elongation of the bilge to the extreme limits of the bow and stern.

The chief characteristic, however, is the fin, or in effect a fixed

Fin-keel and bulb.

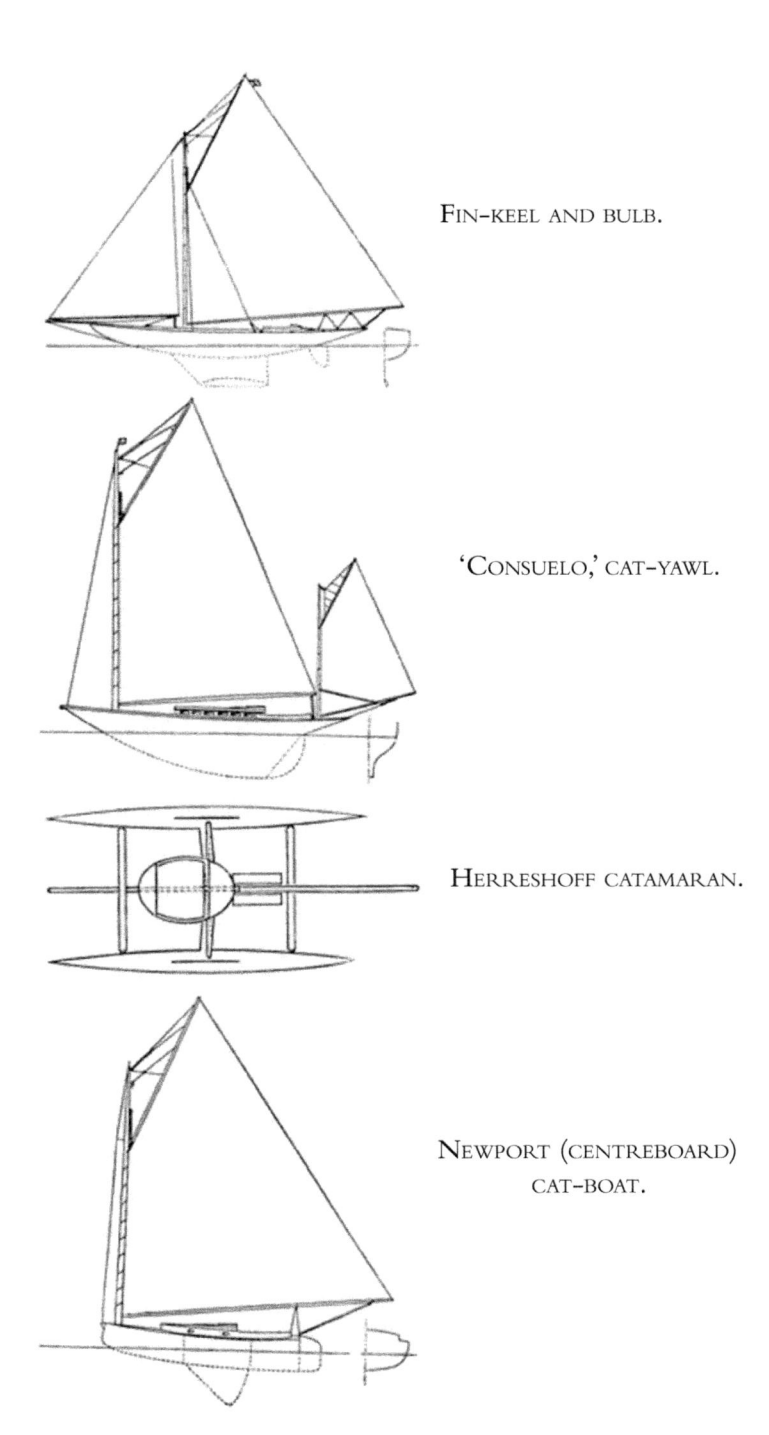

'Consuelo,' cat-yawl.

Herreshoff catamaran.

Newport (centreboard) cat-boat.

centreboard carrying a weight of lead on its lower edge sufficient to give the craft stability enough to balance the rigging and press of wind in the sails.

The most successful fin-keel boats have a length on water equal to three-and-a-half beams, and as the section of the hull is round or nearly so, stability is gained in a manner already explained.

The first of this style of craft was built and launched in the autumn of 1891, and was called *Dilemma*; she had a very moderate-sized rig, the jib-stay being secured to the extreme point of the bow, but with this she easily beat the old style of cat-boat, and showed, besides unusual speed, many other desirable qualities.

In 1892 the fin-keel boat was generally introduced, three or four sailing in Boston waters, while New York, the Lakes, and Buzzard's Bay claimed one each to two in their home waters of Narragansett Bay.

The *Wenona* and *Wee Winn*, the first in the North and the latter in the South of England, showed our friends on the other side of the sea what their racing qualities were, which are soon told by referring to their record. Out of twenty starts made by *Wenona* she won 17 first, 2 second, and 1 third prizes, and her sister in the South was even more fortunate, winning 20 first and 1 second prizes out of twenty-one starts. The fin-keel type at home was almost as successful, except when brought into competition with a centreboard boat of sloop rig, 21 ft. length on water-line, called *Alpha*. She was built and designed by the projector of the fin-keels, and was the chief member of a large 21-foot class that was fully exploited in Boston during the season of 1892, where the *Alpha* won in every race she entered.

The value of the fin-keel type in adding to the resources of yachting is limited; the type does not contribute anything of living value to yachting, it serves only as a means to show that old types can easily be beaten, but that it takes a 'machine' to do it. Fin-keels are, it is true, very pleasant to sail in, and they work beautifully, but the design is probably limited in size to 35- or 40-ft. water-line in length, for above that size the fin becomes a very troublesome adjunct in its handling and adjustment. When the boat is afloat the fin is not objectionable, but in taking the bottom by accident, or in hauling it out, it makes the boat most troublesome to handle.

Larger fin-keel boats have been projected, and one of 45 ft. length on water-line has just been built, but their success from a general view-point is highly questionable. Mr. N. G. Herreshoff, in 1883, introduced a very useful rig, which was first tested to his complete satisfaction on *Consuelo*. These boats are styled 'cat-yawl,' and since their introduction the type has become very popular, and most deservedly so, as for ordinary sailing, and particularly cruising, the rig offers many important advantages. In reefing the mainsail is accessible, and the absence of the long boom of the cat-boat is readily appreciated.

The rig of the cat-yawl has been applied successfully to all designs of yacht, deep and moderate beam as well as the shallow broad type, and always with increasing satisfaction. The rig, however, seems to be confined to boats not over 40 ft. length on water-line, as, the mainmast being placed so near the bow, it is impossible to stay it, and too large a mast unstayed is not desirable in a cruising boat.

The proportions between the mainsail and jigger as recommended by the projector is 4 in the former to 1 in the latter—that is, the dimensions of the jigger should be exactly one-half those of the mainsail. Mr. Herreshoff is also responsible for another marine curiosity that appeared in 1876. This was a catamaran or double-hulled boat—intended to be handled by one man. This boat differs from its kinsfolk of the southern ocean, the point of widest departure being that the hulls are connected by flexible means, so that each hull can adjust itself to the surface of the water it moves in.

The means employed in forming this flexible union were through the agency of a complex system of ball-and-socket joints which had range of motion enough, so that one hull might be riding a wave, whilst its sister would be in the depths of a hollow.

A small tray-shaped car for passengers, and the mast and rigging, were supported between and above the hulls by a system of trusswork with adjustable tension rods of iron.

These catamarans carried a mainsail and jib, and in smooth water made wonderful speed; 21 miles an hour has been attained under favourable conditions. This aquatic marvel was not destined to become popular; the boats required special skill in their management, and were best calculated for an afternoon's sail in smooth, sheltered water. The absence of anything like cabin accommodations was also against their use, but cruising has been successfully accomplished in them through the use of a tent to make shelter, covering the car, and of sufficient height for one to stand under it.

The respect of all dwellers on the shore is due to the cat-boat. She is distinctly American, and whilst her use may be more and more circumscribed, still the old cat will live and continue to fill a place that no other rig could do. But the cat-boat in the usual acceptation means something more than its simple rig; it stands for a shallow, wide boat, with one mast crowded into the extreme bow, and a boom reaching far over the stern, as in the cut in the diagram. The 'cat' is seen on our seaboard from Maine to Florida, but 95 *per cent.* of all yachting and boating is done north of the capes of the Delaware. In this connection it is not out of place to speak of our very large fleet of small yachts and of boats for sailing and cruising which from their size may not properly be called yachts.

The number of these craft is legion, they swarm in every northern port, and in a few places in the south are frequently met; their rig is always of the sloop for the larger, and for the smaller—say below 25-ft. water-line—the cat-rig is in preponderance. The value of this 'Mosquito fleet' as a school for yachting cannot be over-estimated.

The fancy for cruising in small sloops or cat-boats has increased greatly of late, and as the type of craft for this work improves it will become a very general pastime.

It is not here intended to cast too deep a slur on the cat-boats; seeing that the wind and weather are so generally moderate and dependable on our coast, cruising can safely be done in a cat of moderate rig. Even in heavy weather, if properly handled, a cat is sure to come in to port with flying colours, as the writer can attest by his own experience.

There are several other types of boats seen on the Atlantic coast of the United States and British Provinces; they vary in design of hull as well as in the rig, and are adapted to the work required and the surrounding condition of weather and water. They are mostly modifications of the old pirogue, and as a rule are more used in trade or some occupation than for pleasure.

Since yacht and boat racing began, there have been many different plans suggested for measurement, and for allowance between contending craft of different length.

The same questions still agitate the mind of the yachtsman, and doubtless will for all time; but if the subject be wisely considered, it will be found that that system of measurement that conduces to the best form of hull and moderate-sized sail-spread is to be preferred.

It is mainly owing to the differing systems of measurement that the English and American designs are so widely separated; extreme depth with a minimum breadth in the first, and broad, shallow vessels in the latter. It must be said, however, that sailing conditions had quite as much influence in dividing the types as measurement, but in the new compromise design all differences are happily united, and, be the water rough or smooth, the weather light or heavy, the new types will answer all requirements of speed or seaworthiness.

The present idea of measurement that embraces sail-area and length is without question a very sensible one—surely, indeed, the best yet devised—but the tables of allowance cannot make just equality between vessels of widely different size, nor do they make just allowance between yachts of varying size in or under all conditions of wind. A system of measurement that will conduce to the construction of vessels of normal design and rig, and a table of allowance that will equalise yachts in any force of wind and condition of sea, are desiderata most devoutly wished for by all who are interested in the development of the yacht, and especially in racing. The sail of a yacht is such an essential factor in its performance that some words respecting makers of duck and of the sails themselves are not out of place.

The quality of duck as to evenness of the spinning and weaving of the component yarns, and also the equality in the staple itself, are both factors of the utmost importance when the ultimate 'set' of the sail is considered. These inequalities in material, in conjunction with the personal differences of the men employed in sewing, all combine to make the set of the sail a very unknown quantity, and the differences can be removed only by the utmost care in making duck and in selection of sewers. A wholly satisfactory setting sail is a very rare sight on an American yacht, mainly on account of the uncertain characteristics of the duck, and only within the last year, as a result of the highly commendable efforts of Mr. Adrian Wilson, of the firm of Wilson & Silsby, sailmakers of Boston, has duck been produced that can stand comparison with that made in England for the exclusive use of Lapthorn. The thanks of all earnest yachtsmen are due to Mr. Wilson for his interest and untiring labours in inducing the makers of yarn and weavers of duck to produce an article that will meet the difficult requirements of a racing sail.

Wilson & Silsby of Boston and John Sawyer & Co. of New York are considered the best sailmakers in America; but many others enjoy a good reputation: and now that really good duck can be obtained, it is hoped that better setting sails will be more easily obtained than heretofore.

Many of our yachtsmen possess skill in designing, and are also fully capable of supervising and directing the construction of a yacht as well

'Constellation,' 1889, New York Club.
Designed by E. Burgess.

The ubiquitous cat-boat.

as her rigging and fitting out; and when that is done they can take the helm, and under their guidance their craft will be as well handled as by the best professional skipper.

Prominent among these skilled yachtsmen in New York is Mr. E. D. Morgan, Commodore of the New York Yacht Club, who in the height of his yachting career owned a whole harbour full of yachts, ranging from an ocean-cruising steamer to a naphtha launch in machine-propelled craft, and from a first-class schooner yacht to a cat-yawl amongst the sailing vessels. Others but a degree less devoted and skilful are Messrs. J. R. Maxwell, A. Cass Canfield, L. A. Fish, Archibald Rogers; and, in Boston, General Charles J. Paine, Mr. C. H. W. Foster, Com. J. Mal. Forbes, Messrs. George C. Adams, C. F. Adams, jun., Bayard Thayer, Charles A. Prince, John Bryant, Henry Bryant, Gordon Dexter. The chief designers in New York are Messrs. Winteringham, Gardiner, and A. C. Smith; whilst in Boston, Messrs. Stuart & Binney and Waterhouse & Chesebro are amongst the best known; but many others scattered along our seaboard have designed and built most creditable yachts, and occasionally a craft is turned out that rivals the productions of the best and most experienced designers.

Yachting on the waters of the British Possessions in North America has developed rapidly, and, fostered by the formation of clubs, and the establishment of regular seasons for racing and cruising, there is no doubt that the improvement of design and rig will progress satisfactorily.

The seaboard of the British Provinces is well adapted for cruising and racing, and due advantage is taken of all yachting facilities on the coast as well as on the Great Lakes, and to a considerable extent on the St. Lawrence River.

In glancing over the yachting situation in the United States there is every reason to feel satisfied with what has been accomplished; all improvements in design and rig have been eagerly adopted by our yachtsmen, and if we have drawn from the English in some points, they have been fully repaid by gleanings from American practice. Yachting is appreciated in other localities than on the seaboard, with its bays and rivers; the great lakes have a small fleet of pleasure vessels, and on some of the smaller lakes, as Minnietonka in Minnesota, racing is carried to a degree of perfection wholly unsurpassed by the owners' salt-water friends.

During the season of international matches, in 1885-87, the public interest awakened was extreme; reports of the racing were read with interest from Maine to California. When there is no international work on hand, the chief yachting event of the year is the cruise of the New York Yacht Club. Following the lead of *Gimcrack*, in 1884, the cruise always takes place during the first week in August, embracing also a part or whole of the second.

Starting from a port on the Sound easily accessible from the city of New York, the squadron makes its way eastward, stopping at several of the principal places of resort along the Sound.

Of late years it has been the custom to race from port to port, regular entries being made and prizes awarded.

At every port along its course the New York Yacht Squadron receives large augmentations of both sailing and steam yachts, so that at last, when the fleet anchors in the harbour of New London, it is an armada of pleasure craft laden with pleasure-seeking yachtsmen, all in accord to make this demonstration the brightest and gayest event of the season. The entrance of the squadron into Narragansett Bay is one of the most beautiful of all imaginable marine pictures; the ranks are then complete, often numbering 200 vessels, by steam and sail. Every available craft is pressed into service by the dwellers of Newport and vicinity to go out to meet the arriving yachts; steamers laden with passengers, tugs, trading schooners with their decks black with unusual freight, the ubiquitous cat-boat, all assemble in waiting off the Lightship at Brenton's Reef to welcome the approaching fleet that is already coming into view off Point Judith.

The yacht squadron is escorted to the beautiful harbour of Newport by the motley fleet in attendance, and anchors there with a flutter of canvas and the booming of cannon.

At evening the fleet is illuminated with coloured lights, the steam yachts contribute electric glare, forming a scene worth many miles of journeying to witness. Then follow races in the open sea outside Newport, after which the cruise is continued to New Bedford, and Edgartown on Martha's Vineyard Island; more racing, and then a cruise around Cape Cod to Boston, where more racing and much festivity is enjoyed, after which the squadron disbands, most of the yachts return to Newport, whilst others cruise to Mount Desert Island and beyond. About the middle of August it is usual to have more racing off Newport under the auspices of the Atlantic and Seawanhaka Clubs, and this usually closes the season for racing; a few matches, however, are generally expected in the autumn, but by the middle of October nearly all the yachts go out of commission.

Winter cruising to Florida and the West Indies usually begins soon after Christmas, returning early in April, whereby the rigours of our northern winter are avoided.

As a rule, the American yachtsman is not inclined to racing to an extent that would afford the best information and knowledge as to the design and rig of his craft. At times, however, when under the stimulus of rivalry of designers, as occurred in 1891, or particularly when there is an international contest on hand, our marine phalanx stand forth in battle array, sacrifice no end of personal effort, and stake willingly their bottom dollar.

It is the earnest wish of every American yachtsman to encourage frequent and friendly intercourse with his English cousins who are working for the true interest and advancement of yacht designing. The breadth of the interlying ocean and the disparity between the winds and water of the two countries should make no barrier to closer relations, to the end that the noble science of naval architecture and its most useful teachings may find in the progress of yachting a fit subject to bind more and more closely two nations of one blood, one language, and one desire—to attain to that which is highest and best even in sports and pastimes.

The valuable assistance of Mr. Niels Olsen, superintendent of the New York Yacht Club, and of Mr. E. A. Stevens, of Hoboken, nephew of Commodore J. C. Stevens, is hereby gratefully recognised. But for them my work would have been difficult, and in many respects impossible.

Steam Yachting in America

The rapid development of the steam engine as a motive power, and its widely distributed application, soon attracted the attention of the lovers of nautical sports, and before the year 1860 the all-conquering engine began to be used for the propulsion of pleasure craft. The invasion of fields of sport by the engine did not then recommend, nor has it since recommended, itself to the hearts of true yachtsmen; all that is so attractive in yachting seems to vanish as soon as the element of uncertainty is eliminated: all the poetry of motion, all the sense of freedom from disagreeable surroundings, as well as all interest in winds and water—all are sunk when the sail is changed for the engine as a propelling force.

The steam yacht should be considered chiefly in the light of a very agreeable mode of locomotion, and as such it is unquestionably a very

'AMERICA' CUP COMPETITIONS

Year		Name	W.L.Length ft.	Beam ft.	Draught ft.
1870	{	*Magic*	78.11	20.9	6.70
August 1870		*Cambria*	100.00	20.5	12.40
1871	{	*Sappho*	114.40	27.40	12.80
1871		*Columbia*	96.00	25.10	6.00
October 1871		*Livonia*	107.50	23.30	12.80
1876	{	*Madeleine*	95.20	24.00	7.40
August 1876		*Countess Dufferin*	107.20	24.00	6.60
1881	{	*Mischief*	61.00	19.10	5.40
Nov. 1881		*Atalanta*	61.00	19.00	5.50
1885	{	*Genesta*	81.00	15.00	13.00
Sept. 1885		*Puritan*	85.1½	22.70	8.80
1886	{	*Galatea*	87.00	15.00	13.03
Sept. 1886		*Mayflower*	85.70	23.60	9.90
1887	{	*Thistle*	86.46	20.03	13.80
Sept. 1887		*Volunteer*	85.88	23.02	10.00
October 1893	{	*Vigilant*	86.19	26.25	14.00
		Valkyrie 8	6.80	22.33	16.30

desirable adjunct to our resources, filling as it does a place that would be wholly impossible for sailing craft, when the uncertain character of winds and water is considered.

The first idea of steam yachting in America was realised in the famous cruise of the *North Star*, a side-wheel steamship of 2,004$^{25}/_{95}$ tons, built for Mr. Cornelius Vanderbilt in 1852. She was the most handsomely appointed vessel of her day, and sailed temporarily under the flag of the New York Yacht Club, which fixed her identity as a yacht, although she was built for merchant service.

The *North Star*, brigantine rig, was built by Jeremiah Simonson, of Green Point, Long Island. Length over all, 270 ft., 38 ft. beam, 28 ft. 6 in. depth, 16 ft. draught. She was fitted with two vertical beam engines, cylinders 60 in. diameter by 10 ft. stroke; two boilers, 10 ft. diameter by 24 ft. long; paddle-wheels, 34 ft. in diameter. She was broken up at Cold Spring, Long Island, in 1870. The Aspinwalls were the first promoters of real steam yachting, and as early as 1854 the *Firefly* was launched by Smith & Dimon, of New York, for Messrs. W. H. Aspinwall and J. L. Aspinwall. Her length was 97 ft. 8 in. over all, 19 ft. beam, 5 ft. 2 in. hold, 3 ft. 9 in. draught, engines built by the Morgan Iron Works, oscillating cylinders 20 by 36 in., locomotive boiler, paddle-wheels 8 ft. 8 in. diameter, size of paddles 17 by 45 in. She was sold to the United States Government for duty on the Coast Survey Service—89$^{93}/_{95}$ tons. *Clarita*, built for Leonard W. Jerome by Lawrence Faulkes Williams, 1864; length over all, 125 ft.; 121 ft. 9 in. water-line, 22 ft. beam, 9 ft. depth, draught 11 ft. 6 in., 231$^{30}/_{95}$ tons. Engine by Novelty Iron Works, 2 cylinders 22 by 22 in., diameter of screw 9 ft. 6 in. Sold to Pacific Mail Steamship Company, and is now doing towing duty on the Kennebec River, Maine.

The *Ocean Wave* was built for Mr. R. T. Loper by Reany & Naeafy, of Philadelphia, in 1865, iron. She was 87 ft. over all, 19 ft. beam, 7 ft. depth, 2 cylinders each 12 by 18 in., 38 nominal horse-power. The Police Department of Philadelphia bought her.

Day-Dream, composite construction, built by the Continental Iron Works, Green Point, Long Island, for W. H. Aspinwall, 1871. Length over all, 115 ft.; length on water-line, 109 ft.; beam, 19 ft.; depth of hold, 5 ft.; draught of water, 7 ft. Her engine was built by the Delamater Works of New York, vertical condensing, 2 cylinders each 14 by 14 in., one boiler 8 ft. long, diameter of screw 7 ft. 6 in., with 10 ft. pitch. She was sold to the United States Government for postal service in the Gulf of Mexico, and is now at New Orleans.

The *Day-Dream* was really the first successful steam yacht, and set the type of pleasure craft for many years; in fact, it is but a few years ago that the style called 'deck-house' yachts went out of use, and they are at present almost entirely superseded by the deeper-hulled, flush-deck yachts.

During the early Seventies the steam launch, or open yacht, rapidly multiplied in numbers and seemed to fill a demand for afternoon sailing in the sheltered waters of our seaports, and as preparatory to something better they did good service.

The open steam-launch as then used was from 25 to 45 ft. long, and 6 to 8 ft. wide, usually with vertical engines, and used a pipe condenser and boiler of upright form, generally of tubular construction. After the open launch came the small yacht, having a small cabin enclosed mostly by glass with a standing room aft. This very popular form is still much used, and answers a widely sought demand for day sailing or short cruising; the boats are usually about 45 to 70 ft. long, and from 8 to 10 ft. wide. This style of small yacht had no deck room that was available for real use, but the standing room with an awning over it with adjacent cabin made a very serviceable craft, in which cruising could be done from May until October on our coast with perfect safety.

In those days 8 miles an hour was thought fast enough for anybody, but in a few years, when the engine and boiler were both more perfected, more speed was demanded, so that the type in question attained to 12 or 13 miles an hour, which in some cases has been pushed to 15, whilst the speed of the open launch which at first was but 8 to 10 miles an hour, reached, under the stimulus of popular desire and better motive power, to 16 and even 20 miles an hour in quiet smooth water.

About 1885 the flush-deck yacht became more popular, and most deservedly so, as the style is superior in all essential points to the old deck-house form. It is true that the cabin of the older form is pleasanter, being lighter and more airy, but the strength of construction gained by the flush deck, its broad expanse of deck everywhere available for sitting and promenading, all these points of advantage give the present form decidedly the first place in the estimation of all lovers of steam yachting. Since 1880, steam yachting has increased with prodigious rapidity, and, particularly since the introduction of naphtha as a factor in motive power, our waters fairly swarm with craft propelled by a machine.

In about the year 1884 a club was formed for steam-yacht owners only, called the American Yacht Club, and for several years it offered prizes to be run for in Long Island Sound; but steam-yacht racing did not become popular, principally because of the danger of forcing machinery to its utmost limit of safety, and also the difficulty of classifying yachts of different size and power of engine. For the most part the devotees of steam yachting are drawn from the general public without special regard of the situation of their home, as a yacht can be kept on the seaboard or on the lakes, whilst the owner may live far from the sight and sound of the sea; the restless spirit of our countrymen prompts them to embark into every scheme of pleasure-making, as well as business enterprise.

Naturally, however, by far the greater number of steam-yacht owners have their homes on or very near some navigable water, upon which they pursue their favourite sport as a pastime only, or in connection with the daily engagements of business life.

Many men of large means and wide business interests who may be seen daily on Wall Street or in other centres of trade in New York have homes on the head waters of Long Island Sound, or on the lower stretches of the Hudson, whence they daily run to the city of New York in a steam yacht, which, after landing its luxurious owner, waits until his day is done in the city, and bears him again to a home of comfort and quiet retreat.

Yachts used chiefly for such purposes are always fast; when the speed falls below 20 miles an hour, their owners fret and fume, and wonder why she is not doing as well as she might.

Steam yachts having abnormally high speed are occasionally seen in a large yachting fleet. There are always a few men, who, from a love of seeing their names in print and their movements and those of their yacht recorded in the newspapers of the day, find that by tearing up the waters of our bays and harbours with yachts which show a speed of 25 miles an hour, their fondest hope is realised; for every eye follows them, and every reporter wastes his pencil in recording the performances of the speedy craft. It is their delight on regatta days to dart about amongst the fleet of yachts and craft of the lookers-on, and astonish everybody by some new flight of speed or some skilful evolution. I am happy to record, however, that the number of these flyers is small, and becoming less: such speeds are attained only by great danger to life and limb of those in charge of the machine, and an entire loss of comfort from the violent vibration of the vessel; for she must be built as light and carry as powerful machinery as possible, to give the results desired by these morbid lovers of notoriety, who are no more yachtsmen than is the man who takes a balloon trip so as to be seen by the crowd.

It must be admitted that comfort and pleasure can be, and doubtless are, found on many steam yachts; for instance, a yacht of 125 ft. water-line, by 19 ft. beam, with a well-kept flush-deck, a comfortable deck-house forward, a large awning spread over all, the deck set out with Persian rugs, tables, and comfortable rattan chairs, and a number of congenial friends present, who are not tired of life and each other—I think no one will deny that pleasure in the highest degree could be realised with such surroundings.

Our prevailing pleasant weather during the yachting season, and the uniformly sheltered character of our waters, have had their effect on the form and construction of steam yachts as well as those by sail. Nearly 95 *per cent.* of all steam yachts in America are built expressly for bay, harbour, and river work, and when it is necessary to make any extended trip, as for instance to the coast of Maine, they usually creep close along shore, moving cautiously from port to port.

We can, however, boast of a few deep-sea craft, as fine and seaworthy as any pleasure vessels in the world, such as those owned by the late Jay Gould, Mr. W. W. Astor, the Vanderbilts, and few others. The general dimensions of many steam yachts are ruled by the probability of their taking the passage through the Erie Canal, the locks of which are 100 ft. long and 17 ft. wide, and admit a vessel drawing 6 ft. of water.

There is a marked advantage in taking the Erie Canal to reach the great lakes; with a vessel of proper size the passage of the canal is safe and easy, whilst the trip around by the Gulf and River of St. Lawrence is very long and surrounded by difficulties, although the voyage will richly repay one for taking it, as it affords greater variety in sea and landscape than any other possible in America. Steam yachting on the great lakes is also increasing rapidly, and in the harbours of the large cities, as Buffalo, Cleveland, Toledo, Detroit, Milwaukee, and Chicago, many steam pleasure craft may be seen, usually of a length of 100 ft. or less, so as to make their way to the salt water by the canal.

As in the case of sailing yachts, 95 *per cent.* of steam craft are to be found north of the capes of the Delaware, but their numbers are increasing south of that point more rapidly than their sailing sisters. The Gulf and tributary waters as yet show very few pleasure craft of either sort, and the Pacific coast, on account of the high cost of fuel, is not the scene of steam yachting to any considerable extent.

In the Bay of San Francisco, however, are a large number of naphtha launches that find very favourable water in that shallow sea. There is far less variety of form and rig among steam yachts than in any other pleasure craft. The accepted form at present is a flush-deck vessel with pole masts, triple-expansion engine, and some modification of the old Belville boiler, a form that has many varieties, none of which are satisfactory in more than a few points. They are generally safe from explosion, but very short-lived, and difficult to manage.

The compound engine was introduced into yachting craft about the year 1875, and its success was as marked as in all other branches of marine construction.

The triple-expansion engine was first used in 1884 with increased success over its ancestor, the compound, and in 1888 the quadruple engine was put into a few yachts; but it may be questioned if it possesses any advantages over the triple for the general uses of yachting.

The use of high-expansion engines not only results in a marked economy of fuel, but, through a wide distribution of power and strain, far greater durability is attained, as well as greater freedom from vibration, which often imparts discomfort to the passengers, and injury to the hull of the yacht.

With regard to the designing and construction of steam yachts, it seems to be the aim of every designer and builder to try his hand at this branch of naval architecture, and, as might naturally be expected, the resultant vessel is too often an example of semi-successful work of the novice, clumsy in form, construction, and machinery, rude in design and ill fitted to its duty. Nearly all the deep-sea pleasure craft are built on the Delaware, and as a rule are staunch, seaworthy vessels with good speed, and generally satisfactory performance in all situations. The Herreshoff Co., of Rhode Island, have passed No. 180 in steam vessels, the larger number of which are small launches, a good proportion small cabin yachts, and the rest of the every-day class of along-shore craft which satisfy the desires of nearly all who find pleasure on our coast in steam yachts.

The Herreshoff Co. turns out the fastest vessels of their class, and for general qualities are the best examples of careful designing and construction as applied to both hull and machinery. They have the advantage of building every member of a yacht, hull, engines, and boiler, so the result is more harmonious, and in the main is more conducive to speed and that condition, called 'well balanced,' which is so desirable in all steam vessels.

During the last five years naphtha engines, as applied to launches, have been greatly improved, so that their use has become immensely popular. They vary in size from 20 to 45 ft. in length, with speed from 6 to 10 miles an hour; in a measure they have displaced small steam launches as tenders for yachts, and in many places where no great degree of skill is required to run them; in fact, the ease of running and little time required to start a launch are the chief reasons of their popularity, in spite of the fact that they are noisy and malodorous.

The use of the steam yacht will, without doubt, continue to increase more rapidly than the sailing craft, but there is not the least probability that the latter will be superseded. In so large a community of sea-loving people there will always be a few whose good taste and love of true sport will guide them toward the sail as a means of motion, and the forces of nature as motive power; but happy is he on whom fortune smiles to the extent of enabling him to keep both a steam and sailing yacht, for times do come when to reach an objective point is highly desirable, and at other times nothing can give so much pleasure as the quiet and peaceful sensation that is found only in a sailing craft. There is room then for every yacht, both steam and sail; each contributes to the pleasure of its owner, and each deserves our best efforts to develop and make perfect that which contributes so largely to our resources of enjoyment and healthful pastime.

Chapter 7

Yachting in New Zealand
By the Earl of Onslow, G.C.M.G., &C.

As has already been said, there exists every facility in our Australasian Colonies both for cruising and racing. These colonial waters are indeed the only ones in the world where yachting can be enjoyed among our fellow-countrymen on summer seas and in a temperate climate during that portion of the year when yachts are laid up in the mud in England and yachtsmen shiver in the bitter winds, the fogs and frosts of Northern Europe.

The travelling yachtsman may either take out his yacht with him, if she be large enough, or if this be deemed to involve too great trouble and expense, he will find but little difficulty in making arrangements to hire a comfortable craft at the Antipodes.

The southern coast of Australia, though it possesses many beautiful harbours, is washed by the great rollers of the Pacific, coming up through the 'roaring forties' without anything to break their force, straight from Antarctic regions, to dash themselves in mile-long breakers against the Australian coast. Yachting is therefore better confined to the sheltered harbours, and specially to those which have been selected for the sites of the capital cities of Adelaide, Melbourne and Sydney.

No more lovely sea exists in the world on which to cruise than that part of the eastern coast of the Australian continent, sheltered as it is from ocean storms by the Great Barrier Reef, extending for miles from Rockhampton to Cape York, along the Queensland coast. Numberless coral islands, the roosting places of countless Torres Straits pigeons that spend the hours of daylight feeding on the mainland, afford abundant sport for the gunner. These pigeons are quick-flying black-and-white birds about the size of the blue rock; they twist and turn in their flight with great rapidity, and tax the gunner's quickness of eye and hand not less than the best blue rocks from the pigeon-cotes of Mr. Hammond. Unfortunately this long stretch of calm blue water is beset with perils from coral reefs so numerous that the traveller is lost in admiration at the skill of Captain Cook as well as at the good fortune which enabled him, in complete ignorance of the dangers now carefully marked on our charts, to escape with but one mishap. Among the apt terms which he applied in all his nomenclature only one, Cape Tribulation, bears witness to the risks which he ran.

Still, an enterprising yachtsman, choosing the time of year when the monsoon, blowing softly on these confines of its influence, is in the favourable direction, may start from any of the ports touched by vessels of the British India Steamship Company, and, by careful study of the chart coupled with information obtained from local mariners, may enjoy without great risk a prolonged cruise amid tropical scenery and vegetation as far south even as Brisbane.

It is to New Zealand, however, that the yachtsman will turn as the paradise of his sport—abounding in harbours, offering every variety of climate from semi-tropical Auckland to the equable temperature of Cook's Strait, and on to the colder harbours of Stewart's Island—he will find as great variety in scenery as in climate. But let him not imagine that after cruising in Australian waters he may trust himself to the tender mercies of the Tasman Sea, or cross to New Zealand in a small yacht. No more terrible sea exists in either hemisphere.

Once arrived in the harbour of Auckland, however, the potentialities which lie before the amateur navigator are boundless. As he passes down the coast from the lighthouse on Cape Maria van Diemen, he will see the entrance to the singular harbour of Whangaroa, where masses of limestone rock lay piled one above another, dominated by the cupola-shaped dome of Mount St. Paul. Either this or the historically more interesting Bay of Islands may be visited in a yacht from Auckland. The Bay of Islands is one of the most beautiful yachting bays in the colony. It has a width of ten miles at the entrance, and is divided in two by a peninsula, while, with the exception of the Onslow Pinnacle rock, which has 19 feet on it at low water, it is devoid of all dangers. Here is the scene of the earliest settlement of the colony. In this bay the fleets of whalers, who trafficked in dried and tattooed human heads, and who had dealings of all kinds with the Maories (not always the most reputable), conducted a lucrative business, which has now ceased entirely.

Here the first missionaries established themselves, and here was signed the treaty with the natives which brought the islands under the sovereignty of the queen, a sovereignty which was not to remain undisputed, save after many bloody contests, and after a loss of life and treasure which still burdens the New Zealander with a load of war taxation, happily not imposed on his neighbour of the Australian continent. In this bay many days may profitably be spent in studying the interesting Maori tribes who dwell on its shores, and of whom none have stood more loyally by the English settlers than those who fought under Tamati Waka Nene. Every sort of provision may be obtained in the bay from the once flourishing town of Russell, while a sufficiently good cheap coal may be procured at Opua.

It is around the harbour of Auckland, in the Hauraki Gulf, and the Firth of Thames, however, that the perfection of yachting may be enjoyed. As the traveller approaches the earlier capital of New Zealand he will observe how the aptly named Great and Little Barrier Islands protect the Gulf from the heavy seas of the Pacific, and as the steamer wends its way through the islands that dot the Gulf and opens up the land-locked Firth of Thames on one side and the Waitemata Harbour on the other, he will realise the advantages afforded by the situation of Auckland.

Two comfortable and well-managed clubs exercise the proverbial hospitality of colonists to properly accredited arrivals from England. In addition to which the Auckland Yacht Club is an association from which all information as to both cruising and racing will readily be obtained.

The history of yachting in New Zealand is of but recent date; for, although for many years races have taken place and regattas been held annually, the competitors were rather the cutters, schooners, and scows that did the coasting trade of the colony before the Union Steamship Company inaugurated their line of well-found, fast and regular coasting steamers to and from every port of New Zealand. These were assisted by the boats and crews of Her Majesty's ships, whose presence was, and still is, ardently in request on Regatta days. The era of pleasure yachts dates from the last eight or ten years, and the Auckland Yacht Club now occupies, in the number of yachts belonging to the squadron, the first place among the Australasian Colonies. The club has one hundred members and the register of yachts exceeds sixty, which does not by any means exhaust the number of vessels used solely as pleasure-boats in the harbour.

Colonial yachts, like the great majority of colonial incomes, are not large, and nearly all the boats used are built locally. Shipbuilding is a trade extensively carried on at Auckland. During the year 1875, when the prosperity of that part of the colony was at its highest, not less than forty vessels were built, their aggregate tonnage being 1,930. A few steam yachts, such as the *Sunbeam*, the *St. George*, and the R.Y.S. schooner *Blanche* with auxiliary screw, used by Sir James Fergusson when Governor of the colony, have cruised in New Zealand waters; but a vessel of 20 tons burden is considered among the Tritons of colonial pleasure craft. The *Thetis*, a small yacht of 10 or 12 tons, was built on the Clyde, and was brought out by five gentlemen, her owners, to the Antipodes.

Perhaps the most interesting yacht now sailing in New Zealand waters is the *Mascotte*, both on account of the circumstances under which she was built, as well as for the remarkable success which has attended her during her sailing career.

In the year 1890 a strike in the shipping trade broke out in Australia, and after a few days was extended to other trades connected with shipping, finally spreading to New Zealand. During the enforced idleness of certain shipbuilding hands at Lyttelton, the port of Christchurch, some of the men bethought themselves of laying down the lines of a yacht for themselves. The *Mascotte*, commenced under these circumstances, was found, when finished, to be an exceptionally fast sailer. Within eighteen months of her completion she was manned and sailed by her owners in six regattas, netting for them 395*l.*, besides numerous smaller prizes in club races—not a bad outcome of work which, at the time, was doubtless done with no little amount of grumbling, because no wages were coming in weekly on account of it. The result, however, has been a very considerable falling off in the entries for the races last year. For the Champion Cup at Lyttelton only the *Tarifa*, rated 8, the *Mima*, 10, and the *Maritana*, 14, put in an appearance. The First Class Championship race for 100*l.* at Wellington, the capital, was among those secured by the *Mascotte*.

It is, however, in the cruising opportunities to be found in New Zealand that readers of the Badminton Library will be chiefly interested. Taking Auckland as headquarters, it may safely be asserted that throughout the season the yachtsman may lie in a different creek, harbour, or estuary every night that he is out.

He may coast up the north shore till he reaches Waiwera, where he will find an excellent hotel. He can bathe in a large and luxurious hot swimming bath, formed from the thermal springs rising close to the sea, or he may go on to the beautiful island of Kawau, once the property of Sir George Grey, which has been so graphically described by Mr. Froude in 'Oceana.' He may lie in the harbour of Bon Accord, which indents the island a mile and a half, and affords shelter in all weathers.

On landing he will find planted by the erstwhile owner of Kawau every sort of tree, shrub, and rare plant that will live either at Madeira or the Cape.

He will see the wallaby from Australia, deer, sheep, and wild goats. The beautiful Pohutukawa, or Christmas-tree, covered at Christmas-tide with scarlet blossom, feathering down to the clear blue sea till its lowest branches are covered by the rising tide, so that oysters cluster on them with all the appearance of being the natural fruit. In the rocky depths of the clear water great lazy stingarees may be seen floating along with the tide, like sheets of brown paper flapping idly from side to side in the tide race. A perfectly appointed English country gentleman's house fronts the harbour. Its lawn and park-like slopes are timbered with the forest trees of Europe. The opossum of Australia may be seen nimbly springing from the boughs of an English oak to those of the silver tree of South Africa, the whole being a combination of the flora and fauna of all continents, bewildering to the brain of the naturalist.

As the total population of the island is thirty-two, and consists of the family and dependents of the owner, visitors, unless they wish to run the risk of abusing hospitality which is always cordially accorded, must bring a sufficiency of provisions with them.

The Little Barrier Island, though possessing no harbour, has several yachting anchorages. It is uninhabited, and is chiefly interesting from the fact that it is the last remaining stronghold of many rare species of New Zealand birds. This is attributable in some degree to its distance from the mainland. The bee has not found its way across to Little Barrier, and the honey-eating birds, driven away from elsewhere by the stings of bees seeking a common food, have made this island their last habitat. It is greatly to be hoped that the New Zealand Government will complete the pending negotiations for its purchase from the natives, so that it may be made into a national park for the preservation of these unique ornithological specimens.

Great Barrier Island is larger than the Isle of Wight, being 21 miles long. It is about eight miles eastward of the Little Barrier, and possesses in Port Fitzroy one of the finest harbours in New Zealand. Yachts enter by a channel 1¼ mile wide, pass under a remarkable rock resembling the Duke of Wellington's head, and come to Governor's Pass, a narrow channel, 178 feet across, which opens out into an inner harbour three miles in length and more than half a mile wide, surrounded on all sides by high mountains which give complete security from every wind. The harbour is full of fish of every kind, from the little New Zealand herring to the flat stingaree resembling an enormous skate with a formidable spiked tail. Unless the fisherman cuts this off before he proceeds to deal with the fish, he may find one blow from it compel him to seek for several weeks an asylum in the Auckland Hospital.

If the yachtsman has on board a seine net, he may realise something of the miraculous draught of fishes mentioned in the Bible. Let him also bring his rifle, for the island is swarming with wild goats, and if he can steel his heart against the piercing and humanlike screams to which they give utterance when wounded, he may, by getting up to the highest ground and stalking them down the mountain-sides, secure more than he will find it possible to get back to his yacht, be he never so impervious to powerful odours. He will, moreover, earn the gratitude of the settlers by so doing, for the goats eat not a little of that pasture which would more profitably be utilised in affording sustenance to the domestic sheep of the island farmers.

Many years ago Selwyn Island, at the entrance to the harbour, was stocked with the large silver-grey rabbit, and a good day's shooting may still be had among them, though the skins are no longer of the great value they were when first acclimatised.

Having explored the creeks of the Waitemata, which open into the harbour of Auckland to the north, the yachtsman may proceed to cruise in the southern waters of the Hauraki Gulf. On his way he may run in for a few hours to one of the Maori villages, where he will find some very well-to-do natives, owners of valuable property close to Auckland, but who still practise all the old-fashioned Maori customs of cooking and manufacture. He will be interested, too, in the long war canoe with its carved prow, one of the few now remaining in New Zealand.

All the islands between the mouth of the gulf and the Firth of Thames are interesting. The most remarkable in appearance is Rangitoto, guarding the entrance to the Auckland harbour. In shape it is a perfect cone. The mountain is an extinct volcano, rising to a height of 920 feet, and presents a precisely similar appearance from whatever aspect it is regarded. The summit of the mountain is composed of masses of scoria, but there is no fresh water on the island. Rangitoto is connected by a sandy neck, a quarter of a mile long, dry at high water, with Motu Tapu, the Sacred Island. Whatever odour of sanctity may have attached to it in earlier days, it is now the island most profaned by the feet of Auckland yachtsmen. Herds of deer scamper across its grassy slopes, and afford excellent stalking to the hospitable owner and his guests. No one who takes care to keep on the shores of the island and refrain from disturbing the deer is likely to be forbidden to shoot a few rabbits. From some of the higher points round the coast he may espy the acclimatised emus stalking over the hills; the pheasants feeding round the edges of the patches of woodland, and the flocks of turkeys, once tame, but which now require the persuasion of the fowling-piece before they can be brought to table.

From the Thames the yacht may be taken round to the harbour of Tauranga; this is a quiet and comfortable little town, the harbour land-locked by an island running down to meet a sandy spit. From this spit rises the Mawayanui Rock, 860 ft. in height, conspicuous for miles, both from the land and sea sides of the harbour.

The entrance is tortuous, narrow in places, and liable to gusts and eddies when the wind is blowing from the sea, but of considerable capacity inside. Tauranga is close to the scene of a conflict between the Maories and English troops, in which the 68th Regiment lost more officers than did any regiment at Waterloo. It is the best harbour whence to visit the volcano of White Island, and is the nearest also to the Maori Settlements, the hot lakes and springs of the interior of the North Island.

White Island is sixty miles off, and the steam blowing off the crater to a height varying from 2,000 to 10,000 feet is clearly visible in fine weather. This island is well worth a visit, though great care must be exercised in landing, for the whole island is so hot that walking is not pleasant, while the clouds of sulphurous steam blowing to leeward are suffocating. It is about three miles in circumference, having in the centre a crater about a hundred yards in circumference, surrounded by steam geysers, which make a roaring, deafening noise, like a hundred engines massed in one engine-room. Although there is no vegetation on the island, the base of the crater gives the appearance of a well-watered meadow in spring. This effect is produced by the bed of crystallised sulphur traversed by the streams from the several geysers.

Myriads of sea birds, chiefly gannets, circle round the island, and the remarkable Tuatara lizards may be seen crawling on the hot rocks. There is no harbour in the island, but there is shelter between the principal islet and a little islet half a mile to south-east.

Yachting on the west coast of the North Island of New Zealand is less agreeable; there is no convenient centre from which to start on many cruises, and between the harbours are long distances of usually stormy sea.

Once inside the Kaipara Harbour a large expanse of rather uninteresting water is available, but the rivers which flow into it are wide and picturesque, afford excellent wildfowl shooting, and are the home of the trade in Kauri timber. The huge logs are cut up by sawmills with giant circular saws. The trunks of the Kauri trees may be seen floating down the rivers from the forests above till they are caught, as they pass the various mills, by baulks stretched at an angle across the stream to intercept their progress. In the same way, once you get across the bar of the Hokianga River, many days may be spent in the land of oranges and lemons.

Travelling to the southern end of the North Island to the harbour of Port Nicholson, we come to Wellington, the capital, where the Port Nicholson Yacht Club have their headquarters.

An annual regatta is held here in January. The harbour, though magnificent for steamers or vessels of large tonnage, is subject to the gales and sudden squalls which blow through Cook's Strait as through a blast pipe, and therefore not always to be trusted. Not a few sad accidents have happened to small craft sailing on the waters of the harbour.

Most enjoyable excursions may be made from Wellington to the sounds on the northern shores of the South Island, but great care should be exercised in crossing Cook's Strait, though the distance to the first sound is but a few miles. The winds are local, and almost invariably north-west or south-east. Yachts running through the Straits should, therefore, be on the look out for a rapid change from the south-east to north-east, or from north-west to south-west, as they open out either entrance. Queen Charlotte and the Pelorus are the most picturesque of these sounds. They resemble somewhat the fiords of Norway, and though they have not the grandeur of the sounds on the west coast of this island, they are remarkable for the soft green contour of their slopes and the striking contrast between sky, shore, and sea which they present in clear weather.

Picton, at the head of Queen Charlotte Sound, is picturesquely situated, with a good wharf. Like those in the south, the sounds are so deep (20 to 25 fathoms) that, except in the coves, of which, fortunately, there is no lack, vessels have difficulty in finding an anchorage. Like the harbour of Wellington across the strait, these sounds are liable to many gusts from the mountain gullies, and care should be exercised whenever it is known to be blowing hard outside.

Pelorus Sound has even more coves and bays than Queen Charlotte Sound, and no inconsiderable time is necessary to explore the whole of it.

There is abundance of both wood and fresh water; in every part excellent fishing with the line may be had. Most of the catch will be new to English fishermen. Rock cod, blue cod, schnapper, the giant hapuka, a sort of cod, and the game kahawai, which will run like a salmon, are the best from a gastronomical and sporting point of view. Enough has been caught by a single line in a day to feed the whole crew of a man-of-war. Every sort of necessary provision is obtainable both at Havelock and Picton, at the heads of the respective sounds.

From the northern sounds every traveller will wish to proceed through the remarkable French pass to Nelson in Blind Bay. This bay is singularly free from gales and storms. Often, while a hurricane is tearing and raging through Cook's Strait, calm weather will be found to prevail without disturbance in Blind Bay.

The harbour of Nelson is formed by a very remarkable bank 4½ miles in length, covered with huge boulders and forming a natural breakwater to the harbour. There are one or two gaps in the bank at high water where boats and very small vessels may pass over, but the tide runs with such force that it is not advisable to attempt it.

The entrance is not more than 50 yards wide, and lies between the bold pinnacle of the Arrow Rock and the barrel beacon at the edge of the Boulder Bank. The entrance is easily effected on the flood, but the tides run very strong in and out of the narrow entrance. The climate of Nelson is perhaps the most perfect in all New Zealand, and the scenery of the bay, with its blue waters and background of snow-covered mountains in winter and early spring, excels anything that can be seen on the Riviera, while the climate closely resembles that of the French littoral of the Mediterranean; the only unpleasantness being the Waimea wind, felt in early spring down the valley of the Waimea, but it is neither so continuous nor so unpleasant as the Mistral of the Riviera.

Very pleasant expeditions may be made to Motueka and Collingwood, on the opposite shores of the bay. The Californian quail exists in great abundance on these shores; so much so that the little steamers plying weekly bring sackloads of the birds to Nelson, where they are preserved whole in tins for export.

The yachtsman should spend a sufficient length of time in exploring the indentations of the northern coast of the South Island, for next to that of the surroundings of Auckland he is likely to meet with the best weather for his pursuits to be found in New Zealand.

If he then wishes completely to exhaust the opportunities which the colony affords him, he may, choosing a fine day and favourable barometric indications, venture on the ocean to the southward. Let him, however, avoid the west coast, where the harbours are few and far between, and where those that exist are rendered difficult of access, save where great expense (as at Westport and Greymouth) has been incurred by the local authorities to erect breakwaters and dredge the bars. It is noteworthy that the harbours on the west coast of both islands, where they are also the estuaries of rivers, have dangerous shifting sand-bars, while those on the east coast are comparatively free from this objection.

If the yacht be taken down the east coast to Lyttelton, the traveller will pass in full view of the grand range of snow-covered mountains, the Kaikouras. With a north-easterly wind the sea does not get up to any extent, but if it should change to south there is convenient shelter for small craft at Kaikoura.

The harbour of Lyttelton is an indentation of considerable depth and width in Banks Peninsula, which, rising from the flat plains of Canterbury to a height of some 3,000 feet, juts out into the ocean and extends twenty miles from the mainland with an average width of sixteen miles. This peninsula affords plenty of facilities for yachting. Lyttelton has a yacht club, and is connected by eight miles of railway with Christchurch, a town that has always borne the reputation of resembling those of the old country more closely than any other in New Zealand.

Inside the harbour are many pleasant anchorages for yachts, especially Quail Island and Ripa Island; also Governor's Bay, a favourite holiday resort of the people of Christchurch. It should be borne in mind that with a north-easterly wind a heavy swell comes rolling up the harbour, but a secure inner harbour of 107 acres has been formed by moles of rubble, where there is perfect safely for vessels of every kind.

There are many pleasant cruises to be made from Lyttelton to the various bays and harbours in the peninsula, such as to Port Leny and to Pigeon Bay, formerly a favourite station for whaling vessels; but the most interesting as well as the most beautiful is the harbour of the old French settlement of Akaroa. This harbour penetrates the peninsula to a distance of eight miles. The town of Akaroa is the centre of a fine pastoral district, most picturesquely situated on the slopes of green hills turned into fertile gardens. The French language is no longer to be heard in the streets, but the green *'persiennes'* and the white fronts of the older houses bear witness to the nationality of their builders. Lucky it was for the Anglo-New Zealander of today that Captain Hobson, Lieutenant-Governor at Auckland in 1840, was both of hospitable intent and impressed with the necessity of 'pegging out claims' for the future of the English race.

Lucky, too, that Captain Lavand, on his way to prepare for a shipload of French colonists, stayed to enjoy Captain Hobson's hospitality in Auckland, while the latter, having ascertained his guest's intentions, had time to despatch H.M.'s brig *Britomart* with all possible speed to Akaroa, so that when the gallant Frenchman arrived he found the smart sailors of the *Britomart* sitting at the foot of a recently erected flagstaff admiring a Union Jack flying from the top; by virtue of which they claimed the South Island of New Zealand for Queen Victoria in the same manner as Captain Hobson had recently done in the case of the North Island.

These same French emigrants, stopping at St. Helena on their way out, visited the tomb of Napoleon, and piously preserved sprays cut from the weeping willows that surrounded it. From these sprays, planted and cherished on their arrival at Akaroa, sprang all the beautiful willows which grow with such rapidity, thrive so remarkably, and are so conspicuous a feature throughout New Zealand. In December of every year a regatta is held at Akaroa, and yachts from all parts of New Zealand, as well as boats' crews of one of H.M.'s ships, come to take part in it.

The yachting grounds proper of New Zealand may be said to be completed by the exploration of the peninsula below Christchurch, and yet the most remarkable waters of the colony remain unvisited.

These are the sounds of the south-western extremity of the island. To get to them, however, many miles of open ocean must be sailed over. Rarely does the wind blow from the east, and hard threshing against the wind is the usual condition of sailing from the 'Bluff' to the sounds. When they are reached, the giant mountains which hedge them in on every side shut out from some, for days and weeks together, the least puff of wind to fill the sails of the yacht; while the deep gullies running down the sides of the mountains in others admit sudden and violent gusts of wind full of danger to the small sailing craft.

There are interesting places to be visited on the way, such as the harbours of Timaru and Oamaru, where man at vast labour and expense has wrested from the violence of the ocean a small space of calm water in the long straight coast line, well named the Ninety-mile Beach, on which the rollers break and roar with ceaseless monotony; or the beautiful harbour of Port Chalmers, leading to Dunedin, the Scotch capital of Otago. The uninviting looking harbour of the Bluff, where the traveller may touch the most southerly lamppost in the world, lies opposite to Stewart's Island, and is separated from it by Foveaux Strait, one of the most extensive oyster beds in the world. There are several fine harbours in Stewart Island, especially the spacious port of Paterson's Inlet, full of coves and bays.

Yachts bent on visiting the sounds should be warned that a strong current consequent on the quantity of water pouring down from the mountain torrents is usually found to oppose the entrance of a yacht into each sound, and that it is very rarely that the wind blows strong enough to bring yachts in. Generally speaking, within a mile of the entrance a dead calm with heavy swell will be found, rendering it both difficult and dangerous to make the entrance.

Once inside the depth is so great that, except where a river runs in at the head, there is little chance of anchorage, and the vessel must be made fast by tying her to a tree.

There is land communication with one sound (Milford) alone, and that only by a foot track. One or two men manage to eke out a hermit's existence in certain of the sounds, but are chiefly dependent on the periodical visits of the Government steamer; otherwise the only living things on the land are the wingless kiwis and kakapos, and an occasional seal lying upon the rocks. Probably no one visiting New Zealand will care to omit a trip to these sounds; but let the yachtsman leave his vessel snugly berthed in the harbour of Lyttelton or Port Chalmers, and pin his faith to the screws of the Union Steamship Company's well-found vessels, rather than to the sails of his own craft.

For a yachting expedition to New Zealand the month of January,

February, March, or April should be chosen. During these months in the northern parts of the colony and on the coast a N.E. sea breeze sets in daily about ten in the morning, and dying away at sunset is succeeded by a westerly or land wind. The yachtsman may generally reckon on these winds; but if the land wind should not set in towards evening the sea breeze may increase to a gale, when he can remain safe at his anchorage till it has blown itself out—a proceeding which generally occupies not more than twenty-four hours. These gales occur on an average but once in six weeks, and should be looked for when the moon changes or comes to the full.

I have already spoken of the winds of Cook's Strait; those likely to be met with between it and Banks Peninsula will be chiefly north-easterly and light in summer. Southerly and south-easterly gales, known as 'southerly busters,' often last three days, and bring cold rain and dirty weather. Very strong, hot north-westers blow across the Canterbury plains to Banks Peninsula, and are particularly drying and unpleasant. Their approach can generally be foretold by a remarkable clearness of the atmosphere, and an arch of cloud over the Southern Alps, showing blue sky between the cloud and the snow peaks.

The climate in the central and southern parts of the colony is remarkably like that of Great Britain, with more wind and more sunshine, while the northern part resembles that of the shores of Europe washed by the Mediterranean. Indeed, if one takes the map of New Zealand and turns it upside down, imagining the two islands joined together at Cook's Strait, its general similarity in outline and configuration to Italy will at once become apparent. The Southern Alps, the Spencer Mountains, and the Ruahine Mountains, like the Alps and Apennines in Italy, form the head and backbone of the country. The rich plains of Otago and Canterbury answer to those of Lombardy and the Campagna, while the palms and fern-trees of Auckland wave against a sky as blue as that of Naples.

The coast is more indented, the harbours more spacious than those of the Mediterranean; the islands in the north are more numerous, and though the winds blow stronger and the sea runs higher when gales come on, the weather is far less treacherous than that of the Mediterranean, and gives better warning of its approach. For those who wish to enjoy two summers without a winter, to see some of the most remarkable natural phenomena of the world, and the most interesting and most developed savage race with which Englishmen have come in contact; to explore fresh waters; to find an ample supply of good provisions, suited to European requirements; to live among fellow-countrymen who will assuredly give a hearty and hospitable welcome, and to realise something of the extent, the variety and the vastness of the Queen's Empire, I can suggest no better nor more enjoyable cruise during the English winter months than one round the beautiful islands of Antipodean Britain.

CHAPTER 8

Foreign and Colonial Yachting
France
By R. T. Pritchett

The year 1891 will be memorable in the history of French yachting as the date of the beginning of a thorough organisation for the encouragement of what in France is called '*navigation de plaisir*,' a term which will soon contract to our simpler word 'yachting.' The French have long, however, had a taste for the sport. For half a century at least Havre has been *en fête* in the month of July with a great deal of rowing and sailing, encouraged by crowds on the quays of the port, whence they could enjoy the sport much more than if they were afloat. All this is due to the energy and encouragement of the *Société des Régates au Havre*, under the patronage of the Minister of Marine and the City of Havre.

In the year 1891 the regatta was first conducted in a business-like manner. A yachting tribunal was instituted in Paris to make rules and arrange the details of racing. The society, styled '*Union des Yachts Français*,' 45 Rue Boissy d'Anglas, Paris, was very heartily taken up by all the best men in France, and absorbed the other clubs. The President is Contre-Amiral Baron Lagé; Vice-Presidents, M. E. Pérignon, Baron Arthur de Rothschild, Comte Alain de Guébriant, and M. Henri Menier, with a Council of twenty-eight, and a tremendous administration of commissions or committees for everything. The list of members amounts to 520, and their yacht list comprises over 300 vessels of sorts and sizes.

After Havre, Nice ranks as a French yachting centre. The regatta is always held about the 12th to 15th of March—a time of the year when we are generally experiencing a kind of weather which totally

FRASCATI AND PIERHEAD AT HAVRE.

HARBOUR AT HAVRE.

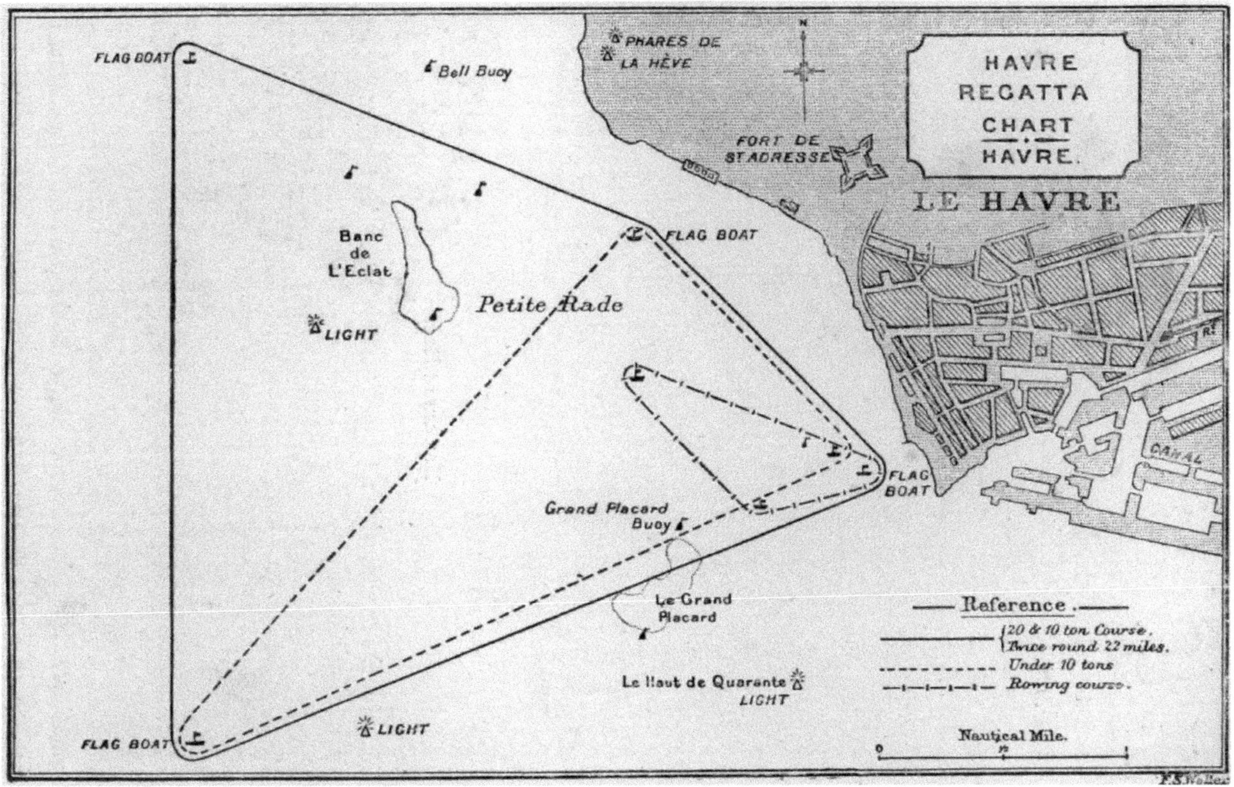
HAVRE
REGATTA
CHART
HAVRE.
LE HAVRE
PHARES DE
LA HÈVE
FORT DE
ST ADRESSE
FLAG BOAT
Bell Buoy
Banc
de
L'Eclat
Petite Rade
LIGHT
FLAG BOAT
FLAG
BOAT
CANAL
Grand Placard
Buoy
Le Grand
Placard
Le Haut de Quarante
LIGHT
LIGHT
FLAG BOAT
Reference.
20 & 10 ton Course.
Twice round 22 miles.
Under 10 tons
Rowing course.
Nautical Mile.
0
½

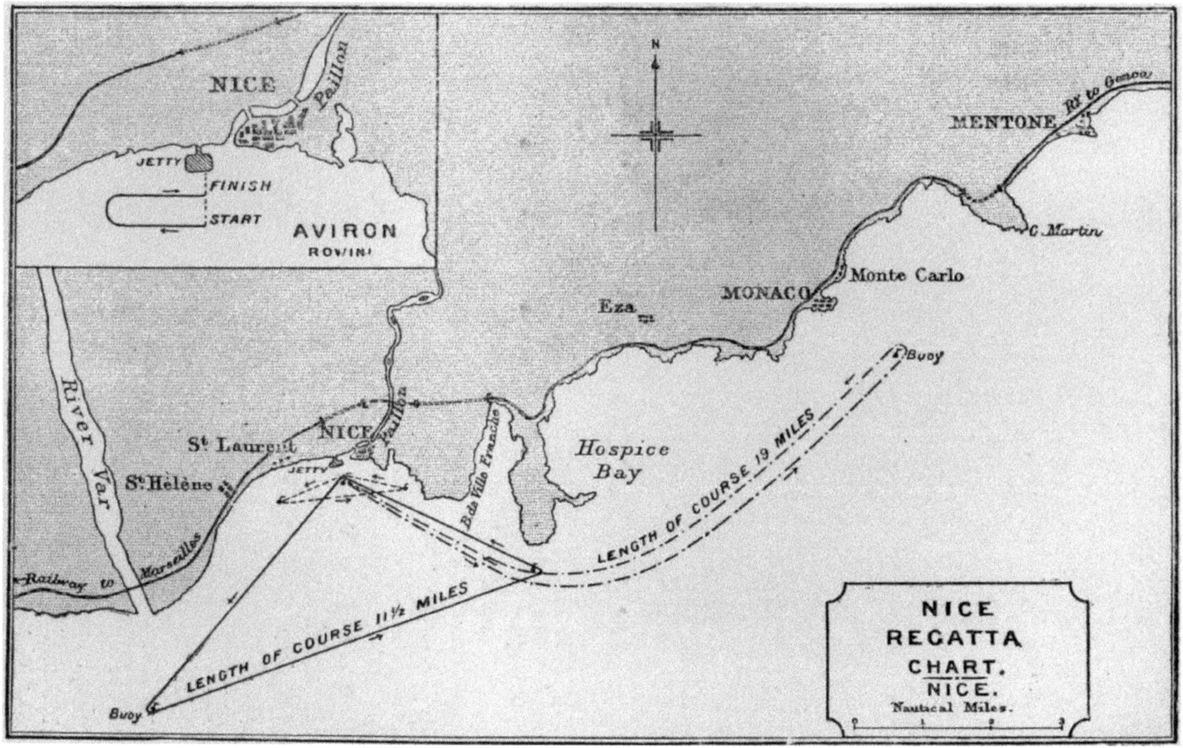
NICE
REGATTA
CHART.
NICE.
Nautical Miles.
0
1
2
3
N
NICE
Paillon
JETTY
FINISH
START
AVIRON
ROWING
MENTONE
Ry to Genoa
C. Martin
Monte Carlo
MONACO
Eza
Buoy
Hospice
Bay
Bde Villa Franche
NICE
Paillon
St Laurent
St Hélène
JETTY
River Var
Railway to Marseilles
LENGTH OF COURSE 19 MILES
LENGTH OF COURSE 11½ MILES
Buoy

removes any idea of yachting from our minds. The *Union des Yachts Français* patronise this *fête nautique*, which is sometimes assisted by English yachts that are in the Mediterranean; for instance, Lord Dunraven's *Valkyrie* has been amongst them, and Lieut. W. Henn's *Galatea*, he being a member of the *Club Nautique,* 8 Quai Masséna, Nice, a club founded in 1883, with rather more than one hundred members. At the present time several English gentlemen belong to it. Their '*Siège*' is No. 12 Rue St. François de Paula à Nice. These foreign yacht races do not offer any inducements to our finer and larger craft, as few of the competitors are over 20 tons. The City of Nice gives good prizes, as under:—

Above 20 tons

	Francs
1st Prize for yachts above 20 tons, 'City of Nice'	5,000 and gold medal
2nd Prize for yachts above 20 tons, 'City of Nice'	2,500 and silver medal
3rd Prize for yachts above 20 tons, 'Société des Bains de Monaco'	1,000 and silver medal

Under 10 tons

1st Prize for yachts under 10 tons, 'Monte Carlo'	1,500 and gold medal
2nd Prize for yachts under 10 tons, 'Monte Carlo'	750 and silver medal
3rd Prize for yachts under 10 tons, 'Monte Carlo'	400 and bronze medal

The courses are very short—about 11½ miles in the triangle once round; and in the race from Nice to the flagboat off Monaco the course there and back is only about 19 miles. The whole arrangements are carried out according to the rules and regulations of the U.Y.F., which have given great satisfaction at Nice as well as at Havre.

It was at Nice that the idea of a race for steam yachts was first carried out. Two vessels entered, and only two; and as the 2nd prize and medal was 120*l.*, they both had something to try for. The two were the *Eros*, 850 tons, Baron A. Rothschild, and *Francisca*. The *Eros* won the first prize, 600*l.* and medal.

'VALKYRIE,' NO. 1.
53 TONS (COMMENDATORE FLORIO, NICE YACHT CLUB).

Germany

His Majesty the Emperor William having bought the English yacht *Thistle*, 170 tons, and Prince Henry of Prussia having built a new 40-rater, the *Irene*, designed by G. L. Watson (as also a small rater, the *Niny*, from Arthur E. Payne), the idea of an Imperial German Yacht Club naturally arose, and in 1891 one was established at Kiel, a place admirably adapted for the purpose. The whole matter was taken up so heartily along the coast that there are at the present time more than 550 members belonging to the club. Of course the number of yachts is not in proportion as yet, but this will gradually develop, and in the meantime it is very pleasant to know that the *Thistle* has become the mother of such a club.

Sweden

The Swedish Club, established 1832, is very strong, having five yachting stations—Stockholm, Goteborg, Norrköping, Malmö, and Ornskoldsirk—the members owning vessels of good tonnage, schooners, screw steamers, cutters and yawls, numbering over 170.

Canada
By G. L. Blake

Yachting in Canada dates back as a pastime almost to the first days of its colonisation. Halifax, Toronto, and Quebec can boast of yacht clubs which were formed long before the seventies, one of the oldest, if not the oldest, being the Royal Canadian Yacht Club at Toronto, which was started as far back as the year 1852, and now has a fleet of forty yachts and more. On Lake Ontario, a superb sheet of water some 200 miles long by 40 in breadth, with a depth in places of over 100 fathoms, and well adapted for either cruising or racing, the sport has been cultivated as a science for many years, so much so in fact that, in 1873, a leading authority on such matters wrote, 'Yachting is fast becoming the national pastime of Canada.'

In 1872 there were yachting stations at Toronto, Coburg, Kingston, Hamilton,—the club at Hamilton was made a Royal Club in 1888—Belleville, and other ports on the confines of the Lake, where numerous regattas have been held each season; but, as the prosperity of colonial yachting entirely depends on the state of trade, these small communities have seen many ups and downs. During Lord Dufferin's tenure of office as Governor of Canada a great impetus was given to things maritime, and the author of 'Letters from High Latitudes,' who owned and sailed a small 7-tonner at the time, lent a very able helping hand to all that concerned yachting in Canadian waters. Yachts of all descriptions are to be found there, from the small skimdish of a 'sharpie,' with its enormous centreboard and cloud of canvas, to the stately schooner of 200 tons and over.

In 1872 there were only one or two vessels of English design or build on Ontario (which is practically the chief yachting centre), of which the best known was the little *Rivet*, 17 tons, that had been built at Glasgow and was brought out in frame some years before. At the present time, however, anyone visiting Ontario would see many old Scotch and English favourites cruising about; more than one of our smartest 10- and 5-tonners are now registered on Canadian books, while most of our principal yacht designers have representatives of their skill flying racing flags and built to the Canadian tonnage rule.

As there is communication with the ocean by canal and river *viâ* Montreal, Quebec and the St. Lawrence, besides through canal with New York, yachts from outports are not infrequent visitors, and they take part from time to time in the several local regattas. The lake, as might be expected, is often troubled by severe squalls, which now and then, if of long continuance, create a very heavy sea disturbance. Luckily, this does not occur very often, though moderately greasy weather sometimes has its advantages in giving tone and colour to the enjoyments of open sea navigation.

Of the principal Canadian outports, Halifax and Quebec are the oldest and most sporting. The Royal Nova Scotia Yacht Club, which was established in 1875, and is stationed at Halifax, is one of the leading clubs in the Dominion; that at Quebec dates back over twenty years; and the St. Lawrence Club, at Montreal, with its fleet of eighty yachts, some five years. At Halifax there used to be a very sporting club, called the Royal Halifax Yacht Club, which would hold precedence of the R.N.S.Y.C., as one of the oldest societies of the kind in Canada, did it exist as such, but it is believed to have been blended into the latter club and to have assumed its new name.

Canada is rich in all the necessaries that are called into play in ship- and yacht-building, the woods she provides for the purpose being some of the finest in the world. Nothing can come up to her timbers, such as the spruce, yellow and red pine varieties, either for length, evenness of grain, or freedom from knots, and it is to Canada that we in England are so deeply indebted for most of the timber used in our shipbuilding yards.

AUSTRALIA

In Australia yachting has had, and in some places still has, a hard fight to assert itself against the exciting sport of horse-racing. The oldest yachting community is that stationed at Sydney, New South Wales, where the two leading clubs date back to the years 1863 and 1867, *viz.* the Royal Sydney Yacht Squadron, and the Prince Alfred Yacht Club. Yacht-racing, however, was carried on long before those years, and perhaps owing to the fine piece of water, some twelve square miles in area, enclosed within Port Jackson Heads, which lends itself to aquatic pursuits, yachting here has taken greater hold of the inhabitants than at any other place in the Southern Ocean. No finer boat sailers exist anywhere than at Sydney.

There are a goodly number of yachts connected with the Port, and no money or care has been spared to keep the Sydney fleet up to date. Both Messrs. G. L. Watson and W. Fife, jun., to say nothing of other well-known designers, have from time to time given a helping hand towards furthering this end. The classes, however, which give the most sport, and which can draw together 5,000 or more onlookers during a racing day, are those that include the open boats. These are altogether a speciality of Sydney.

The limits of the three principal classes are—for the:

First Class.—24 ft. length, with not less than 7 ft. beam, and 3 ft. depth.

Second Class.—19 ft. length, with not less than 6.5 ft. beam, and 30 in. depth.

Third Class.—17 ft. length, with not less than 5 ft. beam, and 20 in. depth.

These boats are all centre-boarders. When in Australia the writer was shown the *Victor* as the finest example at that time of the large class. She was 34 ft. long, had 8 ft. beam, and a depth of 3 ft. A description of her was given in *Hunt's Yachting Magazine* some years ago. She was built of colonial cedar, and of ½-in. planking. Her frames were of bent elm, the sternpost and knees of tea-tree, while her keel was of tallow-wood. Her draught aft was 21 in., and forward 2 in., with the crew of sixteen men on board. She carried a racing centreboard of ¼-inch plating, 9 ft. long, and 6 ft. deep, with a double drop, allowing the plate when lowered to hang with its length horizontal to the keel. For ordinary occasions the racing centreboard was unshipped, and a smaller one substituted in its place. No dead ballast is allowed in these boats, and two air-tight or cork cushions are carried under the thwarts, because no boat is permitted to start for a race unless she possesses sufficient buoyancy to keep afloat should she happen to turn turtle or capsize.

The *Victor* was fitted, like all the boats of her class, with stringers running fore and aft, about two feet from the gunwale, which allowed the crew to sit double-banked, the outside contingent on the weather gunwale, with their feet under the stringer, the inside on the stringer itself. When shifting from the starboard to the port tack, or *vice versâ*, both outside and inside men go over at the same time, the inside men becoming outside, and the outside of the previous tack becoming inside. The *Mantura* and *Craigielee* are also fine specimens of the 24-feet class. Photographs of these two boats under way are hung in the billiard-room of the Royal Clyde Yacht Club House.

The wood these boats are planked with is fine, hard, durable stuff; and lends itself, when finished off, to the formation of a beautifully smooth surface, which readily takes a good polish. This colonial cedar is used for deck-fittings, &c., and takes the place of mahogany with us. New South Wales is certainly very bountiful to yacht-builders in its supply of timber for all purposes connected with their trade, though New Zealand has to supply the pine-wood for yachts' decks. For floors three native woods are employed—honeysuckle, white mahogany, and tea-tree—while iron bark, so well known for its value in the building of whalers, is excellent for knees and suchlike. All these woods offer strong, naturally grown shapes, and forks of the most acute angles. Spotted gum is generally employed for bent timbers; another wood is found in the tallow-tree, which is very suitable for keels, owing to its hard yet oily nature.

From its position the harbour suffers from uncertain winds, but should there be a clear sky and a hard north-easter there need be no fear that the racing will not prove of the very best. The regatta course forms an obtuse-angled triangle, and as a short stretch has to be taken across the mouth of the harbour, it not infrequently happens that a very uncomfortable sea has to be negotiated before the second buoy can be rounded for the run home.

Hobson's Bay is a much larger tract of water, being close upon ninety miles in circumference. It is not, however, navigable in all parts owing to extensive shoals. These, though very much in the way of navigation, help to form a kind of breakwater to the anchorages off

Sandridge and Williamstown, which are open to southerly and south-westerly winds, and would accordingly, but for them, be often swept by very heavy seas. The principal yacht club is the Royal Yacht Club of Victoria, established at Melbourne; but there are numerous small yacht and boat clubs scattered about the colony at various towns, such as Sandhurst, Bendigo and Ballarat, where there are lagoons or lakes varying in size from three to many miles in circumference. The Albert Park Yacht Club, at Melbourne, is a good type of one of these inland institutions. The yachts or boats employed on the Albert and Ballarat lagoons range from 14 feet to 30 feet over all, They have great beam, and because the depth of water is as a rule shallow, have rarely over 4 feet to 5 feet draught. Good sport is obtained out of them, and races are continually taking place.

At Geelong, which is a fine natural harbour about forty miles from Melbourne, and off the open anchorages of St. Kilda and Brighton, yachts are moored during the season, and at these places are to be found any number of yachting enthusiasts.

The club course is a very good one for trying the respective merits of competing yachts, and many an exciting race has been sailed over it. Intercolonial regattas have been held, which have proved great successes, and for these, owners of yachts of 40 tons and under think nothing of working their way from port to port over an expanse of a thousand miles or so of ocean. The yachts built in the colony are framed and planked with the wood of the red gum-tree, which is, in fact, the only wood the colony produces that is of any real value for the yacht-builder's use. It takes the place of larch or pitch-pine with us.

Both Adelaide, in South Australia, and Auckland, in New Zealand, possess yacht clubs, and are the homes of many keen lovers of yacht racing. The Royal South Australian Yacht Squadron, at the former place, has been in existence for almost a quarter of a century. The New Zealand yachtsmen can boast of possessing in their midst perhaps the finest woods in the world, and nothing can beat the kauri pine for decks, though in England and other countries it is generally known only for the excellent masts and spars that can be got out of it. A Scotch builder once reported that he found it very apt to twist and warp; but most likely the wood had been cut badly, for that is not the general opinion regarding it in the colonies, where it is almost invariably employed for decks. New Zealand, however, has been treated at length in the preceding chapter.

BOMBAY, ETC.

At Bombay, Malta and Hong Kong regular annual regattas are held, besides numerous matches and races during the yachting seasons. British built or designed yachts, to say nothing of those produced by local talent, are to be met with in all three ports. At Malta and Bombay very flourishing Royal Yacht Clubs exist.

The yachts at Malta are principally cutter or Bermuda rigged vessels, and range from 20-tonners downward. The Royal Bombay Yacht Club possesses a house beautifully situated near the Apollo Bunda, or main pier, and the yacht anchorage is within hail of the club lawn. About two dozen or more yachts make use of it, among them being steamers and vessels of every method of fore-and-aft rig. Two or three are British built, and among these is the easily recognised little 3-tonner *Senta*, so well known in Kingstown during the palmy racing days of the 3-tonner class. One of the latest additions to the fleet is a small Clyde-built yacht something under 5 tons, with the fashionable fiddle-headed bow. This boat the writer saw under way. There were a number of *dhows*, large enough to carry three or four such yachts inboard, making up harbour with a fine sailing breeze just a point abaft the beam, which placed them on one of their best points of sailing. They appeared to be slipping through the smooth water at a high speed, leaving it as clean as if it had never been disturbed, and everything was in their favour for making a quick passage.

The little Clyde boat had been knocking about the harbour and was well astern of the dhows, when she was hove round and made to stand on after them. Favoured with the same wind, gradually she began to draw up to them, and bit by bit overhauled and passed each one, leaving them in a manner which made me doubt very much whether the rate of speed with which dhows are so often credited can really be so great. The *dhow*-rigged racing yachts make very good reckonings. They have considerable draught forward, with a small draught aft, and the foremast (the masts rake forward) has its step almost over where the largest body and the greatest draught happens to be. These yachts, like all vessels of a similar rig and build, are never tacked, but are always gybed, and naturally in a triangular course they lose much time when racing against cutters and schooners.

The rules of the Yacht Racing Association, with the measurements, regulations, and time allowances, have been adopted by most of, if not all, the clubs mentioned in the Australias and elsewhere, and nothing can equal the cordial reception accorded to all lovers of yachting who

Lateen yachts, Bombay Club, 1887.

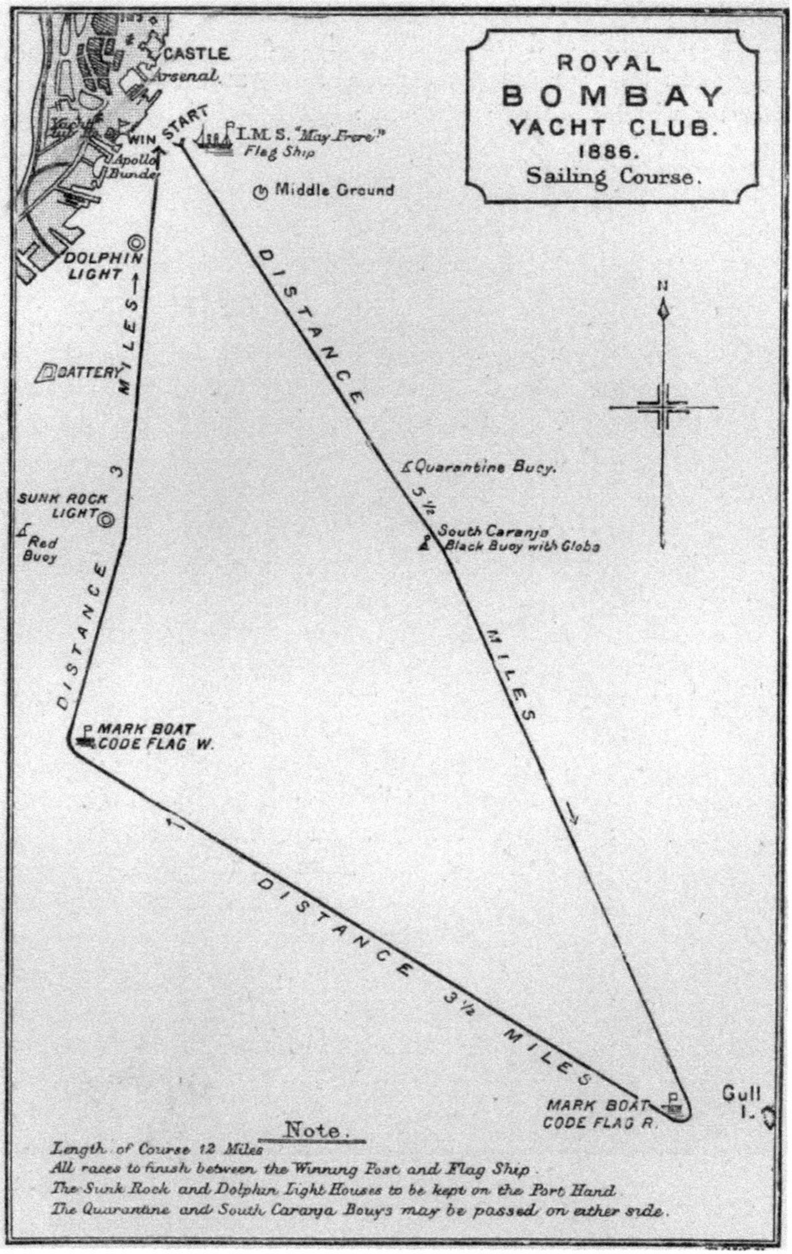
ROYAL
BOMBAY
YACHT CLUB.
1886.
Sailing Course.
CASTLE
Arsenal.
WIN
START
I.M.S. "May Frere"
Flag Ship
Apollo Bunder
Middle Ground
DOLPHIN LIGHT
BATTERY
MILES
3
DISTANCE
SUNK ROCK LIGHT
Red Buoy
DISTANCE 5½ MILES
Quarantine Bucy.
South Caranja Black Buoy with Globe
N
MARK BOAT CODE FLAG W.
DISTANCE 3½ MILES
MARK BOAT CODE FLAG R.
Gull I.
Note.
Length of Course 12 Miles
All races to finish between the Winning Post and Flag Ship.
The Sunk Rock and Dolphin Light Houses to be kept on the Port Hand
The Quarantine and South Caranja Bouys may be passed on either side.

visit their colonial cousins. It is only to be desired that, as in rowing and cricket, so in yachting, a systematic and frequent interchange of friendly contests may soon be inaugurated between them and their mother-country which shall eventuate in a general enlightenment all round on things pertaining to yachting.

Bermuda
By R. T. Pritchett

The Bermudian's hobby is going to windward, and to be really happy he must have a semicircular fin or plate on his keel like that described by Lord Pembroke. Bermuda has a Royal Yacht Club which gives prizes and holds regattas at Hamilton. There is also a Dinghy Club, of which the Princess Louise is Lady Patroness. Lord and Lady Brassey each presented a Challenge Cup when they visited Hamilton in 1883 in the *Sunbeam*. One class here deserves special notice.

'Fitted Races' are the chief joy of the true Bermudian. The owner apparently gives up his boat to the fiendish devices of his 'pilot,' as the nigger boatman is called, who gets the biggest mast, spars and sails he can find, often a 50-foot mast in a 25-foot boat, and a 35- or 40-foot boom topping up with a huge square-sail as big as a ship's maintop-gallant-sail. He then collects all the other niggers he can find, dresses them in striped jerseys and caps, puts them up to windward, over a ton and a half of shifting ballast, serves out a lot of rum all round, and off they go, generally with the head of the mainsail lashed (no halliard) to the masthead, so that she must carry her whole sail all through the race or swamp. The present writer's experience is confined to many good dustings in that admirable craft the *Diamond*, with her very able skipper Burgess, coloured gentleman (*bien culotté*), both of which were lent to Lady Brassey by Admiral Sir Edmund Commerell. She was built of cedar, and her lines and midship section are given in Dixon Kemp's *Boat-sailing*.

Dimensions of average Bermudian boat of 5 tons:

Length	25 ft.
Mast	44 ft.
Boom	33 ft.
Bowsprit	19 ft.
Spinnaker boom	25 ft.

General rule, greatest girth + length = height of mast and hoist.

Mr. Charles Ricardo, Secretary of Upper Thames Sailing Club, who sailed with the owner of the *Cara*, a 28-foot boarder, kindly furnishes the following description of a Fitted Race.

The morning of the race it blew hard, and we sailed out to the leeward mark-boat half under water, the *Cara* having only about 14 in. freeboard, and on board there were six hands, a big spinnaker boom, and some two dozen so-called sandbags for shifting. These had been apparently filled with mud, not sand, and as they rapidly got soaked, we looked more like navvies fresh from a clay-pit than boat sailers. There are many gradations of dirt and various degrees of saturation from salt water, but this combination is unapproachable. We caught a line from the mark-boat and shifted jib, owner going out on the bowsprit for this function, and getting a couple of green seas well in the small of his back—it didn't matter. We were well soaked already, so more or less was quite immaterial to us.

We were hanging on to the stake-boat some time, waiting for the other craft to arrive, with nothing particular to do but bale out and try to dodge the things kicking about in the bottom of the boat. I had no shoes on, and there was one baler. I thought I had put it into a locker three times, and was watching the wretched thing edge out again and prepare to fall on my toes, sharp edge down of course, when the owner sung out lustily, 'Boat bearing down to hang on!' She was a regular Bermudian with 'fitted' gear, enormous spars, and her big sail up, a crew of coloured gentlemen crowded up to windward, and foaming through it like a tugboat after a homeward-bounder. She had to gybe under our stern and run lip alongside the mark-boat, and— Swish, over came the boom again; swish, went the end of it into the water. She heeled over tremendously, and did not seem to right, as she ought to have done.

We guessed at once what had happened: her ballast was to leeward—those mud bags—it had not been shifted in time as she came round, and of course kept her on her beam ends; she gradually settled down and sank in about four minutes. The water was full of yelling niggers, who mostly swam for us; there seemed to be some hundred of them—anyway they yelled like it. They nearly swamped us scrambling in; finally we got rid of them on to the mark-boat, and very glad we were, as a few dozen damp niggers all asking at the same time for drinks are not much fun in a small boat with a bit of a sea on. At the time it was not enjoyable; still it is an episode in yachting experiences which grows more pleasant to refer to as it looms astern and becomes ancient history. When one starts for a day's sport, it is weak to allow a

FITTED RACES AT BERMUDA, 1863.

BERMUDA RIG.

DUTCH ICE BOAT OF PRESENT TIME.

trifling incident like this to mar the even tenor of its way, and at Bermuda one dries so soon.

A great deal of dinghy racing is done at St. George's, and it will be well to notice here the peculiarity of these boats and their gear. The normal dimensions of the dinghy are as follows:—

Length	14 ft.
Beam	4 ft. 6 in.
Draught	2 ft.
Mast	25 ft. to 30 ft.
Boom	25 ft.
Bowsprit	15 ft.

Dinghies are fearfully and wonderfully made things, with their plate on as in the big boats, the sails lashed up and set in. Five lunatics come next in the prescription; these embark very gingerly indeed—quite a bit of fancy work—while some one holds on to the mast from the top of the wharf to prevent accident, and when they think they are ready and balanced they are shoved off. Directly she feels the wind over she goes, and four hands stretch out to windward as far as possible, the fifth being busy baling, which is a most important feature of dinghy sailing.

A very exciting amusement it is. As long as the boats can be kept right side up they do go a tremendous pace. Waiting about before the race and gybing are the most exciting and dangerous times, as three dinghies have been known to capsize in one race before starting. Bathing costume is considered the correct thing, and is well adapted to the climate; it is also desirable in this sport to be able to swim, as there is no room in the boats for such superfluities as life-belts. The *Diamond* was a very fine boat, and splendid in a wind; as the mainsail represents the usual mainsail and jackyarder all in one, the whole sail-area forms the desirable equilateral triangle a little aft to send her up to the wind.

The fitting of the boom is different from any other rig, as it passes on one side beyond the mast; a tail block hauls the boom right aft, and counteracted by the mainsheet gives a very flat sail indeed; great results are obtained, all the advantages of a standing lug on a large scale being secured, while the tension can be increased and the canvas made flatter. Space cannot be afforded for her lines, midship section and sail-plan, good as they are, still *Diamond* is decidedly a good cedar-built representative craft:—

Length on water-line 34 ft.
Beam 11 ft. 2.5 in.
Draught 6 ft. 6 in.

The extravagances of Bermudian water frolics have been given here as very extreme instances of yachting enjoyments; still Bermuda is a splendid place for sailing. You can leave the island on a Friday for New York, arriving on Monday; leave New York on Tuesday, and in a week more be back in the old country.

Chapter 9

Some Famous Races
By R. T. Pritchett

In former days, matches were made between yachts as between horses on the turf, and the stakes were often heavy, but such events are now almost unknown; the increase in the number of craft has divided the attention of the public, and the performance of each vessel is so well known that there are no dark sea-horses to bring out as a surprise. The records of bygone matches are, however, far from easy to obtain, if, indeed, they are obtainable. Newspapers were formerly less numerous than they are at present, nor did there apparently exist much thirst for information and minute detail on the part of the public. Accounts remain, however, of some few of the most important matches. One for a thousand guineas, August 29, 1771, sailed between the Duke of Richmond and Sir Alexander Smith, the course being from Brighton to Beachy Head and back, has been already mentioned, but from this date much search has yielded scanty results.

The war must have interfered greatly with the sport, for there is a long lapse of time when yachting scarcely came at all under the notice of the press. The Royal Yacht Squadron's fine class of schooners and vessels of large tonnage, however, created and revived rivalry. On September 1, 1834, a great race for one thousand guineas took place between *Waterwitch*, brig, 331 tons, belonging to the Earl of Belfast, and *Galatea*, schooner, 179 tons; in this race Mr. Charles Ratsey sailed, and he is now hale and hearty in Cowes. The course was from the Nab Lightship, round the Eddystone Lighthouse, and back. The start took place at 10 a.m., on the Monday morning, when the weather was fine, wind tolerably fresh from south and west. The first day, in the afternoon, the wind fell light, almost a calm at 7 p.m., the yachts being then only off Dunnose, Isle of Wight. The schooner at this time was

'Waterwitch,' 331 tons (Earl of Belfast) and 'Galatea,' 179 tons.
The start for a race for 1,000 guineas, September 1, 1834.

'Corsair' and 'Talisman' race round Eddystone, August 1842, 'Corsair' winning.

'Talisman,' 84 tons, and 'Corsair,' 80 tons, race, 1842.

two miles to windward. On Tuesday, at 7 p.m., the two yachts were off Berry Head, Torbay, the schooner *Galatea* still to windward.

About this time, as the breeze freshened, she had the misfortune to carry away her jibboom, and got too close under Bolthead by the Start, thereby losing her tide. They rounded the Eddystone nearly together; from which point, both running large, the brig gradually drew away from the schooner, and finally reached the Nab Lightship at 2 p.m. on Wednesday, September 3, *Galatea* coming in at 2.20 p.m. The course was about 130 miles, and the time occupied 52 hours. The race, in August 1842, also round the Eddystone, in an easterly gale, between *Corsair*, 80 tons, and *Talisman*, 84 tons, is justly celebrated. *Corsair* won by 1 min. 30 secs. Two pictures of this race were painted by Condy, of Plymouth. Running down channel *Corsair* is represented with a mizzen, which Mr. Charles Ratsey informed the writer was stuck in at the last minute and was carried away turning to windward; she is therefore shown without one on her return.

There was talk of a race between the Marquis of Anglesey's *Pearl* and Mr. J. Weld's *Alarm* for a thousand guineas, but it never came off; in fact, the marquis never raced her from the time *Pearl* was built in 1821 to the year of his death, 1854. The *Mosquito*, with Captain John Nichols at the tiller, once came out on his weather, and the marquis very politely dipped his ensign to the yacht that weathered him for the first time in all his years of cruising. The *Arrow* and *Mosquito* once finished a fine race, which was a marvellously close thing between them, *Arrow*, 6 hrs. 59 mins. 30 secs., *Mosquito*, 6 hrs. 59 mins. 31 secs.!

A very good account is handed to us of how yachtsmen more than half a century since—in 1830—enjoyed a real rough day's sailing on the Thames. A cup had been subscribed for of the value of fifty guineas, and all the cracks of the day entered for it:—

	tons
Matchless	19
Vixen	19
Lady Louisa	13
Fairy	13
Daisy	19
Venus	13
Rob Roy	16
Brilliant	8
Donna del Lago	9
Ariel	8

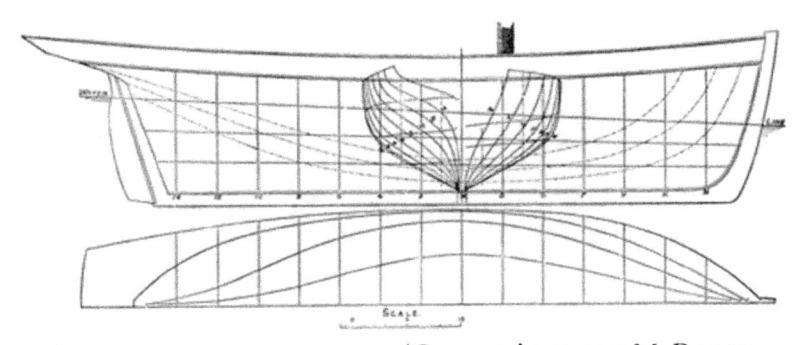

LINES AND MIDSHIP SECTION OF 'CORSAIR,' BUILT BY M. RATSEY, COWES, 1832.
Length for tonnage, 57 ft. 9 in.; breadth, 18 ft. 6 in.; tonnage, $84^{84}/_{94}$.

'YSEULT'
10-RATER (P. DONALDSON, ESQ.) DESIGNED BY FIFE, 1892.

The race was from Greenwich to Gravesend and back, and it certainly was not lacking in interest. The sport began early. *Matchless* carried away her boom, running into *Lady Louisa's* quarter; *Lady Louisa's* bowsprit caught *Rob Roy's* backstay, and she followed *Matchless* ashore, dragging *Lady Louisa* after her. At this time *Daisy* was leading. Soon after *Brilliant* became first and *Ariel* second boat. In Erith Reach on the return *Venus* was waterlogged. *Donna del Lago* carried away her bowsprit; *Vixen* carried away outhaul, and when she got into Erith Roads *Vixen's* mast went by the board. Finally *Brilliant* won by 1 minute from *Ariel*, who was second. They were both reefed down to the balance-reef, as shown in the illustration taken from an old print. Balance-reefs are seldom seen nowadays, although they are occasionally carried by fishing craft.

There was one day's racing in 1892 which should be handed down as a remarkable instance of what the new boats can do in a stress of weather. It was Largs Regatta, July 12, when the Largs men witnessed and took part in the kind of sport they so dearly love; they are severe critics, but give honour where honour is due, especially to weatherly craft and good seamanship. The wind was from the east, freshening up towards the time for the start. Unfortunately *Meteor* and *Iverna* were not competing, the former having damaged her gaff. The forties were there, four in number—*Queen Mab*, *Corsair*, *Varuna*, and *White Slave*—the *Mohican* was flagship, in line with a flag on Largs Pier. It was a truly wild morning, white squalls being frequent and severe. The Firth was all spoondrift; *Queen Mab* and *Varuna* had housed topmasts, one reef down, *Corsair* topmast on end. Under Knockhill the squalls were tremendously heavy, very patchy and local.

Off Skelmorlie the racers got the true east wind hard, and found the flagboat dragging her anchor. They rounded, however: *Queen Mab* was timed 11 hrs. 8 mins. 16 secs., *Varuna*, 11 hrs. 8 mins. 52 secs. Coming over towards Largs they got into a lull, when *Corsair* set her gaff-topsail, *Mab* and *Varuna* getting topmasts on end; the latter set her topsail, the former did not. Soon a mighty rush of wind burst down from between Tomont End and Largs. At the 'Knock' again there was a kind of vacuum-cum-Mäelström.

Soon after, in a wilder phase of Clyde weather, *Mab* and *Varuna* were caught by a fierce squall and laid down to it. *Corsair*, unfortunately, was the victim of a squall spout, which carried away her mast close to the board—such was the strain that something must have gone. The *White Slave*, belonging to Mr. F. W. L. Popham, was at this

'Brilliant' and 'Ariel' race, 1830.

'Iverna' (J. Jameson, Esq.) and 'Meteor'
(H.I.M. the Emperor of Germany).
Dead heat in the Clyde, July 4, 1892.

time off the Knock; she took in her topsail, and nearing *Corsair* further reduced her canvas, lowering her mainsail to assist her. Ultimately *Corsair* was towed by Duncan, of *Madge* fame. Skelmorlie mark was rounded at 12 hrs. 42 mins. 30 secs. by *Queen Mab*, at 12 hrs. 45 mins. 12 secs. by *Varuna*.

After this all was flying spoondrift and canvas reduced to two sails—the wind harder than ever. Smoking bows were the order of the day, clouds of spray soaked the mainsails nearly to the peak, gaffs were like rainbows in curve, all hands were warily standing by to lower foresail or meet the next emergency. *Queen Mab* finished in 1 hr. 43 mins. 35 secs., *Varuna* 1 hr. 49 mins. 33 secs.

Parker sailed *Queen Mab*, Gould *Varuna*, Sycamore *Corsair*. It was indeed a hard blow, and a fine display of yacht handling and good seamanship under most trying circumstances; the *Yseult*, 10-tonner, lost her bowsprit, and everybody lost something. All credit to the skippers, who never lost their heads.

The '6-rater' match seemed to be the joy of Largs, especially on this occasion, when the weather enabled the crews to show what the Irish boats could do. So much damage had been done that three only were left to start: *Red Lancer*, Col. Crawford, *Savourna*, Mr. H. L. Mulholland, and *Windfall*, Mr. Gubbins. They seemed to revel in the storm; 'blow high, blow low,' was all the same to them. More would have started had they not been unhappily crippled in one way or the other, but those that did were nearly blown out of the water. The maxim of 'Batten down' was in every case emphasised. After a tremendous experience of what the Clyde can do to encourage real seamanship and fearless daring *Savourna* came in at 2 hrs. 3 mins., and *Red Lancer*, 2 hrs. 3 mins. 39 secs; *Red Lancer* taking 1st prize, *Savourna* 2nd prize. Largs Regatta in 1892 will long be remembered; it was no flat racing, but real steeplechasing in the Clyde.

1892 also leaves us a dead heat between the two champions of the season, the *Iverna* and the *Meteor*. This occurred at the Royal Clyde Club, July 4, 1892; wind W.N.W., a fine breeze, both carrying jibheaders at the finish, as shown in the illustration. *Iverna* led by 19 seconds—3 hrs. 25 mins. 28 secs., allowing *Meteor* 19 seconds; *Meteor* finished at 3 hrs. 25 mins. 47 secs. Dead heat.

This was sailed off, July 8, in the Wemyss Bay programme, and resulted in a very fine race, topmasts struck, first reef down in mainsail—real going, both vessels made the most of and thoroughly well handled. Mr. William Jameson and O'Neil were on *Iverna*, and Gomes was at the tiller of *Meteor*. It was a grand exhibition of yacht-racing, and finished, *Iverna*, 4 hrs. 18 mins. 26 secs., *Meteor*, 4 hrs. 21 mins. 22 secs.

CHAPTER 10

Racing in a 40-Rater in 1892
By R. T. Pritchett

Most of the races described in these volumes are from the standpoint of the looker-on ashore, or else on board some vessel which was not competing; the present chapter describes a race from that point of vantage, the deck of the winning yacht.

Cowes in the early morn is not generally known to visitors. The 'wood and brass work'—a term better known on board than on shore—is now in full swing, for this admirable function must be completed by eight bells. If cleanliness be next to godliness, surely yachts have very much to commend them, with their spotless decks, bleached runners, and immaculate canvas. In leaving the pontoon for the offing, the various craft increase in size as the water deepens. First the small raters are passed, ½-, 1-, 2½-raters, *Wee Winn*, *Polynia*, *Hoopoo*, and *Kitten*—described by 'Thalassa' in his Solent chapter. Passing the tens and twenties the French yachts are reached, for of late years the burgee of the French club is often seen at Cowes, and the American flag is more frequent than of yore. The Guard-ship now looms. The Royal yacht, *Victoria and Albert*, is at her buoy, the Royal Yacht Squadron nobly represented. Eight bells now strike.

Immediately the morning flutter of bunting flies to the mastheads, where all the burgees should arrive simultaneously, taking the time from the flagship—but they do not, unfortunately. (N.B.—Racing flags can be lashed before eight bells, as they have no halliards.) By this time we see the 40 just astern of a yawl and ahead of a Frenchman. *Queen Mab* is basking and glistening in the bright morning sunshine, in perfect repose, yet rather fretting to be off, for with her colour she knows what is coming. Having come alongside very carefully, without touching the varnish, we are soon on board, and find all in

GOING ALOFT.

motion. The business of the day has begun, the preliminary functions are completed, such as sending the gig away with the superfluous gear of squeegees, mops, oars. The 12-ft. dinghy is already lashed over the skylight, with the stem wedged up to the coaming abaft of the companion. The tyers are off the mainsail, and it is soon on the hoist. The crew are going aloft, to string down on the throat halliards; gradually the peak rises, well up, about 45°, and with the modern lacing down to the boom the sail soon becomes fairly set.

Next, the gaff topsail. In America, in the *Puritan* and other racers, photography shows that they start with two, jibheader and jackyarder or club foresail, so called from the club or yard at the foot. In the *Vigilant*, the jackyarder was set most cleverly over the jibheaded topsail when running back in the final race. In joining a racer there is nothing so comfortable for host and guest too as being on board in good time. With a flying start it is very important to be under way to the minute, especially in light winds and with a tide running, such as the swill in Cowes Roads generally is, whether spring or otherwise. It is no joke for a boatman to catch a racer once under way, even without her head sails, in the offing, to say nothing of the anathemas of the owner, and the skipper's suppressed comments.

Soon comes the welcome of the owner of *Queen Mab*, Col. T. B. C. West, well known in the yachting world in connection with that grand yawl *Wendur*, 143 tons, T.M., built in 1883, his famous 10-rater *Queen Mab* in the Clyde, and now the *Queen Mab* of 1892. The forties are a very prominent class and justly so; they emphasise the sport of class racing over handicaps.

About this time the racing flags of other craft are a subject of intense interest, and the crew are immensely keen. Should an old adversary not be getting under way, the why and wherefore will be at once discussed; this generally brings out prominently any hand of the 'sea lawyer' class, if the owner has unfortunately shipped one. The head sails have now been set, and we are curvetting and pirouetting about waiting for preparatory gun. There is no doubt that wonderful skill is shown in the handling of the various craft. A dexterity and firmness are apparent which could never be secured with the American system of adjusted time: thus if *Vigilant* were four minutes late at the start, that time would be deducted from the winner at the finish.

Now comes the full excitement of the start. 'First gun, sir; fifteen minutes to go!' is the word, and for the next eighteen minutes all is extra wariness, sometimes fourteen yachts under way, manœuvring,

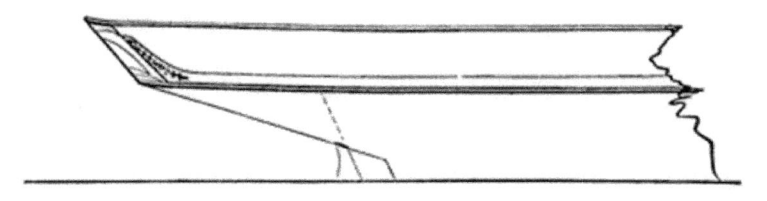

OLD STYLE.

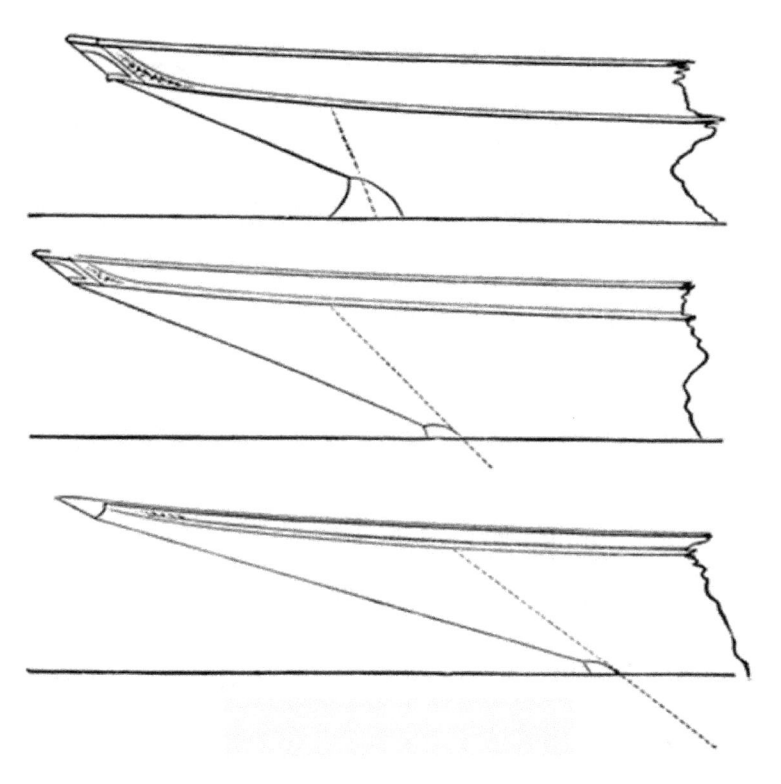

NEW STYLE.

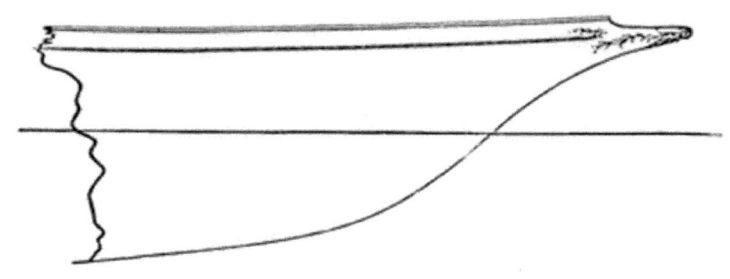

'Reverie,' 1891.

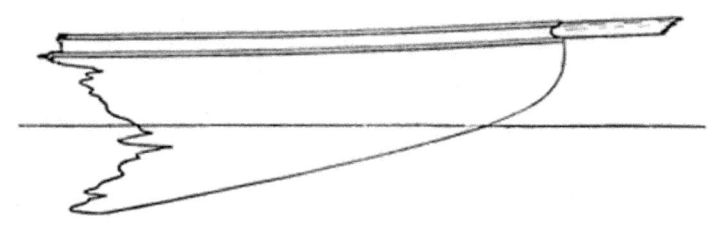

'Corsair,' 1892.

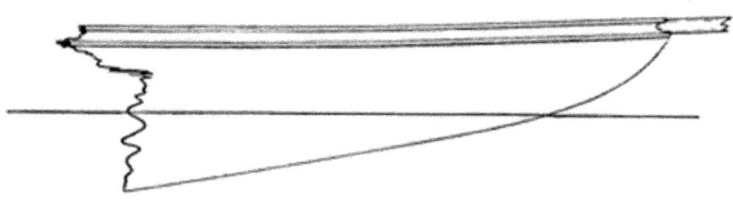

'Queen Mab,' 1892.

'Doreen,' 1892.

and keenly watching each other. 'Blue Peter, sir, five minutes!' is next heard. The owner, watch in hand, by the skipper, records the fleeting moments as they pass, calling out the minutes: at length it comes to 1 min., 50 secs., 40 secs., 30 secs., 20 secs. 'How much, sir?' 'Ten seconds'; then 'Let her go!' and she goes—with her cranse iron over the line directly after the gun. Everyone now turns attention to the recall numbers. Are there any? There has been such a thing as three over the line out of four starters, so great is the eagerness for a lead.

Among the larger classes everyone looks out for Mr. Jameson being first over line, with O'Neil at the tiller, famed for his special gift for quick starting and weather berths. A good start is a grand beginning. So long as one is leading no explanation is required why the good ship is not showing her best form, or how it is that she is not in her right trim. By this time the fleet is getting sorted; with a good sailing breeze the large craft draw out ahead in many cases, and it is well to do so; the large cutters are started, say, a quarter of an hour ahead, and the forties together.

In 1892 the forties were very strongly represented, *Thalia, Reverie, Queen Mab, Corsair, Creole, Varuna, White Slave*. This gave most interesting sport, far preferable to handicapping, which is only adopted to bring vessels of different tonnage together. A curious instance of this occurred at Cowes, when *Irex, Genesta,* and *Lorna* all came in together within five minutes, and having brought up, stowed canvas and dined, it was discovered that *Sleuthhound* was coming in, almost saving her time allowance of about 53 min. It is certainly most uninteresting to the spectators on shore to see the first fine craft come in close together, and returning from afternoon tea to perhaps discover that the real winner is just sailing in round the flagboat and getting the gun.

By this time the 'sun is over the foreyard' and all are settling down for a fine race. Sailing in a race affords excellent opportunity for noticing the other competing craft and admiring the goodly company assembled around. The big cutters are leading, and some of the forties astern. That *Queen Mab* will hold her own with the best is a point upon which we feel happily confident, her racing flags being proof of her capacity—thirty-six is the number she showed at the end of the season. This yacht, as mentioned elsewhere, was built with a centreboard, but instead of a huge partition in the centre of the saloon, the board came under the main companion, and was quite unnoticeable. As with Mr. Jameson's *Irex, Mab's* centreboard was discarded, and each became the crack of her respective season.

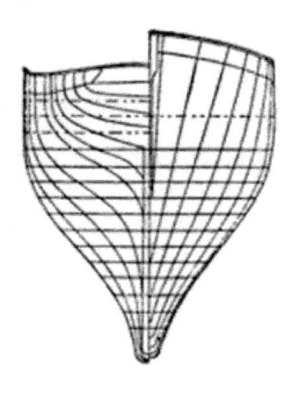

'IREX,' MIDSHIP SECTION.

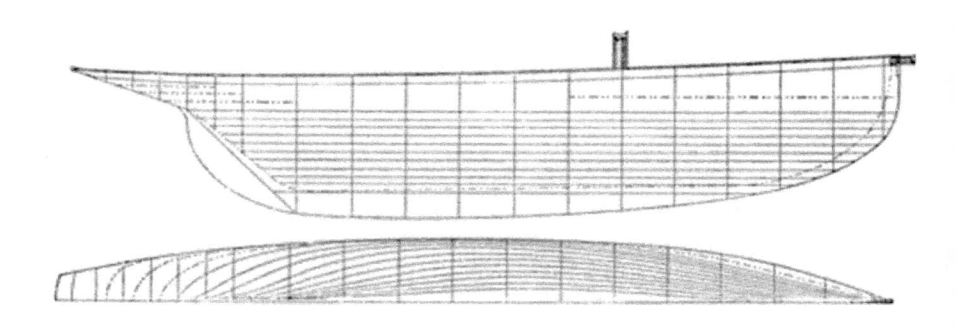

'IREX,' BUILT FOR JOHN JAMESON, ESQ., 1884.
Length B.P. 88'0"; length L.W.L. 83'6"; beam extreme 15'0".
Tonnage R.T.Y.C. Rule 88. tons; tonnage register 74.67 tons; Y.R.A. Rating 98 tons.

Varuna, also a new boat this year, designed by Mr. G. L. Watson with a Watson bow, as in *Mab*, was a beautiful craft, really perhaps the designer's favourite. These bows, with those in *Corsair* and others, elicited sighs and groans from the old school of yachting men; for what with the schooner bow, the Viking bow, the inverted Roman nose bow, the bottle-nose bow, the Fife bow, and the canoe bow, one's idea of what a bow should be became somewhat confused. However, overhang forward carries the day up to 200 tons. *Corsair*, 40-rater, designed by Mr. Arthur Payne of Southampton, was a grand boat, with less beam than *Mab*, beautiful counter, long boom, very workmanlike all round. She was built for that enthusiastic yachtsman, Admiral the Hon. Victor Montagu, a dear lover of all good English sports. *Thalia* was a fine craft, by Fife of Fairlie, splendid sea boat. Many is the good race Mr. Inglis has sailed in her, with Carter, who sailed *Britannia*, 1893, at the tiller.

We live in an age of rather rapid development; 1892 becomes ancient history in 1893, still it seems sad that when one has a good vessel like *Thalia*, she should so soon be outclassed. Fashion always runs to extremes; now that fashion has attacked yachting, the belle of one season is extinguished in the next. '*Sic tempora et naves mutantur.*' In old days enthusiastic yacht-owners lengthened their pets, almost rebuilt them sometimes, as in the cases of *Alarm* and *Arrow*; the associations were retained and duly cherished.

We have started, it should have been said, for the Australian Cup, value 50*l.*, presented by Mr. Gibson Miller for yachts exceeding 20 tons and not exceeding 40 tons. The second prize, 30*l.*, is given by the Royal Squadron. The westerly wind turned out very light, and without a good sailing breeze racing becomes peaceful repose. Much interest, however, is felt in the performance of *Irene*, 40-rater, designed by Mr. G. L. Watson for Prince Henry of Prussia, who was at the tiller all day, heart and soul in it, longing for a breeze, and probably keeping up the old superstition by giving an unintentional whistle for one; but still it would not come. At 4 hrs. 0 min. 35 secs. *Queen Mab* came in the winner, *Thalia* taking second prize.

For real racing a true wind, such as we had in the race for prizes given by the Royal Southampton Yacht Club, August 6, is indispensable. This was a small but sporting muster. *Iverna* and *Meteor* were sent away at 10.45 a.m., *Iverna* crossing the line to a second. The forties, *Corsair*, *Queen Mab*, and *Thalia*, were despatched half an hour later at 11 a.m., to a perfect start and a whole-sail westerly breeze, *Mab*

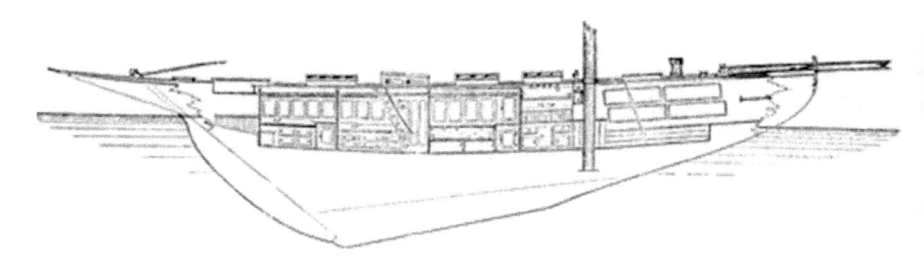

LONGITUDINAL ELEVATION.

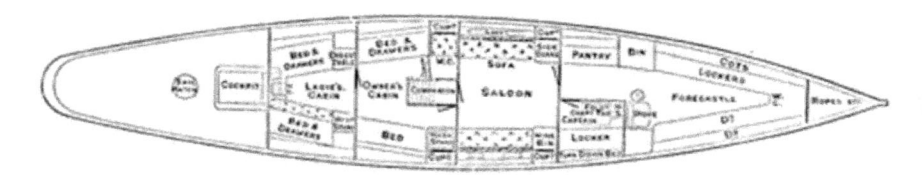

CABIN PLAN.
'CORSAIR' (ADMIRAL THE HON. VICTOR MONTAGU), 40-RATER, 1892.
DESIGNED BY ARTHUR E. PAYNE.

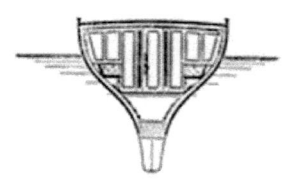

'CORSAIR,'
MIDSHIP SECTION.

crossing two seconds after the Blue Peter was hauled down. The gun missed fire. We hailed the Committee Boat, 'Are we all right?' when the pleasant echo returned, 'All right, go on,' and away we went.

It was a fine reach down Southampton Water, the three close together in single file. Passing Calshot Lightship we hauled our wind and stood over for Cowes, feeling the westerly breeze which came sweeping up from the Needles; below Egypt we went about and took our jumps merrily—a nasty sea, if the sea can be nasty; our working topsail relieved her somewhat—for *Corsair* and *Thalia* were carrying jackyarders. It was a grand beat down to Lymington; the rain was heavy, but after a few hard squalls the sun came out and the Lymington mark-boat was rounded, *Queen Mab* 12 hrs. 45 mins. 10 secs., *Corsair* 12 hrs. 46 mins. 20 secs., *Thalia* 12 hrs. 47 mins. 35 secs. As the mark-boat was neared all were astir. 'Get your gear on your spinnaker boom, my lads, and top him as soon as you can. Will you take the time, sir, of *Meteor* and *Iverna* rounding?' Before this our masthead man George had gone aloft by an acrobatic performance which is always interesting to the beholder: on the port tack with the port foot on a hoop, and the starboard foot on the sail, as indicated in the illustration. George was a good compact cheery hand, and must have been born for this particular function. By this time we are round.

'Down spinnaker boom,' and now every thread draws and the whole sail is pulling hard. 'All aft, my sonnies!' and the skipper Parker seems to smile upon his pet. At this time bread and cheese and beer are served out, and form a very pleasant pendant to 'all aft' except the look-out, who took his mid-day in solitude by the unfilled foresail. A splendid dead run from the Lymington mark back to Cowes now takes place. See! *Corsair's* spinnaker is here suddenly taken in, Sycamore, her skipper, having discovered that her mast was sprung, and he therefore went into Cowes. This was a great disappointment to us, and must have been to Admiral Victor Montagu, who so dearly loves racing, especially in a true wind. We were now cracking on for the Warner, our enjoyment only once disturbed by a hail from the look-out, 'Boat right under bow, sir,' and in the same breath, 'Only a photogger, sir,' and on we sped.

Rounding the Warner *Thalia* carried away her throat halliards, but soon continued the race. Rounding mark-boats and lightships is thrilling work, and beautifully it is done on *Queen Mab*. It is delightful to see the judgment and decision, and how cheerily the hands haul on to the mainsheet; truly this is sport and excitement not easily beaten.

OUR MASTHEAD MAN.

LASHING THE EMPEROR'S RACING FLAG.

'All aft, my sonnies!'

'Another pull at the mainsheet, my lads!'

Close hauled.

Queen Mab bends gracefully to it, and well it suits her; we are hissing through it. It is generally supposed that racing yachts are regularly gralloched and cleared out below; it is so in America and was done to *Navahoe* in her races; but it is not so here. Everything is in its place, and when the head of the steward appears at the companion with the welcome words, 'Lunch, sir!' we find that all is well—but look out for the swinging table: touch that and there will be a ghastly crash. The 40-rater has the owner's cabin and the lady's cabin, with a very comfortable one for a guest, to say nothing of accommodation for sea bachelors who do not require shore luxury.

The ladies' conning tower is generally the top step of the companion, but in the *Seabelle* Mrs. Taylor had an armchair swung like a gimbal compass, in which she knitted comfortably at whatever angle the yacht might be in a seaway. After lunch we are close-hauled lying for Calshot Castle, hissing through it with a pleasant swish of spray, ever and anon making some of the hands duck their heads as they lie up to windward. Many is the dry remark and cheery yarn that one hears under these circumstances; not many words but much to the purpose, old recollections are revived, and there is always something to be learnt.

Each hand is on the look-out in calm weather, scouring the horizon for a wandering catspaw, or in bad weather, watching the other craft to see how they take it. To note the skipper's face is a study; his eye on every leach and every sheet, keen and ready for any emergency, entirely absorbed in 'her' and how she is going and how he can best cosset her. Such was the impression left of Ben Parker at the tiller of *Queen Mab*. He had done good work in Mr. Hill's *Dragons* of the 20's. His first command was the *Ulidia*, Fife's 10-tonner, after having sailed for some years under Tom Diaper and O'Neil, and his Channel race from Dover in 1892 will never be forgotten. It was a merry close haul back from the Warner to Southampton Water.

As the wind was drawing down the river we had a beat up to the Committee-boat, which was reached, *Queen Mab* 4 hrs. 9 mins. 57 secs., winner, 40*l*. and silver medal; *Thalia* 4 hrs. 58 mins., second prize 10*l*. *Thalia*, built by Fife of Fairlie, had a rare good crew, and Mr. I. A. Inglis has sailed many a famous race in her with his skipper, Carter, whose season of 1893 in H.R.H. the Prince of Wales's *Britannia* speaks for itself. We get the 'gun,' that great joy at the end of a good race. 'Down foresail,' and round she comes. The cheering is over, so now to clear up. Unlash the dinghy, get back the cutter and gear, and fill in the

TORQUAY.

'QUEEN MAB'
40-RATER (T. B. C. WEST, ESQ.)
DESIGNED BY G. L. WATSON, 1892.

Declaration, which has to be sent in by every owner or his representative immediately after a race is won. It runs thus:

Y.R.A. Declaration that Rules have been observed
I hereby declare that yacht whilst sailing in the race this day has strictly observed the sailing rules and regulations.
Date.   Signed

The gig is by this time alongside, and it must have been delightful to the owner as he stepped into her and left the side of the victorious *Queen Mab*, to look up and see five winning flags flying, representing five first prizes in five starts in one week.

It is not the purpose of this chapter to record all *Queen Mab's* victories, but it may be noted that she won the 40*l*. prize given by the Royal Dorset Yacht Club in August of this year—1892. The club was founded in 1875, and holds forth many inducements to yacht-owners to visit Weymouth. For small raters it is admirably adapted, as the Esplanade is of immense length, and the short courses can be seen from one end to the other.

At Dartmouth also *Queen Mab* had two fine races, in a hard wind round the Skerries. The first, August 26, was very good, but the second, August 27, was better, though only one round, at the end of which we found the flagboat bottom up. *Queen Mab* won first prize on both days. At Plymouth, in the following week, continuing the 'Westward Ho' procession, *Mab* sailed over, with double-reef mainsail No. 3 and jib, no foresail, *Thalia* and *Corsair* not caring to start. Outside the Breakwater it was very grand, and outside Rame Head grander still, as the rollers came in after a 48 hours' gale. The pilot admired *Mab* immensely, she made such good weather of it. The gale was great sport for us, and it was surprising to see how the small boats thrashed through it. *Dis* carried away her bowsprit, and there was much harmless wreckage of gear.

One lesson might be learnt, that with the short bowsprit produced by the overhang forward there is much strain taken off that very important spar. Plymouth often gets a hard blow about this time, which is the more to be regretted from the extraordinary variety of boats and classes, from the *Britannia* class down to the rowing matches of the bum-boat women. Devonport and the navy training brigs and colleges all join the water frolic, and great is the disappointment when the weather is unfavourable.

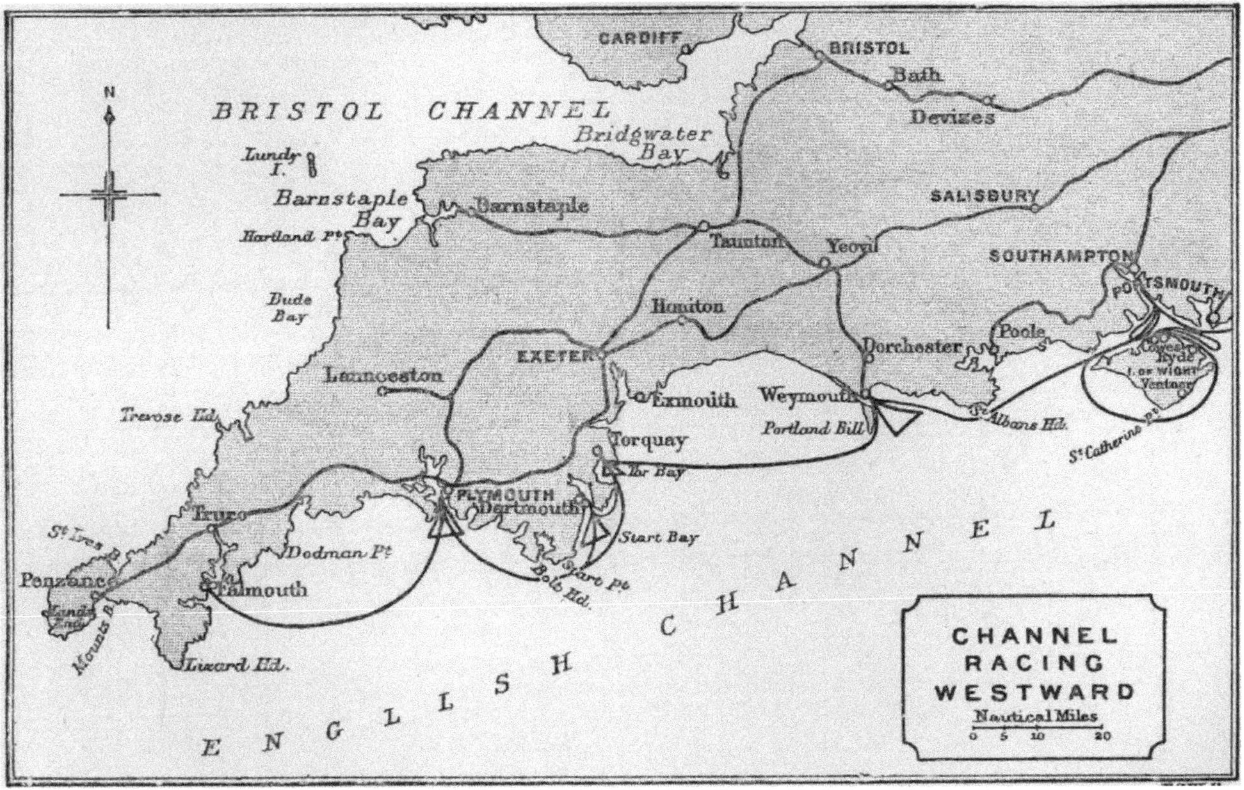
CHANNEL
RACING
WESTWARD
Nautical Miles
0 5 10 20
N
BRISTOL CHANNEL
ENGLISH CHANNEL
CARDIFF
BRISTOL
Bath
Devizes
Bridgwater Bay
Lundy I.
Barnstaple Bay
Barnstaple
Hartland Pt.
Bude Bay
SALISBURY
Taunton
Yeovil
SOUTHAMPTON
PORTSMOUTH
Honiton
EXETER
Launceston
Trevose Hd.
Dorchester
Poole
Cowes
Ryde
I. OF WIGHT
Ventnor
Exmouth
Weymouth
Portland Bill
St. Albans Hd.
St. Catherine Pt.
Torquay
Tor Bay
PLYMOUTH
Dartmouth
Start Bay
Start Pt.
Bolt Hd.
Truro
St. Ives B.
Dodman Pt.
Penzance
Falmouth
Lands End
Mounts B.
Lizard Hd.

REAL BUSINESS.

A CLOSE FINISH, 'QUEEN MAB' AND 'CORSAIR,'
R.T.Y.C., MAY, 1892.

Chapter 11
Yacht Racing in 1893
By H. Horn

An exceptional year, alike in regard to weather and sport, for not within living memory has there been so fine a spring, summer and autumn, and there is no previous record of such a sequence of eventful and stirring racing. It is highly gratifying that sport so truly national in character as yacht racing enlisted more general interest during the past season than has ever previously been the case; in fact, it can further be said that the doings of the *Britannia, Valkyrie, Satanita, Calluna, Navahoe,* and *Iverna'* arrested world-wide attention.

Lord Dunraven's commission, given in the fall of 1892, for a new *Valkyrie* of about double the rating of his first cutter of that name, heralded a revival of big-cutter racing, and later on yachting enthusiasts were almost delirious with joy when authentic announcements were made that the Prince of Wales had given orders for a sister ship to the *Valkyrie*, and that a big cutter was to be built at Southampton for Mr. A. D. Clarke, and one on the Clyde for a syndicate of Scotch yachtsmen.

Mr. G. L. Watson had a free hand in designing the *Valkyrie* and *Britannia*, which were built side by side at Partick by Messrs. Henderson, and parenthetically it may be said they fitted out, moored together, and kept singularly close company in all their matches. The *Satanita*, which was designed by Mr. J. Soper to sail on a 94-feet water-line, was built by Fay & Co., while Mr. W. Fife, junr. was responsible for the *Calluna's* model, and the vessel was built by Messrs. J. & A. Inglis of Pointhouse, Glasgow, in an incredibly short space of time. Although very certain that the *Iverna* would be quite outbuilt by the new ships, Mr. John Jameson determined to bring her out, and *Iverna's* well-tried antagonist, the *Meteor*, was under orders to join the fleet later on.

Just before the advent of the new year, Lord Dunraven's challenge for the new *Valkyrie* to sail a series of races for the America Cup was accepted by the New York Yacht Club, and about the same time came a notification from Mr. Carroll, a prominent American yachtsman, that he was having a sloop (the *Navahoe*) built by Messrs. Herreshoff, with which he intended to challenge for the Royal Victoria Gold Cup, and also make an attempt to win back the Cape May and Brenton Reef Cups.

The year was thus launched auspiciously enough in respect to big ship racing, and prospects were reassuring in regard to sport in all the other classes except the tens. There was a fining down however in number of the 40-rating division compared to 1892, and regrets were general that the sale of the *Queen Mab* had led to her expatriation. But Admiral Montagu was replacing the absentee *Corsair* with the *Vendetta*, a fin-bulb and balance-rudder craft, with a beam of about 17 feet, and Mr. John Gretton, jun., who did not get much fun out of the 10-rater *Doreen*, had determined on having a 40 from a Fife design, the outcome being the *Lais*. *Varuna* was being fitted out again by Capt. Towers-Clark, and the *Thalia*, which had passed into the possession of Judge Boyd, was to be raced, but not to go all round the coast.

The second class was thus virtually made up of *Vendetta*, *Varuna*, and *Lais*, which verily proved a militant trio, and their owners had plenty of racing, and no end of exciting and eventful sport. With the new *Dragon*—the third of that name Fife's had built for Mr. F. C. Hill—Lord Dunraven's *Deirdré*, by *Valkyrie's* designer, and the *Vigorna*, by Nicholson—which Lord Dudley intended to take the place of the 5-rater *Dacia*—there was promise of keen competition for the 20-rating prizes; but it was not in the best interests of sport that a joint arrangement was made that this class would not be raced outside the Isle of Wight—at least from the beginning of the season, until the Western meetings came on in the fall.

The *Zinita*, a new 20 by Fife, had things pretty much her own way on the Clyde, and it was a pity that she did not meet the new boats which starred in Southern waters. *Idalia*—the first *Dragon*—was the *Zinita's* most formidable opponent on the Clyde, and the *Molly*—*Dragon* the second—after a good spell of Solent racing, went North, but found the *Zinita* as bad to beat as she did the *Dragon* and the *Deirdré*. There were no new boats in the 10-rating class, and racing in this division was confined to the Clyde, where the *Dora*, *Ptarmigan*, *Maida*, *Phantom* and *Woodcock* had some good sport. The 6-raters, which were a feature in the Clyde and Irish regatta programmes in 1892, had gone out of fashion, and 23-feet 'lengthers' were the reigning favourites with small shipmen on the Clyde, Mr. Robt. Wylie's *Vida*, a Watson design, being the crack in a fleet of eight. The Solent 5-rating class could not boast of a new boat, and the *Dacia*, although she headed the list of prize-winners in the South, did not sail up to her 1892 form. The *Red Lancer*, which went all round the coast, was the pride of the season of the fives, and she was equal to taking down *Dacia* pretty easily. The *Fleur-de-Lis* and *Quinque* also frequently lowered *Dacia's* colours, and honours were about easy with the trio at the end of the season.

In the 2½-rating class the *Meneen*, a Herreshoff boat, had a better average than the over-year Nicholson boat, *Gareth*, and in the 1-rating class the *Morwena*—another Herreshoff—was the principal winner. It cannot be said that the branch of the sport known as handicap sailing flourished during the season, though there were some keen and interesting battles with the ex-racers. The most successful vessels in this division were the *Creole, Castanet, Columbine, Mabel* and *Samœna*.

The big-cutter contests were of such exceptional interest that a review of the season would not be complete without a history of all the races sailed, and the opportunity is embraced of embodying many unreported incidents in the subjoined *résumé* of the first-class racing.

There was a thoroughly representative assemblage of yachtsmen afloat the first day the big cutters had racing flags lashed up, and it may be said that never during the half-century the Royal Thames has been an institution has a more critical company, collectively, been present at a river match of the premier metropolitan club. A white haze was hanging about the lower Thames on the morning of Thursday, May 25, and when the *Valkyrie, Britannia, Calluna* and *Iverna* were ready to answer the starting gun, a breeze from the west-north-west of balloon topsail strength was blowing. The quartet began the race at 12.5, and went reaching down the Lower Hope, with flowing sheets and carrying a swirl of ebb-tide with them. *Valkyrie* had made a clever start, and keeping to the Essex side was first to square away in Sea Reach, and get spinnaker set to port.

Britannia had been edged off to the heart of the fairway, but about Thames Haven she was drawn in across *Valkyrie's* wake, and straightened on a down-river course directly she had angled the latter's wind. *Valkyrie's* first racing burst was satisfactory, inasmuch as she kept pride of place for about 14 miles, albeit she never held more than a clear

'SAMŒNA'

94 TONS. BUILT FOR JOHN JAMESON, ESQ., BY INMAN, 1880.

length's lead of *Britannia*. About a couple of miles below Southend the wind had a hank off the sands, and, with square canvas gathered and sheets trimmed in a little, *Britannia* raced up broad on the weather beam of *Valkyrie*, while wide away *Calluna* was booming along with a rally of wind aft, and for a few minutes certainly led the fleet. On an easy reach *Britannia* gave evidence that she had the foot of the sister ship, yet it was a marvellously close race, the Prince of Wales's cutter drawing by the wind round the Mouse at 2.10 with about three lengths lead of *Valkyrie*, while the *Calluna* was only 1 min. 11 secs. and *Iverna* 2 mins. 5 secs. astern of the leader.

With a beat back over a lee tide in perspective the lead round the lightship was an immense advantage, and, in order to keep weather gauge, *Britannia* was kept shooting so long that *Valkyrie* had no chance of a successful hug, and it would have been suicidal for her to have turned about in the body of the tide. The alternative was sailing hard to get the wind clear to leeward; but when *Valkyrie* came round outside the edge of the tide rift, *Britannia*, drawing a foot less water, was able to cast about dead in the wind's eye of her rival. A grand breeze squeezing trial went on right up Sea Reach, *Valkyrie*, although the quicker of the pair in stays, getting now and again a staggering weather bower. It was a racing treat, however, and, despite the duel, the *Calluna* and *Iverna* were getting a hollow beating. The breeze freshened with the flood, and from off Shellhaven *Britannia*, which was a bare hundred yards to windward of *Valkyrie*, was, on starboard, pointing clear of the Blyth, and did not therefore follow her rival on an inshore cast.

After passing the Lower Hope point, sheets were checked, jib topsails and balloon staysails were set, and, with a puffy breeze broad off the Essex side, they went straight up the fairway pushing on a big bow wave. *Britannia* going thus free was dropping *Valkyrie* a trifle, yet the race looked open until *Valkyrie's* bowsprit snapped short off close to the stem head. She was eased in to the weather shore, and her topmast saved in a wonderful way, and eventually she followed *Britannia* home. *Calluna* had split her big jib across the diagonal seam in Sea Reach, but got another set, and looked likely—consequent on *Valkyrie's* mishap—to gain second honours. An attempt, however, to pass inside the Ovens ended by *Calluna* sticking deep in the mud, and *Iverna* got home soon enough to save her time on *Valkyrie*. This, the first race, was a fair trial to leeward and to windward, and it showed *Britannia* and *Valkyrie* to be wonderfully evenly matched, while *Calluna's* début was disappointing.

'Iverna,' 1890. (John Jameson, Esq.)

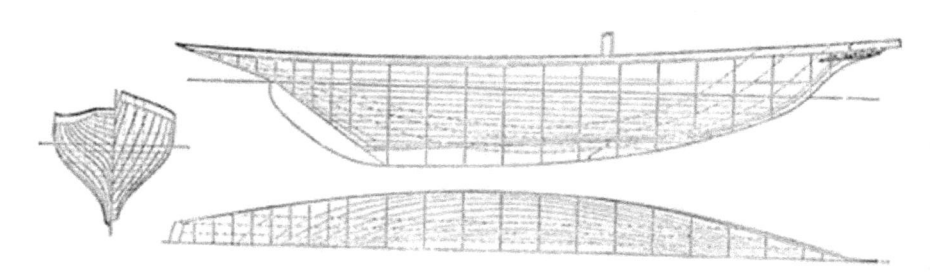

Lines and midship section of 'Iverna.'
Dimensions, &c.: Length (on L.W.L.), 83.50 ft.; beam, extreme, 19 ft.; depth, 10.70 ft.; tonnage, registered, 84.40 tons; tonnage, y. m. 152 tons; Y.R.A. rating, 118 tons. Designed by Alexander Richardson for John Jameson, Esq.

The valedictory match on the river on May 27 proved the best racing test, and furnished the most stirring sport of the trio. *Valkyri* was ready to join in, and the fleet was similarly constituted to the opening day. The race was under the Royal London burgee, and was sailed in gloomy weather and a smart north-east breeze. A sensation was served up before the contest proper had been started, and directly after the heavily freighted official steamer had got down to the Lower Hope, through *Calluna's* mast breaking off short as a Jersey cabbage-stalk. With her whole canvas pile carrying away over the side it was feared some of the crew might be entangled; but luckily everything went clear and no one was hurt. It was 12.45 before the Commodore started the race, and at the time the Hope was full of trading craft.

A bulky hopper barred *Britannia's* way, and both *Valkyrie* and *Iverna* had to be shoved up in the wind; and while the two last named were hovering, *Britannia* stood away for the Kent side into the full scour of the ebb, and came off on the starboard tack in weather berth. *Valkyrie* had to short tack at the top of Sea Reach to clear her wind, and as a long leg could be made, *Britannia* reached away with the lead, *Valkyrie*, half a dozen lengths astern, pointing high for her weather quarter. The wind was puffy and both dropped *Iverna*, but the two leaders were sailing a grand race, and made a long stretch as far as the East River Middle without breaking port tack. Hereabout, however, the wind suddenly shortened on them from the eastward, and the *Valkyrie* most unluckily was thrown dead under the lee of *Britannia*. With the tide soaking them bodily to windward, they both fetched under the Nore Sand, which had to be stood from for water, and by short turnings they then made a fine race to the Nore Lightship.

Here they got in deep water, and after a short hitch and a rap-full stretch to clear had failed, *Valkyrie* went in for short boards of about twenty seconds, and ended by being given lee helm directly she was full. This meant that *Britannia*, being slower in stays, had not got sheets in before she wanted to go about again, and she would to a certainty have been weathered by *Valkyrie*, before getting as far on as the West Oaze, had not the Prince of Wales's cutter been treated to longer boards. *Britannia* then got away and weathered the Mouse, after as fine a display of short tacking as has ever been seen on the river, with a lead of 39 seconds, and the duel had let *Iverna* get within 10 minutes of the leader. They ran back against the tide with spinnakers to port; but it was dead running, and *Valkyrie*, edging in to the Maplins, got through into first place above the Admiralty mile.

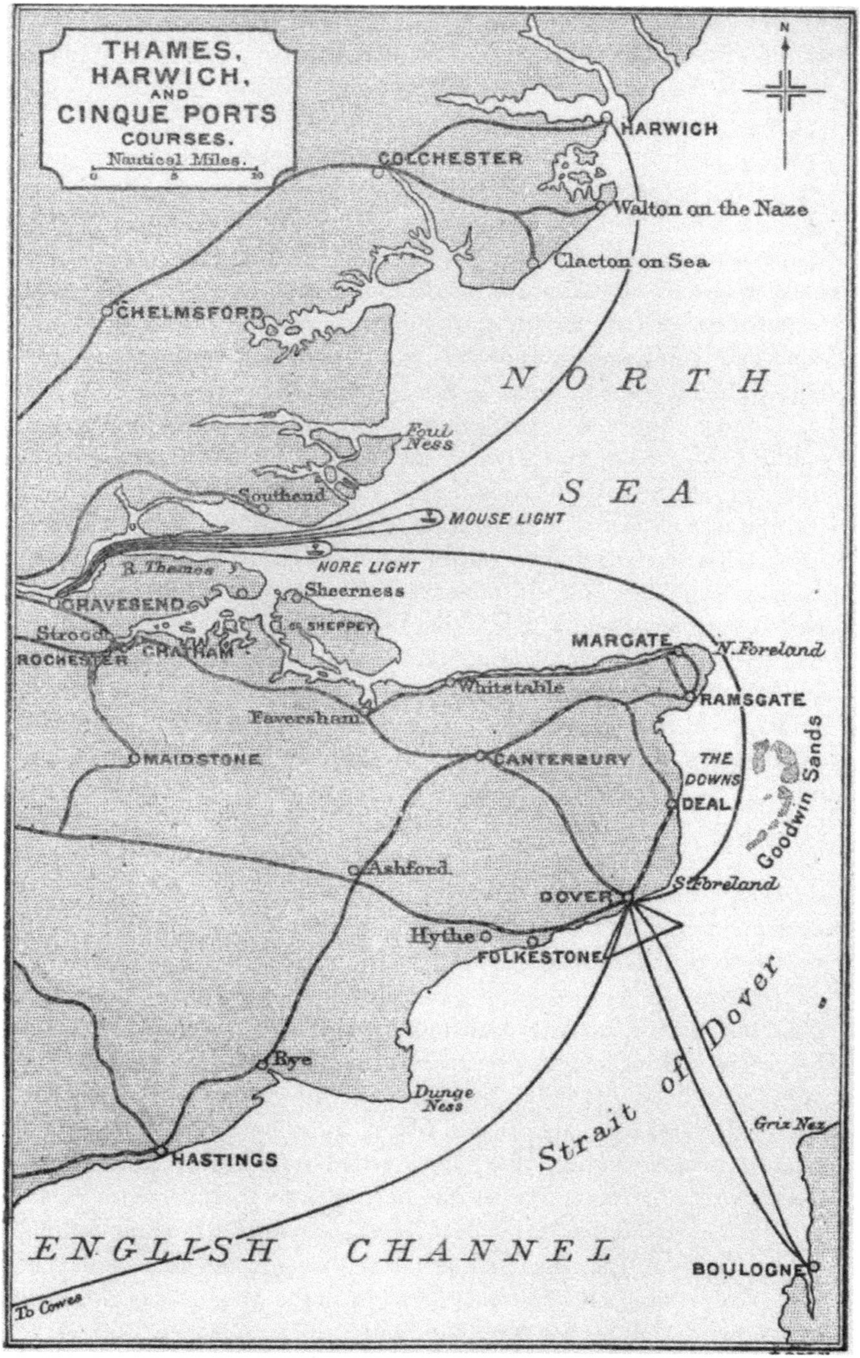
THAMES, HARWICH, AND CINQUE PORTS COURSES.
Nautical Miles.
0 5 10
N
HARWICH
COLCHESTER
Walton on the Naze
Clacton on Sea
CHELMSFORD
NORTH
SEA
Foul Ness
Southend
MOUSE LIGHT
NORE LIGHT
R. Thames
GRAVESEND
Sheerness
SHEPPEY
Strood
ROCHESTER
CHATHAM
MARGATE
N. Foreland
Whitstable
RAMSGATE
Faversham
MAIDSTONE
CANTERBURY
THE DOWNS
Goodwin Sands
DEAL
Ashford
S. Foreland
DOVER
Hythe
FOLKESTONE
Strait of Dover
Rye
Dunge Ness
Griz Nez
HASTINGS
ENGLISH CHANNEL
BOULOGNE
To Cowes

The wind then came off shore, and *Britannia* at once began to luff in. *Valkyrie* was determined to keep her weather wind clear, the pair had a match up to Southend, and on keeping away both touched the ground, the *Britannia* bumping three times hard on the north head of Leigh Sand. The Prince of Wales's cutter, however, keeping wide, slipped past *Valkyrie* about the Chapman, drew to, and came fair ahead. The pair kept up a grand race on the Essex side of the river, but *Iverna*, greatly favoured by the wind and her opponents' jockeying, had got within a couple of minutes of the leaders when off Holehaven. Spinnakers were carried through the Hope, and a grand race finished with a free reach from Coalhouse Point home, *Britannia* beating *Valkyrie* by 73 seconds; but *Iverna* won the prize by time.

A very fine open-water match was that of the Royal Thames Club on June 10 from the Nore round the back of the Goodwins to Dover. The usual tale of five of the national rig and the schooner *Amphitrite* made up the entry, and all mustered at the rendezvous. It was a cheerless morning, the sky being heavy and of slaty hue, whilst a brisk north-easter blew cold off the water. The schooner had a yard-topsail set, *Calluna* her No. 2 jackyarder, and the *Britannia*, *Valkyrie*, *Satanita*, and *Iverna* their jibheaders. Reef-tackles were ready to pull earings down, but the breeze veered to the east north-east and did not harden. They had a beat to the Tongue with a swinging weather tide, *Britannia* made a capital start, and twice crossed ahead of *Valkyrie*; but exactly half an hour after the start, off the *West Oaze*, *Britannia* found her sister marching clear ahead. *Calluna* had been in Tilbury Dock since her inglorious performance at Harwich; she was there lightened of tons of dead weight, and the syndicate ship was very much livelier, and infinitely more able at breeze squeezing; while the turnings were too short for *Satanita* to be cutting a dash.

Britannia jumped up on *Valkyrie* every time the long leg on port came, and at the entrance of the Alexandra Channel *Valkyrie*, on the bearing tack, had to come about under the lee bow, the Prince of Wales's cutter thus becoming 'bell wether.' *Valkyrie* stayed for *Britannia*, which was however on port, but the former was clear enough ahead before getting abreast of the beacons on the Girdler. The two leading boats worked shorter tacks than the rest down the Alexandra to the southern pitch of the Shingles, and they were consequently getting picked up a little by *Calluna* and *Satanita*. After a long leg on port, the last tack was made for weathering distance of the Tongue Lightship, and on passing this mark after a beat of 19 miles with a weather tide, the *Valkyrie* led *Britannia* 2 mins., *Calluna* 7 mins. 30 secs., *Satanita* 9 mins. 30 secs., and *Iverna* 15 mins. 30 secs. It may be said that the distance was covered by the leader in 2 hrs. 18 mins.

After allowing for a sweep of fair tide they had a broad reach off to the North Sandhead, and although *Britannia* raced up on *Valkyrie*, she stopped directly she began to yaw about on the leader's quarter sea, and was half a minute astern at the North Goodwin Lightship. *Satanita's* was a remarkable piece of sailing, as according to the 'distance table' it is 14¾ miles from the Tongue Lightship to the North Sandhead, and she was timed officially as taking just over one hour to do the distance; it should be added that the tide was running about two knots, and setting under the weather quarter, whilst it is worthy of note that between the marks *Satanita* had two luffs with *Calluna* and shifted her jibheaded topsail for a jackyarder. In a run to the East Goodwin main booms were carried to starboard, and *Britannia*, running the nearer to the sands, was placed to cover *Valkyrie*, when an inevitable gybe came off at the East Goodwin.

Valkyrie came over all standing just after passing the lightship, and unluckily for her the parts of the mainsheet got under the counter. '*Britannia*' was also gybed in a hurry, and, covering her opponent, she slipped past into pride of place, while *Valkyrie* was unable to pull her boom in and luff; oddly enough, however, *Britannia* was in the same mess as her sister, and it was some time ere both had mainsheets running free through the blocks. With the North Sea tide swinging along hot, a fine head of speed was kept up, and about the Calliper headsails were taking well and spinnakers were got in. Although the wind was quarterly from the Southsand Lightship home, *Britannia* made but a very trifling gain on *Valkyrie*, and, according to official clocking, crossed the line with a lead of 17 secs., and, having 13 secs. to allow, thus won with 3 secs. to spare—a remarkable finish of a grand race. *Satanita* was 5 mins. 52 secs. astern of the leader, '*Calluna* 7 mins. 26 secs., and *Iverna* 18 mins. 32 secs.

A smart easterly wind on the morning of the cross Channel match from Dover to Boulogne very naturally gave rise to anticipations that the time record for the course would be broken. The breeze came unsteady, however, and put a veto on the accomplishment of a fast journey either way, whilst a serious collision at the start, in which the *Valkyrie*, *Britannia*, and *Vendetta* were involved, had the effect of utterly spoiling the race. A fleet of eight responded to the starting gun—namely, *Britannia*, *Valkyrie*, *Calluna*, *Iverna*, *Mabel*, *Lais*, *Vendetta*, and

Varuna—and they ran in close flight for the line before a north-east wind, with booms to starboard and having a gybe to make immediately after crossing. *Vendetta* got away first and was reaching off on her course when *Valkyrie's* bowsprit end took the 40 on the port quarter and forced her round until she filled on the starboard tack, her topmast being carried away as she was slewing. There was not much room between the outer flagboat and the port side of *Valkyrie*, but *Britannia's* helm was drawn down—after gybing—to give her a chance of finding a passage. She fouled the mark, however, and through *Valkyrie's* way being deadened when she fouled *Vendetta*, *Britannia* had the alternative of steadying her helm and giving *Valkyrie* a sliding blow, or of keeping it a little a-lee and crashing right through the 40.

The *Britannia's* helm was eased, and she put her bowsprit inside *Valkyrie's* rigging, while *Vendetta*, after getting her bowsprit broken off by *Britannia*, got some of the gear foul and dropped alongside the Prince of Wales's vessel, with her counter up about level with the big cutter's main rigging, and the stem even with the taffrail. The three vessels, locked together, sidled away towards shore, *Britannia*, listing to the wind, pressed her mainsail on to *Vendetta's* port crosstree, and the sail split up from boom to gaff. The trio laid thus entangled for ten minutes, but meantime *Valkyrie's* crew had chopped away at *Britannia's* bowsprit and headgear; eventually the spar broke, and then the three vessels at once got clear. Meanwhile *Calluna* and *Iverna* had been racing away for the French coast with a fine leading wind, and twelve minutes after they had crossed the line *Valkyrie* started in pursuit.

The wind was shy and very puffy after getting inside Grisnez, and *Valkyrie* picked up six minutes on *Calluna*, which had beaten *Iverna'* only 3 mins. 45 secs. in going across, and *Varuna*, the leading 40, by 24 mins. *Calluna* hung on to her jackyard topsail in a wonderful way, as some of the puffs laid her over until the lee decks were full. *Valkyrie* passed *Iverna*, but *Calluna* well kept her lead, the wind easting enough for all to fetch clean full home. *Calluna* beat *Valkyrie* by 5 mins. 27 secs., *Iverna* by 8 mins. 52 secs., and *Lais*, the first of the 40's, by 46 mins. 6 secs.

There was a full muster of the heavy-weight cutters at the Royal Southern rendezvous, the club having a first-class match on June 17, the second day of its 'Jubilee' Regatta. *Satanita's* light blue banner was carried nearer the water-level than in her previous racing essays, owing to the lower mast having been clipped 3 feet, and additional lead had been put on her keel. '*Britannia*' had made good the damage sus-

'CALLUNA,' 141-RATER (PETER DONALDSON, ESQ.)

tained at Dover, and with *Valkyrie, Calluna,* and *Iverna* the fleet was brought up to normal strength. It was a lovely morning, glorified by fervent sunshine, and softened by a gauzy haze, but a southerly chill was not strong enough to 'carry' the smoke of the starting gun, and the surface of the Solent looked smooth as burnished steel. With flying airs filling jackyard topsails, they started the race, and ere going half a mile *Calluna* got aground on the Calshot Spit. *Valkyrie* was lucky to strike the first of a gathering breeze, and went reaching fast from the fleet down the West Channel. She afterwards gave a fine display by the wind, and showed matchless form on a dead run. *Valkyrie* eventually beat *Britannia* by 5 mins. 32 secs., and *Satanita* by 16 mins. 4 secs., *Calluna* and *Iverna* both being miles astern. *Valkyrie's* was a good performance, but she was distinctly lucky in getting the first of the wind, and she likewise was kindly treated subsequently by Dame Fortune.

Rather singularly the Jubilee Regatta of the Royal Southern Club was followed by the Jubilee of the Royal Mersey; but the latter meeting, on June 24, did not open under such exhilarating influences as the Solent gathering, particulars having just come to hand of the *Victoria* disaster in the Mediterranean, while the weather was dismally dull, and a tearing north-north-west wind blowing. Consequent on the prevailing stiff breeze an alternative course—three times round the Formby—had been plotted off overnight—probably not, however, from any tender consideration whether the racing vessels could cross the bar safely, the anxiety more likely being in regard to the Committee-boat and her freight. The inside course was named on the day, but, in spite of foresight and precaution, the racing was disappointing. The *Valkyrie*, which had come round from Cowes with her mainsail an underdeck passenger, could not get the sail bent owing to the rain and wind; then *Calluna* got her anchor foul, and being 25 minutes late, did not start.

Britannia alone was near the line when the Blue Peter came down, yet she lost 1 min. 50 secs., while *Satanita* came 2 mins. later, and *Iverna* a minute after *Satanita*. There was wind enough to warrant second earings being hardened down, all topmasts were housed, and with the tide flying to windward the ground was sidled over very fast. The start meant victory—barring accidents—in beating out of the narrow Mersey channel, and although *Satanita* worked right up under *Britannia*, she was kept safely pinned. There was a short jump of sea, and the two new ships were giving a free display of the fore body, smashing the tidal combers into blinding clouds of sea dust. *Satanita* had a rare drilling from *Britannia*, and although she also ran the faster, she could not get through in such a limited stretch of water.

Thus the game was played to the end, it being a flog out from New Brighton to the Formby, and a run back each round. Had the *Satanita* got her opponent's start, she would probably have beaten the Prince of Wales's cutter fully 5 mins., as in such a breeze she was clearly the faster to windward. *Iverna* was very soon done with, and at the finish '*Britannia*' finished 2 mins. 19 secs. before *Satanita*.

The Royal Northern Regatta opened on July 1 with a piping breeze strong enough for slab reefs to be pulled down; before noon, however, jackyard topsails were wanted, and calms and partial breezes made tiresome work afterward, flukes being as plentiful as motes in a sunbeam. The *Calluna* put in an appearance, and when viewed broadside on her big sail-plan gave her quite an over-hatted look. *Satanita*, *Britannia*, *Valkyrie*, and *Iverna* all made their number, and the match commenced in a rush of wind, *Satanita* clearing out of Rothesay Bay faster than any steamboat ever left it—perhaps a madder burst of reaching was never seen. The Southampton boat was at the head of affairs for some time, but after some fluking *Valkyrie* led.

At the end of the second round, however, *Satanita*, through a sheer slice of luck, got 3 mins. ahead of *Britannia*, and as it was then 4.30 and clock calm in the Clyde, it was thought the match would be stopped. The Committee, however, wanted the distance done, and *Britannia*, being the faster in light airs, got home late in the evening 1 min. 49 secs, before *Satanita*, *Valkyrie* which was nearly 20 mins. astern of the latter at the end of the first round, getting in 1 min. 32 secs, after, and saving her time for second prize. The *Calluna's* wide wings did not seem to help her as they should have done in flaws and catspaws.

The Mudhookers opened the ball on July 5 at Hunter's Quay, and a very capital sailing programme was put forward by the exclusive 'forty' which constitute the club, the leading event being a prize value 100*l*. for big cutters. With *Britannia* and *Calluna* disabled, the affair virtually resolved itself into a match between *Valkyrie* and *Satanita*, although the *Iverna* was a starter. It was imperative that the helmsmen should be amateurs, and Mr. W. G. Jameson shipped for the day as timoneer of *Satanita*, Lord Dunraven having Mr. George Watson to relieve him on *Valkyrie*. Starting with a free sheet in a smart breeze, *Satanita* went away so fast that *Valkyrie* looked likely to have a stern chase; but the wind got baffling, in beating up the Firth from Ascog *Valkyrie* worked up, and off Dunoon, in standing off on port, she had to come round under the lee bow of her rival.

A wind-jamming trial then followed, and *Satanita* either sidled away and dropped down on *Valkyrie,* or the latter ate up under her rival, as the end of *Satanita's* gaff hooked *Valkyrie's* topmast shrouds, and Lord Dunraven's cutter was towed along for some minutes. After getting clear, it was thought *Valkyrie's* topmast was slightly sprung, and there were cross protests at the finish of the round. A desperately close race was sailed on the second turn round the course, and *Satanita,* which was only 27 secs. ahead at the finish, got beaten on time by *Valkyrie. Iverna* finished 26 secs. after the leader.

Amateur helmsmen were in request for the big ships on Clyde Corinthian Club day, when the *Britannia, Valkyrie, Satanita,* and *Iverna* responded to the starting gun. The weather was very uncertain, the breezes being so light that only one round of the course could be sailed.'*Valkyrie'* was the lucky ship as she rounded the Kilcreggan flagboat, two and a half miles from the Commodore, last boat. Standing off in the Firth, along the edge of a flaw, whilst her opponents were lying becalmed, she tacked into a breezy lane, and, passing *Iverna, Satanita,* and *Britannia* in turn, carried her way up to the line, getting the winning gun 30 secs. before *Britannia* struggled through, and 2 mins. 15 secs. in advance of *Satanita.* The *Valkyrie* was steered by her owner, the *Britannia* by Mr. W. G. Jameson, and the *Satanita* by Mr. R. Ure.

A more unfavourable racing day than that which opened the Royal Club Regatta has never been experienced even on the unutterably fluky Firth. Sudden spurts of wind, calms, a very long spell of what was quite a deluge of rain, deafening thunder, blinding lightning and depressing gloom, made up the sample of weather vouchsafed to the competitors during the time that the 'sport' was progressing. The big cutters mustered in full force, and had a light easterly breeze, which gave a reach down the Clyde. Just before the start, *Britannia* on the port tack, with the wind pretty broad abeam, made *Calluna,* which had run down from the eastward with boom over the port side, come round; and this was deemed cause for *Calluna* to pursue a protest, on the ground that a breach of the rules of the road had been committed. *Valkyrie,* too, made a mark of *Britannia,* the latter getting the stem, and sustaining damage to the port bulwarks aft and the taffrail.

After an unsatisfactory start *Britannia* and *Satanita* went round the Ascog mark together, but just as the latter was stepping out in style, and apparently in first place, her bobstay pendant burst and the bowsprit broke off short to the stem-head. Topsails had been shifted, as there was a prospect of a strong breeze, but the outcome was a tempest without a rattle of wind. *Britannia* sailed in fine form, and simply lost her opponents directly *Satanita's* accident had put that boat out of the way. It was a wretchedly poor time, however, and, thanks to not a little good fortune, *Britannia* beat *Valkyrie* by 41 mins. 40 secs., and *Calluna* by 62 mins. 17 secs., while *Iverna* gave up. Protests were lodged against *Britannia* on behalf of both *Calluna* and *Valkyrie*.

The *Calluna's* objection was considered, and about midnight the Sailing Committee decided to disqualify the *Britannia*, only one witness, be it said, from the last-named vessel having been called. There was really not a semblance of racing on the second day of the Royal Clyde Regatta, which was the valedictory fixture in the so-called 'Clyde fortnight.' Flying chills and draughts out of every 'airt,' with long spells of calm, kept the vessels hanging about the lower part of the Firth until the shadows were well slanting eastward. An evening breeze helped *Valkyrie* home, but it took her nearly seven hours and a half to cover one half the course, and she finished 54 mins. 9 secs. before the *Calluna*, 1 hr. 31 mins. 30 secs. before *Britannia*, and about 2 hrs. 40 mins. before *Satanita*, the last named taking 10 hrs. to cover 25 miles.

Inspiriting racing marked the opening of the Irish fixtures at Bangor, and the Royal Ulster Regatta attracted all the big cutters. The wind was fresh from the north-north-east, slab reefs were down in mainsails and sharp-headed topsails set. A thrilling and eventful contest followed a perfectly judged start, and *Britannia*, *Satanita*, and *Valkyrie* formed first flight in a plain sail round the Lough as far as the South Briggs flagboat, where the last named lost her place through one of her hands getting knocked overboard in a gybe. At the same mark in the second round *Britannia* got the inside turn, when the main boom had to come over; but *Satanita* at once began to luff, and with mainsheet blocks together on both they went heading out in the Lough. Foot by foot *Satanita* came up, off Ballyholme Bay she had ranged broad on the weather-beam of her rival, and was thus able to claim room at the home flagboat, which she luffed round with 5 secs. lead, and Jay then kept her shooting almost as long as she would to keep weather berth.

Britannia unluckily got her mainsheet jammed, and as she could not in consequence be sprung to the wind—at once—so high as *Satanita*, she dropped under the lee quarter, and got a severe blanketing all the way up the Lough. The pair sailed an exciting match round the

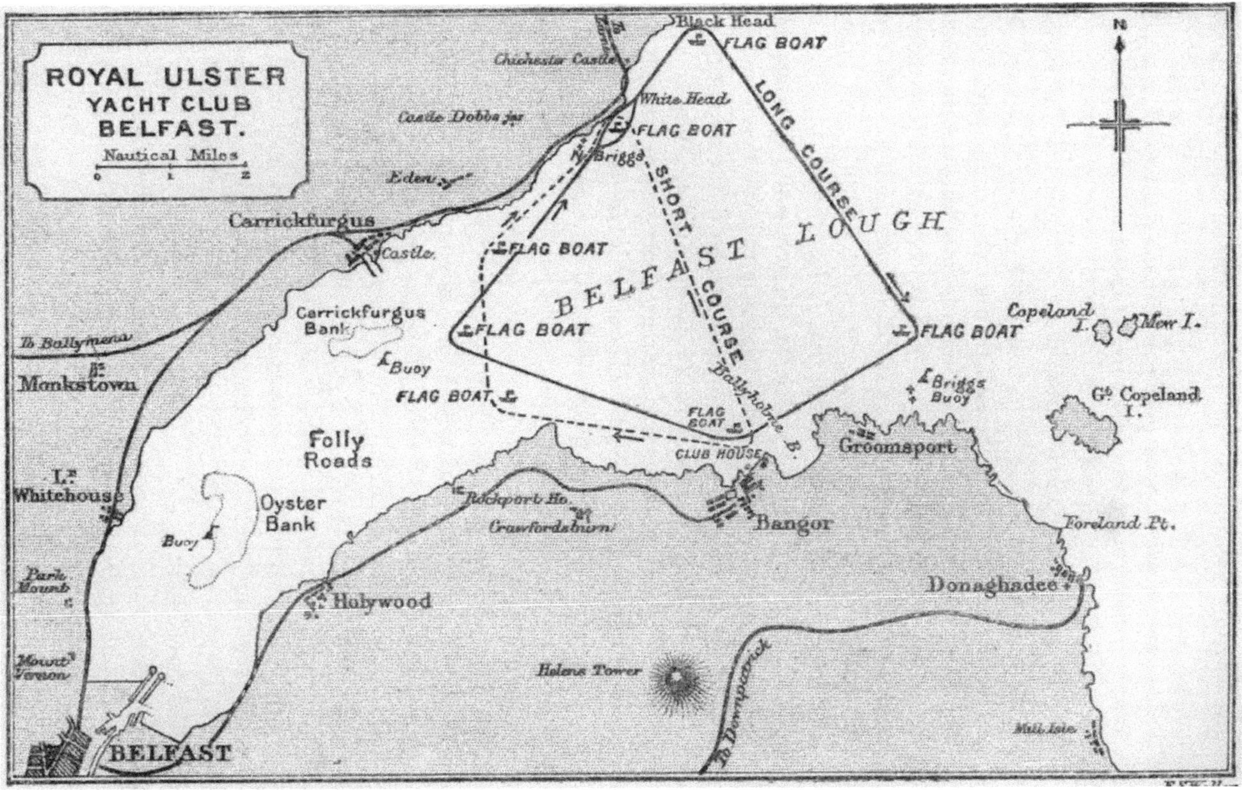
ROYAL ULSTER
YACHT CLUB
BELFAST.
Nautical Miles
0 1 2
N
Black Head
FLAG BOAT
Chichester Castle
White Head
FLAG BOAT
Castle Dobbs
N. Briggs
LONG COURSE
SHORT COURSE
Eden
Carrickfurgus
Castle
FLAG BOAT
BELFAST LOUGH
Carrickfurgus
Bank
FLAG BOAT
FLAG BOAT
Copeland I.
Mew I.
To Ballymena
Buoy
Monkstown
FLAG BOAT
Ballyholme B.
Briggs Buoy
Gt. Copeland I.
FLAG BOAT
Folly
Roads
CLUB HOUSE
Groomsport
Lt. Whitehouse
Oyster
Bank
Rockport Ho.
Crawfordsburn
Bangor
Foreland Pt.
Buoy
Park Mount
Donaghadee
Holywood
Mount Vernon
Helens Tower
To Downpatrick
Mill Isle
BELFAST

rest of the course, and *Satanita* travelling like a shooting star reached home winner with 5 secs. in hand. It may be said that the feat was accomplished in one third of the course, 16½ miles, and that she beat *Britannia* 2 mins. 29 secs. in that distance, which was a very high tribute indeed to *Satanita's* speed. *Calluna* finished 7 mins. 19 secs. after the winner. *Valkyrie* never regained any of the time lost in picking up the hand who got overboard.

The breeze steadied down during the dark hours, and the *Valkyrie* had a day just to her liking. *Iverna's* well-known racing banner was missed for the first time in the season, owing to her rudder-head being twisted. Spectators were treated to a magnificent light-weather match between the *Valkyrie* and *Britannia*. The former took the lead directly after the flash of the starting gun, but she did not seem to ghost along in the usual peerless style. *Britannia* was with difficulty kept pinned under the lee; in fact, it was evident that *Valkyrie* could not allow her opponent a cross-tacking chance, or her quarry would certainly have slipped her. The breezes were paltry and patchy, with plenty of white water spots about, and the course was shortened to the extent of one third the distance, *Valkyrie* eventually crawling home winner about three lengths ahead of *Britannia*, although there was 1 min. 56 secs. difference between them in time. *Calluna's* big sail-plan availed her little, and *Satanita* never once really woke up in the prevailing zephyrs. *Calluna* finished 16 mins. 53 secs. astern of *Valkyrie*, and *Satanita* struggled in against the tide 8 mins. 6 secs. after *Calluna*.

There was a piping breeze from the westward on the opening day of the Royal Irish Regatta, and a stirring struggle with *Satanita*, *Britannia*, and *Calluna* for Her Majesty's Cup was accordingly anticipated. *Calluna* risked a whole mainsail, but *Britannia* and *Satanita* had the baby reef in and all set jibheaded topsails. Perfect judgment was shown on the *Satanita* and *Britannia* in manoeuvring for the start, but *Satanita's* skipper scored first honours as he gave his ship a wipe away at the nick of time, and she reached through the line, fairly foaming a length ahead of the Prince of Wales's cutter, '*Calluna*' being about a hundred yards astern.

They went along the wind at a tearing pace to the Muglins Mark, jib-topsails being cracked on, and on going to the Kish the wind was brought on the quarter, a nasty roll tried spars and gear, and an ugly gybe came on before making the Lightship. At this mark *Satanita* had given a startling illustration of her speed with a free sheet, as she led the *Britannia* 2 mins. 5 secs., with *Calluna* only 19 secs. astern of the latter. A very fast piece of close reaching was done between the Kish and the Rosebeg, then came a dead peg across the Bay. *Britannia* tried hard to get *Satanita* into short tacking, and the latter, having to turn about more often than suited her, found *Britannia* settling up, enabling *Calluna* to profit by the game her opponents were playing. In a hard squall the second round commenced, and through a backing of the wind they had a run with spinnakers to the Kish.

A gybe had to be made, and it was a heavy one. *Satanita* and *Britannia* got their booms over all right, but *Calluna's* came in a hurry, and while the boom-end was buried deep in the water, the inner part came with a surge against the runner and broke off, the outer half of the spar launching in board and lying square across the deck. Luckily no one was hurt, which was simply a miracle. The *Satanita* and *Britannia* sailed a desperate race during the rest of the round, and this time the former had the better of her rival beating across the bay. In going free to the Kish on the last turn, *Satanita* sailed in peerless form, and had a lead of 4 mins. 44 secs. at the Lightship. In a close reach to the Rosebeg, *Satanita* lost a few seconds, and then followed a splendid race tack and tack home. *Britannia* was the better on this point, but *Satanita* kept her under the lee and weathered the line with a lead of 2 mins. 47 secs., winning the Royal trophy and scoring a brilliant victory with 69 secs. to spare.

The Royal Irish Regatta finished on Thursday, July 20, in changeable weather and baffling breezes. With *Calluna* crippled, the *Satanita* and *Britannia* had a match for the club prize, and not at all unexpectedly *Britannia* was winner. She scored by no means a bloodless victory, and her crew had a scare when *Satanita* struck into a breeze about half water between the Muglins and Kish, and went streaking past like a flash of greased lightning. *Satanita* was pluckily sailed, but had not wind enough to wake her up and, when the match was stopped at the end of the second round, *Britannia* had a lead of 4 mins. 4 secs.

Most auspicious was the opening of the Cowes racing week in regard to wind and weather, there being every indication of the morning breeze of Monday freshening when the stream bent westward, and of lasting sunshine and a clear atmosphere. The match was under the Royal London burgee, and the club had adopted a new course of which it may be said that a better could not have been marked off inside the Isle of Wight. The big cutter entry included the *Valkyrie*, *Britannia*, *Satanita*, *Calluna*, *Iverna*, and the Gold Cup challenger *Navahoe*, and there was general rejoicing on the morning of the day that the

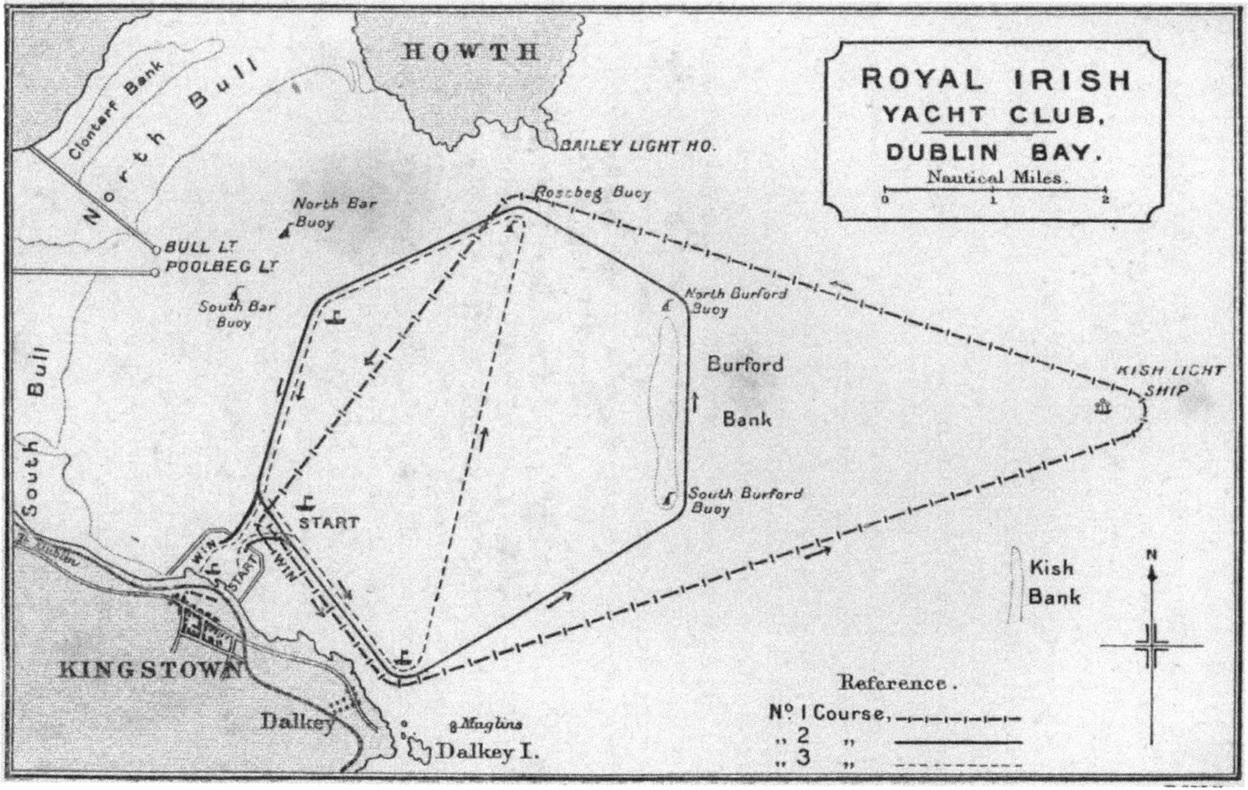

American would be certain to get a trustworthy test of speed in her first racing essay. Curiosity to see how she would acquit herself under the circumstances ran high.

The match commenced with a free reach to the eastward on the back of a fair tide, and the wind followed and gave a run, but it came in streaks and the fleet were all together at the Warner, the *Valkyrie* being leader, with *Navahoe* 75 secs. astern. A nice breeze was found to windward, and in turning in to the Noman *Valkyrie* worked away from the Yankee and then went for *Britannia*, which, with *Satanita*, stood away for the north shore. *Valkyrie* was then left with *Navahoe*, and the latter along Ryde Sands and on to the Motherbank got more wind and a slacker tide, inside *Valkyrie*, and forereached so much the faster that on coming off she crossed comfortably ahead of Lord Dunraven's cutter. *Navahoe* performed this feat 'on her uppers,' while *Valkyrie* was stiff as a tree, perhaps through having less wind than there was to leeward.

The breezes continued to be served out partially in strength and direction, and *Britannia, Satanita,* and *Calluna* were having a bad time in working the north shore down. *Valkyrie* picked up *Navahoe* in beating on to Calshot, and went round that mark with just a clear lead. The breeze was unsteady and puffy in reaching to Lepe, but for the most part sheets were checked, and *Navahoe's* big sail-plan dragged her by to windward of *Valkyrie*, and she was first round Lepe buoy, but she made a wide sweep in the gybe and *Valkyrie* ran on to the fore. With a leading wind *Navahoe* slipped through to leeward into first place before getting to Cowes, and thence they squared away. *Valkyrie* was not raced with the same spirit as *Britannia* was on the first run eastward, or the *Navahoe* would have been luffed out into Spithead; the latter was, in fact, allowed to keep the even tenour of her way, and she rounded the Warner with 10 secs. lead of *Valkyrie*, *Britannia* having run up on both, while *Satanita* had taken the American in nearly 3 mins.

With a weather tide and truer and fresher breeze, they had a fair test to windward, and a couple of boards sufficed for *Valkyrie* and *Britannia* to weather the American. *Valkyrie* was sailed to bother *Britannia*, while the *Navahoe* was fairly let run loose. Had the sister ships been simply sailing boat against boat, they could not have carried on a keener duel. *Britannia* beat *Valkyrie*, but instead of having a substantial lead at Calshot Lightship, she was only just to windward of *Valkyrie*, and but 1 min. 33 secs. ahead of *Navahoe*. In reaching to Lepe, *Britannia* and *Valkyrie* gained in distance on the American, but nothing in time, owing to the rushing lee-tide. There was a smart breeze to blow

'NAVAHOE,' 161-RATER: N.Y.Y. CLUB (ROYAL PHELPS CARROLL, ESQ.)

them home against the boiling stream, and the *Navahoe's* big sail-plan helped her. Both *Britannia* and *Valkyrie*, however, kept to the fore, and *Britannia* finished winner of a hard race, 63 secs. ahead of *Valkyrie*, 1 min. 23 secs. of *Navahoe*, 3 mins. 50 secs. of *Satanita*, and 7 mins. 36 secs. of *Calluna*. It may be said that *Satanita* gained 4 mins. 34 secs. and *Calluna* 6 mins. 18 secs. on the *Navahoe* in sailing the second round; the pair picked up on *Britannia* and *Valkyrie* simply owing to the suicidal tactics adopted in racing the sister ships.

A breeze was wanting on the opening morning of the Royal Yacht Squadron Regatta to put animation in the scene afloat, still in the flood of sunshine it was a brilliant spectacle. There was a galaxy of private yachts, and quite a fleet of fighting ships of various nationalities riding on the Solent dressed in bunting the German emperor's new *Hohenzollern* looming up a very Triton amongst the host, through which the racing fleet had presently to thread their way eastward. The starters for Her Majesty's Cup were the *Meteor, Britannia, Valkyrie, Viking, née Wendur,* and *Mohawk*. An alteration in the course had been made by substituting the Bullock patch buoy for the Nab, and with thoughtful consideration for the length of leg of the modern craft, the three-fathom North Bramble Channel was left out.

A dreadfully slow run was made eastward, the 16½ miles from Cowes to the eastern limit of the course taking about 2½ hours to cover. The breezes came in puffs out of every cloud, but mostly from the north or north-west, and in this sort of weather it was absolutely humiliating that the aspirant for America Cup honours should be led round the lee mark by the seven-season-old *Meteor*. With a better and fairly true breeze westerly *Valkyrie* and *Britannia* on a close reach in to the Noman passed the emperor's cutter, and, from mark to mark eight miles, *Valkyrie* beat *Meteor* exactly 4 mins. After fetching well up to Cowes, they turned through the roads, and then got a northerly slant in the west channel; a flying weather-tide settled them bodily to windward, and at Lymington mark *Valkyrie*, which had gone in grand form to windward, was 3 mins. ahead of *Britannia* and 15 mins. 40 secs. of *Meteor*, the time allowance of the last named having thus run out by 68 secs.

The wind was breezing up, and they ran through a roaring ebb tide at a fair speed, the modern boats pushing out a tremendous bow wave. The *Meteor* unquestionably had a stronger following breeze than the two leaders, and with about 3½ ft. less draught than *Valkyrie*, she could be edged inside the tide rift on the north shore, the result being that she gained 50 secs. on *Valkyrie*, yet with an allowance of 14 mins. 32 secs. she thus lost by 18 secs. On the question being raised that *Valkyrie* had not followed the track marked on the official chart furnished, it was admitted that she had left the Nab on the wrong hand, and the Sailing Committee disqualified her and declared the *Meteor* winner of Her Majesty's Cup. It may be said that the *Wendur* after rounding Lymington mark attempted to set her spinnaker, but lost the sail, which was picked up by a pilot boat. Worse still, the boom was let drop in the water, and on it breaking two of the crew were badly hurt.

Wednesday, August 2, was chosen by the Royal Yacht Squadron for the match for the Meteor Challenge Shield presented by the German Emperor, the course being from Cowes round the Isle of Wight (outside Nab), thence round the Shambles Lightship and back through the Needles passage to Cowes, a distance of 112 miles. According to the conditions four yachts were to start or no race, but out of an entry of six only '*Britannia*' and *Satanita* went for the trophy. The start, which was fixed for seven o'clock, was delayed an hour owing to the card and sailing directions differing. At 8 o'clock, when *Britannia* and *Satanita* got away, the *Valkyrie's* crew, which had made a show of getting the vessel ready, had proceeded as far as hoisting a jib in stops and lashing up the fighting colours, the vessel subsequently lying listless at anchor all day.

A charmingly bright clear morning with a bonny breeze from the north-west sent the two ships scudding out in hot haste to the eastward. Spinnakers were on and jackyard topsails, and at the Nab *Britannia* had run out a lead of 4 mins. Coming on a reach the east stream was faced, and *Satanita*, doing a wonderful stretch of sailing, had almost drawn level with her rival, when the wind came ahead and gave a beat of about forty miles to the Shambles. In order to shun the tide the Island shore was worked, but *Satanita* got too close and bumped hard several times on Atherfield Ledge. In working on a nasty short jump of sea was trying the vessels, and off Swanage the breeze came in such hard puffs that big topsails were got down.

Britannia worked away from her rival, and after a pretty considerable amount of pile-driving got round the Shambles at 4 o'clock with a lead of 10 mins. They had to face a west tide, and as the evening closed in the wind almost entirely failed. In the west channel it was mere tide-work, and at 9.30 *Britannia* drove across the line winner, *Satanita* at the time being barely discernible astern. It was an uninteresting match, but a hard one for ships and crews, and in the heavy plunging which went on between the Needles and St. Albans *Britannia* sprung her mast.

Thursday morning opened with a fine singing breeze from the west-south-west, and the match for the Cowes Town Cup gave promise of stirring sport. *Britannia's* absence, owing to her mast being sprung, was generally regretted; but *Navahoe, Valkyrie, Satanita,* and *Calluna* appeared under fighting flags. All had a single reef in mainsails, and *Valkyrie's* topmast was struck, the rest keeping theirs on end. They were sent first to the westward, and had a clean reach to the first mark, a capitally judged start being made. *Satanita,* nearest the Hampshire shore, was first on the line, with *Valkyrie* overlapping the western quarter, and *Calluna* and *Navahoe* broad to windward. Laying down to the hard breeze, *Satanita* was given the weight of it, and went smoking away, while *Navahoe* in weather berth was getting comparatively very lightly sailed.

A hard breeze, however, caught the Yankee, making her curl up to an ugly angle, and as she went off her helm, *Calluna's* crew were getting scared that she would either drop down flat on them or make a wild shoot into their ship. A heavier slam than the first put the *Navahoe* fairly out of control, and she went down on her side and wallowed helplessly in a smother of foam, until a gripe up to the wind relieved her and she came upright, when particular care was taken not to fill on her again. The weight of the wind had burst the mainsail at the clew, and, after getting the sail off the vessel ran away up Southampton Water, International rivalry thus coming to a summary end for the day. Owing to the strong wind and flood tide, the mark-boat had driven about a mile eastward, so it was soon reached down to, and *Satanita* was first round, then *Valkyrie* and *Calluna*.

It was a broad reach to the Warner, and cracking on a jibheaded topsail *Satanita* was ploughing along at an astounding speed; in fact, she was doing 14½ knots when crossing the Admiralty mile. With a jibheader on, the leader was leaving *Valkyrie,* which had lost *Calluna's* close company through the latter, when careening to a squall, fouling the jibboom of the steam yacht *Cleopatra,* the cutter getting mainsail split and gaff broken. *Satanita'*stayed round the Warner at 10.52, 1 min. 18 secs. before *Valkyrie,* and the former had the benefit of a reach back as far as Cowes. Heavy squalls came off the Island, and *Satanita* had lee decks full, *Valkyrie* by comparison standing up manfully. Owing to the flagboat drifting, they went round Lepe buoy, and having to nip to fetch, *Valkyrie* gained a trifle. Coming back free, *Satanita* was driven along with jibheader, and she held a lead of 7½ mins. at the Warner. The homeward track could be laid clean full, and the wind coming off with canvas-splitting force, *Satanita's* lee decks were washing like a porpoise's back, but she was travelling at a tremendous speed and would have gone much faster and on a more even keel had the topmast been struck. It was a wonderful display of fast sailing on her part, as she finished 8 mins. 13 secs. before *Valkyrie*, and covered the distance, 48 miles, allowing for the drifted flagboat at Lepe, in 3 hrs. 40 mins. 50 secs., thus averaging a little over 12½ knots.

An exceedingly brilliant wind-up of an eventful regatta was made at Cowes on Friday, August 4, when the Royal Yacht Squadron prize was sailed round the Warner-Lepe course. The competitors were *Satanita*, *Valkyrie*, *Calluna*, and *Navahoe*, and they started on a short beat down the west channel in a rising breeze from the west-south-west, jibheaded topsails being set over whole mainsails. In the first board *Navahoe* was weathered by each of her rivals, the Yankee being kept hovering in the wind, instead of being made to feel the weight of it, the previous day's experience perhaps being the cause. A heavy squall with sheets of rain passed over before the Western mark-boat was weathered, and they drove back to Cowes with spinnakers, all but the Yankee being run on the wrong gybe.

From a run they came to a free reach off Osborne, and went streaking out at a great pace to the Warner, all except *Satanita* cracking on jackyarders, but *Valkyrie* shifted back to jibheader off the Sandhead buoy. The latter kept pride of place going east, but in coming back clean full the wind came off the Island in savage puffs and *Satanita* was racing up. A regular flame of wind struck off above the Peel, and *Satanita* went by the windward into first place, leaving *Valkyrie* fairly stuck up. *Navahoe* and *Calluna* hung on to big topsails too long, the Yankee continuing whipper-in and falling down flat on her side in the hardest of the gushes. *Satanita*, too, crabbed up badly, but did not heel to such an angle as *Navahoe*, and was always lively and manageable in the puffs; she also got up a higher head of speed the fresher the wind piped.

On the second round it was harder driving between *Satanita* and *Valkyrie* than with *Calluna* and *Navahoe*, and after the free reach to the Warner the first named was 2 mins. 2 secs. ahead or 3 secs. short of her allowance. It was just a clean reach from the Noman to Cowes, and some of the puffs came off the Island with the rush of a white

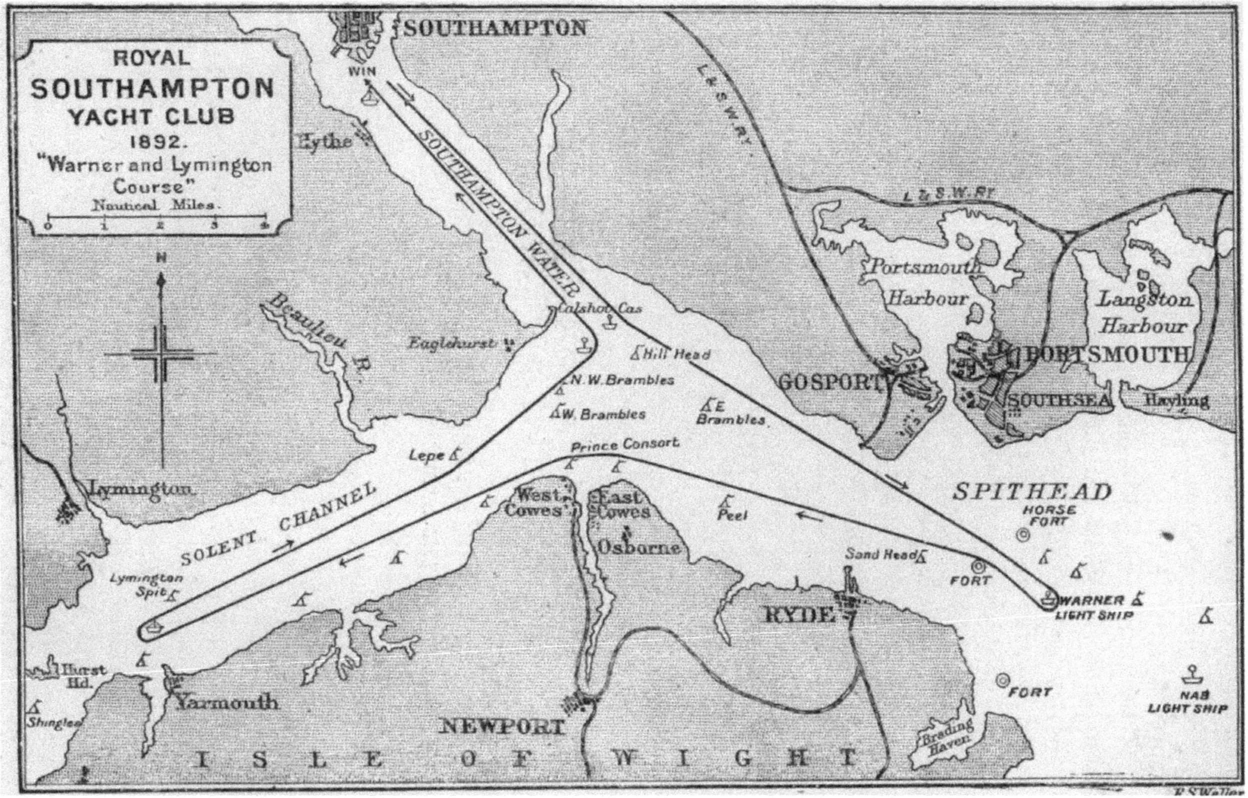
ROYAL
SOUTHAMPTON
YACHT CLUB
1892.
"Warner and Lymington Course"
Nautical Miles.
0 1 2 3 4
N
SOUTHAMPTON
WIN
Hythe
SOUTHAMPTON WATER
L & S. W. RY.
L & S. W. Ry
Portsmouth Harbour
Langston Harbour
PORTSMOUTH
GOSPORT
SOUTHSEA
Hayling
Beaulieu R.
Eaglehurst
Calshot Cas
Hill Head
N. W. Brambles
W. Brambles
E Brambles
Prince Consort
Lepe
Lymington
SOLENT CHANNEL
SPITHEAD
HORSE FORT
West Cowes
East Cowes
Peel
Osborne
Sand Head
FORT
Lymington Spit
WARNER LIGHT SHIP
RYDE
Hurst Hd.
Shingles
Yarmouth
NEWPORT
FORT
NAB LIGHT SHIP
Brading Haven
ISLE OF WIGHT

squall. *Satanita* was knocked down flatter than *Valkyrie*, but she did not steady her speed, and finished a splendidly fought and most exciting race with 2 mins. 9 secs. lead of *Valkyrie*, *Satanita* winning with 4 secs. to spare. *Calluna* was 5 mins. 22 secs. astern of the winner, and *Navahoe* 7 mins. 36 secs.

Ill fortune has of late haunted each annual Saturday fixture of the Royal Southampton Club, and that of August 5, instead of attracting the fleet of heavy weights, was reduced to a match between the *Navahoe* and *Calluna*. The *Britannia* had her new mast in, but was not ready, *Satanita* was getting a strengthening band shrunk on her masthead, and *Valkyrie*, which had come across from Cowes to Southampton Water, did not start, fearing there would be too much wind for her sprung main-boom. A north-wester came shooting down Southampton Water fresh enough for *Navahoe's* small reef to be pulled down, *Calluna*, however, had whole mainsail and both jibheaders. The Scotch clipper was unluckily sailed through the line too soon, and the *Navahoe* got two minutes start; but *Calluna* bringing quite a rattle of wind, nearly nailed her rival at Calshot Spit.

The breeze got light in the west channel and came bare, while the tide had to be stemmed. *Navahoe* kept sailing into the first of the wind, and, getting a fine lift near the Lymington Mark, led by 3 mins. *Calluna* was sailed without heart or judgment in the run up the west channel, and so on to the Warner. She might well have carried her jackyard topsail going west, and certainly wanted it, coming back with sheets off. *Calluna* was gybed in Cowes Roads for some reason; and while her opponent was running clean with boom the other side, the Scotch boat was 'by the lee.' *Navahoe* at length was first to shift her big topsail, and had 6 mins. lead at the time, but when *Calluna* did go to work sail shifting, it took her crew eighteen minutes to get down the jibheaded topsail and replace it with jackyarder. In the beat from the Warner up past Browndown there were some flukes lying under the north shore which might have been picked up for the seeking, and *Calluna's* poor attempt at match sailing ended by *Navahoe* weathering the line off Netley with a lead of 11 mins. 25 secs.

The racing fleet mustered in force on the Royal Albert Station, and cruisers swarmed thick as bees to do honour to the last of the Solent racing fixtures. A light gauzy haze in the early morning of Monday, August 14, did not bode well for sport, but an air came just before the starting hour for the Albert Cup, and stretched out the fighting flags of *Britannia*, *Navahoe*, *Calluna*, and *Satanita*. A south-east breeze of about

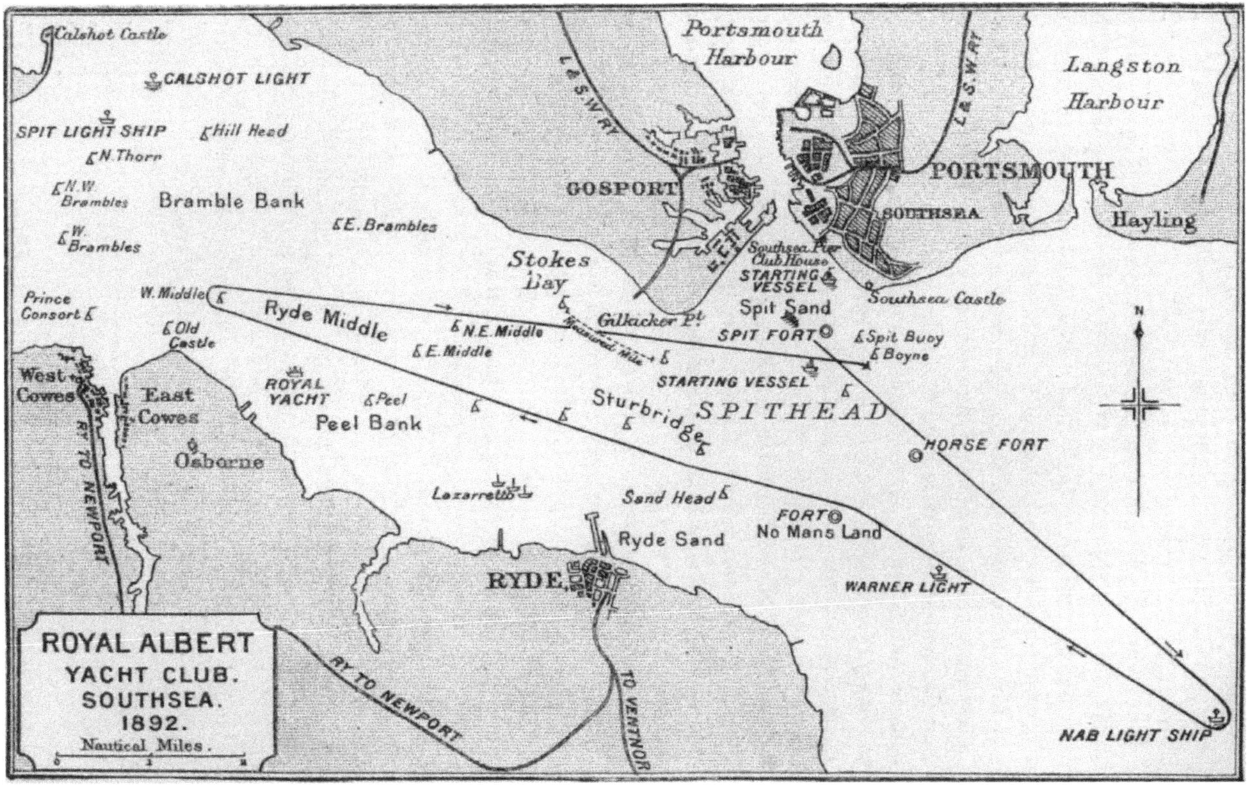
ROYAL ALBERT
YACHT CLUB.
SOUTHSEA.
1892.
Nautical Miles.
Calshot Castle
CALSHOT LIGHT
SPIT LIGHT SHIP
Hill Head
N. Thorn
N.W. Brambles
Bramble Bank
E. Brambles
W. Brambles
Prince Consort
W. Middle
Ryde Middle
N.E. Middle
E. Middle
Old Castle
West Cowes
East Cowes
RY TO NEWPORT
Osborne
ROYAL YACHT
Peel
Peel Bank
Lazarretto
Stokes Bay
Gilkacker Pt
GOSPORT
L&S.W.RY
Portsmouth Harbour
PORTSMOUTH
SOUTHSEA
Langston Harbour
Hayling
Southsea Pier Club House
STARTING VESSEL
Southsea Castle
Spit Sand
SPIT FORT
Spit Buoy
Boyne
STARTING VESSEL
Sturbridge
SPITHEAD
HORSE FORT
Sand Head
FORT
No Mans Land
Ryde Sand
RYDE
WARNER LIGHT
NAB LIGHT SHIP
TO VENTNOR
N

weight enough for small jib-topsails to be carried with profit to windward was drawing in against the last of the east-going stream, when an eventful race commenced with *Satanita's* bowsprit end showing first across the line; the others were close at hand, and a pretty start was made.

The wind freshened at night after Weymouth Regatta, and on Sunday morning there was an ugly sea off the Bill. The yachts which made the passage to Torquay had a coarse time, some of them ran back, others did not leave the Dorset port, the consequence being that there was a poor muster in Torbay. The *Satanita, Navahoe, Britannia*, and *Calluna* were ready to answer the starting gun on Monday morning when the wind was piping loud from the westward. All had a reef in mainsails, and topmasts were housed when anchors were broken out, but *Satanita's* was very unwisely got on end, and she subsequently set a jibheader. *Satanita*, over-eager, sailed the line too soon, and her opponents had been racing for the off mark nearly 3 mins. before she followed them across. With the wind quarterly, she soon smoked out to the first flagboat, where *Navahoe* was leader and *Calluna* second. Then came a beat in a little head jump, and the full drift of the wind was felt.

Navahoe's performance in beating to Brixham was far and away her worst display, as she simply crabbed on her uppers and sidled away, while *Satanita,* crippled as she was with jibheader, was—truth to tell—not shaping a whit better, and seemed to be simply wallowing in dead water. Off Brixham, *Satanita* had another set back, through one of her extra hands slipping overboard, but a very smart job was made in picking the man up. *Satanita* was punished with jibheader again on the second round, and *Britannia, Calluna*, and *Navahoe* were waltzing away from her. On the third round the sail was pulled down and the spar housed, but it was too late in the day to pick up the first flight. *Satanita*, however, began to tramp away, and in addition to reaching her rivals beat the lot going to windward.

The wind fairly whistled offshore as they reached on for Goodrington, but *Calluna* and *Navahoe* did not lower staysails as on the second round. The *Britannia's* jib, however, burst, and *Navahoe* shifted hers. The latter was in the way of a regular canvas splitter as she kept away round the Goodrington mark, and falling down flat she swept the mark-boat with her mainsail, but continued the match. At the end of the third round *Navahoe* was 8 mins. astern of *Britannia*, and 4 mins. of *Calluna*, while *Satanita* had gained 4 mins. on the Yankee in 10 miles.

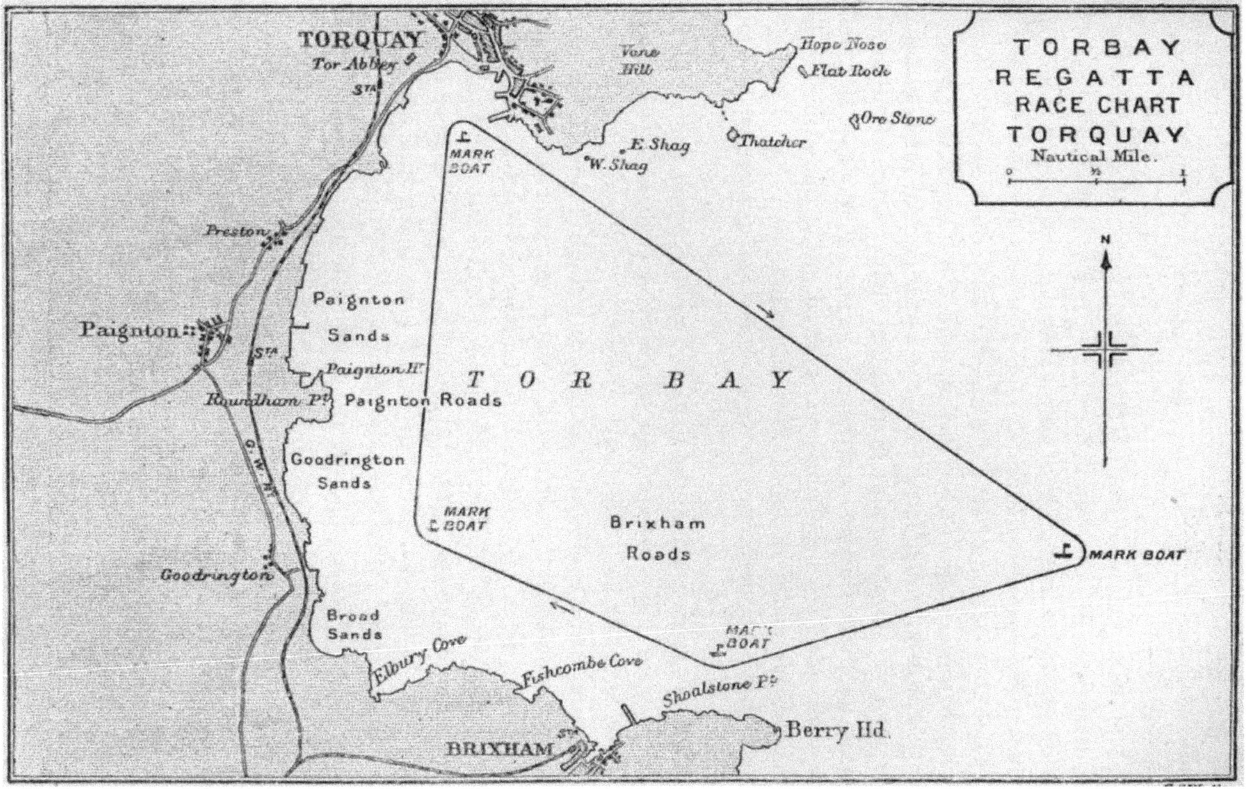
TORBAY
REGATTA
RACE CHART
TORQUAY
Nautical Mile.
0
½
1
N
TORQUAY
Tor Abbey
STA
Vane Hill
Hope Nose
Flat Rock
Ore Stone
Thatcher
E. Shag
W. Shag
MARK BOAT
Preston
Paignton
Paignton Sands
STA
Paignton Hr
Roundham Pt
Paignton Roads
TOR BAY
Goodrington Sands
Goodrington
G. W. R.
MARK BOAT
Brixham Roads
MARK BOAT
Broad Sands
Elbury Cove
Fishcombe Cove
MARK BOAT
Shoalstone Pt
Berry Hd.
BRIXHAM
STA

The *Navahoe's* mainsail was found to be damaged at the clew, and to be giving out at the reef lacing, and just as *Satanita* was collaring her off the Imperial she drew to the wind and gave up. On the last round *Satanita* gained 1 min. 42 secs. on *Britannia*, the latter finishing an easy winner 4 mins. 30 secs. ahead of *Calluna*, and 7 mins. 9 secs. of *Satanita*.

The wind hardened during the dark hours, and was blowing a moderate gale from the south-west at sunrise. It had veered westerly and moderated a little an hour before the start, and the *Britannia*, *Calluna*, and *Satanita* housed topmasts, got first reef in mainsails, and set third jibs in anticipation of a dusting. *Navahoe* could not start, owing to her damaged mainsail; but had she joined in there is no reason to suppose that she would have shaped better than on the previous day, as the wind was about the same in strength and direction, and the course almost identical. *Britannia* and *Satanita* made a grand start, but with the wind abaft the beam the latter cleared out at once from under her rival's lee, and gave a really phenomenal display of speed going to the flagboat outside Hope's Nose, covering the distance in 13 mins. 50 secs.

She was at the mark in the thick of a passing squall, and when the tiller was put down to bring her by the wind it broke off close into the rudder-head, Jay, who always steers from the lee side, being just saved from going overboard. The mishap was alike annoying to crew and spectators as the vessel would, without doubt, have established a record over the Torbay course. The *Britannia* and *Calluna* then had a match, and, curious to state, *Calluna* in the hard wind which prevailed during the first, second, and third rounds, fairly beat *Britannia* on each turn while sailing with a free sheet, the advantage gained by the latter being on the beat between the sea mark and Brixham. On the last round the wind took off a little and *Britannia* made an all-round gain, eventually beating her antagonist by 4 mins. 17 secs.

In contrast to the tearing pipe-up at Torquay, variable breezes, flaws, catspaws, and calms prevailed in Start Bay when the Royal Dart matches were decided. Owing to the death of the Duke of Coburg the *Britannia* did not start, but *Navahoe* was under racing colours again, and she was opposed by *Calluna* and *Satanita*, Mr. Crocker, of New York, having arrived just in time to sail the American. All light kites were set, and *Satanita* led the race on a reach to the Skerries buoy, at which mark *Navahoe* was whipper-in. *Calluna*, through luffing out to cover *Satanita*, let *Navahoe* through into second place, and the lat-

'SATANITA,' 162-RATER (A. D. CLARKE, ESQ.)

ter ran up close to the leader. The breeze got so soft that they could hardly gain on the tide, and getting a flaw first on one quarter and then on the other positions kept changing, till at the last mark *Satanita* was just clear ahead of *Calluna*; the tide, however, hooked the latter and set her on to the mark-boat, and she at once gave up. *Satanita* and *Navahoe* reached along in a trickling air with all light kites set, and *Satanita* finished the first round with a lead of 1 min. 18 secs. Both got in the doldrums near the Start mark, but taking a chill *Navahoe* got away with a long lead. *Satanita*, however, brought enough wind to drag her by to windward, and give her a good lead at the east mark. *Satanita* was lucky enough to get a new wind first, which kept pretty true and steady afterward, and she eventually beat *Navahoe* in a fluky race by 7 mins. 45 secs.

The rising Start Bay Club, to its credit be it said, catered for the big ships, and in return secured the entry of the familiar quartet. After a breathless morning an opportune breeze from the south-east travelled in from sea and put a little life into the start. The *Satanita*, however, had just before drove on to the outer flagboat and she was then kept lying with staysail to windward. *Navahoe* crossed the line first, and in a soft breeze went clean full and by for the Torcross flagboat, *Britannia* and *Calluna* being sailed finer. *Satanita*, when told by the committee to 'go on,' crossed the line 11 mins. 20 secs. after *Navahoe*, and getting a better breeze than the leaders she gained about 7 mins. on *Navahoe*. The last named went stealing along in the gentle breeze and finished the first round 33 seconds before *Britannia*.

The breeze freshened and they came on a taut bowline, and after *Navahoe* had tried her best to wind *Britannia*, the latter squeezed through her lee and in the next board crossed ahead, while *Satanita* closed up. After a run from the west to east mark, they had a broad reach home in a fine breeze, *Britannia* keeping bell-wether. *Navahoe* held second place in the beat to Torcross, but *Satanita* went past in going down wind for the next mark. It was a curious finish, as after reaching in fairly foaming, the wind cut off within a quarter of a mile of the winning line, and *Britannia* came upright. She then got a cyclonic cooler, which filled the lower sails one way and the topsail the other.

Britannia's long lead looked likely to be wiped out, as the *Satanita*, *Navahoe*, and *Calluna* were meanwhile tearing in foaming. They in turn got stuck up, however, in the same vortex, and *Britannia* was logged winner with a lead of 7 mins. 16 secs. of *Satanita*, 9 mins. 20

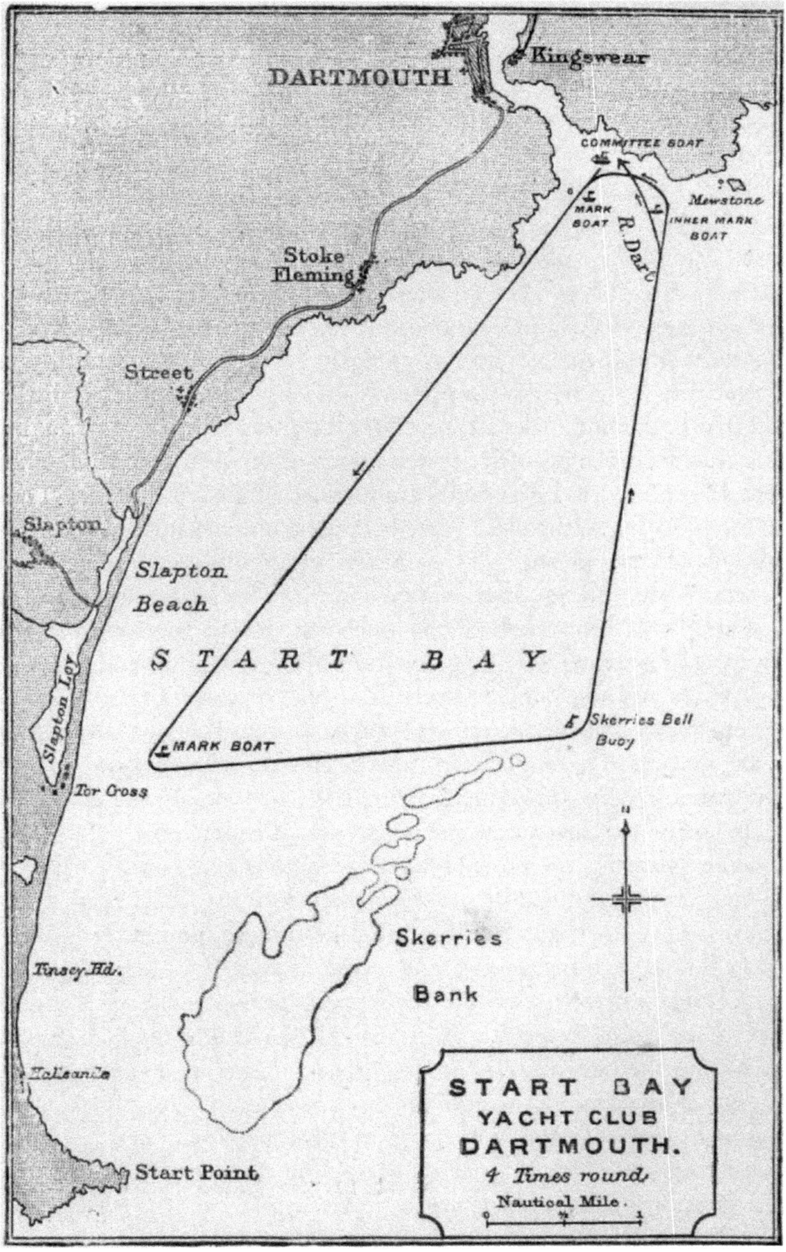
DARTMOUTH
Kingswear
COMMITTEE BOAT
MARK BOAT
Mewstone
INNER MARK BOAT
R. Dart
Stoke Fleming
Street
Slapton
Slapton Beach
START BAY
Slapton Ley
MARK BOAT
Skerries Bell Buoy
Tor Cross
Skerries Bank
Start Point
START BAY YACHT CLUB DARTMOUTH.
4 Times round
Nautical Mile.
0
½
1

secs. of *Navahoe*, and 12 mins. 44 secs. of *Calluna*. *Satanita's* was a remarkably fine performance in such weather; but, after all, she had a bootless journey, the *Navahoe* taking second prize.

The *Navahoe* did not go further west than Dartmouth, but gave topsail-sheet for Cowes to get her wings clipped and a thorough brush up before the Gold Cup and other challenge cup matches with *Britannia*.

Had the matches for the Royal Victoria Gold Cup been set for decision earlier in the season, and the challenger and defender not previously gauged their speed, deeper and wider interest would very naturally have been taken in the contests. As matters stood, the result appeared a foregone conclusion, yet many were warned by the *Navahoe's* admirers that a little clipping and other alterations would be found to have wrought an improvement both in stability and speed, and that she would make a closer fight than was generally anticipated. The club arrangements for the first match of the series, on Wednesday, Sept. 6, appeared to be as perfect as possible, and excitement ran high on the morning of the day. There was a great crowd on Ryde Pier, and the official steamer which embarked ticket-holders at Southampton, Cowes, Ryde, and Southsea carried a large and critical company.

Friday was appointed for the final match over the long Victoria course, and it turned out a very coarse time, the wind coming in tearing squalls and the rain in sheets. *Navahoe's* mainsail gave out at the eyelet lacings, and the second reef was got down, the start meanwhile being delayed. The American, however, eventually brought up, and Mr. Jameson, who was acting for the Prince of Wales on the '*Britannia*,' declined, under the circumstances, to take advantage of a 'sail over,' it being mutually agreed subsequently to race on Monday. Monday opened with a rattling breeze from the eastward, but it had toned down at 11 o'clock, and was then a typical time to test the rivals under lower canvas with mainsails single reefed.

As usual with the wind out there was a tumble of sea off Spithead. They started to the eastward at 11.5, and had a beat to the Nab, *Britannia* having the best of it, as she was broad to windward at the flash of the gun. The west tide was going, and a long stretch was made across Spithead, *Britannia* giving her rival a blistering for a time. She was too far ahead off the Warner to be spilling *Navahoe's* head-sail, and, smashing through the short sea in peerless style, beat the American 9 mins. 5 secs.—or a minute a mile—turning to the Nab. Spinnakers Irish-reefed and hoisted to masthead were set after they had reached

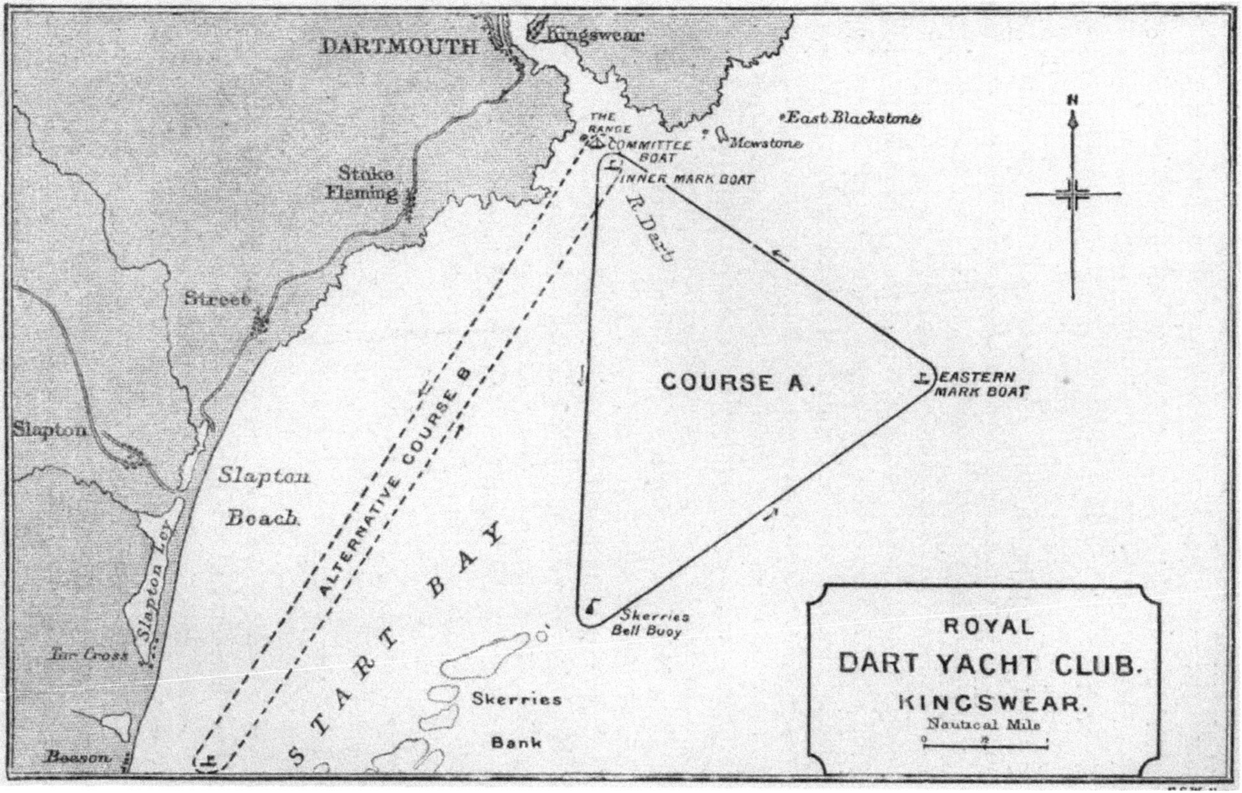
DARTMOUTH
Kingswear
THE RANGE
COMMITTEE BOAT
INNER MARK BOAT
East Blackstone
Mewstone
N
Stoke Fleming
R. Dart
Street
COURSE A.
EASTERN MARK BOAT
ALTERNATIVE COURSE B
Slapton
Slapton Beach
START BAY
Slapton Ley
Skerries Bell Buoy
Tor Cross
Skerries Bank
Beeson
ROYAL
DART YACHT CLUB.
KINGSWEAR.
Nautical Mile

on to the Spit mark, and a gybe was made off Lee, the western flag being tacked round, and here *Britannia* led by 9 mins. 7 secs. *Navahoe* after rounding appeared to be starved for wind, while *Britannia* was getting rammed along. Soon the jibsheets of the American ran out, and the sail had to be secured, sheets rove, and the sail reset, *Britannia* meanwhile having hopped a long distance away; and she weathered the home flagboat and finished the first round with a lead of 17 mins. 7 secs.

The Nab was turned to in a lighter breeze and smoother water, and *Navahoe*, getting a northerly slant when off the Elbow buoy of the Dean, made a long leg out, while *Britannia* had been pegging away at short turnings. The latter, however, weathered the lightship holding a lead of 14 mins. 5 secs., and she only added 10 secs. in going free to the western mark. The wind having backed to the eastward, they could lay clean for home, and with a fair tide the ground was covered very fast. *Britannia's* masthead had gone aft, and the heel of her housed topmast was sticking out so far that it had torn the staysail just inside the tabling, and the sail split up from foot to head just before she crossed the line victorious in her defence of the Royal Victoria Gold Cup. The *Britannia* finished at 4 hrs. 29 mins. 17 secs., and *Navahoe* at 4 hrs. 44 mins. 25 secs.

After having finished the deciding match for the Royal Victoria Gold Cup, conqueror and conquered sailed away westward and rode the night out at anchor in Cowes Roads. Tuesday, Sept. 12, was fixed for the race for the Brenton Reef Cup, and it turned out a bright crisp morning, with a fine singing breeze easterly, and, gauged by the loom on the seascape, it appeared probable the wind would prevail from that quarter. According to conditions the course was from off the Needles Rocks round Cherbourg breakwater, passing in at the west end and out at the east, and returning to the Needles, the distance being computed at 120 miles. The antagonists were towed away after breakfast to the rendezvous, and going down the west channel a reef was put in mainsails, No. 3 jibs hoisted in stops, and flying jibs stowed at bowsprit ends, while jibheaded topsails were set after the last pull had been taken at purchases.

The owner of the *Navahoe's* wish that 5 mins. be allowed for crossing the line and the difference corrected at the finish of the match was acceded to, and about 11.30 the official steamer was in position, Mr. R. Grant, secretary of the Royal Yacht Squadron, being officer in charge. The imaginary starting line was formed by bringing the three

Needles Rocks in one, and at noon the Blue Peter was lowered and the match commenced. *Britannia* reached across the line at 12 hrs. 1 min. 6 secs. p.m., the *Navahoe* at 12 hrs. 2 mins. 5 secs., the Prince of Wales's cutter thus having 54½ secs. to allow at the finish. Sheets were trimmed for a beam wind, and with flying jibs and balloon staysails set they went racing fast across the down-coming ebb. There was a nasty ground swell, and on getting clear from under the lee of the land the full weight of the wind was felt, the sea getting crested and heavy. Jibheaders were handed, flying jibs lowered, and working staysails set, and travelling upwards of twelve knots there was plenty of drift knocking about. *Britannia* continued to keep *Navahoe* astern, and two hours after the start 25 miles had been logged.

The wind kept true and they continued to sail a punishing race, the vessels labouring a good deal in the lumpy sea, and yawing in all directions. Keeping up an even speed of about twelve knots, they made the breakwater about four and a half hours after the start, and up to this time *Britannia* had kept her lead. When about five miles off, *Navahoe* was let come up sharp across the leader's wake, and, making a shoot afterward off her helm, she looked like coming in to her opponent. *Britannia* dropped back after being thus covered up, and then came into her rival's wake, and they raced on into the comparative smoothing under the land, with *Navahoe* holding a few lengths lead. Topmasts were housed, and they passed into the breakwater ready for the two-miles beat through Cherbourg Roads. This was at 5 o'clock, and *Navahoe* had a lead of 25 secs. *Britannia* drew to close round the buoy,

Navahoe found her opponent beating out broad on her weather, and in the first board *Britannia* held a clear lead. In the last tack *Britannia* stood on until she could spoil her opponent, and it took *Navahoe* a few minutes to recover the winding. *Britannia* headed out of the eastern end with about 2 mins. lead, and on getting in the open the ebb was still going west. It was a clean fetch back, but the wind was heavier and the sea steeper than on coming over. When night closed in they were about half-way across Channel, the vessels then getting fearfully punished. They raced together, however, in a wonderful way, *Britannia* keeping the lead, with *Navahoe* about 150 yards astern, the latter running wildly about, pointing one minute wide of the leader's weather quarter and anon for the lee side. Foresails had with difficulty been lowered when the vessels were about two miles off the breakwater, but with the wind more moderate, when they were about five miles off St. Catherine's they were reset.

The flood tide was streaming hard, but *Britannia* on closing in to the Needles was hauled up a bit for fear the wind should draw off the land, while *Navahoe* was sailed hard along and closed on the leader. As the club steamer could not be anchored in the fairway outside the Needles, she was brought into Alum Bay and moored, and according to official timing *Britannia* showed 'on' with the Needles Light at 10 hrs. 37 mins. 35 secs. p.m., the *Navahoe* at 10 hrs. 38 mins. 32 secs., *Britannia* thus being winner on corrected time by 2½ secs. Mr. Carroll protested that the judge's steamer was not in position, and that the difference between the vessels at the finish was not so much as 57 secs. A meeting of the Royal Yacht Squadron Sailing Committee was called, and it was decided to adjudge *Navahoe* winner. It need hardly be said that this ruling was thought hard on *Britannia* after such a grand race, and no explanation of the finding was forthcoming. It was understood that the owner of the *Navahoe* would not agree to the match being re-sailed.

It was arranged to sail for the Cape May Cup on Friday, Sept. 15, under precisely similar conditions to those which governed the Brenton Reef Cup, and over the same course. In order to obviate any difficulty about timing in the dark, it was agreed that the start and finish should be from Alum Bay, and Col. J. Sterling undertook the duties of starter and time-keeper. Seven o'clock was named for a beginning, but the vessels could not move out of Cowes Roads until 9.30, owing to a dense fog choking up the west channel.

On getting down to Alum Bay a further wait had to be made, owing to a glass calm prevailing, and it was not until 12.30 that the preparatory flag was broken out. There was a soft westerly breeze at the time, which gave a short beat out to the Needles. Fine generalship was displayed on *Britannia*, which was intentionally sailed through the line before the gun, and *Navahoe* was allowed the honour of showing the way. *Britannia* followed 10 secs. later, and on meeting *Navahoe* standing off on port tack put her round, and presently stayed dead in her wind. *Navahoe* got a terrible shake-off, and was 2½ mins. astern at the Needles. They then had a close reach off into the Channel, and with the light breeze narrowing only slow progress was made.

An hour and a half after the start *Britannia* held a lead of about a mile, and at 7 o'clock she was judged to be three miles ahead. At 8 o'clock there was not a breath of wind, the vessels laid in a perfect calm for about two hours, and it was reckoned that *Britannia* was then about twenty miles off the Wight. At 10.15 a north-east breeze gathered in, *Britannia* ran away with it, and in the pitchy darkness *Navahoe* could not be made out.

The breeze kept up, and the spinnaker was carried on *Britannia* until Cape Barfleur lights were made out right ahead. Owing to an alteration in the character of the lights not being noticed on the chart for a time, it was thought *Britannia* was too far to the westward, the spinnaker was then got off, and the vessel hauled up a little. The western end was made in the grey of the morning, and on entering at 5.29 *Britannia* was holding about three miles lead, but *Navahoe* was closing up fast. The wind was drawing through Cherbourg Roads, a few boards were made to get weathering distance of the east end, and *Britannia* was going out at the one end while *Navahoe* was about entering at the other, the distance between them being a trifle over two miles.

The breeze, which came from the northward by east, was growing, and jib topsails were pulled down when about ten miles off. *Britannia* was sailed to keep her opponent fair in her wake, and she might have been made fetch Christchurch head, but Durleston was the landfall, and the leader tacked off the Dorset headland at 10.15, *Navahoe* following at 10.45. It was a beat hence home with a weather tide, and *Britannia* at this game made a terrible exhibition of her opponent, weathering the line winner of the Cape May Cup with a lead of 36 mins. 13 secs. The official timing was, *Britannia* 12 hrs. 57 mins. 19 secs. p.m., *Navahoe* 1 hr. 33 mins. 32 secs. p.m. It may be said that *Britannia's* sail-area in the Gold Cup, Brenton Reef, and Cape May races was 10,327 square feet, and the *Navahoe's* 10,815 square feet, the latter having been clipped to the extent of 270 feet.

In summing up this review it may be said there is little reason to doubt that the *Britannia* was the best all round vessel of the fleet; the *Valkyrie* was a trifle the quicker in stays and in light breezes, the better vessel to windward, or even on a long close reach, and also in a dead run. In hard winds and plain sailing the *Satanita's* 10 ft. greater length on the load-line gave her the mastery over the Prince of Wales's cutter, but on any point and in any weather *Britannia* was equal to lowering the *Calluna's* colours. The *Britannia* and *Navahoe* were desperately close matched whenever the latter could get a broad reach or run and keep the lee rail out of water, but the Prince of Wales's cutter was immeasurably her superior on the all-important point—going to windward.

Perfect handling contributed not a little to *Britannia's* success, and, sailed as she was by John Carter and Mr. W. G. Jameson, it is certain nothing was given away or lost. She had a peerless record in her class—namely, 33 prizes in 43 starts; the gross value of the prizes won, including challenge cups, being in round numbers 2,500*l*.

It must have been highly gratifying to the *Valkyrie's* designer that the vessel excelled in the very weather and sailing points desired—namely, going to windward and dead running. Her trials with *Britannia* showed how wonderfully evenly matched the vessels were in moderate weather, and artistic handling was always conspicuous whenever Lord Dunraven's cutter was under a racing flag. *Valkyrie* made her mark in the short season she had in home waters, her record being 15 prizes in 24 starts, her winnings amounting to 955*l*.

The *Satanita* was a particularly unlucky boat, and on the Clyde her ill fortune passed into a proverb. After breaking the spell with a victory in Belfast Lough, she, however, scored several notable victories, and it was a great feat to win two events at a Royal Yacht Squadron regatta. Her fastest reaching display was no doubt in the Nore to Dover race, but for a short burst the speed she attained in going from the New Pier, Torquay, to the flagboat outside Hope's Nose has perhaps never been equalled by anything of yacht kind. *Satanita* was not such a handy boat to get round marks or herring-bone through a crowded roadstead as *Britannia* and *Valkyrie*, but Jay is deserving of the highest praise for the able way he sailed his charge. *Satanita's* winnings included a Queen's Cup and the Albert Cup, and in 36 starts she won 13 prizes, value 760*l*.

The *Calluna* was a disappointing boat; indeed, her designer got into a way at last of calling her 'My unlucky boat,' for which expression there was all-sufficient reason. The best of *Calluna* perhaps remains to be got out of her, yet she went by fits and starts in a wonderful way, but could rarely maintain her form to a finish. She had very strong opposition in *Britannia*, *Valkyrie*, and *Satanita*, but likely enough she would have been an all-round better boat, and perhaps a real flier, with 2½ ft. less beam and 2½ ft. more load-water length. Her skipper, A. Hogarth, is exceptionally smart in handling a small craft; *Calluna* was his first charge of the heavy-weight line, and she certainly was not the sort of craft to serve an apprenticeship in. The Clyde cutter managed to win 10 prizes in 36 starts, but it was only on two occasions that she sailed home in the van.

To small details in a racing vessel's outfit the Americans give much more consideration than British yachtsmen think necessary. Many a wrinkle might have been picked up, however, in making a careful study of the *Navahoe's* outfit, and there is no doubt that much of the gear and ironwork in English yachts is too heavy. *Navahoe's* failing was want of stability, and this was found out on the other side before she set out from home. Her iron skin was not in her favour, and we, on this side, have yet to learn that a vessel can be properly laid on a wind when steered with a wheel. The *Navahoe* started 18 times and won 6 prizes. Including the Brenton Reef Challenge Cup, her gross winnings amounted to 445*l*.

The record of broken masts and other spars in connection with first-class vessels was a remarkable one. It is likely that poor quality wood brought about the majority of the breakages; in fact, last season's spars were a rank bad lot. The case was different in *Thistle's* year, that vessel having a really splendid lot of sticks. It may be said that the *Britannia* had no fewer than three masts in her forty-three racing essays, one topmast, two bowsprits, and one gaff; *Calluna* two masts, one main boom, and one gaff; *Valkyrie* one mast, one topmast, one boom, and one bowsprit; and *Satanita* one bowsprit and one boom.

Referring to the 40-rating class, it was feared at the outset of the season that neither *Lais* nor *Vendetta* was any improvement on the over-year *Varuna*. The last named had quite a triumphal march at the outset, winning four class matches right off. It was at Lowestoft that *Lais* first gave *Varuna* a taste of her quality, as she beat the latter by 13 mins. 34 secs. in moderate weather. *Lais* was afterwards victorious at Dover, Southampton (R. Southern), Largs Regatta, Royal Western of Scotland, Mudhook, Royal Ulster, Royal Irish, Royal Alfred, Royal Yacht Squadron (Australian Cup), Royal Victoria. Altogether she made up a string of 29 prizes in 39 starts, and the gross value of her winnings was 827*l*. *Varuna* gained first honours in the Royal London match (Thames), Brightlingsea Regatta, Royal Harwich (both days), Royal Mersey (both days), Royal Clyde, Royal Ulster, Royal Cornwall (S.O.), Royal Southampton (2), Royal Albert (2), Royal Dart, and Royal Western, her winning total being 23 prizes in 40 starts, value 605*l*.

The *Vendetta* won her maiden race, and only one more (R. Southern), before leaving the Channel. She was an improved boat when she joined in on the Clyde and won round the Royal Northern course, and she was subsequently to the fore in the Clyde Corinthian Regatta, Royal Clyde, Royal Irish, Royal London (Cowes), Royal Yacht

Squadron, Royal Dorset and Torbay (2). In all she gained 18 flags in 33, and the value of her prizes amounted to 490*l*. The *Thalia* only carried Judge Boyd's colours ten times, and won six prizes, value 150*l*.

The *Dragon III.* was crack of the 20-rating class, and she had a very brilliant record—namely, 31 prizes, value 445*l.*, in 34 starts. The *Dragon* did not go through the season without a little doctoring, her formidable opponent, the *Deirdré*, being found very hard to beat after being shortened about 10 in. on the water-line, and getting 45 square feet more sail-area; so *Dragon* was altered in like manner, and *Deirdré* had again to take second place. The new *Vigorna* was a failure, and *Dragon* and *Deirdré* were too good for the *Molly* (*Dragon II.*). The *Zinita* would perhaps have proved equal to tackling the *Dragon III.* by the wind, but Mr. Hill's boat would certainly have been able to score heavily with checked sheets. *Deirdré's* record was 21 prizes in 35 starts, and the *Zinita's* 18 in 24 starts. The *Phantom* was the crack of the tens, with 14 prizes in 24 starts; and the 5-rater *Red Lancer* in going round the coast managed to win 24 flags in 34 racing essays.

This review would not be complete without some reference to sails, and it may be said that those made by the joint firms of Laphorn and Ratsey were really wonderful and perfect specimens of the art. Still, *Valkyrie's* canvas elicited the greatest praise in America, and especially from General Paine, who said her suit 'fitted like a glove; the most perfect canvas he had ever seen in America.' The quality of the material and workmanship was strikingly evident in *Britannia's* mainsail, which lasted a season through, and after all the fagging and rough work it had, it kept its shape to the end of the season. The *Valkyri'* had a mainsail made of Sea Island cotton for the America Cup matches, but most people would vote flax good enough after seeing such a sail as *Britannia's*. The *Satanita*, *Calluna*, and *Valkyrie's* mainsails stood equally well as *Britannia's*, and those of the 40-raters *Lais* and *Vendetta* could not have been better. The twenties were quite as well done by; but the plan of giving the last-named class wide cloths in a measure spoils the beauty of the sails. The patent jibs introduced by T. Ratsey were very pretty sails, but they seemed liable to go across the diagonal seam in a gusty wind.

Mr. Hill's 'Dragon III,' 20-rater.

CHAPTER 12

The American Yachting Season of 1893

By Lewis Herreshoff

The yachting season of 1893 was inaugurated by the laying of *Navahoe's* keel in the autumn of 1892, at the construction shops of the Herreshoff Company, in Bristol, R.I.

Interest was soon centred in her, for it was clear that she was intended for some unusual service, and when her owner Mr. R. P. Carroll, announced his programme for the season of 1893, of going to England to try for the American cups there, and to take part in what racing he might, there was an astonishing awakening of enthusiasm on both sides of the Atlantic, which culminated in the international contest off New York in October 1893, that being without question the most exciting and interesting series of races ever witnessed. Early in December 1892 the challenge from Lord Dunraven was finally settled and adjusted, creating a patriotic ardour in all English and American yachtsmen.

Almost simultaneously the *Valkyrie*, *Britannia*, *Calluna*, and *Satanita* in England, and *Colonia*, *Vigilant*, *Jubilee*, and *Pilgrim* in America, were begun, the last three English yachts being expressly intended to defend the American and other trophies against the attack of *Navahoe*, as well as more fully to test the value of *Valkyrie*, on which rested the herculean task of returning the America Cup to its native shores. The early months of 1893 were spent by the yachting circles of both England and America in discussions on and comparisons of the merits of their favourite design and construction, rig and so forth.

All attempts by the designers and builders to keep their work secret were utterly futile, for all essential information as to dimensions and chief characteristics found their way into the newspapers, giving zest to the public interest and discomfiture to the builders, who set seals on the mouths of their workmen and watchmen, and blocked every door and window where the prying public might steal a view of the coming wonder; but seals and watchmen could not evade the desire to know what was to be the form and outline of the 'Defenders,' as the American yachts were popularly called.

The table gives important information concerning the five American yachts of 1893, to which is added *Valkyrie*, her dimensions being important for comparison with the American vessels. *Navahoe* was built under restrictions that precluded all expectations of attaining the highest speed; she was intended for a cruiser which in the event of necessity could be rigged and sailed so as to make a good show with yachts then in existence. Her performance in English waters, although disappointing, was but little below the anticipations of those who knew her and understood the value of her opponents, whose lines were not drawn when *Navahoe* was begun.

The yachts *Navahoe*, *Colonia*, and *Vigilant* are all after the type of *Gloriana* and *Wasp*, but differing widely in some points, the first and last being centreboard vessels, and *Colonia* a keel, but of not sufficient lateral plane, rendering her windward work faulty.

Vigilant represents perhaps more nearly than the others the so-called American type; she combines a broad beam with good depth, and with her centreboard down draws about 23 ft.

The chief characteristic of her construction is the employment of Tobin bronze for her plating (save the upper row of plates, which are of steel), and her centreboard, also of bronze, is made of two plates set apart with ribs between, the space of 2½ in. being filled with cement; the structure weighing 7,750 lbs., and being operated from the cabin by means of differential lifts, capable of raising 6 tons.

Jubilee is of unusual design and construction; her body is wide and shallow, with a fin attachment carrying about 40 tons of lead at a depth of 13 ft. below the water's surface, and to increase the lateral plane she has a centreboard that works through the fin and its bulb of lead, exposing surface enough to ensure most excellent windward work, dropping about 8 or 10 ft. below the bulb. *Pilgrim* is an out-and-out fin-keel yacht, the largest vessel of that type ever built. Like *Jubilee*, she is broad and shallow of body, the fin being of a separate construction, and this with its bulb of 15 tons weight was attached to the vessel in New York, the hull having been built in Wilmington on the Dela-

Cutter	Designer	Owner	Builders	Length Overall	L.W.L.	Beam	Draught	Sail-area	Sail-makers
				ft.	ft.	ft.	ft. ins.	ft.	
							13 0	.	
Navahoe	R. P. Carroll, N.Y.	N. G. Herreshoff	Herreshoff Manufacturing Co.	123	—	23	23.0	—	Wilson and Silsby
Colonia	Arch. Rogers and others, N.Y	"	"	128	85.48	24	15.3	11,340	"
							14.0		
Vigilant	E. D. Morgan and others, N.Y.	"	"	127	86.12	26	24.03	11,312	Wilson and Griffen, N.Y.
Valkyrie	Lord Dunraven	Geo. L. Watson	Henderson	117.25	85.50	—	17.6	—	Ratsey
							13.9		
Jubilee	Chas. J. Paine, Boston	J.B. Paine	L a w l e y Corp., Boston	125	84.47	23	22.0	11,342	Wilson and Silsby
Pilgrim	Bayard Thayer and others, Boston	Stewart and Binney	Pussey and Jones	123	85.28	23	22.6	10,261	"

ware. She carried her bulb 23 ft. below water, which gave her good stability and power to hold her course when sailing to windward; but with her, as in some measure with *Jubilee*, they did not represent any authorised, well-tested type of yacht, and though their performances were interesting and highly instructive, they did not fill the mind of the true yachtsman with glowing satisfaction, seeing that the work that was in hand was one of national importance and required designs of equally high character.

The middle of July found all four yachts in sailing, if not racing, trim; their owners scrupulously avoided contact with each other; each claimed unheard-of speed and other noble qualities; and each felt that his craft was that on which would rest the honour of defending the America Cup. It was soon found that the booms of *Colonia* and *Vigilant* were not satisfactory; they were not stiff enough to hold the sail where it should be to ensure a flat set, and when swung off their weight was found to list the yacht too much, both of which difficulties were to be expected in spars of their length and diameter (100 ft. long by 16 in.).

Hollow booms of different construction were tried. Those where the spar was sawed lengthwise and the core dug out, then glued and trenailed together, were found to be the best. Booms of highly elaborate construction made for *Colonia* and *Vigilant* were tried and found unsuitable. They were built up of long staves, having double skins which were well glued and fastened, and weighed less than half the solid spar; they were 30 in. at slings, 18 in. at after, and 15 in. at forward ends, but they evidently were lacking in material enough to endure the tension on one side and the compression on the other, and were condemned after a short trial.

In the first regatta of the N.Y.Y.C. cruise on August 7, *Colonia* and *Vigilant* met; it was at the head of Long Island Sound, triangular course.

There came a puff of wind a moment after starting, and before the defenders sailed a mile *Vigilant* broke down and withdrew, leaving *Colonia* without an opponent, as *Jubilee* and *Pilgrim* did not join the fleet until later.

The race for the Goelet Cups off Newport on August 11 was famous for first bringing together all four of the 'Defenders,' and infamous in the annals of yachting for being the most disappointing occasion that was ever remembered. Calms varied by light baffling breezes, generally from the east; mists mitigated by clearing moments,

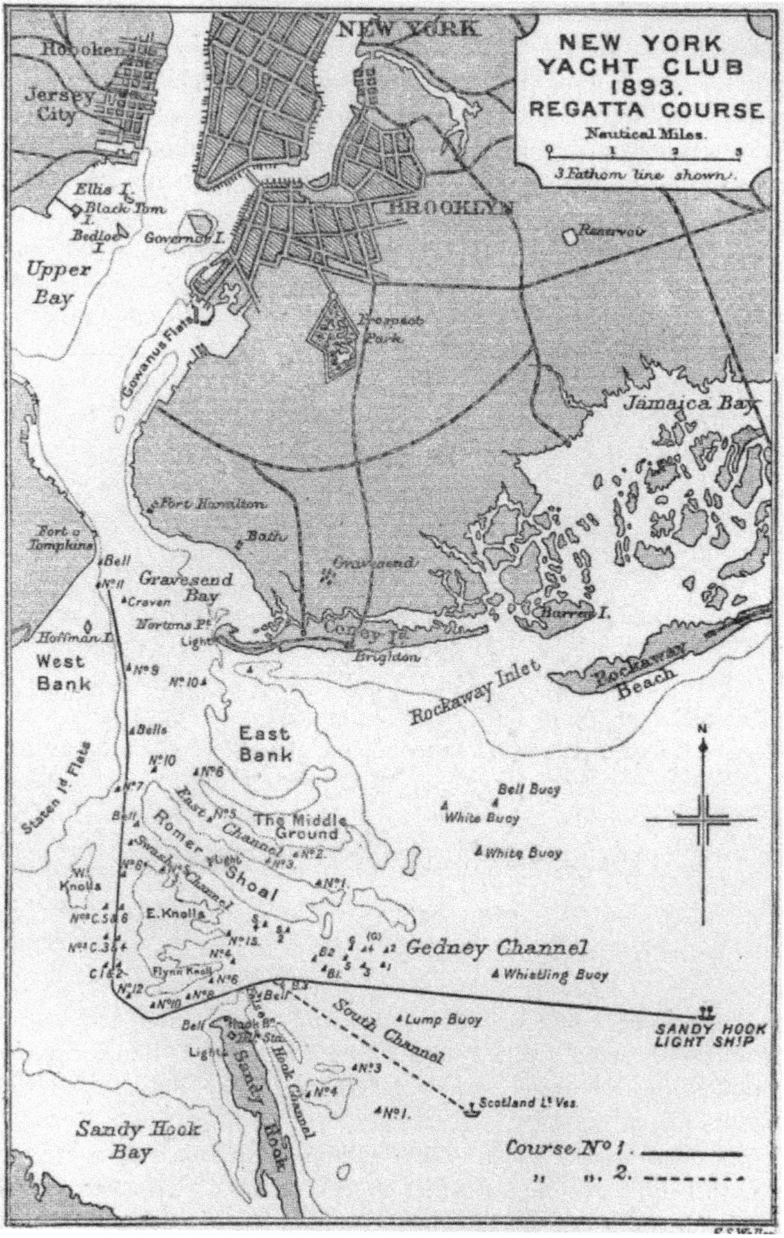
NEW YORK YACHT CLUB 1893. REGATTA COURSE
Nautical Miles.
0 1 2 3
3 Fathom line shown.
NEW YORK
Hoboken
Jersey City
BROOKLYN
Ellis I.
Black Tom I.
Bedloe I.
Governor I.
Upper Bay
Reservoir
Prospect Park
Gowanus Flats
Jamaica Bay
Fort Hamilton
Fort Tompkins
Bath
Gravesend
Gravesend Bay
Craven
Nortons Pt.
Light
Coney Id.
Brighton
Barren I.
Hoffman I.
West Bank
Rockaway Inlet
Rockaway Beach
East Bank
Staten Id. Flats
The Middle Ground
East Channel
Romer Shoal
Swash Channel
W. Knolls
E. Knolls
Flynn Knoll
Bell Buoy
White Buoy
White Buoy
Gedney Channel
Whistling Buoy
Lump Buoy
South Channel
SANDY HOOK LIGHT SHIP
Scotland Lt. Ves.
Hook Channel
Sandy Hook
Sandy Hook Bay
N
Course No. 1.
" " 2.

which finally settled into a hopeless calm and densest of fogs. *Colonia* came drifting home nearly fifteen hours from the start, with *Vigilant* and *Jubilee* an hour or two behind. *Pilgrim* had long before withdrawn. The course was from Brenton's Reef light-vessel to that at the entrance to Vineyard Sound, thence a short leg to the light-vessel at the entrance of Buzzard's Bay, and thence to the point of starting—about thirty-six miles.

The only fact disclosed by this race was that *Jubilee* was as good as *Vigilant* in beating out to the Vineyard Light, and that *Vigilant* was faster than *Jubilee* in reaching, for the latter was caught and passed by *Vigilant* a few moments before the wind wholly disappeared.

During the continuation of the cruise there were several tests of speed in going from port to port, in which *Vigilant* showed herself to be the fastest.

The races for the Astor Cups off Newport were in the main unsatisfactory as real tests of speed and desirable qualities, but in all it was more and more assured that *Vigilant* was the best, and also that *Pilgrim* was far from fulfilling the expectations of those responsible for her. The August races ended without affording any definite information as to the comparative value of the 'Defenders,' but there was a growing opinion that *Vigilant* was best, with *Colonia* and *Jubilee* about even, and *Pilgrim* well astern; this classification, however, was from inference rather than any absolute test. *Jubilee* and *Pilgrim* went to Boston to prepare for the final trial, to take place off New York in a series of races beginning September 7.

It was decided by the owners of *Pilgrim* to give her more power; lead was added to her bulb, spars lengthened, and sail-spread increased. *Jubilee* underwent only minor alterations, whilst *Colonia* and *Vigilant* tried to improve the set of their sails (a hopeless task) and otherwise prepared for the all-important final race. In the first of the trial series *Colonia* and *Vigilant* were about even, the Boston boats being disabled by damage to their gear. The second and third races were victories for *Vigilant*, the last race being sailed in a fine wind and fairly rough sea.

Those who wanted to see an actual test of qualities were again bitterly disappointed, for the Boston boats did not show as they might have done had their rigging and spars remained intact; but in the case of *Pilgrim* it was clear that her increased sail-spread and consequent augmentation of weights below and aloft imposed too severe strains on her hull and rigging, so that structural weakness became alarmingly evident before the close of the race, when she was at once put

'Vigilant,' Cup defender.

Earl of Dunraven's 'Valkyrie.'

out of commission, since which she has been sold, and will appear next as a harbour steamer for passengers.

The choice of *Vigilant* to defend the cup was a wise one—in fact, the committee could decide nothing else, for it was clear that *Colonia* could not do good work to windward, through lack of lateral resistance; and *Jubilee*, although unquestionably a very fast yacht—in some instances the equal of *Vigilant*—was rigged with such untrustworthy material that she could not be depended upon to enter so important a struggle as the defence of the America Cup. After the trial races and consequent choice of *Vigilant* as defender, public attention was centred on the coming of *Valkyrie*. Day after day passed and yet no news of her; at last anxiety was felt for her safety, seeing that she had not been positively reported since her sailing. But, after a thirty days' voyage, she appeared at sunrise off Sandy Hook, none the worse for her stormy passage.

Valkyrie was quickly put in racing trim, and on the arrival of Lord Dunraven all the final arrangements for the contest were settled and both yachts prepared for the struggle, the last act being the docking of them to make their wetted surfaces as smooth and repellent of water as possible.

The America Cup races were set to begin on October 5 and four following alternate days, the first, third, and last to be 15 knots from the lightship off Sandy Hook and return in a course parallel with the wind; the second and fourth races to be triangular, 10 knots on each leg, to start from the same point, and to have one leg to windward; all races to be started from a single gun, and to be sailed in a limit of six hours.

As the day approached the excitement became intense; yachtsmen and sportsmen flocked to New York from all parts of the country. Betting ran in favour of *Vigilant* (3 to 2), some bets being taken at large odds against *Valkyrie's* not being able to win a single race in the series.

First Race, October 7, 1893

	Start	Turn	Finish	Elapsed	Corrected
	h.m.	h.m.s.	h.m.s.	h.m.s.	h.m.s.
Vigilant	11 25	1 50 50	3 30 47	4 5 47	4 5 47
Valkyrie	11 25	1 58 56	3 38 23	4 13 23	4 11 35

Vigilant wins by 5 mins. 48 secs.

Second Race, October 9, 1893

	Start h. m.	First mark h. m. s.	Second mark h. m. s.	Finish h. m. s.	Elapsed h. m. s.	Corrected h. m. s.
Vigilant	11 25	1 6 35	1 56 55	2 50 1	3 25 1	3 25 1
Valkyrie	11 25	1 11 20	2 5 52	3 2 24	3 37 24	3 35 36

Vigilant beat *Valkyrie* on first leg 4 mins. 35 secs., on second 4 mins. 12 secs., and on third 3 mins. 26 secs. *Vigilant* won by 10 mins. 35 secs.

Third Race, October 13, 1893

	Start h.m.	Turn h.m.s.	Finish h.m.s.	Elapsed h.m.s.	Corrected h.m.s.
Vigilant	12 27	2 35 35	3 51 39	3 24 39	3 24 39
Valkyrie	12 27	2 33 40	3 53 52	3 26 52	3 25 19

To windward *Valkyrie* gained 1 min. 55 secs. Off the wind *Vigilant* gained 4 mins. 8 secs. *Vigilant* won by 40 secs.

Every steamer, tugboat, or anything propelled by an engine within 250 miles of the scene of the contest was pressed into service; and the fleet by sail and steam started for New York, bearing eager, interested men who had laid aside every business or social engagement to witness what was felt to be the greatest yachting event the world had ever known.

The 5th came. The bay and surrounding waters were alive with craft loaded with excited spectators, but all were doomed to the bitterest disappointment. It was a perfectly exasperating day—light winds varied by calms; and spectators saw the nation's hope absolutely forsaken by the treacherous breeze, whilst her opponent sailed away with favouring flaws until the American was hopelessly distanced. The time limit was reached before two-thirds of the course were covered, and yachtsmen as well as spectators returned utterly disgusted. The abortive race of the 5th afforded not the slightest clue to the comparative value of the contending yachts, so on the 7th the prospects of the coming race were as uncertain as ever.

The day was again disheartening; a waning westerly wind gave no promise of a good race; the attendance was still large, but there was a decided falling off in numbers from the first day.

The yachts were sent off east by south at a six or seven mile pace, the *Vigilant* slowly gaining; but when about half-way to the outer mark *Vigilant* took a start and rapidly drew away from *Valkyrie*, so that when within three miles of the mark she was one and a quarter mile in the lead. Here a soft spot in the wind occurred, and *Valkyrie* drew on the brass-bottomed boat; but at that moment the wind shifted more southerly, blowing over the quarter rail of the yachts, and *Vigilant* again drew away from her pursuer, turning nearly a mile and a half in advance.

The wind having changed in direction there was no windward work, the yachts returning two or three points free, and maintaining the same relative distance at the close as at the outer mark. The race of the 7th, although a decided victory for the American, was not generally considered as a satisfactory test of sailing qualities; the wind was unsteady in force and direction, and to some extent fluky, but in the opinion of those who were competent to judge, the 'luck' was rather more on the side of the *Valkyrie* than the *Vigilant*, the English, however, stoutly declaring the reverse.

The real value of the two yachts in windward work was still unknown, and although *Vigilant* had scored by a good margin one race, still the result was then quite uncertain.

October 9 opened with a fair promise of wind; the interest was still deep and the attendance large; the course was triangular, ten miles each side. The first leg was to windward; the yachts started about equal as to time and position.

At first *Valkyrie* seemed to lead—that is, she outfooted the American; but the latter was slowly edging up toward the wind, and later, when a good weather position was gained by '*Vigilant*,' her skipper gave her more power, and with the increasing wind she rapidly left her opponent astern, rounding the first mark well in the lead.

The next leg was a broad run, and all that witnessed it unite in declaring that yachts never made such time in a race before. They flew; but *Vigilant* flew the faster, and nearly doubled the handsome lead that she had obtained on the rounding of the first mark.

The home leg was with a freshening free wind two points forward of beam. It was made without incident, save that *Vigilant* had to favour her bowsprit that was sprung on the windward stretch, her jib-topsail was lowered, and head-sails eased in regard for the weakened spar. On the home stretch *Vigilant* still further widened the distance between her and the English yacht, and made a most decided point in her favour. The race was a fine one, but it seemed to seal the fate of *Valkyrie*; still with native pluck her undaunted owner made ready for the next race. By a most masterful stroke a new mainsail was bent, and more lead given the cutter, so that she lost fifteen seconds of time allowance from the American.

October 11th proved another disappointing day. Light breezes and calms ruled; the beat of fifteen miles resulted in no decisive difference in the sailing of the yachts, for when the time-limit was reached the yachts were far from home, with the American yacht leading.

On the 12th a gale was reported as working up the coast, and great hopes were entertained of a fresh wind for the fifth start. Many thought that the American yacht would beat her opponent more easily in a strong wind and rough sea, but they were disappointed, as the sequel proved. When October 13 dawned an easterly gale was blowing up; early in the morning the wind began to pipe and the sea to roughen, and by the time of starting the wind had set in strong and steadily from the east. After some delay caused by an accident to the rigging of *Valkyrie*, that was speedily repaired on board, the two yachts shot away for a fifteen-mile thresh to windward, the *Valkyrie* at the south end of the line, and *Vigilant* at the north end—a fair start.

At first *Vigilant* outfooted *Valkyrie* and held nearly or quite as well to the wind; but when the windward work was about half finished the wind drew more from the south of east, it soon began to increase in good earnest, and from that moment *Valkyrie* got further away from *Vigilant*, and turned the outer mark nearly two minutes ahead. On starting, the yachts had each a reef down, *Vigilant* a whole reef, *Valkyrie* a half reef in her mainsail, each her working topsail set, with usual head-sails. After the mark was turned it became apparent that if '*Vigilant*' were to win she must work, and, as it proved, no lack of energy was displayed on either yacht. The reef was turned out of *Vigilant's* mainsail, and her No. 1 club topsail set over it. The storm that had been threatening all day now began to increase, the wind rose rapidly and the sea became very rough.

Vigilant gained noticeably on her opponent, and passed her when about half-way to the home point. The contest was now most exciting; the rigging of both yachts was strained to the last degree. Soon after the *Valkyrie* was passed by *Vigilant*, her spinnaker, that was torn in setting, became disabled by splitting; another but smaller one was set in its place, but that also soon gave way to the ever-increasing force of the wind. The last three miles of the race were a mad rush for the *Vigilant*; she carried all the sail that could be spread, and it seemed that an inch more of canvas would carry everything by the board. She gained more quickly than ever on her crippled follower, and crossed a close winner in the midst of the most exciting scene that yachting annals have ever recorded.

It is hard to say if the *Vigilant* would have won had *Valkyrie* not lost her light sails; but if the latter claims that her race was thus lost, *Vigilant*, with equal sense of right, can claim that a maladjustment of her centreboard lost her at least five minutes on the beat out.

Closely following the termination of the races both yachts were put into winter quarters, and owners as well as crews took breath, enjoying a well-earned rest. It is not possible at this early moment to draw any absolutely settled conclusions as to the merits or demerits of the contesting yachts. Fortunately Lord Dunraven decided to leave *Valkyrie* in the States for a continuation of the contest in 1894, when if the races that are now hoped for occur, and all the yachts take part that now promise to do so, it will be a far more useful and interesting contest than was afforded by the races of 1893.

A few points that are worth considering force themselves on the close observer of the international races of 1893.

October is one of the worst periods of the whole year for racing, at least during the first half of the month; the winds then are light and inconstant in force and direction, and calms are of longer duration than at any period during the yachting season.

From August 15 until September 20 is without doubt the most favourable time for racing, and when another international contest is contemplated, it is to be hoped that the races will be set at least three weeks earlier than those of 1893.

This international sport awakens such a widespread interest, serving, as it were, as a great national school in yachting and racing, that it is to be hoped as much facility as possible may be afforded the public for witnessing them; therefore, let all international races be held in New York waters, where they were in 1893, as that point is more accessible than any other to those interested. We in America must establish some school for the training of skippers and crews; there is not to-day a professional skipper in the country, nor a crew that is capable of sailing a yacht against the English. The best school possible is actual racing, and when we present to our yachtsmen a racing list as long as that published in England, then we can hope to have captains and men fit to hold their own. The English may learn of the Americans how to design a yacht that will bear pushing to extreme speeds without making such a disturbance in the water as did *Valkyrie*.

They can also take lessons in staying the mast and masthead, and in proportioning the sizes of spars and standing rigging more closely to the labour assigned them. The Americans may learn of the English how to make canvas that will stand where it is desired; and when it is made they can also learn of them how to make sails and how to set them; and in general to copy the management of their yachts when racing, that when we meet the English in international races we may be able to rig and sail our yachts in such manner that an expert would be able to say whether any advantage on either side was due to design, or if not to that factor alone, to place the cause of advantage where it belongs, so that the lesson set by such races may be of some benefit to those who have the improvement of yacht-designing and sailing near their hearts.

The long-mooted question of keel *v.* centreboard still remains unanswered, and in fact it never can be determined as a general rule. In close windward work there seems little or no difference between the keel and centreboard as to speed; the latter has some advantage when sailing free by raising the board, thus lessening the wetted surface of the yacht.

The great and undeniable superiority of the centreboard lies in the fact that a yacht possessing it can essentially reduce her draught of water so as to work in depths that would be wholly impossible for the keel vessel. It would seem, therefore, that the advantage gained in the use of the centreboard is mainly not one of sailing qualities, but one of desirability for use in certain locations where shallow water prevails.

The interest exhibited in the international races by those who were able to be present has already been mentioned, but it yet remains to notice the astonishing degree of excitement as to the result of the races evinced by the public at large.

From Maine to California, and from Michigan to Florida, news of the struggle was eagerly awaited, and in all the cities, towns, and even villages the exact position of the yachts was exposed on a bulletin board, the news being sent by telegraph every five or ten minutes, or more often if the change of position of the yachts demanded it. In some of the larger cities where the interest was most intense such crowds collected in front of the bulletin boards that traffic had to be suspended; in New York City the stock-board was deserted, and business generally was at a standstill.

CHAPTER 13

The America Cup Races, 1893
By Sir George Leach, K.C.B.

[1]On October 5th, the opening day of the races, the first thing to strike the observer was the extraordinary number and diversity of craft attracted by the spectacle. Near the Sandy Hook Lightship we find the racers were under way, with whole mainsails and jackyarders set. *Vigilant* looks a bigger ship than *Valkyrie*, with a more numerous crew, and four battens in the leach of her mainsail and three in her staysail. The two vessels were easily distinguished one from the other, *Vigilant* being painted white above her bright yellow Tobin bronze, *Valkyrie* black with gilt line. The starting-line was between the commodore's steam yacht *May*, the New York Club's flagship, and Sandy Hook Lightship. There was no tide. The wind was a little east of north, and the course 15 miles to leeward round a mark and back. *Vigilant* allowed *Valkyrie* 1 min. 48 secs.

The first gun was at 11.15 a.m., the start gun 10 mins. after. Just prior to the start the yachts set their head-sails. *Vigilant* sent up a large bowsprit spinnaker, a very favourite sail in American waters, and *Valkyrie* a large jib-topsail. The crowd was immense, excursion steamers, tugs, yachts; and at the start came the horrible screech of steam whistles, customary on these occasions, but dreadful all the same.

Spinnakers were at once run up on the starboard side, but the wind was so light that, in spite of the enormous sail-areas, little progress was made. By noon the sky was clear and the sun came out, but at 1.30 there was a marked change. The wind shifted, and a light air came

---
1. Though the subject is so ably treated by Mr. Herreshoff in the previous chapter, the editors, recognising the extraordinary importance of these races, have thought well to include a detailed description of events kindly furnished by a prominent English yachtsman.

from S.W. *Vigilant* took in her bowsprit spinnaker a little too soon, for *Valkyrie*, holding on somewhat longer, ran up, and passing to windward so effectually blanketed *Vigilant* that she lost steerage way for some ten minutes. During this time *Valkyrie* crept up to the S.W. wind, and was going on her way rejoicing. The S.W. wind held true; it became a close haul to the mark, which *Valkyrie* rounded at 3 hrs. 37 mins. 20 secs. The 15 miles took 4 hrs. 12 mins. *Vigilant* rounded at 4 hrs. 2 mins. 30 secs., twenty-five minutes after *Valkyrie*, whose performance created great disappointment to English sympathisers. At 5.10 the committee stopped the race—if race it could be called.

The excitement on shore as well as afloat was intense. Upwards of 200 steamers of various kinds accompanied the race, all crowded with spectators, and some of them got terribly in the way at the start of the race, the police-boat warning them off, and *Valkyrie* holding up from her deck, in large letters, 'Keep further off.' On the whole, the course was fairly kept, and there was certainly no intention to injure *Valkyrie's* chance—quite the contrary. I am happy to say the spirit of *fair* play appeared to animate all; the anxiety of the captains of the steamers to show their friends as much as possible was really the sole cause of trespass.

This day's race was another example of the frequency with which races to windward and leeward and return fail in their object, especially in early October in these waters, when the wind is more fluky and lighter than at any other time of the year. If the S.W. wind had piped up a little, it would have been a reach both ways. On the whole, triangular races are best courses.

On the second day, October 7, after rain in the early morning, it became fine and bright as the New York Club's steamer left No. 8 Pier at 9.15. Not quite so many steamers appeared, although there were probably over 150, many large excursion ones, and yachts. One yacht stood prominently out, and was conspicuous for her taut brig rig and large tonnage, 2,400—a grand vessel, the *Valiant*, designed by St. Clare Byrne for Mr. Vanderbilt, and built at Liverpool. There was also a large yacht of the *Chazalie* type; and I may also mention Commodore Morgan's steam yacht *May*, designed by Mr. G. L. Watson. The wind, W. by S., was still very light, with a gentle swell from the southward. Course, 15 miles to leeward, round mark, and return.

The start at 11.25 was admirable. *Valkyrie*, beautifully handled, out-manœuvred *Vigilant*, and crossed the line to windward about 10 secs. ahead. Spinnakers were at once hauled out on the starboard side, both setting balloon jib-topsails and lowering foresails. Bowsprit spinnakers are more correctly to be termed balloon jib-topsails, the difference being that the balloon jib-topsail is hanked on the stay. *Vigilant* drew ahead, and at 12.25 was a quarter of a mile in front. *Vigilant*, a quarter of a mile to the eastward, got a streak of wind and increased her lead, her balloon jib-topsail drawing well. At 1.30 *Vigilant* was nearly a mile ahead; she tacked round the mark 1 hr. 50 mins. 30 secs., '*Valkyrie* following at 1.59, when she was bothered by a small steamer. The 15 miles took 2½ hrs. to accomplish, but on the return there was no beating to windward, a close haul with jib-topsails set. The windward work was again frustrated by shift of wind. It was a plain sail home, and

	h. m. s.
Vigilant crossed the line	3 30 16
Valkyrie " "	3 37 57

After deducting time allowance, the English boat lost by 5 mins. 53 secs. One of the members of the committee took the velocity of the wind at different periods of the race, as follows:—

h. m.	Velocity per hour
11 25	10.0
1 56	14.5
2 3	9.0
3 23	9.0
3 35	8.8

It will be well to remember that here velocity does not indicate strength as we feel it at home. As Lord Dunraven particularly noticed, the dryness of the wind reduces the pressure, which the moisture of our climate so materially increases.

The result of the race seemed to show that the two yachts were fairly matched, so that if one got a slice of luck the other was not likely to recover without a slice too, or a good streak. The course was better kept; but, although the race was not affected by it, the *Valkyrie* was favoured by the wash of steamers on the return from the mark-boat.

On the third day, October 9, everything promised well; the weather was all that could be desired to test the relative merits of the two racers; the morning bright, with a good topsail breeze, and the white crests on the wavelets gave hopes of great sport. The club steamer left the pier at 9 a.m.; but on our arrival at Sandy Hook no breeze was there. The steamers were fewer in number; I had, however, no difficulty after the start in counting fifty, besides yachts under canvas. Going down the river we passed one very striking object, the well-known gigantic and magnificent statue of Liberty, which stands on a small island. I must say I never saw anything finer, either in conception or execution.

The wind was from the S.W., the course triangular, round marks placed by steamers with a large red ball hoisted, the steamers remaining near to indicate their positions, which were so stationed as to make each side of the triangle ten miles. Both yachts carried jackyarders and jib-topsails. The start took place at 11.30, after some pretty manœuvring as usual, *Valkyrie* getting the weather berth, and a little ahead. About 12.30 the wind increased, with a little jump of sea, and both went round on the port tack; here *Vigilant's* power began to tell. *Vigilant* bore round the first mark at 1 hr. 6 mins., and *Valkyrie* 4 mins. 50 secs. later. A broad reach on starboard followed, *Vigilant* setting her balloon jib-topsail very smartly. Soon after this *Vigilant* sprung her bowsprit and took in her jib-topsail. The second mark was rounded by *Vigilant* at 2 hrs. 1 min., *Valkyrie* at 2 hrs. 10 mins. 3 secs.

Now came the last ten-mile reach on the port tack to the finish. The wind piped up still stronger; but *Vigilant*, though carrying only a small jib-topsail, still increased her lead, finishing a winner at 2 hrs. 49 mins. 3 secs., *Valkyrie* coming in 12 mins. 20 secs. after her. After deducting time allowance she lost the race by 10 mins. 32 secs.

The wind velocities were as follows:—

At the start	10 miles per hour
" first mark	15 " "
" second mark	22 " "
" finish	29 " "

On the fourth day, October 11, the start was delayed, the competitors hoping for wind, but it was made at 1.45. Course, south by west to windward and back. *Valkyrie*, there is no doubt, was always beautifully handled, and it would be wrong not to recognise the ability Cranfield has shown throughout, whether in manœuvring for the line or in sailing *Valkyrie* during the races in waters far from home. To these he is not a stranger, having had some experience with Sir Richard Sutton in the *Genesta* (1885) when sailing against *Puritan*. This race, October 11, could not be finished within the prescribed time, six hours, and therefore the tugs took the competitors in tow, homeward bound.

On the fifth day, October 13, the course was to windward and leeward. This was the great day, and included many most exciting episodes. *Valkyrie* had altered her trim, but news had arrived of a hard blow in the south, and in heavy weather what could she do against the more powerful boat, the *Vigilant*? The weather was overcast and cloudy, wind S.E., blowing moderately at Sandy Hook Lightship. When *Valkyrie* was below the Narrows her mainsail was lowered, one of the throat-halliard blocks had to be repaired, and it was 11.19 before she neared the starting point. The course, due east, was given from the steam yacht *May*. Signals now came from *Vigilant*, 'Time wanted for repairs.' Her centreboard was jammed, but finally it was lowered about eleven feet. At 12.7 the Blue Peter was run up on the flagship. The two were under the same canvas, each with jibheader over single-reef mainsails, foresail, and jib.

At 12.17 came the preparatory gun, and then began some of the prettiest manœuvring ever seen in these waters as the two big cutters chased each other like a couple of kittens for the weather berth. *Valkyrie* passed the line up to windward 12 hrs. 27 mins. 10 secs., *Vigilant* to leeward 3 secs. later. It was a long tack, some six miles, towards Long Island, *Valkyrie* carrying her canvas decidedly the better of the two; to-day she was notably stiff—in fact, at no time has she ever been tender. She pointed as high as *Vigilant*, and held her weather berth easily. The latter was heeling over much at 1 hr. 18 mins. *Valkyrie* was on her weather bow. *Vigilant's* jibsheet got adrift. The wind was now stronger, and they were getting a head sea, which did not suit *Vigilant's* beam and bow.

This long tack lasted an hour, and at 2.15 *Valkyrie* led by three-eighths of a mile. As they neared the outer mark the time was

	h. m. s.
Valkyrie	2 33 40
Vigilant	2 35 35

In the beat to windward of fifteen miles *Valkyrie* gained 1 min. 55 sec.

Spinnakers were now on both, the wind increasing, and at 2.47 *Valkyrie's* biggest balloon jib-topsail went up. *Vigilant* had some trouble forward with hers, and a hand was smartly sent down the topmast stay before the sail could be sent up in stops. At 2.50 it broke up and revealed that favourite sail in America a balloon jib-topsail, and a rare good puller it is. Some very smart work was now done on board *Vigilant* on the run. The reef in the mainsail was shaken out by a hand slung from the masthead in the bight of a gaut-line, and hauled along the boom by an outhaul as he cast off the stops. Next a hand was out on the gaff.

This led to hoisting the second club topsail over the jibheader left standing to leeward, and just before the club topsail went up she ran through *Valkyrie's* lee. *Valkyrie's* white spinnaker burst. It was most smartly taken in, and the light one set. This split before it was belayed, from head to foot, right down, and *Valkyrie's* chance had now gone. A large jib-topsail was set on her, but was of no use against the sail area of *Vigilant*. Some ten minutes more and

	h. m. s.
Vigilant finished and won	3 51 39
Valkyrie	3 53 52

losing by 40 secs. corrected time.

	m. s.
To windward *Valkyrie* led by	1 55
To leeward *Vigilant* led by	4 5

On this day the course was kept very clear. The wind increased at the finish, but the fact that *Vigilant* carried full mainsail, second club topsail, balloon jib-topsail, and large spinnaker, shows that it was not blowing the gale described by some journalists.

After the finish in the lower bay the wind piped up, the sea got up, and all raced hard for home.

It was a splendid race, nobly sailed, and both yachts admirably handled. There always must be some luck, but it was most untimely for *Valkyrie's* spinnakers to burst. The question at once suggests itself, should they not be sent up in stops? *Valkyrie's* mast was sprung and worse, and that prevented her getting more canvas put on her. When one yacht gains to windward and the other to leeward they must be well matched; in England we consider that windward work should take precedence of running free.

For English waters *Valkyrie* is a most successful and beautiful craft, and for American waters, with light winds and long reaching, *Vigilant* has proved a great success. Certainly this last race was the grandest ever sailed for the America Cup, and we may be proud of our representative. The 1,200 feet of sail-area in *Vigilant*, and extra crew, gave her a decided advantage, and the centreboard was supposed to be a gain to windward; but that good sportsman Lord Dunraven is not disheartened in any way, neither is he won over to centreboard yachts.

Appendix

THE 'GIRALDA'

It chances that while these volumes were being prepared, a steam yacht of a remarkable character was being built, and it seems desirable to include a few words about this vessel, for the reason that she is, perhaps, the most perfect boat ever constructed for a private gentleman. Reference is made to the magnificent twin-screw steam yacht *Giralda*, the property of Mr. Harry McCalmont of Cheveley Park, Newmarket. *Giralda* gives evidence of the perfection to which vessels of this type are now being brought. She is about 1,800 tons yacht measurement, and her principal dimensions are: Length between perpendiculars, 275 feet; breadth moulded, 35 feet; depth moulded, 19 feet. She is built with thirteen water-tight bulkheads of Siemens-Martin's steel to Lloyd's highest class, and so constructed as to be readily converted into a light-armed cruiser or despatch vessel for Admiralty requirements.

A notable point will be her speed of twenty knots, to develop which she is fitted with twin-screw machinery and five boilers, three of which are double-ended, and two single-ended, with sixteen furnaces, all adapted for forced draught. The machinery consists of two independent and separate sets of triple-expansion direct-acting surface-condensing engines, one set to each screw propeller, and will indicate with forced draught 6,500 horse-power, or with natural draught 5,000 horse-power. The bunker capacity is 400 tons of coal, and the fresh-water tanks are ample for Admiralty requirements; in addition to which she is fitted with fresh-water condenser capable of producing 1,200 gallons *per diem*. The yacht is also fitted with large ice-house and refrigerating chamber.

One of the special features in the *Giralda* is that the saloons—consisting of smoking-room, *boudoir*, or library, spacious dining saloon and drawing-room—are all on the main deck, where there are also situated lavatories for cabins and crew, three galleys, and ample pantry and service spaces. Owner's sleeping accommodation is below, fore and abaft the machinery space, having intercommunication on the main deck through the house. The officers and crew are berthed forward, and the servants' quarters are aft. It is almost unnecessary to add that the cabin accommodation has had the most special attention, both in respect of arrangement and fittings, and the greatest care has been taken throughout for ventilating, heating, and insulation where necessary. A large bridge or shade deck extends along about 160 feet of the vessel, on which, forward, is the bridge, and also the chart and wheel houses. The boats are housed on this deck, and there is steam hoisting gear for steam launch and larger boats.

The yacht is lighted throughout by electricity, there being over 200 incandescent lamps. In addition to these, there are fitted two regulation-size search lights, and groups of electric lights for each mast. There are two separate and independent engines and dynamos, connected with large accumulators of sufficient capacity to supply the whole of the lamps for many hours without recharging.

Mr. McCalmont has himself taken the very greatest personal interest in the arrangement of all details, which have been carried out by Messrs. Cox & King, of Suffolk Street, Pall Mall, London, under the direction of Professor Elgar, the designer of the well-known Fairfield Shipbuilding and Engineering Co., of Govan, Glasgow by whom the yacht is being built, (as at time of first publication).

ALSO FROM LEONAUR
AVAILABLE IN SOFTCOVER OR HARDCOVER WITH DUST JACKET

BOOTS AND SADDLES by *Elizabeth B. Custer*—The experiences of General Custer's Wife on the Western Plains.

FANNIE BEERS' CIVIL WAR by *Fannie A. Beers*—A Confederate Lady's Experiences of Nursing During the Campaigns & Battles of the American Civil War.

LADY SALE'S AFGHANISTAN by *Florentia Sale*—An Indomitable Victorian Lady's Account of the Retreat from Kabul During the First Afghan War.

THE TWO WARS OF MRS DUBERLY by *Frances Isabella Duberly*—An Intrepid Victorian Lady's Experience of the Crimea and Indian Mutiny.

LADIES OF WATERLOO by *Charlotte A. Eaton, Magdalene de Lancey & Juana Smith*—The Experiences of Three Women During the Campaign of 1815: Waterloo Days by Charlotte A. Eaton, A Week at Waterloo by Magdalene de Lancey & Juana's Story by Juana Smith.

DESPATCH RIDER by *W. H. L. Watson*—The Experiences of a British Army Motorcycle Despatch Rider During the Opening Battles of the Great War in Europe.

TWO YEARS BEFORE THE MAST by *Richard Henry Dana. Jr.*—The account of one young man's experiences serving on board a sailing brig—the Penelope—bound for California, between the years 1834-36.

A SAILOR OF KING GEORGE by *Frederick Hoffman*—From Midshipman to Captain—Recollections of War at Sea in the Napoleonic Age 1793-1815.

LORDS OF THE SEA by *A. T. Mahan*—Great Captains of the Royal Navy During the Age of Sail.

COGGESHALL'S VOYAGES: VOLUME 1 by *George Coggeshall*—The Recollections of an American Schooner Captain.

COGGESHALL'S VOYAGES: VOLUME 2 by *George Coggeshall*—The Recollections of an American Schooner Captain.

TWILIGHT OF EMPIRE by *Sir Thomas Ussher & Sir George Cockburn*—Two accounts of Napoleon's Journeys in Exile to Elba and St. Helena: Narrative of Events by Sir Thomas Ussher & Napoleon's Last Voyage: Extract of a diary by Sir George Cockburn.

KIEL AND JUTLAND by *Georg Von Hase*—The Famous Naval Battle of the First World War from the German Perspective.

AVAILABLE ONLINE AT **www.leonaur.com**
AND FROM ALL GOOD BOOK STORES

ALSO FROM LEONAUR
AVAILABLE IN SOFTCOVER OR HARDCOVER WITH DUST JACKET

FARAWAY CAMPAIGN *by F. James*—Experiences of an Indian Army Cavalry Officer in Persia & Russia During the Great War.

REVOLT IN THE DESERT *by T. E. Lawrence*—An account of the experiences of one remarkable British officer's war from his own perspective.

MACHINE-GUN SQUADRON *by A. M. G.*—The 20th Machine Gunners from British Yeomanry Regiments in the Middle East Campaign of the First World War.

A GUNNER'S CRUSADE *by Antony Bluett*—The Campaign in the Desert, Palestine & Syria as Experienced by the Honourable Artillery Company During the Great War.

DESPATCH RIDER *by W. H. L. Watson*—The Experiences of a British Army Motorcycle Despatch Rider During the Opening Battles of the Great War in Europe.

TIGERS ALONG THE TIGRIS *by E. J. Thompson*—The Leicestershire Regiment in Mesopotamia During the First World War.

HEARTS & DRAGONS *by Charles R. M. F. Crutwell*—The 4th Royal Berkshire Regiment in France and Italy During the Great War, 1914-1918.

INFANTRY BRIGADE: 1914 *by John Ward*—The Diary of a Commander of the 15th Infantry Brigade, 5th Division, British Army, During the Retreat from Mons.

DOING OUR 'BIT' *by Ian Hay*—Two Classic Accounts of the Men of Kitchener's 'New Army' During the Great War including *The First 100,000* & *All In It*.

AN EYE IN THE STORM *by Arthur Ruhl*—An American War Correspondent's Experiences of the First World War from the Western Front to Gallipoli-and Beyond.

STAND & FALL *by Joe Cassells*—With the Middlesex Regiment Against the Bolsheviks 1918-19.

RIFLEMAN MACGILL'S WAR *by Patrick MacGill*—A Soldier of the London Irish During the Great War in Europe including *The Amateur Army*, *The Red Horizon* & *The Great Push*.

WITH THE GUNS *by C. A. Rose & Hugh Dalton*—Two First Hand Accounts of British Gunners at War in Europe During World War 1- Three Years in France with the Guns and With the British Guns in Italy.

THE BUSH WAR DOCTOR *by Robert V. Dolbey*—The Experiences of a British Army Doctor During the East African Campaign of the First World War.

AVAILABLE ONLINE AT **www.leonaur.com**
AND FROM ALL GOOD BOOK STORES

ALSO FROM LEONAUR
AVAILABLE IN SOFTCOVER OR HARDCOVER WITH DUST JACKET

ESCAPE FROM THE FRENCH *by Edward Boys*—A Young Royal Navy Midshipman's Adventures During the Napoleonic War.

THE VOYAGE OF H.M.S. PANDORA *by Edward Edwards R. N. & George Hamilton, edited by Basil Thomson*—In Pursuit of the Mutineers of the Bounty in the South Seas—1790-1791.

MEDUSA *by J. B. Henry Savigny and Alexander Correard and Charlotte-Adélaïde Dard*—Narrative of a Voyage to Senegal in 1816 & The Sufferings of the Picard Family After the Shipwreck of the Medusa.

THE SEA WAR OF 1812 VOLUME 1 *by A. T. Mahan*—A History of the Maritime Conflict.

THE SEA WAR OF 1812 VOLUME 2 *by A. T. Mahan*—A History of the Maritime Conflict.

WETHERELL OF H. M. S. HUSSAR *by John Wetherell*—The Recollections of an Ordinary Seaman of the Royal Navy During the Napoleonic Wars.

THE NAVAL BRIGADE IN NATAL *by C. R. N. Burne*—With the Guns of H. M. S. Terrible & H. M. S. Tartar during the Boer War 1899-1900.

THE VOYAGE OF H. M. S. BOUNTY *by William Bligh*—The True Story of an 18th Century Voyage of Exploration and Mutiny.

SHIPWRECK! *by William Gilly*—The Royal Navy's Disasters at Sea 1793-1849.

KING'S CUTTERS AND SMUGGLERS: 1700-1855 *by E. Keble Chatterton*—A unique period of maritime history-from the beginning of the eighteenth to the middle of the nineteenth century when British seamen risked all to smuggle valuable goods from wool to tea and spirits from and to the Continent.

CONFEDERATE BLOCKADE RUNNER *by John Wilkinson*—The Personal Recollections of an Officer of the Confederate Navy.

NAVAL BATTLES OF THE NAPOLEONIC WARS *by W. H. Fitchett*—Cape St. Vincent, the Nile, Cadiz, Copenhagen, Trafalgar & Others.

PRISONERS OF THE RED DESERT *by R. S. Gwatkin-Williams*—The Adventures of the Crew of the Tara During the First World War.

U-BOAT WAR 1914-1918 *by James B. Connolly/Karl von Schenk*—Two Contrasting Accounts from Both Sides of the Conflict at Sea During the Great War.

AVAILABLE ONLINE AT **www.leonaur.com**
AND FROM ALL GOOD BOOK STORES

Lightning Source UK Ltd.
Milton Keynes UK
UKHW010051121120
373227UK00003B/767

9 781782 821199